SEVENTIES

ALSO BY HOWARD SOUNES:

Down the Highway: The Life of Bob Dylan

Charles Bukowski: Locked in the Arms of a Crazy Life

Bukowski in Pictures

The Wicked Game

Fred & Rose

SEVENTIES

The Sights, Sounds and Ideas of a Brilliant Decade

Howard Sounes

SIMON &
SCHUSTER

London · New York · Sydney · Toronto

A CBS COMPANY

First published in Great Britain by Simon & Schuster UK Ltd, 2006
A CBS COMPANY

1 3 5 7 9 10 8 6 4 2

Simon & Schuster UK Ltd
Africa House
64–78 Kingsway
London WC2B 6AH

www.simonsays.co.uk

Simon & Schuster Australia
Sydney

A CIP catalogue record for this book is available
from the British Library.

ISBN 0-7432-6859-8
EAN 9780743268592

Typeset in Bembo by M Rules
Printed and bound in Great Britain by
The Bath Press, Bath

SEVENTIES

CONTENTS

PREFACE

Having now finished writing this long and ambitious book, I am looking back to why I started it so many months ago. The impetus, I suppose, was seeing a plethora of television programmes based loosely around a theme of the 1970s, and the popular culture of that decade, and feeling that what I was being shown, and the memories that presenters and pundits were sharing with viewers, were nothing like my own perception of that time in our recent history, or its culture. My impression on watching these retrospective clip-based shows about the 1970s, and also hearing people refer to the '70s on radio and reading comments in the printed press, was that there was a consensus among journalists and other pundits that the decade was somehow a rather stupid, indeed vulgar, one – certainly when compared to the ever-glamorous 1960s – but amusingly stupid and vulgar: a time of endearingly foolish fashions, embarrassingly bad (so bad it is good) music and deliciously trashy TV and films, all of which we are presumed to embrace in collective fond nostalgia. In essence, I felt as if I was being told that the 1970s was all about flared trousers, *Starsky and Hutch*, Chopper bikes and Showaddywaddy, and that this was all great. Well, that is not my impression of the decade.

Even though I was born in 1965 and was therefore essentially a child during the whole of the 1970s, as a precocious teenager towards the end of the decade I took an increasing interest in what was happening in popular culture and the arts generally, and there was a much headier and more significant mix of entertainment on offer than I see portrayed in these television programmes. And of course as one ages, one naturally catches up on the best books, films, art and design of a decade just slipped away. As I did so (and of course I am in no way unusual in this), it became quite evident to me that the 1970s was not at all a trivial or foolish period in art and culture. Quite the contrary; it was more a time of modern classics, to use a publishing analogy. Certainly many exciting new books were published that are now read as modern classics; the '70s was also the decade of countless outstanding films, as well as some of the best rock music and television ever made; there was remarkable achievement in painting, sculpture, architecture, and design of all kinds, work that still enriches the world enormously. The spirit of experimentation that had been a hallmark of the 1960s continued well into the early 1970s, and by the end of the decade a changing, and in many ways more severe, world was reflected in the arts in an equally fascinating way. In short, this was an important and worthwhile decade in the arts: not one to be dismissed as a silly, jokey interlude between the Beatles and the 1980s.

Then one evening I went to see Lou Reed in concert. For me Lou Reed has always been associated closely with the 1970s, primarily because of his classic 1972 album *Transformer*, songs from which remain a mainstay of his live show. The theatre was sold out and as I looked around at the people in the hall I noticed that most were of an age with me, or slightly older, and as Lou Reed performed it was evident that we all still held his music, which we had discovered when young, as dear to us. It was not merely kitsch 1970s nostalgia. These songs, by which I mean tunes such as 'Perfect Day' and 'Satellite of Love', had become part of the core culture of our lives; we take them seriously, in the sense that we think them beautiful and clever and they affect us emotionally. And as I walked home from the theatre that night it occurred to me that, of course, this phenomenon isn't limited to the songs of Lou Reed (a most variable artist, by the way, as we shall come to), or even rock music generally. Millions of people who are now in what might be broadly termed middle life have grown up with certain books, films, music and artwork from the 1970s, culture they discovered in their youth that they still enjoy. They do not do so in an ironic way, but sincerely, for the culture of the 1970s helped to form their tastes and, indeed, their lives.

So the point of this book is to take a journey back through the arts of the 1970s, exploring some of the work (*some*, not all, this is not an encyclopaedia) that can be argued to be among the best of its time; best is very subjective of course, but certainly it is work that can be said to have stood the test of time. The emphasis is on anglophone culture because, frankly, that is what I and, I presume, most readers are most familiar with, though the book does occasionally look beyond the English-speaking world. I start in 1970 and end in 1979, and although that is a slightly artificial structure because life and art are not generally speaking circumscribed so neatly, it is a useful framework in which to study some very interesting people who were at work during those ten years, and to rummage about in ideas and creations that were exciting then and retain their lustre now. I hope the book is entertaining, first and foremost, and that it also goes some way to show and remind us that, at its best, the 1970s offered a vibrant, innovative and fascinating popular culture, much of which remains important and enjoyable.

Thank you to everybody who was interviewed, or contributed thoughts by way of correspondence, including: Allan Arbus, John Bayley, the late Peter Benchley, Celia Birtwell, Karen Black, Chris Blackwell, Angie Bowie, Malcolm Cecil, Candy Clark, Peter J. Conradi, Robert Crumb, Frederic Forrest, Frederick Forsyth, Ray Foulk, Vincent Fremont, Dana Gillespie, Terry Gilliam, Martyn Goff, Carl Gottlieb, Henry Guthard, Pat Hackett, Buck Henry, David Hockney, Antonio Homem, Dennis Hopper, Angela Huth, Miriam Karlin, Kasmin, Jon Landau, Michael Lewis, Maury Lipowich, Si Litvinoff, John Lydon, Norman Mailer, Robert Margouleff, Mardik Martin, Richard Meier, the late Dr Bob Moog, Peter Myers, Graham Parker, Bob Rafelson, Jamie Reid, Tony Roberts, Dave Robinson, Nicolas Roeg, Lord (Richard) Rogers, Richard Romanus, the late Bernice Rubens, Larry Schiller, Peter Schlesinger, Jean Schulz, Ken Scott, TV Smith, Ileana Sonnabend, Ralph Steadman, Professor Ronald Grigor Suny, Anthea Sylbert, Jonathan Taplin, Chris Thomas, Jane Turner, John Updike, Jann Wenner, Professor Stephen Wheatcroft, Gordon Willis and Sir Jack Zunz. Thank you also to my agent Jonathan Lloyd at Curtis Brown and finally, most of all, to Andrew Gordon at Simon & Schuster for giving me the opportunity to write what has been an ambitious, and in many ways very personal, book.

Howard Sanes

1

AUSPICIOUS BEGINNINGS

It became permission-time. Permission was granted in the '70s to behave [and] make work that, in fact, was something you were thinking about doing in the '60s, but nobody gave you permission to do.

BOB RAFELSON

On a bright, cold morning in January 1970 Jack Nicholson crouched down beside an old man in a wheelchair in a field by the Pacific Ocean to deliver one of the key performances in his nascent career as a movie star, a scene in which he had to draw from deep within himself in order to weep on camera. 'I don't know if you'd be particularly interested in hearing anything about me,' Jack began, speaking in character as prodigal son to his screen father, the man in the wheelchair, disabled and rendered mute by a series of strokes. 'My life, most of it, doesn't add up to much that I could relate as a way of life you'd approve of,' he continued, mentally referring back to his own history, particularly his difficult relationship with the man he called Dad, in order to work up the tears the director, his friend Bob Rafelson, insisted must come at the climax of this new movie, *Five Easy Pieces*. Rafelson, or Curly as Jack called him, argued that the audience had to see the vulnerable underbelly of the character, and the only way to show them was to have Jack break down and cry.

The actor resisted at first. 'I'm not going to cry. I don't cry,' he told Rafelson. 'Fucking directors are full of shit when they ask actors to cry.' Curly remembered all the times he had seen Jack break down in private, specifically when talking about his family, but he knew better than to trade on that personal knowledge now. Instead, he cajoled his friend into doing the scene his way by telling Jack he could rewrite the words to suit himself, and that when they came actually to shoot the scene he would send the crew away and hold the microphone personally, so Jack wouldn't be embarrassed in front of a lot of people. Nicholson agreed reluctantly, and this was how they were working that frigid January morning in 1970, in a field by Puget Sound in Washington State: the camera turning over automatically, Curly holding the boom mike aloft, looking in the opposite direction to give Jack as much privacy as possible as he worked himself up to the moment when he hoped that the tears would come.

Jack's character, Bobby 'Eroica' Dupea, was a tragic one. The son of a family prominent in the world of classical music, Bobby had failed to live up to his father's expectations that he would be a concert pianist (the movie title *Five Easy Pieces* refers to a book of elementary piano lessons) and had cast himself adrift to live a peripatetic life. In the process, he had lost sight of who he was as a man. The character was a composite of people Rafelson had known growing up in the 1950s and 1960s: young men who had rejected their backgrounds for whatever reason and gone on a journey of self-discovery. Indeed, Rafelson saw himself in the character of Bobby, and something of Jack, too. Both had turned away from the places where they were born and the lives they had been born to* in favour of drifting out to California, achieving success in the movie business only now as they entered their thirties after several dead-ends.

'I move around a lot,' Jack continued, speaking as Bobby. 'Not because I'm looking for anything, really, but because I'm getting away from things that get bad if I stay. Auspicious beginnings, you know what I mean?' Jack had written that striking phrase, *auspicious beginnings*, referring to the early promise his character showed as a pianist. Auspicious beginnings also described the actor's own life: the early

---

*Rafelson, son of a middle-class New York hat manufacturer; Nicholson raised in working-class New Jersey, as we shall see.

breaks in Hollywood encouraging dreams of imminent stardom, only to be followed by long, dreary years of dispiriting work in B-pictures before finally, recently, getting lucky with a cameo in *Easy Rider* at the age of thirty-two. Now here he was in his first starring role in a classy picture, though it came too late for his nearest and dearest to know about it. The woman he believed to be his sister – but was in fact his mother – had gone to her grave thinking of Jack as a Hollywood bum. Dad died in 1955, a sad old Irish drunk with whom he had never been close. Jack didn't even go home for the funeral, which said a lot about their relationship. 'I don't know what to say,' the actor continued, becoming upset as he reached the end of the scene with his screen father. 'I don't know . . . I didn't . . .' He steadied himself, said in character that his sister had suggested father and son should have this *tête-à-tête*. But it was too late. 'She totally denies the fact that we were never that comfortable with one another to begin with.' The tears did come naturally in the end.

'Are you finished?' asked Rafelson, who was still looking away, after a suitable pause.

'What are you talking about? Yes, I'm finished.'

'Well, let's do it again then.'

'Why do we have to do it again? I just did it.'

'Well, I didn't see it,' replied the director, who wanted another take just in case.

'That's your problem that you don't want to look.'

So that was the take, printed and used as the key scene in a movie that heralded independent, naturalistic American filmmaking in the 1970s, the movie that also presented Jack Nicholson to the public in his first leading role in a picture of consequence, 'starkly resisting his director,' as Bob Rafelson points out with a laugh, adding proudly: 'It has been said that it changes the course of American acting forever.'

In the 1970s, Jack Nicholson inherited Marlon Brando's crown as the king of Hollywood actors. He did so after a slow start, having got his late break in 1969 with a cameo in *Easy Rider*, but moved swiftly thereafter, establishing himself with a series of memorable star turns beginning with *Five Easy Pieces*, building on that success with *The Last*

Detail (1973), then making the excellent private-eye movie *Chinatown* (1974) and capping that with his portrayal of a mental hospital inmate in *One Flew Over the Cuckoo's Nest* (1975). In each of these very different, highly engaging pictures, Nicholson's hipness, his not-too-perfect good looks, and sardonic sense of humour endeared him to 1970s cinemagoers. Jack was somebody they liked, were amused and excited by, and empathised with; a man of his time and someone akin to themselves, or who they would like to be. Certainly that was the case for many of the men in his audience while, for women, Jack was both hip and sexy, and his trademark crooked grin showed how much the actor relished his newfound popularity after years of failure and such a peculiar start in life.

Jack's background was stranger than even he knew when he made *Five Easy Pieces*. He was born in Neptune, New Jersey, in 1937, but his parents were not the people he thought they were. The woman who gave birth to him was June Nicholson, a chorus girl made pregnant at age eighteen by an older man named Don Furcillo-Rose. At least Don was the most likely candidate; nobody was ever *sure* who the father was. In order to hide her daughter's shame, June's mother, Ethel, took the baby in as her own, casting her shiftless husband John in the role of father. Nobody in the family told Jack the truth about his parentage (he later found out from a journalist), and he never managed to forge much of a relationship with John Nicholson, perhaps unsurprisingly as the old man knew the boy wasn't his own. More positively, Jack was raised by women who adored him. In Neptune there was Ethel, whom he called Mud, his fond corruption of Mudder (Mother), and a 'sister' Lorraine (actually his aunt). When he was seventeen Jack went to live with his other sister June (actually his mother) in Los Angeles, where he wormed his way into the movie business with a combination of hard work and charm, making many friends early on who would figure significantly in his adult career. One such was actress Carole Eastman who used to hang out with Jack at Pupi's diner on Sunset Boulevard. Jack had a fearful temper as a young man and one time Carole witnessed her friend creating a hell of a scene at Pupi's with a waitress who had upset him: an altercation Carole recreated when she wrote the screenplay for *Five Easy Pieces*.

As an actor, Jack was fortunate early in his career to get plenty of work, but he was cast almost exclusively in cheap, exploitative films, many of which were produced and directed by Roger Corman. These were pictures such as *The Little Shop of Horrors* (1960) and *The Terror* (1963), in which Corman was assisted by a young Francis Ford Coppola. Many luminaries of 1970s cinema worked for Corman on their way up in the business, and were grateful for the opportunity. Indeed, Corman was a stylish and interesting filmmaker in many ways. But as the years passed Jack found himself making more of these low-rent pictures than he would have wished, and by the late 1960s he had all but despaired of achieving his early dreams of crossing into more legitimate movies. It was then, finally, when all seemed hopeless, that he landed the part of the dipsomaniac lawyer George Hanson in *Easy Rider*. The picture was financed by his friend Bob Rafelson, and Rafelson's business partner Bert Schneider. The two had made a fortune from creating the *Monkees* TV show, and were eager to expand into the movie business. Dennis Hopper was the driving force behind *Easy Rider*: the co-writer, director and co-star of the picture, along with his buddy Peter Fonda. And when Rip Torn dropped out of the cast, Nicholson found himself on screen alongside them. Made on a shoestring budget, *Easy Rider* was a box office sensation in 1969, bringing young audiences flocking back to theatres at a time when cinema attendance had seemed to be in terminal decline, losing out to television and rock music. The lesson was that if you gave young audiences the kind of hip, intelligent, iconoclastic entertainment they wanted, they would buy a ticket. So producers began to release money to make similar pictures and, for a brief time, independent American filmmakers were able to create interesting, idiosyncratic, character-driven films that eschewed the tired old conventions of Hollywood. Jack was one of the actors who benefited because, when Bob Rafelson came to invest some of his and Bert Schneider's profits from *Easy Rider* in their next movie project, they chose their pal Jack as the leading man, having long thought he was deserving of a break. As Dennis Hopper explains the sequence: 'Rafelson and Bert Schneider gave me the money to make *Easy Rider*. Out of the profits of *Easy Rider* they went on to build their company, and Bob Rafelson then made *Five Easy Pieces* [which] made Jack a star.'

In many ways, *Five Easy Pieces* is the seminal film of what became known as the New Hollywood, and it is an even more interesting and accomplished film than *Easy Rider*. The story begins in the dowdy Californian town of Bakersfield, a dusty, rural, unglamorous place where Jack's character Bobby Dupea is living with a waitress named Rayette, working in an oil field, frittering his evenings bowling, watching TV and drinking beer. Bobby's girlfriend is none too bright, and has nothing in common with Bobby in terms of background, but Rayette is an affectionate, warm-hearted girl who believes herself in love with her man. The tragedy of the relationship is that Rayette neither understands Bobby nor realises how unsuited they are as a couple. The part was played superbly by Karen Black, one of a number of young actresses who fitted with the ethos of the New Hollywood, whereby directors like Rafelson prized authenticity in acting above everything. Along with similar actresses such as Candy Clark, Black was attractive but not beautiful, and slightly kooky in personality, less a movie star than a girl you might know. 'There was a tremendous emphasis in the '70s on naturalness,' she explains. 'How that affected the world of movies was there was movie after movie made where people were natural, people were real. [Directors] wanted funny little grins in the wrong places. They wanted idiosyncrasy galore. I think it started with *Easy Rider*.* My opinion is that when [audiences] saw these people really getting high by the camp fire, Doris Day was gone forever. They went, *Oh, we don't want* [those type of actors]. *We want real people. We want to see real emotions.'* The verisimilitude of *Five Easy Pieces* was aided by the fact that Karen had a crush on Jack during the making of the picture ('I really was kind of in love with him,' as she recalls).

In the opening moments of the film, which – unusually – was shot in sequence, we see Bobby and Rayette at home after a hard day's work, bickering sweetly in each other's arms. So natural and convincing is the scene that one feels like a Peeping Tom. The

---

*Which Black also appears in, as an Acid-imbibing hooker.

relationship is then tested when Bobby discovers Rayette is pregnant. Traditionally, in movies of the past, and in society generally, when a man discovers his girlfriend is pregnant he is expected to set aside whatever doubts he might have and marry her, simply to do the right thing. Bobby's reaction, however, is to leave Rayette, and put his own happiness first. This was in fact the way the world was going. The marriage rate had risen throughout the 1960s in many English-speaking countries, reaching an all-time high in the United States in 1970. But after this peak fewer and fewer people married, while the divorce rate rose as the after-effects of the great social and cultural changes of the 1960s – like waves created by rocks tossed into water – rippled out through society. Many more women enjoyed a greater degree of independence now. Also, gay culture became increasingly prevalent. Whereas in the past gay or bisexual men might have married, often unhappily, in order to conform, more now took the option to be essentially what they were by nature. The increase in divorce in America was aided by changes in legislation, including the introduction of so-called 'no fault' divorces (in California initially) in 1969, and divorce became easier legally in other countries, too. So did abortion. To summarise, it was increasingly commonplace in the 1970s to be single, and it was socially acceptable to be concerned with finding oneself and one's own happiness, rather than seeking to please others (a spouse, one's children) first. Though there was a good deal of selfishness in all this, for many it was an improvement on the old ways of sticking with somebody because that was what society expected. 'I always thought *leaving* was like the best invention of the century,' says Karen Black, speaking personally and typically for a young woman born in the early 1940s. From time immemorial, couples in her Midwestern family had mated for life ('like pigeons' as Woody Allen remarks in *Manhattan*, another great seventies movie). Karen and her sister broke that tradition, as did so many others of their generation around the world, and she was glad about it. Because if a relationship wasn't working it was better for everybody if you left. 'I *leave*. If I don't like some one, I leave,' she exclaims. 'Thank God!'

In the movie, just when Bobby has resolved to leave Rayette (absolutely the right decision in Karen's mind, so long as he made a financial contribution to the upbringing of their child), he hears from his sister that their father has suffered a series of strokes and goes home to visit him for the first time in three years. Against his better judgement, Bobby takes Rayette along with him on the trip, unable to summon the courage to dump her just at that moment. This middle section of *Five Easy Pieces* is a mini-road movie, with Bobby and Rayette driving north through California, Oregon and Washington, picking up a couple of eccentric girls *en route*, played by Toni Basil (a good friend of Karen's), and Jack's friend Helena Kallianiotes, the latter as an intense lesbian obsessed with the prevalence of dirt in society. She explains that she is heading to Alaska because she figures Alaska is a very clean place, being all white, judging from pictures. The scenes with these two nutty women in the back of the car are wonderfully funny, and *real* – partly because the actors knew each other well and drove the route together with Bob Rafelson, shooting as they went, a delightful *On the Road*-type adventure for the cast – and the audience – sandwiched between the early scenes in Bakersfield and later scenes on Puget Sound. 'It was like we were always all together. We never separated,' reminisces Karen Black. 'We'd get in the car, we'd go, *Oh, look a big sand hill! Let's go climb it!* We'd stop the car. Rafelson would get out. We'd all go running up this huge sand hill, rolling down it, you know, lying down and rolling down it, all of us, laughing. Then we'd get some oranges, and we toss oranges and play catch in the afternoon light, get back in the car.' Pulling into little towns, they would all book into the same hotel, eat dinner together and then rehearse the next day's scenes.

The most famous of these comes when the travelling companions pull into a highway diner where Bobby attempts to order a cup of coffee, a plain omelette and wheat toast from a waitress who is having none of it. The set menu does not offer toast with an omelette. The waitress suggests tartly that he orders the number two, which consists of a plain omelette with cottage fries and rolls. It's the nearest thing. When Bobby tries to adapt this to suit himself, she snaps: 'No substitutions!' The scene was inspired by a peccadillo of Bob Rafelson's: wherever he went to eat, he stubbornly ignored the menu and tried to order *à la carte*, arguing that if the kitchen had the ingredients why couldn't he order precisely what he wanted? The actual scene however was written by Jack's friend Carole Eastman, who knew Jack's temper of old:

Bobby (Nicholson): *What do you mean you don't make side orders of toast? You make sandwiches, don't you? . . . You've got bread, and a toaster of some kind?*

Waitress: *I don't make the rules!*

Bobby: *OK, I'll make it as easy for you as I can. I'd like an omelette, plain, and a chicken salad sandwich on wheat toast – no mayonnaise, no butter, no lettuce – and a cup of coffee.*

Waitress: *A number two. Chicken salad san'. Hold the butter, the lettuce and the mayonnaise. And a cup of coffee. Anything else?*

Bobby: *Yeah. Now, all you have to do is hold the chicken, bring me the toast, give me a check for the chicken salad sandwich, and you haven't broken any rules.*

Waitress: *You want me to hold the chicken, huh?*

Bobby: *I want you to hold it between your knees.*

Waitress: *You see that sign, sir? I guess you'll all have to leave. I'm not taking any more of your smartness and sarcasm!*

Bobby: *You see this sign?*

Bobby ends the argument by sweeping everything off the table, a cathartic gesture which made cinema audiences get up and cheer in 1970. 'His contempt is not for the waitress, it's for the rules. Rules are something he is having a hard time accepting throughout his life,' comments Rafelson, who always felt uneasy about the gleeful reaction audiences have to this scene, and to a scene that comes shortly after it when Bobby and Rayette get to Puget Sound and Bobby tells a garrulous middle-aged intellectual to *shut-up*. Again, audiences whooped with approbation, though in both cases Rafelson considered that Bobby was behaving loutishly. Cinemagoers liked the rebellion, however, and part of Jack's charm was that he played the rebel very well, with a singular talent for throwing a charismatic fit of rage.

Having cheated on Rayette at the start of the film with a girl he picks up in a bowling alley, Bobby cheats on her again when he gets to the family home at Puget Sound, having sex with his brother's girlfriend. She regrets sleeping with Bobby and declines his offer to go away with him, explaining why he is a bad bet for any woman; how can Bobby expect anybody to love him when he does not love or respect himself, she asks. In contrast, his superficially dull but decent brother is a much more attractive proposition. Having been rejected by a woman of his own social background and comparable intelligence, as opposed to poor dumb Rayette who doesn't understand him at all, Bobby sees finally how wretched he is. It is in this state that he has his final one-sided discussion with his father, breaking down in tears when he comprehends how impossible it is to explain himself or make a connection with the old man. The realism is compelling, underpinned by Jack's real life experiences. For years afterwards the actor would cite the movie as being the work he was proudest of and closest to personally.

One of the pleasures of American cinema in the early 1970s is that pictures were permitted for a brief time to end on an ambiguous, even unhappy note, which gave them complexity and a sense of truth. In the final few minutes of *Five Easy Pieces*, Bobby and Rayette pull into a rain-swept Gulf service station, having left Puget Sound on their return journey to California. Rayette goes for coffee as Jack uses the toilet. When he looks in the mirror he 'sees the inside of himself,' as Rafelson puts it, and realises he is no good, that Rayette would be better off without him, though the poor mutt didn't know it, humming her Tammy Wynette songs and planning their fantasy future together. Emerging from the restroom, Bobby sees a logging truck in the forecourt and on the spur of the moment asks the driver for a ride, getting into the cab before he notices that he has left his jacket behind, his wallet with Rayette. All he has are the clothes he is wearing: boots, jeans and a black turtleneck sweater, a garment which Bob Rafelson had bought for himself as a college boy in the 1950s, making a connection with the existentialist French writers he so admired. To Rafelson, Bobby Dupea was an existentialist character, a man who had cut himself free of his past and rejected society's rules. So Bob gave Jack his sweater to wear in the picture, the symbolism coming into its own as Bobby Dupea huddles for warmth in the black sweater in the logging truck, choosing not to retrieve his jacket but go on as he is, though the driver warns him that it'll be colder than Hell where they're going. And so the movie ends with Bobby running out on Rayette, headed for Canada.

'Everybody feels sorry for Rayette, and thinks what Bobby is doing is somewhat dastardly, but perhaps more criminal would have been for him to mistreat her for the rest of his life,' comments Rafelson, who created the ending after rejecting Carole Eastman's original scene in which Bobby crashes the car and kills himself.* Rafelson didn't think Bobby was a suicidal character. But the way in which Rafelson cuts Bobby loose at the end of *Five Easy Pieces* is uncompromising, made starker by the way the camera lingers on the bleak Gulf forecourt as the logging truck disappears into the North and Rayette emerges from the café, searching around for Bobby with increasing agitation as the titles come up over the melancholy scene. It is a sombre ending to a film that typifies a particular kind of early 1970s American movie, owing much to the European art-house pictures which directors such as Rafelson so admired, and to writers including Jack Kerouac who had influenced them in their youth. For ideas take a long time to gestate and directors such as Rafelson, and others whom we will come to, had been carrying their pet projects in their minds for *years*. Only now – thanks to the change in the business brought about by *Easy Rider* – were they getting an opportunity to bring their ideas to the silver screen. 'It became *permission*-time. Permission was granted in the '70s to behave [and] make work that, in fact, was something you were thinking about doing in the '60s, but nobody gave you permission to do,' elucidates Bob. 'I'm talking about cultural permission.' Jack Nicholson was the perfect leading man for this new era of quirky, naturalistic picture-making, showing in *Five Easy Pieces* how 'dazzling' he could be on screen. As Karen Black puts it. 'You just wanted to see more.'

---

*Eastman had her name removed from the film, and is credited under the pseudonym Adrien Joyce.

2

MR HOCKNEY, MR AND MRS CLARK
AND PERCY

*I said, 'Well, Mr and Mrs Clark and Percy is better than Mr
and Mrs Clark and Blanche.'*

DAVID HOCKNEY

In London in the spring of 1970, the British artist David Hockney
was also working on a naturalistic picture, one that *doesn't move,
doesn't talk and lasts longer*, as he says, arguing the merits of painting
versus the more pervasive form of photography. While many of his
artist contemporaries were moving deeper into abstraction in the early
1970s, Hockney had become fascinated with painting large naturalistic
double portraits of couples he knew in order to try and figure out their
relationships, and he had recently embarked upon perhaps his most
renowned work, *Mr and Mrs Clark and Percy*. (See picture 1.) More than
thirty years later, Hockney and Celia Birtwell (formerly Clark, and one
of the two people in the picture) meet at the artist's London home to
talk about what has become one of the most famous and popular of
all modern paintings, indeed a masterpiece of 1970s art. 'It's very good,
actually, isn't it?' asks Hockney, without false modesty, studying a
small reproduction of the portrait which, in reality, is an enormous
canvas measuring seven by ten feet, showing an elegant young couple,
dressed in the high fashion of 1970, staring out at the viewer with
solemn faces. 'I notice that it stands up incredibly well. It's become a
kind of iconic thing, but you don't know why that happens. I mean,

it could be of course, yes, it's a fashionable couple of the time . . . Mr and Mrs Clark were known then.'

Firstly, there was Mr Clark. Raymond was his given name, but he disliked it and was known to all as Ossie (pronounced Ozzy) after the Lancashire town of Oswaldtwistle where he grew up. Ossie came to London in the 1960s to study fashion at the Royal College of Art, which is where he met David Hockney, a slightly older student, born in Bradford in 1937, making him of an age with Jack Nicholson and many others in our story (the last generation, as Hockney observes, to be brought up without the constant influence of television. David was eighteen by the time his family got a TV, and by then he was making his own pictures). As well as being from working-class families in the North, Ossie and David were both homosexual, and lovers briefly. Gay sex was illegal in Britain until 1967, and something that was mostly hidden for years thereafter. But from college onward, Hockney was remarkably open about his sexuality and made it a feature of his work, almost as a political statement. In 1961 an astute young dealer named John Kasmin (who prefers to travel under his surname alone) attended an RCA student show and recognised the quality and marketability of pictures such as Hockney's *The Most Beautiful Boy in the World* (1961). 'I adored David's work from the start,' says Kasmin. 'I knew he would be a success, and his open homosexuality and use of gay imagery would be to his advantage since gay people always have money to spend on art.' He offered David a yearly stipend to cover his living costs and expenses in exchange for being his dealer, thus launching Hockney as a professional artist.

Embarking on his own career as a fashion designer, Ossie was less comfortable about being gay than David was, as he was generally less sure of himself. For instance, he changed the way he spoke when he came south. 'He got rid of his accent, Ossie. That's the one thing I noticed when I met him. He didn't have a northern accent at all, actually,' recalls Hockney. 'Whereas I did. I was quite strong.' In London, Ossie took lovers of both sexes and tried to live as a straight man at times, which is how he got involved with Celia Birtwell, a young fabric designer also from the North. Ossie and Celia became close while sharing a flat in West London, fell into bed together, as one did, though she knew he was not entirely straight, and became romantically entwined. 'I can't bear that gay scene,' Ossie would complain to Celia, suggesting that they try and make it as a couple. 'Very stupidly, I said yes,' she recalls. 'He moved in with me and for quite a while he was actually rather nice. I mean, he had this lust for boys, but he had this thing about me . . . I suppose it was playing with fire, which was a thing that you would do a lot more then than you would later on.' Rather like David and Angie Bowie, whom we shall meet in due course, Ossie and Celia decided bisexuality was not necessarily an impediment to a happy relationship. As Celia says, such things seemed possible in the '60s and '70s. And when Celia became pregnant, they got married. David was the witness at the ceremony at Kensington Register Office in January 1969. Any misgivings the wedding guests may have had about this union seemed borne out almost straight away when Ossie took off on honeymoon to Barbados . . . without his wife.

Apart from being a married couple, Ossie and Celia were business partners, she designing the fabric which he made into clothes, predominantly but not exclusively for women. In this they were extremely successful, with Ossie becoming as renowned a British designer as his French contemporary Yves Saint Laurent, and Celia was no less talented in her field. When they met, she was creating geometric pop art prints in the style of Bridget Riley, but in the late 1960s Celia began to develop her own more lyrical style, influenced predominantly by nature, with an emphasis on floral patterns in subtle but unusual colours – dead rose, prune and so forth – also with an eye on 1930s design which, together with the look of the 1950s, enjoyed a revival in the 1970s as Celia and other designers were obliged to search beyond the 1960s for ideas less shopworn. Celia specialised in working with diaphanous fabrics such as chiffon, creating bolts of printed cloth which Ossie cut into beautiful, sexy dresses, drawing and snipping with a dexterity that was a delight to behold. 'He always surprised me by what he could do with my prints,' says Celia. 'Nobody was as clever as he was.'

In addition to his skill in the studio, Ossie was the first designer to have his models walk down the catwalk to rock music, thus creating the archetype of the modern theatrical fashion show. 'He was very, very influenced by pop stars,' recalls Celia. 'In fact, I think he felt jealous because they could cut an album and make a fortune from it, where if you were a dress designer you were only as good as your last collection . . . and you're not financially rewarded like you were in the pop world.' Rock was at its apogee in 1970. The Beatles, Simon & Garfunkel and the Velvet Underground all released their final extraordinary LPs that year. Also new in the shops were Frank Zappa's *Hot Rats*, Santana's *Abraxas*, *Tapestry* by Carole King and *Layla* by Derek and the Dominoes. A colossal amount of marvellous music. Ossie named his dresses in honour of the new sounds. There was a Guitar dress, and later a Ziggy dress, when David Bowie became Ziggy Stardust. And Ossie made personal friends of many rock stars and their partners, some of whom modelled for him and Celia. George Harrison's wife, Pattie, the subject of Eric Clapton's new song 'Layla', was a favourite model. Ossie said admiringly that Pattie had ankles 'like glass.' The sight of Mrs Harrison floating down the catwalk to rock music at the Clarks' 'Revolution' show in Mayfair in 1970, wearing a chiffon-print bluebird dress, with David Hockney and Jimi Hendrix in the audience, epitomised the new fusion of fashion, art and music.

As Ossie's designs became more sought-after, Hockney's career was also getting established, his painting style having broadened and developed since college. For a while he had been fashionably semi-abstract, with a fleeting connection to pop art in works such as his 1967 picture *A Bigger Splash*: literally the depiction of a splash of water rising up from an idealised Californian swimming pool the moment after the entry of an unseen diver. In the late 1960s, and 1970s, many of David's contemporaries moved further into abstraction, but he diverged from the mainstream and followed his own artistic tributary into naturalism. While most of the artists who showed their work at Kasmin's Bond Street gallery were creating big colour-field paintings and uncompromising metal sculpture, David showed exquisite drawings and paintings, mostly of human figures, where the subjects were clearly recognisable for what they were, which seemed old-fashioned and twee to fellow artists. 'Some of the artists I showed, like Kenneth

Noland, disapproved of David's work,' concedes Kasmin, who also represented such giants of modernity as the British sculptor Anthony Caro and the American Frank Stella. 'You know, *What am I doing with this frivolous stuff?*' Hockney didn't care what anybody thought of his new work. 'You just go on doing your pictures. I mean, I've always done them for myself, to please myself.' And in the long run the humanity of Hockney's pictures attracted a much larger audience than most of the abstract artists who sniped at him. As Kasmin points out, 'A whole world of people would come in when it was his show who didn't come in to any other show.'

With his pictures selling strongly in Britain and the US, where he spent much of his time, Hockney refurbished a spacious flat-cum-studio at 17 Powis Terrace, London W11, where he lived with his American boyfriend Peter Schlesinger; driving a BMW; smoking Havana cigars; a frequenter of the ballet and opera. Raised on classical music, a regular at concerts given by the Hallé Orchestra in Bradford all his teenage years, Hockney did not share Ossie's infatuation with rock. 'I don't dance for instance,' he says, touching on a subject that would feature significantly in his career in the mid-1970s. 'So I like art music, meaning: music you listen to that's in the foreground.' Dressed in bespoke suits, often with brightly-coloured shirts and ties, his dyed yellow hair contrasting with large, black-framed spectacles, Hockney cut a distinctive and eccentric figure on the London scene. Unlike many artists, he was also a good conversationalist and for all these reasons he was often called upon by broadcasters to appear on television and by journalists for quotes in the newspapers. 'I became aware that I was reasonably articulate as a painter. Some are. Some aren't. You don't need to be as a painter. But that meant if they wanted someone to say something about painting it was me they were getting . . . And, you know, most reporters are lazy: *We'll see if he'll do it.*' In short, Hockney was a wealthy and famous man by 1970. But life was not carefree.

Like most artists, Hockney put his work first and his relationships suffered as a result. The love of his life, Peter Schlesinger, having tired of living in his boyfriend's shadow, began to pull away from him at this time. An added stress was the fact that the documentary filmmaker

Jack Hazan was shooting a movie about David, supposedly about his art, but in the end an account of his disintegrating relationship. (The film, *A Bigger Splash*, an important art film in the decade, also notable for its frank approach to homosexuality, was released in 1973.) As it became clear that Peter was leaving David, and had indeed found someone new, the desolate artist went to his friends for solace, confiding in Celia in particular.

At the time Celia and Ossie were living with their baby son, Albert, and their two cats, Percy and Blanche, in a first-floor apartment at 55 Linden Gardens, London W2, a large Victorian building behind Notting Hill Gate. Influenced by the interior designer Sybil Colefax, Celia had decorated the flat throughout in white, going so far as to lime the oak floors, giving the rooms a luminous quality. Despite having this bright and elegant nest to return to, Ossie would typically stay out late at night, gallivanting in clubs and taking drugs, a vice that would ultimately get the better of him. Many an evening Celia lay on their bed for hours, listening for the returning drone of her husband's Mini. Sometimes David kept Celia company during these anxious vigils, lounging on the Clarks' bed as he talked to her about his problems with Peter. And they became very close during this time, almost intimate. The idea of David and Celia becoming *lovers* was absurd, of course, only it wasn't quite. Somewhat to his surprise David found himself tempted to take his friendship with Celia further. 'I think he got rather keen on me at one time,' reveals Celia. 'I'm rather flattered actually.' The female form was ultimately too off-putting. 'I think it was the breasts that upset him the most,' notes Kasmin, pointing out that Celia was nevertheless one of the only women Hockney has drawn in a state of undress: *Celia Half-nude* (1975).

An even more significant picture came out of this friendship when David decided to paint a double portrait of Ossie and Celia in the light, white bedroom he had got to know so well. As his relationship with Peter failed, the artist became fascinated with couples and had already embarked on a series of double portraits of friends such as Christopher Isherwood and his partner Don Bachardy, who were depicted at home, in great detail on a grand scale. In this sense, the portraits had a classical look. But by using acrylic rather than oil paints Hockney also achieved a modern, poster-like appearance. He took photographs in preparation for these pictures, and worked from photographs much of the time, but these new portraits did not have the quality of the work of the American artist Richard Estes, say, whose pictures of American street scenes around this time look almost exactly like photos. Hockney's pictures were clearly made with brush and paint. (Close-up one can see the drips.) But with the figures almost life-size, depicted in great detail, the subjects became very life-*like*, and something of their relationship is revealed, especially when Hockney knew his subjects intimately. 'I think I might say that of all the portraits [I did at this time] I knew Ossie and Celia better than any of them, and I knew [the room],' comments Hockney, looking again at the reproduction of *Mr and Mrs Clark and Percy*, and trying to fathom why, along with *A Bigger Splash*, it has become the picture he is best known for. Indeed, in 2005 *Mr and Mrs Clark* was voted in one poll as being among the ten most popular paintings in Britain.*

Starting in the spring of 1970, Ossie and Celia posed for preparatory sketches and photos in their bedroom at Linden Gardens, taking positions on either side of the French windows that opened on to a balcony, so daylight enters from the middle of the picture, rather than one side, which is technically challenging because Hockney was painting against light, *contre-jour* as artists say. Because of the light emanating from the centre of the picture and the fact that the room was basically white, the portrait would also have an especially luminescent quality, with a faint green tinge coming from the trees in leaf in the street outside. The key point thematically is that Ossie and Celia posed apart, looking not at themselves but out at the artist – the third, unseen person in the picture – Celia standing and Ossie sitting in a cane-backed Marcel Breuer tubular chair. The pose lends the portrait a pleasing symmetry. 'It's very well balanced, isn't it?' remarks the artist. 'It's a very harmonious picture.' At the same time the pose is part of the enigmatic quality of the picture, raising all sorts of questions about

---

*When it is suggested to Hockney that he is known primarily to the general public for these two paintings, he becomes understandably slightly grumpy, complaining: 'Well, I have done more than a couple of pictures!'

the nature of the relationship and recalling another very famous and popular double portrait.

The composition was inspired partly by one of the masterpieces of the Middle Ages, Jan van Eyck's double *Arnolfini* portrait, which Hockney knew very well from numerous visits to London's National Gallery over the years. (See picture 3.) For centuries art experts have debated the precise significance of this immaculate and ambiguous Flemish portrait of the early fifteenth century, an innovative work in the history of art in its realism and attention to the then recently discovered laws of perspective. 'A simple corner of the real world had suddenly been fixed on to a panel as if by magic,' as E.H. Gombrich writes of the painting in his celebrated book *The Story of Art*. The picture shows a young couple standing together in a room next to a bed. They are wealthy people, as indicated by the exotic fruit ripening on the windowsill, the richness of their clothes and the furnishings and fabrics, as well as the lapdog standing guard at their feet. Giovanni Arnolfini was, in fact, an aristocratic Italian merchant of the day. It is unclear what event precisely the picture commemorates, however. Often referred to as *The Arnolfini Marriage*, the picture would appear at first glance to show the couple becoming man and wife. Yet there are many inconsistencies and apparent contradictions. For one, the woman looks pregnant. She may have been with child when she married Giovanni, of course, but it would seem indelicate to depict her so. Maybe the picture is about something else, something unknown, and indeed some scholars have argued persuasively that the picture does not show a marriage but a betrothal ceremony, with Giovanni solemnly pledging – his right hand raised, standing in front of witnesses (two of whom can be seen reflected in a mirror) – to marry this young lady, in an age when the union of a man and woman was more to do with combining the fortunes of families than as a matter of love. Betrothals were therefore taken very seriously indeed. Still, the picture remains a delightful, playful mystery, with van Eyck apparently inviting us to amuse ourselves by puzzling over its many symbols. As the *Arnolfini* portrait is a riddle, it is also a window into the domestic life of moneyed metropolitan people in Bruges in 1434 (the artist carefully inscribed in the background, 'Jan van Eyck was here/1434'). Similarly, Hockney portrayed Ossie and Celia in an ambiguous way in their bedroom in the middle-class London of 1970, surrounded by fashionable artefacts of *their* time.

Ossie's Breuer chair, a classic late 1920s design, was very much back in vogue in the '70s, recently purchased by the Clarks from the trendy King's Road shop Aram. Similarly, the Bauhaus-style table and Art Deco lamp in the Hockney picture were items with which any sophisticated young couple might have adorned their London home at the start of the new decade. Suitably for two people prominent in fashion, the hair and clothes also tell a story about who they are. Ossie's hair grew fashionably long, down to the collar of his chiffon shirt, which was a garment of his own design cut from one of Celia's most celebrated prints. Although he wears a sweater over the shirt, the collar is exposed and Hockney took great care to paint in Celia's Floating Daisy pattern. Ossie wears flared green suede hipster trousers (green being the dominant colour in the picture: the green light, Ossie's green sweater and trousers, the green stems of the lilies in a green vase). Giovanni Arnolfini is in his stockinged-feet, having removed his clogs, which are seen in the foreground of the van Eyck. In a similar way, Ossie is barefoot. His twentieth-century toes nestle in the tufts of a shag rug, which was another domestic item very much of its time (Celia remembers that David made the tufts shaggier than they were in order to obscure Ossie's toes, which he found difficult to paint). Finally, on Ossie's lap sits one of the Clark cats, its white fur luxuriant. To some eyes the cat is a not-altogether satisfactory detail in the picture, appearing not to sit entirely naturally on Ossie's lap, but almost seeming to float in space. The feline is, however, a key element in the composition. Again there is a parallel with the van Eyck because, of course, the Arnolfinis have their charming little dog with them. In the Middle Ages, a dog was often included in portraits as a symbol of fidelity. In this case, the cat might be seen as a symbol of Ossie's *infidelity*. In this and so many ways, Hockney's wonderful double portrait can be read as an updating of the *Arnolfini*: a very modern union in which some things are the same for a wealthy metropolitan couple as they were five centuries ago, and just as much has changed.

Take the stance of the women in the picture. In the *Arnolfini* portrait the young woman is demure, her head cast down, obviously sub-servient to Giovanni. In Hockney's picture, on the opposite side of the French windows to Ossie and wearing a long black crêpe dress of her husband's design, stands the proud figure of Celia. She is a successful young businesswoman, head up, hands on hips, as if having just admonished her husband for not attending to some important matter. Celia doesn't recall that they had had an argument that day, but it wouldn't be unusual in a relationship that was a business partnership as well as a marriage (and difficult on both counts), and she did charac-teristically stand like that: *Bossy Birtwell*, as she says. That she is on her feet while Ossie sits is also significant. 'I was quite aware that it was the wrong way: that usually the man is standing up,' says Hockney. The pose symbolises consciously or unconsciously an eccentric marriage, with a working wife and a rather lazy gay husband, as does the fact that Celia is wearing her wedding ring on her right hand, not her left as is traditional. That she is standing is especially incongruous because, like the woman in the *Arnolfini*, it appears that Mrs Clark is pregnant. It is not clear even to Celia whether she *was* pregnant precisely at that time, because the picture was painted over so many months (starting in the spring of 1970 and not completed until the following year). She was probably still recovering from her first pregnancy when the picture was begun, which would explain the slight bulge in her form, and she was pregnant again months later, with her second son, George, when Hockney was finishing. The ambiguity is in keeping with the overall enigmatic quality of the picture, and her full figure is also echoed by the curve of the columns on the terrace outside the window.

Couples often touch in double portraits (the Arnolfinis, typically, touch hands), or they seem about to touch, maybe arranging them-selves with their limbs inclined towards one another. This is the body language of people in love. Celia and Ossie are separate, like business partners whose conversation – perhaps fractious conversation – has just been interrupted, which in a sense is what is going on. In this modern relationship, it is Celia who looks sternly out at the viewer and it is the man who hangs his head slightly sheepishly, as with the woman in the *Arnolfini*. Apart from seeming more confident than her husband, it should be mentioned that Celia appears radiantly beautiful, as if painted by Botticelli, a testament to David's skill and affection for her, and indeed the root of a nickname some critics attached to the picture when it first became famous in the early 1970s. Hockney's 'Bottichelsea', they called it, a somewhat sneering pun on his West London social set.

As noted, in comparison to his wife's open, confident expression, Ossie's face appears slightly downcast and guarded. Indeed, his visage caused the painter much trouble. David reworked Ossie's head repeatedly to try and capture something of what Kasmin calls Ossie's 'hard-to-pin-down nature.' Ossie was an exasperatingly difficult character, a puzzle to everybody including himself. 'He had a psychiatrist for many years, but nobody seemed to know who he was or what he was,' laments Celia. And his story would not end happily. When David painted their portrait, the Clarks were at the high point of their careers, their marriage difficult but manageable, their work selling strongly, the future apparently bright. And they were so young, still in their twenties, beautiful and fresh-looking. Soon life began to unravel. Kasmin, who was their business manager briefly, talks of Ossie as 'a wild boy' forever chasing after men, dizzy on drugs, with no idea how to handle money. Even at the height of his success, he was virtually broke, a major handicap being that he never had an entrepreneurial partner – as Yves Saint Laurent did, by comparison, with Pierre Bergé – who could look after the business side of things. And although Ossie would work frantically on his collections, after the shows were done he did not move with alacrity, as he should have, to capitalise on his success, but would become lazy and inactive. 'This is what he did do: he tended to work very, very intensely for the shows, and he did, I mean night and day actually, for the shows,' recalls Hockney, reminiscing with Celia.

'And then crash out,' interjects Celia.

'Then crash out for three months . . .'

'Which was when he should have been with somebody building up the collection, selling it . . .'

'Of course, he'd make a lot of money from the shows . . . Then he was out at nightclubs.'

'*Let them do it*,' says Celia, meaning the assistants. 'But they didn't know how to. That was his downfall.'

In 1974, Ossie and Celia divorced, an inevitable outcome, one might think, to a flawed relationship, but apparently a shock to Ossie who never forgave Celia and seems to have blamed David for coming between husband and wife. Without Celia, the dress-maker's career went into sharp and ultimately tragic decline, exacerbated by a drug habit that affected his mood and impaired his judgement. By the 1990s he was bankrupt, living on state benefit, in trouble with the police and humiliating himself in front of old friends such as Mick Jagger by virtually begging for money. In 1995 he took up with a young Italian boyfriend named Diego Cogolato who, after apparently experiencing a vision, beat and stabbed Ossie to death the following year. The designer who was once as fashionable as Yves Saint Laurent met a violent, squalid end at the age of fifty-four, by which time his work was all but forgotten. 'I think it's rather good of Ossie, actually,' says Celia, of the portrait that freezes her and her late husband at the cusp of their lives on a warm spring day in 1970. 'But it's very *serene* in comparison to what was going on. It's quite calm . . . I think it's a façade.'

The 1970s was a time when the rules of coupledom were changing, when men and women walked away from relationships when they felt stifled (like Bobby Dupea in *Five Easy Pieces*); also when men could be more like women, and the other way around. It became fashionable, in Britain particularly, for men be effeminate. In rock music specifically, Mick Jagger was a distinctly androgynous superstar in his early seventies incarnation, wearing Ossie Clark-designed stage suits; David and Angie Bowie would soon declare themselves the most famous bisexual couple in the world. The Clarks were another odd celebrity couple, their unconventional life belied by the deliberately prosaic title that David Hockney chose for the picture he painted of them. The cat perched on Ossie's knee in the picture was the Clarks' pet Blanche, and when David came to give the painting a name he wanted to include the cat in the title, but didn't like the sound of *Mr and Mrs Clark and Blanche*. There was another family pet, though, with the more euphonic name of Percy. Suitably, for a decade in which sexual ambiguity was such a motif in the arts, David renamed and thereby re-sexed Blanche the female puss as Percy the tomcat. Sold to London's Tate Gallery, *Mr and Mrs Clark and Percy* soon became one of the most famous and popular paintings on public display in Britain. It is also something of a good joke, for Percy – as Hockney well knew – is a slang word for penis: a sly juxtaposition of immaculate art and vulgarity that the Monty Python team would have been proud of, especially the animator Terry Gilliam, who was a frequenter of the Tate at this time, looking for artwork he could copy and subvert with a similar sense of naughty fun.

3

AND NOW FOR SOMETHING COMPLETELY DIFFERENT

. . . I wish to complain about this parrot . . .
MONTY PYTHON'S FLYING CIRCUS

The trouble began when Terry Gilliam finished eating his dinner and cast his cutlery aside just anyhow. 'That's not the way we do it in this country,' expostulated hotelier Donald Sinclair, pouncing on the table where Gilliam and his fellow Pythons were attempting to relax after a day filming at the beach near Torquay in Devon. They had been struggling with a not entirely successful sketch entitled 'Scott of the Antarctic'. Despite the problems, there had been a veritable hum of jolly conversation at dinner that evening at the Hotel Gleneagles, with Gilliam punctuating his contributions, as was his way, with hoots of manic laughter: a noise between that of a barn owl and a loony child. The laughter died on his lips when Sinclair interjected to correct his table manners. 'This is the way *we* do it,' he told the American, picking up Gilliam's scattered cutlery and then snapping the knife and fork together at 90 degrees to his guest in the British style and then – *Finished? Right!* – whipping the plate away to the kitchen.

Gilliam was agape, astonished, horrified. 'The man was crazy,' he shudders with the memory. 'Actually, there's a lot of John [Cleese] in him, before John created Basil. Hahaha-hehehehehe.' Anyway, that was it, the Pythons were leaving. It wasn't the first time that Mr Sinclair had behaved outrageously towards them. The youngest

Python, Eric Idle, left his bag behind at reception one morning in his rush to get out to filming. When he returned and asked Sinclair if he had seen the bag, he was told that it was out by the swimming pool, behind a wall.

'Why did you put it there?'

'We thought it might be a bomb.' A *bomb*, in Torquay? Had the IRA decided to target Devon now? As if by way of further explanation, Sinclair offered this bizarre *non sequitur*: 'We've had some staff problems recently.'

When the comedians came down from London to film the second series of *Monty Python's Flying Circus* in 1970, Sinclair, who was by background a retired naval officer, hadn't wanted to accommodate them. 'They didn't fit into a family hotel,' as his wife Betty explains. 'But it was off-season [and] I argued that it was good money and we couldn't afford to turn them away.' Having checked in, the six Pythons soon succeeded in fulfilling Sinclair's worst fears, driving the militarily correct hotelier to distraction with their demanding behaviour. They kept irregular hours, coming in late, demanding hot baths and drinks from the bar, especially the one who smoked a pipe, Graham Chapman, a doctor if you could credit it, a bloody drunk in truth, and a poof. No, Sinclair would not open the bar so that Dr Chapman could chuck brandy down his throat and chat up men! *What did he think this was?* (In his memoirs, Graham Chapman offered a dry observation on Mr Sinclair: 'The owner of this particular hotel did not like guests.')

Then there was John Cleese, with his superior manner. 'I beg your pardon?' Sinclair asked, taking offence when the comedian asked him to telephone for a cab.

'Could you call me a taxi, please,' Cleese repeated.

'A *taxi*?'

'Yes!'

Sinclair emitted a deep sigh. Then through gritted teeth the grudging reply came: 'I *suppose* so.'

After the incident with Terry Gilliam they all moved to a hotel down the road, all except Cleese that is, who stayed on at the Gleneagles to make a study of this man Sinclair whose livelihood depended on providing guests with a home-from-home. He could not have been less suited to the work, being uncongenial, abrasive and angry. In fact, he was a classic comedy character: the rude hotelier. And so the idea of *Fawlty Towers* was hatched in Cleese's ample brain. That great show was some years off, however, and before it came *Monty Python's Flying Circus.*

Though its roots were in the late 1960s, with the first series broadcast from October 1969 on the BBC, *Monty Python* was a great seventies success story. Building on the popularity of their debut series, the troupe wrote, directed and acted in three further television series between 1970 and 1974, and took their comedy far beyond the parameters of a weekly half-hour show. There were *Python* stage tours, books, records and feature films, including the brilliant medieval comedy *Monty Python and the Holy Grail* (1974), in which England's knights clatter coconut shells together in substitution for actual horses (which the production could not afford); and in 1979 the heretical *Monty Python's Life of Brian*, a supremely funny film that also raised an important theological debate. It is remarkable that the troupe were so creative over such a long period, finishing the decade as strongly as they started it, and that they succeeded in so many different mediums. Furthermore, they created all this work without significant outside help, doing their own writing, acting, most of the direction, and even designing their own titles and graphics. Yet the members also found time for spin-off solo projects, the most accomplished of which was *Fawlty Towers*, though Michael Palin's *Ripping Yarns* (1976–79) and Eric Idle's Beatles' spoof *The Rutles* (1978) were also terrific. And this very British humour travelled abroad, becoming popular throughout Europe and the USA, where the Pythons were an important influence on major comedy shows such as *Saturday Night Live*. For all these reasons, *Monty Python* is a jewel of 1970s television, far more brilliant than the dull cop shows and predictable situation comedies so often pointed to as being classic '70s fare: *Kojak*, *Are You Being Served?*, *Happy Days*, and the like.

In contrast to those programmes, intelligence played a very significant part in *Monty Python*, as John Cleese has remarked. All five British Pythons were graduates of Oxford or Cambridge University.

They didn't get into these institutions by dint of privilege, but as exceptionally able students, mostly from ordinary backgrounds. The comedy of *Python* is neither undergraduate humour, nor is it public school humour, though it is often given these labels. Only Michael Palin attended a British public school. He went to Shrewsbury, as his father had before him. Eric Idle was educated at an RAF-funded boarding school, but only because of the premature death of his airman father, and indeed Idle considered the institution a veritable orphanage. More typically, John Cleese was the son of an insurance salesman (the family name originally, and comically, Cheese), educated at an ordinary grammar school and the first member of his family to make the leap to tertiary education, going up to Cambridge in 1960 to study Law. Here it was that Cleese fell in with the Cambridge Footlights, the venerable student theatre company that in recent years had included such luminaries as Alan Bennett and Peter Cook. As importantly, it was at Cambridge that Cleese met Graham Chapman, a medical student who became his writing partner.

Although he looked very ordinary, Chapman was the most eccentric Python, fundamentally different from the others in at least one significant respect, as became apparent in 1967 when he hosted a party in order to announce to his friends that he was, as he put it, a poof. 'But no mincing,' he qualified, 'a butch one with a pipe.' He subsequently became outspoken on the subject of gay life, using his *Python* wealth to help launch *Gay News* in 1972, and taking to task anybody he thought homophobic, often behaving outrageously in the process. Drink had a lot to do with it. Heavy drinking is commonplace among medical students of course. Chapman also drank, perhaps, to cope with his sexuality, and he drank to medicate himself against stage fright. Over the years his boozing became a chronic problem. As well as making Chapman volatile in everyday life, alcoholism affected his work. Irritatingly, Graham often did not know his lines and was generally unreliable. Yet Cleese considered his old university friend to be the funniest Python, and Graham proved an invaluable member of the team when it came to casting the television skits and films: with his conventional looks and straight face, Chapman was frequently best suited to the leading-man role. All in all, he was a curious and contradictory fellow. (Or as Eric Idle puts it simply: 'Graham was weird.') Idle went up to Cambridge shortly after Cleese and Chapman, and duly joined the Footlights, of which he became president – and in that capacity revoked the no-women rule, thus allowing in a remarkable student named Germaine Greer. While he found Chapman to be a strange fish, Idle considered Cleese the most remarkable performer he had ever seen, Cleese's uncommon height alone making him physically impressive on stage (he stands six feet five inches). As Idle says of Cleese, at Cambridge 'there was nobody like him.'

The common factor among this Cambridge set of future Pythons, particularly Cleese and Chapman, was that they tended to express their considerable intelligence, and perhaps a shared residual anger, in articulate and often hurtful mockery. Terry Gilliam likens talking with the Cambridge Pythons in the early days to engaging in a verbal sword fight with superior rapier wits. In conversation, Gilliam's sentences tend not to make grammatical sense and are replete with slang phrases and Americanisms that Cleese and Chapman would ridicule in an understated but nonetheless cutting English way. For years Chapman would relate this story as an example of what the British Pythons referred to disparagingly as Gilliam's *paucity with language*: 'I do remember on one occasion we were touring Canada and we were flying over Lake Superior and Terry looked down at Lake Superior and turned around to the rest of us and said, "Hey you guys – a whole bunch of water," which I didn't feel adequately summed-up the lake.' The Oxford-educated Pythons – Terry Jones and Michael Palin – were no less eloquent and erudite than the Cambridge contingent, but they were not so cruel. 'That's why I got on better with Mike and Terry, the Oxford side, because they are much gentler,' explains Gilliam. 'It was a *total* Cambridge–Oxford split. The college I went to in the States was Occidental, so I shared at least the first letter. So the Os were on one side and the Cs were on the other.'

In parallel with the Cambridge set, Jones and Palin became stars of Oxford University revue shows and by the late 1960s all were working in television in London, with Palin, Jones and Idle making a particular success of a children's programme entitled *Do Not Adjust Your Set*. It was here that they met Gilliam, an illustrator originally from Minnesota where his grandfather was a Baptist minister. Terry had recently worked in New York with Harvey Kurtzman, founder of *Mad* magazine, on the satirical publication *Help!*, contributors to which included artists of the new underground comix where the conventions of cartooning were being subverted to create characters that were, typically, sexually explicit and satirical. 'It was not a mainstream pop culture phenomenon at the time, nor was it taken seriously at the time by the fine art world,' comments Robert Crumb, the master of the genre and a friend of Gilliam, 'but it was creative and original and produced a large amount of good work (plus a lot of mediocre work, naturally).' Gilliam mentally packed the visual style of *Help!*, and the underground comix, when he went travelling in Europe, winding up in London with a job on *Do Not Adjust Your Set*.

Working with a meagre budget, Gilliam developed a simple and effective animation style for this British kids' TV show whereby he would scour museums such as the Tate for images to copy, cut up, enlarge and manipulate. To his delight, he discovered that there was free access to London's museums and that the curators were happy to help him find what he needed. 'At that time nobody was thinking about copyright, who owned this stuff. It was just there for public use, and I used it.' One of his best early ideas involved the Tate's collection of Victorian and Edwardian greetings cards. Taking a classic image of the three wise men (or Magi) travelling towards Bethlehem by camel, guided on their journey by a star, Gilliam cut out the mounted Magi and animated them so that they chased one another across the Holy Land to a frantic comedy soundtrack. Unexpected, subversive and very funny ideas such as this pointed towards the visual style of *Monty Python*, which came into existence late in 1969 when John Cleese, already an established BBC star and a fan of *Do Not Adjust Your Set*, suggested that Palin, Jones, Idle and Gilliam join forces with him and Graham Chapman to make a new series for the Corporation. Despite lacking a coherent plan of what this new show would be like exactly, Cleese and his friends were given the go-ahead to make thirteen episodes – a testament to the progressive ethos of the BBC at the time. As Terry Jones recalls, Huw Weldon, the controller of BBC1, explained the Corporation's philosophy to the Pythons: 'What the BBC tries to do is keep just one step ahead of public opinion, so we're just pushing the boundaries slightly and not just conforming to the lowest common denominator.' This was wonderfully encouraging.

Aside from having the good fortune to debut their show at a time when the BBC was determined to be bold, the Pythons also had the luck to launch just as colour television was coming into service. In some respects, *Monty Python's Flying Circus* was squarely in a tradition of BBC radio and television comedy. The main inspiration for *Monty Python* was of course *The Goon Show*, the absurdist radio programme of the 1950s. Recent television shows made by Oxbridge graduates such as Alan Bennett and Peter Cook, series including *Not Only But Also* and *On the Margin*, were also not dissimilar. But they were in black and white, dating them quickly. From its first episode late in 1969, *Monty Python's Flying Circus* was filmed and broadcast in colour, making it visually exciting in its day, and an important factor in maintaining its watchability in subsequent years. Colour was also a great boon to Terry Gilliam's graphics, which gave the *Python* episodes a cohesion and sense of identity that contemporary shows lacked and which, over time, have become a visual shorthand for Pythonesque comedy. (See pictures 4 & 5.)

The titles were perfectly matched with the theme music, John Philip Sousa's march tune 'Liberty Bell', which Gilliam seized on with enthusiasm. 'It was the punctuation of that great bell. *Bong!* We are off to something. We are off to the races, it felt like. And I just said, "That's the one."' As the band struck up, the long name of the show – a nonsense which had the initial effect of making studio audiences think they were going to see an actual circus – emerged from the blooms of a flowering plant, an animated sequence which segues into surreal images, including that of a woman whose head blows off and a naked girl pursued by a tricycling cardinal who, in turn, is crushed by a falling cherub, all coloured luridly by Gilliam using felt-tip pens (for speed and cheapness). Finally, all these mad, brightly-coloured characters are obliterated by the descending foot of Cupid, from Bronzino's *An Allegory with Venus and Cupid*, one of the treasures of the National Gallery,* accompanied by a fart. Thus one of the glories of Renaissance art was used to infantile ends, a comedic and artistic coup that made Terry hoot with laughter. And his contribution went beyond the titles. There were also wonderful animated sequences within the episodes, providing a refreshing change of pace, and giving special visual interest to every show.

Gilliam took no part in the writing of the live-action sketches. The British Pythons took care of that, dividing into teams based on university alliances. Cleese and Chapman always wrote together, majoring in sketches whose humour often derived from lists of words or ideas, as in the 'Cheese Shop' sketch, a highlight of the third series. They also wrote the classic 'Dead Parrot' sketch, inspired by a story Palin told them about returning his car to a garage where the mechanic, in spite of all the evidence to the contrary, would insist there was nothing wrong with the vehicle. Cleese and Chapman changed this obtuse fellow into the keeper of a pet shop. A dissatisfied customer brings back a parrot.

> Customer (Cleese): . . . *I wish to complain about this parrot what I purchased not half an hour ago from this very boutique.*
>
> Shopkeeper (Palin): *Oh yes, the Norwegian Blue. What's wrong with it?*
>
> Customer: *I'll tell you what's wrong with it. It's dead, that's what's wrong with it.*
>
> Shopkeeper: *No, no, it's resting . . .*

The humour of this exchange never fades. It has become a classic of comedy, a routine frequently performed live on stage by the Pythons, and other comedians in emulation of them. It is as funny in

---

*Throughout this history of the 1970s we see how disparate figures in the arts were frequently crossing one another's paths. With the *Arnolfini* portrait hanging within a few yards of Bronzino's picture in the National Gallery, here we have David Hockney and the Pythons virtually bumping into each other as they collect ideas for their seminal works of the 1970s.

Germany or America as it is in Britain, because it is simple, delightfully ridiculous, and yet true. We have all encountered aggravating shopkeepers who seem to want to be as perverse as possible. The laughs are caused principally by Cleese's sense of indignation, turning into furious sarcasm – something he excelled at – as in this retort to the pet shop owner's assertion that the Norwegian Blue was probably supine because it was pining for the fjords:

> Customer: *It's not pining, it's passed on. This parrot is no more. It has ceased to be. It's expired and gone to meet its maker. This is a late parrot. It's a stiff. Bereft of life, it rests in peace. If you hadn't nailed it to the perch, it would be pushing up the daisies. It's rung down the curtain and joined the choir invisible. This is an ex-parrot.*

While Cleese and Chapman wrote some of the best *Python* sketches, Palin and Jones were the most productive team. Not all of their material was superb, but their contributions included such highlights as 'The Lumberjack Song', the idea for which came to the duo at the end of a long day in which they had been working laboriously on an idea about a maniacal barber. The boys were stuck for a way in which to end the sketch until they had the notion that their barber's real ambition had been to be a lumberjack, living the healthy outdoor life in British Columbia. So the barber bursts into a song about chopping down trees, 'I'm a lumberjack and I'm OK,' joined for the chorus by a group of stout Canadian Mounties. As the barber veers off into singing of pursuits not normally associated with the life of a lumberjack, including wearing women's clothing, the aghast Mounties stop singing, leaving Palin to conclude with the joyous couplet that he wished he'd been a girlie, just like his dear Mama. Despite the slightly *outré* nature of 'The Lumberjack Song', it has a warmth typical of Palin and Jones' work, in contrast to the furious confrontations of Cleese and Chapman, and indeed the writing of Eric Idle, which was different again. Working on his own, Idle created distinctively bright, cheeky sketches such as 'Nudge Nudge', and wrote many of the team's best songs, which lent themselves particularly well to *Python* LPs. Being the most musical team member, and the Python with the sharpest business brain, Idle took charge of these spin-off projects and produced several comedy albums which helped establish *Python* as a cult in the United States before the TV show was widely seen.

Although the different writing camps had their individual flavours, there was a shared belief among all the Pythons that they should avoid conventional comedy formats. As Chapman said, 'We were fed up with the traditional, well-shaped "sketch", the beginning, middle and the inevitable punch line.' *Python* sequences were irregular in shape and content. They could be epic ('Scott of the Antarctic'), or very short (Palin's wild man in rags, whose one spoken word is 'It's . . .'). Sketches were not introduced conventionally, nor did they take place necessarily in ordinary or even logical situations. (Certainly nobody sitting at home in modern Britain expected the Spanish Inquisition to burst into their lounge!) And sketches frequently stopped abruptly, or took off in unexpected directions, as with the barber/lumberjack, often with a Gilliam animation in-between. Characters stepped outside sketches and spoke directly to the audience (Chapman as an army officer apologising for the silliness of the content). All these innovative devices were copied by later television shows, including notably *Saturday Night Live*, which began broadcasting in the US in 1975, its producer Lorne Michaels and his prodigious cast – including Dan Aykroyd, John Belushi and Chevy Chase – all of them *Python* aficionados. As the British show was a collective effort by six very different and individually brilliant comic talents, *SNL* was another ensemble comedy show of anarchic sketches that launched many distinguished careers, with the furious absurdity of Belushi's 'Samurai Hotel' and his 'Killer Bees' particularly reminiscent of *Python*. Even more in the shadow of the show was *Not the Nine O'clock News*, which began broadcasting on BBC television in 1979, with an early episode featuring a parody of *The Life of Brian* controversy then raging. In the tradition of *Python*, both *SNL* and *Not the Nine O'clock News* subverted and fooled around with the conventional sketch format, eschewing the neat set-up and punch-line, and resisting recurring characters that the viewers became fond of, as one might laugh indulgently at an eccentric uncle. The Killer Bees and so forth did become favourites, but they were not ingratiating, and there was nothing ingratiating about *Python*. Rather, the viewer was challenged to get the joke.

Having written the sketches in isolation, the Pythons would meet to enact their routines in front of the group to see which ideas deserved inclusion in the show. There was a good deal of rivalry at these meetings, and indeed the Pythons did not necessarily get on personally. Terry Jones and John Cleese rubbed each other the wrong way from the start, with Cleese characterising Jones as a 'bit of a control freak.' Jones found that Cleese could be arrogant. Cleese dismissed Gilliam's cartoons initially, and was exasperated by Chapman's lax time-keeping. The team member Cleese found most simpatico was Michael Palin and some of the best *Python* sequences involve the friends acting together. Palin's air of innocence provided the foil to set off the brilliance of Cleese's mania. Each Python had his strength as a performer, and Palin was good in almost every one of his roles, though he could never wholly disguise his innate (now legendary) niceness, even when playing the fiendish leader of the Spanish Inquisition. Chapman was a convincing straight man, ironically. Jones was terrific in drag. Idle had a cheeky charm. Gilliam was confined to his studio most of the time working on his animations, but he was determined to be part of the performances, too, and, as he explains, his comrades would condescend to offer him small parts: 'very patronisingly, graciously, they would allow me to put on an uncomfortable suit of armour and hit somebody with a rubber chicken.'

As he was the dominant personality in the team, John Cleese was also the outstanding performer. Dressed in a dinner jacket, solemnly intoning the link, 'And now for something completely different,' his mournful appearance was perfect for parodying old-style BBC announcers, who would say such things when introducing programmes of the utmost banality. He could be meek when the part required, but he was best-suited to playing men who could barely control their contempt for a world fallen lamentably short of expectations, the basic Basil Fawlty/Donald Sinclair type, the pet shop customer so frustrated and maddened by the world that his eyes glitter and the veins on his neck bulge with rising blood pressure, a character set to go *BANG!* Partly because of his unusual height, and skinniness, Cleese also made a fine physical clown, most famously in 'The Ministry of Silly Walks' sketch first broadcast in September 1970, a simple routine which had enormous impact. The sketch begins with Cleese, dressed as an archetypal City gent, carrying a briefcase and wearing a bowler hat (as many men still did in England in 1970), calling in at his corner shop on his way to work. Rather than enter the emporium normally, he half-hops, half-prances into the shop, keeping his upper body erect, his expression betraying no hint of anything being out of the ordinary.

'*Times*, please.'

'Oh yes, sir, here you are,' replies the shopkeeper, played by Terry Jones, without letting on that anything is amiss. It wouldn't be polite to draw attention to a customer's eccentricity. Cleese turns, one leg aloft, and hops out, whereupon he proceeds to half-lope, half-goose-step (with back-steps and twists) to the train station. We meet him again, making his eccentric progress up Whitehall, past the offices of state, before turning in at The Ministry of Silly Walks.

Nothing he would ever do, even the creation of Basil Fawlty, would eclipse the few minutes that John Cleese spent prancing down the street in 1970 – to his dismay because it was such a slight piece, lacking any clever words. 'Oi, Monty,' fans would often shout when they saw Cleese in public, 'let's 'ave yer funny walk then.' Why was there such a strong and enduring response to this sketch? It is perhaps easier to refer to Cleese's 'Silly Walk' than to recall some of the more intricate verbal exchanges in *Monty Python*; the routine becomes a shorthand way of conjuring up the show in conversation. Also, the physical humour crosses language barriers, and thus works internationally, while part of the particular British delight in 'The Ministry of Silly Walks' is that it lampooned a type who lingered on in society in 1970 as a hangover from the days of Empire. In his uniform dress, with his copy of *The Times*, his aloof and predominantly correct manner, Cleese's character was representative of the regimented, frustrated Rule Britannia generation, then passing into late middle-age. The country was still full of them: Donald Sinclair of the Hotel Gleneagles; all those men marching to work in the City of London each day; the Pythons' own parents were of that same generation. They had not disappeared from British life during the 1960s, but were only now being usurped as their sons and daughters came to maturity, the younger generation represented at gatherings such as the 1970 Isle of Wight Pop Festival.

4

EAST AND WEST

One word of truth shall outweigh the whole world.

ALEXANDER SOLZHENITSYN

Having learned her trade in coffee houses, the sight that greeted Joni Mitchell when she took the stage at the Isle of Wight Festival on the afternoon of Saturday, 29 August 1970, was overwhelming. 'It looks like they're making *Ben Hur* or something,' she commented nervously, surveying the vast accretion of humanity spread across East Afton Farm and rising on the downs behind. Close up, you could identify individuals, but the further Joni looked the more people seemed to be like dots of colour – the blues and reds and yellows of their jackets and tents – an estimated 600,000 pixels. And they were a rowdy crowd, quick to heckle the singer, who was *Vogue*-model beautiful in a citrine summer dress and armed only with her guitar and songs. Nervously, she complained from the stage: 'You know, maybe I'm kinda weird, but when I'm sitting up here and playing and I hear all those people growling out there . . . it really puts me uptight, and I forget the words, and then I get nervous, and it's really a drag!'

The days preceding the third and last Isle of Wight Festival – which forms a semi-colon between the music scene of the 1960s and the new decade – had been fraught. The organisers struggled to resist militant fans, including a contingent of French students, veterans of the recent Paris demonstrations, who wanted the five-day event to be free.

As the promoters tried to form an enclosure around the stage, students tore up the fences. They also seized an adjacent hill as a vantage point from which to watch the show at no cost, which affected ticket sales and contributed to the financial failure of the event (which is why it was the last Isle of Wight Pop Festival, until 2002 when the idea was revived on a much smaller scale). A great many acts were on the bill, some already forgotten; others, such as Jimi Hendrix and Jim Morrison of the Doors, artists in the last lap of their careers, slowed-down and fucked-up by success and over-indulgence; and a third group of musicians, paid relatively little attention at the time, who have come to seem ever more impressive. For instance, on Saturday at *the bottom of the bill* was Miles Davis, blowing his horn the summer he released *Bitches Brew*, a truly classic album in the sense that it sounds as modern now as it did when it was made. A few hours later Joni Mitchell took the stage. Known primarily at the time as the hippie-chick singer of such songs as 'The Circle Game', Mitchell matured greatly in the 1970s, releasing a series of more sophisticated records, notably her albums *Blue* (1971), *The Hissing of Summer Lawns* (1975) and *Hejira* (1976).

On that Saturday, in front of that pixilated sea of people, Mitchell performed several songs that would appear on *Blue*. The work was highly personal: songs such as 'Little Green' about the baby daughter she gave birth to back in Canada in 1965 when she was an art student, and had reluctantly given-up for adoption; and 'The Last Time I Saw Richard', concerning her brief subsequent marriage to folk singer Chuck Mitchell, with whom she worked for a while as a double act, taking her name from him, and then moving on. The lyrics to these songs, and indeed all her seventies' work, are highly poetic, subtle and emotionally persuasive. Joni was at the piano picking out the opening chords of another new song, 'My Old Man', about her relationship with the singer James Taylor, when she lost her composure and turned on that huge audience again. 'Listen a minute, will ya? Will ya listen a minute?' In the moment when the hecklers – and those who had just been talking among themselves – paused and took notice, wondering whether to barrack Joni from the stage as they had Kris Kristofferson earlier that day, she managed to settle them. Then Joni held their attention as she completed her set with more of these accomplished new songs, including 'A Case of You', in which she deftly incorporates a quote from Shakespeare, singing the beautiful line, 'I am as constant as a northern star.'*

The Doors played on Saturday evening, their lead singer Jim Morrison almost unrecognisable as the iconic youth of the posters and album covers of 1967–68: bearded, heavy-set, sombre. Following the Doors, the Who by contrast were exuberant, with singer Roger Daltrey in his Messiah-like pomp as the rock-opera character Tommy, and Pete Townshend thrashing his guitar against the thunderous rhythm created by bassist John Entwistle and drummer Keith Moon – the latter beloved of British press and public for his eccentric, boozy antics. Finally on Sunday night, actually at two a.m. Monday, the festival having run madly over schedule, Jimi Hendrix appeared, along with the original Jimi Hendrix Experience drummer Mitch Mitchell and bass player Billy Cox, the great guitarist flamboyant in his multi-coloured Butterfly stage costume, a kind of bird of paradise in flares. Close to the front, Ossie Clark helped welcome the American musician back to a British stage after an absence of almost a year and a half. 'Yeah, thank you very much for showing up, man,' said Hendrix in acknowledgement of his vast audience, many of whom were huddled for warmth in sleeping bags in the dew-damp early hours. 'It has been a long time, hasn't it?'

Hendrix launched into a set that was under-rehearsed and bedevilled with technical problems, resisting an audience who evidently wanted him to play his hits in the theatrical style of old, when he would perform such tricks as plucking his Stratocaster with a plectrum clutched between his teeth. By 1970, Hendrix was beyond all that, was tired of performing the old songs. He really didn't want to be on stage at all in fact, preferring to spend his time in his New York studio, Electric Ladyland. It was partly the cost of the studio that had forced him out on the road, where his weariness was apparent – a mental and physical exhaustion, partly caused and certainly

---

*Though more correctly, and even more powerfully: '. . . I am constant as the Northern Star' (*Julius Caesar* {III, I, 60})

exacerbated by his drug use. Few artists gave so much to popular music in so short a time as James Marshall Hendrix, but by 1970 he was almost used up. And it is for this reason that the two hours or so he spent on stage at the Isle of Wight, recorded and preserved as they are for posterity, retain special interest. It is the last work of a master, performing for one of the biggest audiences of his career but seemingly preferring to play for himself. In contrast to the rambunctious Who, flinging themselves about wildly on stage, Hendrix stood almost like a statue, losing himself in long experimental jams, the most successful of which were based on new songs, murky, bluesy numbers that sounded like a man trying to find his path home. Here was music slurred and blurred by dope, but beautifully so. In the introduction to 'Midnight Lightning', his guitar sounded like the slow, doom-laden toll of a great bell. Hendrix thanked the audience sarcastically at the end of the number for their lacklustre applause, telling them that they were *outta sight*, adding amid shrieks of angry feedback, 'if you want the same old songs, we can do that,' before plunging into a perfunctory 'Foxey Lady' from his first album. Finally, Mitch Mitchell rolled out a wonderful percussive overture to another fine new song, 'In From the Storm'. On the count of four, the big electric sound of Hendrix and Cox slammed together, forming a mighty connection, and after six minutes of howling sound – a *Lear*-like storm of sound – Hendrix thanked the fans one last time, said somewhat sadly that they must do it again some time, and walked off stage, dropping his Fender discontentedly as he did so.

Jimi Hendrix died three weeks later in London, having mixed alcohol with barbiturates: a sloppy, ugly and wholly unnecessary death, for it was almost certainly unintended. Less than a month later Janis Joplin died of an overdose in Los Angeles. Jim Morrison expired in Paris the following year – all three by coincidence at the absurdly young age of twenty-seven – and by the end of the 1970s that prankster Keith Moon would also meet a pitiful end. All were musicians of exceptional talent who were fortunate to enjoy artistic and commercial success, fame and acclaim, yet they threw everything away. Their deaths are among the least attractive aspects of rock in the '70s. And if one steps outside Western pop culture for a moment, the decadence and waste appears nothing less than obscene. Contrast the lives of these pampered musicians with, say, that of artists living behind the Iron Curtain during this era. 'I put no hopes in the West,' Alexander Solzhenitsyn wrote around this time, holding much of Western culture, certainly its popular culture, in contempt. 'Excessive ease and prosperity have weakened their reason.' What an extraordinary contrast Solzhenitsyn's story is to these rock idols, a true rebel versus a simulacrum of rebellion, and illustrative of the gulf that existed between East and West during the long years of the Cold War, which of course spanned the 1970s, making the citizens of the free world and those of the Soviet empire mutually and ineffably mysterious to one another as if they lived not on different sides of border posts, but on different planets.

Enter another world, frozen in time, painted in muted tones, where fear and secrecy reign. It is October 1970 and a bell jangles insistently at the home of the cellist Mstislav Rostropovich, summoning his house guest Alexander Solzhenitsyn to the telephone. Instantly he is on his guard. 'No one had phoned me there for ages,' the writer later said, 'and suddenly there were several calls in a few minutes.' For Solzhenitsyn, every waking moment was pregnant with suspense. An unexpected telephone call was a reason to catch his breath. For he was a marked man in the USSR, watched constantly by the KGB who wanted to throw him back in jail for writing books that exposed the Soviet Union as an empire of lies, a state with the deaths of millions of its citizens on its conscience. So difficult had the writer's life become in recent months that he had taken sanctuary in the Moscow dacha of his friend Slava Rostropovich, knowing that the powers of darkness would hesitate before bursting in and dragging him from the home of one of the world's pre-eminent classical musicians. That would be a story that the Western press would seize upon, and despite the corruption of the USSR the Soviets still cared about incurring the opprobrium of the international community. Solzhenitsyn lived in a guest apartment above Slava's garage, rising early each day to write by hand his illicit and incendiary books and pacing the garden furiously between bursts of activity, as he had once paced his prison cells. A thick-set man of fifty-one, with a bushy reddish beard, his top lip shaved clean so that the beard formed an inverted horseshoe under his face, with hair thinning on the crown of his head, Solzhenitsyn's expression was invariably solemn as he paced. But his eyes glittered as thoughts, emotions and memories swarmed through his mind. Then back to his table and more words flooded forth. Any interruption was unwelcome, a phone call was something to make him think *What now?*

He picked up the receiver and murmured *Hello?* A Norwegian journalist was on the line, one based in Moscow who spoke Russian, calling with momentous news: Solzhenitsyn was to be awarded the Nobel Prize for Literature. Would he accept?

'Yes, I accept!' exclaimed the writer, forgetting his customary caution in his surprise and excitement.

Would he go to Stockholm to collect the award?

Yes, again, in his joy. 'At that moment I had no doubt.' But to leave the USSR was no simple matter in 1970 – if one wanted to return.

How inspiring it is to think that the greatest Russian writer since Leo Tolstoy has lived in our time, and what a remarkable and noble story Solzhenitsyn's is! It is a sobering and inspiring one to recall at the start of a decade where so much was glittery and ephemeral. Alexander Isayevich Solzhenitsyn, known by the patronymic of Sanya, was born in 1918 during the violent aftermath of the Bolshevik Revolution. His soldier father was killed in a hunting accident just before his birth and the lad was raised by his mother, a former member of the bourgeoisie, with the help of a coterie of devoted female relatives. Like the young Jack Nicholson, Sanya thrived in a household run by women and he grew up to be a serious-minded boy of exceptional intelligence, a loner with a grand ambition to be an author of the stature of Tolstoy, whose *War and Peace* he read and reread. Remarkably, an outstanding facility for language was matched with a brilliant mathematical mind and it was maths that Sanya studied at Rostov University, where he met his first love, chemistry student Natalya Reshetovskaya, whom he married in 1940. Sanya presented Natasha, as she was known, with a curious wedding gift which reveals two aspects of his character: his intensity and his ego. It was a photograph of himself, on the back of which he wrote a penetrating question: 'Will you, under all circumstances, love the man with whom you have joined your life?' The answer proved complex, for theirs was a tragic love of Tolstoyan proportions.

As a young man, Solzhenitsyn was an ardent Communist who believed that Lenin had saved Russia. Later, he saw Lenin as the Devil. He volunteered with alacrity when the Soviet Union plunged into war with Germany in 1941, wanting to fight for his country and for Communism, and like his father before him he became an artillery officer, a brilliant and successful one, admired by his men and decorated for his service on the Eastern Front. Yet, as the Red Army turned the tide of war and surged into Germany in 1945, Solzhenitsyn was disgusted by the havoc wreaked on Germany and its people, outrages inspired by Josef Stalin's vengeful call for 'blood for blood.' Rashly, Solzhenitsyn criticised Stalin in letters to a childhood friend serving on the Ukrainian Front, suggesting that a further Socialist revolution might now be in order. The letters were intercepted and on 9 February 1945, Captain Solzhenitsyn was arrested.

'Arrest! Need it be said that it is a breaking point in your life, a bolt of lightning which has scored a direct hit on you?' Solzhenitsyn wrote with characteristic verve in his 1973 masterpiece *The Gulag Archipelago*, detailing how his epaulettes were ripped from him, divesting him of rank, and how he was then taken to Moscow to be swallowed by 'the black maw of the gates' of Lubyanka Prison. After interrogation, he was sentenced to eight years in the labour camps. 'Eight years!' Solzhenitsyn protested. 'For what?'

The unspoken reason was that Stalin was paranoid about soldiers such as Captain Solzhenitsyn, believing they would band together after the peace to force him from power, and so pre-emptive arrests were being made on a massive scale. Indeed, Sanya was fortunate not to have been summarily shot. As it was, he was found guilty without formal trial, with no means to appeal, even obliged to sign a bogus confession.

'Sign it.'

'It's not true.'

'Sign.'

'But I'm not guilty of anything.'

This black comedy was the prelude to the life that became his work, as a *zek* (inmate) in the network of Soviet prison camps to which Solzhenitsyn himself gave the name *gulags*, a noun derived from a longer bureaucratic term. Largely unknown to the world, from the hinterland of Moscow to the frozen extremities of the Soviet empire there existed hundreds of forced-labour camps into which millions of men, women and even children – anybody and everybody perceived for whatever reason to be a threat to Stalin – were sent. Some were executed swiftly, but most were made to work for their rations on colossal building projects, such as the Belomor Canal where Solzhenitsyn estimated that 250,000 died, a huge number but only a fraction of the *sixty million* he calculated had perished over the years in the camps. If true, this would be the greatest crime in the history of the world. Many thousands were employed in herding and working these millions of prisoners. Yet the camps seemed to exist in secret, buried somewhere out of sight. No news of this underworld appeared in the press. If one went to a Moscow train station and asked to buy a ticket to any gulag the response would be a blank look. Still millions were transported there, and when Solzhenitsyn joined them in their misery he was met with a curious question: 'Are you from freedom?' *Freedom* was a place, a state of mind. How different a use of the word this is to the way it would become bandied about in the West.

Solzhenitsyn believed he became a better man for the experience of being so unjustly sentenced, having his youthful officer-class arrogance knocked out of him and finding in the camps a subject that demanded to be written about. It was a question of whether he was man enough for the task, because it was perilous to even think of such a thing, also unrealistic. Even if he got out of the camps there would be no way of publishing such books. This challenge forged steel from an iron character. 'I hate to think what sort of writer I would have become,' he wrote in his memoir *The Oak and the Calf*, which was first published in Russian in the mid-seventies, 'if I had not been put inside.' In fact, when he came to analyse his life, he saw that he had passed through three stages in the forging of man and writer. Firstly, the fire of war. Then the searing experience of the camps, where he recognised his

vocation. Finally, in his seventh year of incarceration, came the cool-
ing acceptance of the Christian god. Raised as a Communist in what
was officially an atheistic country, Solzhenitsyn shared the official state
disdain for religion into his early thirties. But in the camps he met
prisoners who maintained the beliefs and the rituals of the Russian
Orthodox Church and Sanya, too, came to adopt these, becoming
moreover a religious zealot whose world view was based essentially on
Christianity.

Communism was certainly evil in his mind, but he had little time
for democracy either, believing that Westerners were spoilt by an
excess of freedom (the decadence of certain rock stars of the 1970s
providing a persuasive example of this). What Solzhenitsyn hankered
after was a Bible-based authoritarian regime, which was something his
Western readers took a while to appreciate. In his own life, he came
to feel that his writing was guided by the hand of his Maker. 'And that
is why I turn back to the years of my imprisonment and say, sometimes to the astonishment of those about me, "Bless you prison!"'

Sanya's descent into and journey through the gulags is analogous to
the tribulations of Job in the Old Testament; also to Dante's imaginary
journey into Hell, which he describes in his *Divine Comedy* as being
drilled down into the core of the Earth in diminishing circles, each
level having its own tortures. Similarly, there were circles of torment
within the gulags. The first circle (a term Solzhenitsyn borrowed
from Dante for the title of one of his novels), had him working in a
clay-pit. Briefly, he was set to do research, which was work more
suited to his education and intellectual powers, but for the most part
Solzhenitsyn did manual labour. As he descended through the circles
of his punishment, he worked on building sites, as a foundryman, and
spent a year as a mason in remote Kazakhstan where conditions were
particularly brutal. As he endured these many ordeals, he composed
verse and wrote stories in his head. Phooey to those Western writers
who needed inspiration to write, a comfortable chair, a particular
grade of paper! Solzhenitsyn wrote as he marched, wrote as he laid a
course of blockwork, sometimes literally jotting down words on
paper, but mostly composing in his mind for fear that a permanent
record would be discovered. In this way, he memorised thousands of

lines of verse and planned a shelf of books that would tell the story of Russia's descent into Communism, the setting-up and running of the gulags, the millions who died in them, some deaths he had witnessed, others described to him by fellow zeks: an epic and truly important work that would address history in broad terms and be illustrated by the detail of individual stories, including, not insignificantly, his own.

It was this project – it became a monomania, with touches of megalomania – that kept him going through the years in the gulags, though Natasha was also a source of support. She and Sanya had shared just one year of married life when he went to war. Then Sanya disappeared into the camps. Yet Natasha maintained contact with her husband and saw him whenever she could. In return, he told her that she should get a divorce if it made her life easier. Many wives did so in their position, and Natasha was a talented woman with a career as a chemist, latterly head of a chemistry department at an institute in Ryazan, 100 miles from Moscow. She therefore had her work to consider. At first Natasha would hear nothing of it, but she was young and lonely and having a husband who was a political prisoner *did* cause problems. In the early 1950s she began living with another man and, though she kept this news from Sanya for some time, eventually they divorced. Despite having advised her this was what she *should* do, it seems that Sanya was hurt deeply by what was in effect a betrayal. Returning to the analogy of Job, it was also another test. They came thick and fast. As Satan smote Job with painful boils, so Sanya developed a cancerous tumour in his groin. After the cancer was removed, his original sentence came to an end, but rather than being freed he was 'exiled for life' to a village in a desert region of southern Kazakhstan where he worked as a school teacher, and here the cancer flared up again. He underwent a course of radiation and was warned that he probably had only weeks to live, but he survived even that ordeal, and came to use the experience for his novel *Cancer Ward* (first published in English in 1972) in which the disease becomes a metaphor for Communism, spreading through the body of the state, corrupting its vital organs.

In 1956, three years after Stalin's death, Solzhenitsyn succeeded in having his sentence annulled and was set free: he was thirty-seven, a veteran of war, the gulags and cancer. As he wrote poignantly, 'The grass has grown thick over the grave of my youth.' Entering mid-life he had no place in society, no money, no wife or family – he had never wanted children when he was young, and now presumed himself rendered infertile by radiation treatment. Most men might despair in his situation, but Solzhenitsyn was exceptional. 'I've always been an optimist. When I was dying of cancer I was always an optimist.' He was reunited with Natasha and, despite all that had happened, very remarkably, they remarried, establishing a home together in Ryazan. It was here that Solzhenitsyn began transcribing the books that he had composed in his mind during his long years in the camps, first setting down *One Day in the Life of Ivan Denisovich* in forty days, naming it at first *Shch-854* – the prison number of his character, Ivan Denisovich Shukhov, and a slight variation on his own camp number.

Typically, *Ivan Denisovich* reads as the work of someone in a hurry to unburden himself of a story he is compelled to tell, in the manner of Samuel Coleridge's Ancient Mariner (another bearded man with glittering eyes). Solzhenitsyn's style is simple and urgent with frequent dramatic exclamations, liberal use of colloquial expressions, proverbs, and metaphor. The author excels at detail. Take food, a vital part of camp life: 'The skilly was the same every day,' Solzhenitsyn wrote in *Ivan Denisovich*, describing the filth served for breakfast. 'Its composition depended on the kind of vegetable provided that winter. Nothing but salted carrots last year, which meant that from September to June the skilly was plain carrot. This year it was black cabbage . . . The worst time was [when] they shredded nettles into the pot.' To augment this thin soup, they added putrid fish. 'The little fish were more bone than flesh; the flesh had been boiled off the bone and had disintegrated, leaving a few remnants on head and tail.' Imagine subsisting on such muck! There was no choice. Indeed, Ivan Denisovich begged and stole extra portions in order to survive.

For six years Solzhenitsyn worked on his stories in secret until finally, at the age of forty-two, he decided he had to try and get published, and so sent *Shch-854* to *Novy Mir*, the most liberal of the state-sanctioned monthlies, a publication edited by Alexander

Tvardovsky, a poet and Soviet courtier who enjoyed the friendship of Premier Nikita Khrushchev. Tvardovsky started reading the manuscript in his bed one night at his Moscow apartment. But he quickly became so involved with and moved by the story that he got himself up again and dressed before continuing. It seemed disrespectful to read such an account while lounging about. In fact he read the manuscript straight through twice that night, staying up all night in order to do so. Tears sprang to his eyes as he took in the tale of twenty-four unexceptionally hellish hours in the life of a camp inmate towards the end of Stalin's reign, a man imprisoned on a trumped-up charge of treason, like so many had been, detailing Ivan Denisovich's quotidian struggle to maintain dignity, sanity, and health, from the clanging five a.m. reveille through a day of gruelling work, laying blocks in freezing conditions as Solzhenitsyn had, to the moment when the prisoner returns to his barracks and lays down his head to escape his problems in sleep. 'Almost a happy day,' Solzhenitsyn concludes the tale. 'There were three thousand six hundred and fifty-three days like that in his stretch . . .'

Under Stalin, writing and publishing such a book could bring a death sentence upon one's head. But there had been a thaw under Khrushchev, a loosening-up that made it possible such a book might be published. Tvardovsky succeeded in getting a lightly-edited version read aloud to Khrushchev and the Premier was moved to tears as Tvardovsky had been, giving his consent to the work being published in November 1962. Overnight, Alexander Isayevich Solzhenitsyn was transformed from an anonymous former zek, one of millions shuffling around the country, into a famous Soviet citizen, congratulated in person by Khrushchev, and feted by his fellow citizens, with one of whom Sanya had an affair – the turning point in his marriage to Natasha. She had betrayed him, now he her. So it would go on.

For a short time, Solzhenitsyn was allowed to publish further stories in the USSR, but then Khrushchev was deposed from power and a harsher regime was ushered in under the leadership of Leonid Brezhnev. The KGB put Solzhenitsyn under surveillance and reported to Brezhnev that the author was working on a new book he spoke of as *The Gulag Archipelago*, not a work of fiction but a hugely ambitious history of the prison camps based on accounts collected from witnesses. Solzhenitsyn predicted that when *Gulag* was published it would be like an erupting volcano burying the Party bosses under a lava-flow of truth. In a series of raids, the KGB seized his manuscripts (though not the *Gulag* itself), plunging the writer briefly into suicidal despair. But he recovered his sense of hope and fought back. Indeed, Solzhenitsyn thrived during the next few years by engaging the Party and KGB (headed at this time by future Soviet leader Yuri Andropov) in a one-man guerilla war. His only weapons were words, but they proved surprisingly mighty. His hand was strengthened immeasurably by the fact that his stories increasingly found their way into translations in the West, often crude translations, it was true, made as they were without his direct co-operation, for that would be too dangerous, but nevertheless he was being read around the world. Indeed, it became fashionable to read Solzhenitsyn, even though the work was challenging. *Ivan Denisovich* is a slim book that can be read in an afternoon. Later books were typically very long, somewhat repetitive and written in an (excusable) tone of self-righteousness. Yet for Westerners to read such books in the early 1970s was to have a secret world exposed to them. The Soviet empire, that seemed so austere and imposing on the television news reports, especially when its military hardware was displayed in Red Square, was apparently a broken-down lie, built on slave labour, its zeks treated worse than animals, while ordinary citizens subsisted in poverty. And the man who was revealing this story – one that bolstered the prejudices of many Western readers, of course – was doing so at risk to his own life, so Solzhenitsyn was a brave and even heroic figure to these readers.

There was, however, growing anger and concern about Solzhenitsyn within the Kremlin. In November 1969, the writer was punished by expulsion from the Soviet Writers Union, an ominous warning that arrest might follow. Solzhenitsyn's fearless reply was an open letter to the Secretariat of the union. 'Dust off the clock face,' he jeered. 'You are behind the times.' Next, the authorities forced his editor Tvardovsky to resign from *Novy Mir*. As the wolves closed in, Rostropovich offered Solzhenitsyn sanctuary at his dacha, a splendid building on the outskirts of Moscow in what was known as Zhukovka 2, a special residential zone adjacent to Zhukovka 1, where the Party leaders resided. Rostropovich and his wife, the soprano Galina Vishnevskaya, had a spacious property on a quiet, tree-lined street next to composer Dmitri Shostakovich. Their other neighbour was the nuclear physicist Andrei Sakharov, who had become another outspoken dissident. 'At first when Solzhenitsyn was in trouble, I was a very good Soviet citizen,' says Rostropovich. 'But when I heard of his plight, I went to see him and he was being treated like a dog. He was afraid for his life. I offered him refuge and that is when my troubles started.' Concert tours were cancelled and Slava's conductorship of the Bolshoi was taken from him. Still he and his wife did not betray their friend, and Sanya found their home to be a congenial place to work. Unlike the neighbourhoods he was used to, the special zone was clean and quiet, devoid of unsightly Soviet posters, also without Big Brother-type speaker announcements urging workers to the factories. Here, he found a tranquil place to write, paradoxically within a stone's throw of Yuri Andropov's home. And so he turned his attention to *August 1914*, a historical novel similar in tone and scope to *War and Peace*, dealing with Russia's disastrous clash with Germany in the First World War, under the inept direction of the Tsar, a calamity which foreshadowed the Bolshevik Revolution. The writer envisaged this as the first in a series of books – a vast undertaking that became *The Red Wheel* – explaining Russia's plunge into ideology. He also worked on *The Oak and the Calf*, a blow-by-blow account of his struggle to get published in Russia: Solzhenitsyn being the calf butting its head against the apparently implacable oak tree of the state.

The move to the special zone coincided with Solzhenitsyn's marriage reaching its crisis. There was a new woman in the writer's life now, a thirty-year-old mathematician named Alya Svetlova who, having volunteered to work as Solzhenitsyn's typist, had become pregnant by him. The writer informed Natasha by letter of this state of affairs in September 1970, and the news struck his wife like a thunderbolt. All the time they had been together Sanya had told her that he didn't want children, or couldn't have any. Now he was to be a father in his fifty-second year *with this woman!* Her emotions in tumult,

Natasha dashed to Rostropovich's property, half-minded to destroy herself. When she arrived, to find her husband not home, she took up a knife and cut her hand, opening a small wound but one that bled sufficiently for her to use the blood to daub a mark on a piece of paper – *I* – which she struck out angrily and followed by a question mark. She fixed the bloody page to the wall over her husband's bed as an expression of her anguish. This was the extraordinary domestic drama that preceded news of the Nobel.

It was a political award, given for the 'ethical force with which [Solzhenitsyn] has pursued the indispensable traditions of Russian literature,' as the citation read, rather than as recognition of a body of work. Only a fraction of Solzhenitsyn's writing was in print, hastily, and sometimes crudely, translated Western editions of his early books – *Ivan Denisovich*, *Cancer Ward*, a version of *The First Circle* – not his opus *The Gulag Archipelago*. The Politburo was enraged. The state press responded by ridiculing the Nobel Foundation and defaming Solzhenitsyn as *treacherous scum*, a man apparently guilty of shabby, unpatriotic behaviour all the way back to the Second World War (when, in reality, he had been decorated for bravery). Some courageous friends stepped forward to defend Sanya in the face of such libels. 'I know many of the works of Solzhenitsyn. I like them,' Rostropovich wrote in an open letter, suppressed in the USSR but published abroad. 'I consider he seeks the right through his suffering to write the truth as he saw it.' Sanya began to understand that the Party wanted him to leave the country to collect his award. That way they could portray him as a traitor to the Russian people, and prevent his return. One might have thought Solzhenitsyn would be happy to see the back of the USSR. On the contrary, his heart and soul were Russian. To be an exile in the West would be yet another punishment.

The 1970 Nobel ceremony was held in Stockholm on 10 December. That evening Solzhenitsyn and Rostropovich huddled around a long-wave radio that the cellist kept secretly in his attic to gather news from the West. Although he chose not to attend in person, and therefore could not deliver the customary Nobel lecture, Solzhenitsyn was not prevented from writing a lecture. In this essay, later published, he described the grim times in which much of the world was living at the start of the 1970s, when, let us remember, very large parts of Europe, Africa, Asia and South America were under the boot-heel of totalitarian rule – of the extreme right-wing kind (Nicaragua for example) as well as Communist regimes. 'Violence, less and less embarrassed by the limits imposed by centuries of lawfulness, is brazenly and victoriously striding across the whole world.'

The suppression of literature was one of the greatest of state crimes, Solzhenitsyn wrote, because it robbed a people of their collective memory. But literature would prevail. 'In the struggle with falsehood art always did win and it always does win!' By reading his books, ordinary people whom he did not know had supported him with what he described as 'the invisible dumb tension of a sympathetic public membrane.' When the iron fist of the state was poised, ready to smash him, that hand was stayed by the fact that he had a readership – especially a foreign readership. And no matter how often he was besmirched in the Soviet press, he was confident that he would prevail. 'One word of truth,' he concluded his lecture, 'shall outweigh the whole world.' And so the author worked on through the winter of 1970. He did so in defiance of the men who ran the Soviet Union, the dread weight of whose authority remained suspended above him. Their power was poised as if to crush him, but somehow, miraculously, it did not come down. It stayed in suspension.

5

MONUMENTAL

to roll, to crease, to fold . . .

RICHARD SERRA'S VERB LIST

The threatening weight of the Soviet Union, poised above its dissidents, was echoed in the new prop-piece sculptures of the American artist Richard Serra, whereby thick, heavy sheets of metal were balanced together precariously so that they stayed upright – just – giving the viewer the unsettling feeling that one false move might send them crashing down. The work embodied dread, causing one to stop and think, initially perhaps: *Is that damn thing safe?* But then more generally and deeply, which is the most any artist can hope for. 'It's not going to change the world,' as Serra says of his work. 'But it can be a catalyst for thought.'

The art came from Serra's early life in San Francisco, where he was born in 1939. As a boy, he was deeply impressed by watching a vessel launched at the shipyard where his father worked as a fitter, later recalling the exhilarating moment when the huge metal hull '. . . bounced into the sea, half-submerged, to then raise and lift itself and find its balance . . .' In adult life Serra would make a specialty of working with very large pieces of metal, putting the dead weight of the material in balance, emphasising its inherent power. He developed his knowledge of metal-working doing shifts in steel mills during summer breaks from the University of California at Berkeley. The iron and steel industry would be decimated in the USA during the 1970s, but Serra had opportunities beyond those of the men he laboured alongside. After UC Berkeley, he went East to study painting at Yale and in 1965 received funding to spend a year studying in Europe, an experience he shared with his friend and fellow student, the composer Philip Glass. Although Serra seems to revel in the image of *the worker* – a tough-looking, shaven-headed fellow with a short temper – he is very much the intellectual, and when he returned home from Europe he took his place in the *avant-garde* of the New York art world, experimenting with film (he was one of the first artists to use video) and in 1967–68 creating his *Verb List*, a conceptual artwork consisting of a hand-written list of verbs relating to manipulating material: 'to roll, to crease, to fold . . .' This he began to do with rubber before moving on to lead, a metal he found delightfully malleable.

Serra hurled molten lead at walls, where it solidified into pleasing shapes; he ripped and cut sheets of lead into strips, then rolled these to form cylinders to prop up other bits of metal. The obvious but nonetheless surprising fact that enormously heavy lumps of metal could be made to stay upright simply by being leaned together in a state of balance opened a whole field of new work. A seminal piece from 1969, *One Ton Prop (House of Cards)*, consisted of four lead squares (each four feet square and weighing 500 pounds) leaned together so they stood up like a house of cards. The sculpture was placed not on a pedestal or plinth but, following the example set by Anthony Caro, sat on the ground where there is a more direct relationship with the room and the viewer thus increasing the sense of drama. Walking past Serra's prop-pieces, one looked to see whether they were welded in place, and if not (early works were not secured in this way) there was real danger. The bigger the piece, the greater the drama, and Serra's sculpture grew to be enormous.

Around 1970 Serra began to concentrate on using steel, the material of the shipyard which, although experimented with by Picasso and others, was not commonly used in sculpture because of its industrial connotations and because, simply, it rusts. This quality is precisely what excited Serra, who came to specialise in using Cor-Ten steel because of the specific way it corrodes, changing from blue-grey when new to orange in about eight years, then turning brown, amber and finally stabilising as a blackish-brown. The artist knew that he had found his element. 'I started as a painter and I started using rubber and lead and a lot of other things, and when I finally picked up a piece of steel I realised that the way steel had been used in the Industrial Revolution, the way it had been used for making bridges or silos or whatever, hadn't been used in sculpture.' The sculpting of the material became a matter of giving direction rather than manhandling materials; the sheets of steel were too large to cut in the studio, and required professional riggers to move them. A typical Serra of the early 1970s would be a massive single slab, such as *Strike* (1969–1971), a sheet of hot-rolled one-inch-thick steel, eight feet high and 24 feet long, which Serra had jammed into the corner of a gallery room so its vertical position, combined with the fact that one end brushed against the angle of the walls, kept it up. (See picture 7.) This monumental work divided the room, causing the beholder to wonder and fear, again, *What if it fell?* Sometimes they did. In 1971, at the Walker Art Centre in Minneapolis, a gallery worker moving a two-ton Serra piece, titled *Joplin*, was killed. In another accident, a man lost a leg.

As his work grew in size and weight, Serra took it outside the gallery where, partly for the sake of safety, pieces were welded discreetly together and/or rooted in the ground. There was also an aesthetic reason for burying the sculpture. In the 1970s there was a return to landscape art in America, a notable example being Richard Smithson's earthwork *Spiral Jetty* (1969–70), a spiral isthmus of rock, 1,500 feet long, built out into Utah's Great Salt Lake. Like Smithson, Serra worked in bucolic settings, putting his steel slabs in fields, but he became most famous for his urban installations. In 1970, he inserted a steel ring 26 feet in diameter (*To Encircle Base Plate Hexagram, Right Angles Inverted*) at the end of a dead-end street in the Bronx, a 'sinister [place] used by the local criminals to torch cars,' as he described it. Few took much notice, considering the low-rent location. But Serra was soon receiving commissions to erect larger works in city centres. There were notable failures: a 100-ton piece commissioned for the new Pompidou Centre in Paris was never installed, partly because it was feared the weight of the artwork would damage the building. Most famously, in 1981, Serra sited *Tilted Arc* in Foley Square, downtown New York, a wall of steel 120 feet long. There were vociferous complaints from office workers irritated by the fact that they had to walk around this ugly thing (they said) in order to go about their business, which was in fact Serra's idea. He wanted to force people to think about sculpture, and the site it was created for. Serra lost the battle of Foley Square. Eight years later *Tilted Arc* was removed. Still his sculpture was installed in many of the great cities of the world from the early 1970s onward, and remain for the most part in place. The best examples – massive slabs of steel, oxidised to a mellow rust brown, bone-dry in the sunshine, darkly wet in the rain – are enduringly effective and dramatic works of 1970s art.

Although his sculpture was sited increasingly in city plazas, Richard Serra disliked most modern architecture, especially modernist skyscrapers which, by 1970, had become a standardised building-type based on principles developed shortly after the First World War by the German-born architect Mies van der Rohe. The classic high-rise is Mies' Seagram Building (1954–58), designed with the help of his American disciple Philip Johnson, on Park Avenue in New York. From a concrete and steel core, containing lifts and other services, radiate 38 floors on which hang amber-tinted glass curtain-walls, creating a massive rectilinear box and, typically for such a building, concealing the steel and concrete that makes the structure stand up (which is the aesthetic deception which niggled Serra). Twenty years after the Seagram was built, New Yorkers watched as two new landmark towers arose in their city, Mies-inspired towers but wearing some of their steel on their sleeve. Experimental in engineering, and also a monumental work of art before they became associated primarily with the events of September 2001, the twin towers of the World Trade Center were architectural wonders of the 1970s.

At eleven a.m. on Wednesday, 16 December 1970, the first tenants moved into the North Tower (Tower One) and, although both towers would not be completed until 1973, the World Trade Center was already the largest and tallest structure on Earth, which was an achievement in itself. The development was not initially popular with the public or the business community, however. Residents of the

Bronx and Westchester County complained that the towers inter-
fered with their television reception; some insisted that they could feel
Lower Manhattan sinking under the weight. Real estate experts
doubted the towers would ever be fully occupied, and warned that the
rental market would be depressed by so much office space being made
available at one time. Despite these critics, the World Trade Center
became over the next three decades one of the primary symbols of
New York City, and moreover of the United States; far from being a
commercial failure, it was the most successful real estate development
in the country; and the towers drew tourists like a magnet. The
Seagram Building is beloved of architects and students of art, but it is
more or less ignored by the public who pass by every day without
pause. In contrast, every gift shop and souvenir stall in New York sold
postcards of the World Trade Center.

For many years a large proportion of visitors to the city went out of
their way to take a closer look at the complex, typically having their
picture taken with the towers behind them, or riding the express elevator to the observation gallery on the 107th floor of the South Tower
(Tower Two), from where there was a remarkable panorama of
Manhattan, the East River, Hudson River and the outlying boroughs
of New York. A further escalator ride discharged visitors on to the
roof itself, 1,350 feet in the air, where the sense was of being part of
the sky rather than the city: buffeted by wind, dazzled by sunlight, or
shrouded in cloud; and, no matter what the weather was doing, feeling disconcerted by the motion of the tower now swaying, weirdly,
under one's feet. Emerging on to this platform, some fearless souls
almost skipped around the perimeter in their excitement. Others,
frozen with vertigo, clutched the hand-rail grimly as they staggered to
the exit, looking like they wanted to vomit. Visiting the summit of the
World Trade Center was an unforgettable experience, and in common
with the other important 1970s buildings featured in this book – the
Pompidou Centre, the Sydney Opera House, and Lloyd's of London –
the twin towers were hugely and enduringly popular: not an insignif-
icant accolade when so much modern architecture is reviled or
ignored.

An American icon, the twin towers were created by an architect who drew on European modernism and antique Indian and Italian architecture, as well as the aesthetic ideas his parents brought from their motherland of Japan, notably origami. How all this came together in the world's tallest building is a remarkable story. Minoru Yamasaki was born in Seattle in 1912, a Nisei or second-generation Japanese-American. To fit in, he shed his difficult first name and insisted everybody refer to him simply as Yama, and was known as such to all except his mother who continued to address him, often sternly, as *Minoru*. A diminutive man, Yama was – in contrast to many notable architects – a gentle and amenable soul, possessed of a self-deprecating wit and a sense of poetry. He was, however, deceptively tough. Born poor, he helped pay his way through college, at the University of Washington, by working in canning factories, and he overcame anti-Japanese feeling during and after the Second World War to win senior design jobs at leading architectural firms in New York and Detroit, becoming known as one of the leading architects of his generation.

In his work, Yama was influenced heavily by Mies van der Rohe. The Miesian maxim 'less is more' was his first principle. In the early 1950s, he established his own firm in Detroit, with a satellite office in St Louis, Missouri, where he designed many buildings. Not all of them were successful, but they included a renowned airport terminal in St Louis, featuring a spectacular shell-like concrete roof, for which Yama was awarded his first American Institute of Architects Gold Medal. (This structure influenced Jørn Utzon when he came to design the Sydney Opera House.) Yama overworked during this period, damaging his health. Apart from professional stresses, he had a torrid personal life: in 1941 he married Teruko Hirashiki, with whom he had three children, divorced her, and married and divorced two further wives, before remarrying his first spouse! In early 1954, the architect decided he needed to take a sabbatical and went on a contemplative journey around the world, looking at favourite buildings as well as seeing other wonders for the first time, such as the Taj Mahal, a building that bewitched him. For years Yama had been trying to reconcile Miesian and Japanese minimalism with the self-evident fact that in buildings such as the Taj Mahal less was *not* more.

Ornate decoration worked beautifully, as it did in nature. *Was the rose with its elegant structure less beautiful because of its rich ornamentation,* Yama would ask rhetorically. On the other hand, *Could the wing of a gull be less wonderful for its incredible structure?* These were the aesthetic architectural paradoxes he struggled to resolve on his travels. Wending his way around the globe, he fetched up in Venice on a grey and rainy day when St Mark's Square was all but deserted, and looked upon the familiar façade of the Doge's Palace, his eyes scanning the wide base arches at the plaza level transferring to a colonnade of closer-spaced arches above, a system that elegantly carries the heavy entablature of the load-bearing walls. It struck him that there, in this fifteenth-century masterpiece, was the perfect marriage of engineering and ornamentation. 'That was his epiphany really,' says Henry Guthard, a close friend of Yama and senior engineer at his firm Yamasaki, Inc. 'The World Trade Center was Yama's destiny.'

Returning to Detroit, Yama began to design major new buildings in which he moved away from the modernist tradition of glass curtain walls, that have no structural strength, and increasingly used steel arches and columns to create load-bearing walls that embodied the lessons he had learned on his world tour. These were commissions such as the IBM building in Seattle, and the Michigan Consolidated Gas Company in Detroit, '*astonishingly* beautiful buildings', in Guthard's opinion. Certainly they spread Yama's reputation as an architect who could design very large, efficient office buildings that were also pleasant places in which to work, typically surrounded by plazas planted with gardens, something which he considered to be very important. Then, one morning in 1962, Yama received an extraordinary letter which he brought to the attention of Henry and other senior staff at their Monday meeting. It was from the Port Authority of New York, inviting Yamasaki Inc. to submit plans for a major development in Manhattan. 'Now, guys, I want to show you something about letter-writing,' Yama told his colleagues (by Henry's recollection). 'I just got a letter to come to New York and be interviewed for a project for $280.00 million. Now, we all know the decimal point is in the wrong place.' Everybody around the table laughed, for virtually no building cost $280 million (£154 million) in 1962. Even a $28 million building would be a substantial commission. 'Henry, you know as an engineer how serious that is,' warned Yama, passing the letter around. 'Watch that damn decimal point.' But when Yama wrote back to New York questioning a typist's error, he was informed it was no mistake. After all, the client wanted the world's largest and tallest structure – and in fact the completion cost would balloon to $650 million (£357 million).

For several years billionaire brothers Nelson and David Rockefeller had been working with the Port Authority to build a massive office complex in Manhattan, a part-private part-government project, and had gone so far as to engage three leading New York architects to design a complex that included offices described grandly as a 'world trade center,' on the east end of Wall Street. The Rockefellers eventually became disenchanted with this scheme, and attention switched to another site, a seventeen-acre plot of land downtown, between Vesey Street and Liberty Street, that was in need of redevelopment. Indeed, the whole of lower Manhattan was due for a shot in the arm, and with the Rockefellers possessing substantial real estate interests in the neighbourhood it was in their interests that the area be upgraded. The Port Authority and its investors essentially required buildings that would provide between eight and ten million square feet of office space – a huge amount (ten times the capacity of the Seagram tower by comparison) – most of which would be let to private tenants, as well as integrated subway links to bring commuters into the city from New Jersey. It was essentially the Rockefellers who chose Yamasaki for the job, having wearied of trying to collaborate with three architects on the aborted Wall Street plan, and having heard good reports of Yama's agreeable nature.

It was apparent from the first that ten million square feet of office space could not be enclosed in a single building. There is a ratio between the size of a building's core and its height and a tower of ten million square feet would require a core so massive that solid concrete would take up practically all the space in the lower floors, while the building's height would be a hazard to aircraft. So there had to be more than one tower. But how many? Five? Three? Ten? Yama and his staff drew up 108 schemes. Around the seventeenth, it was more or less decided that two monumental towers was the solution (though the architect had his staff complete all 108 alternatives so that he could counter anybody who queried, 'Didn't you think of doing it *this* way?') Each tower would be 110 storeys, set in a garden-like plaza. With many existing skyscrapers, classically the Empire State Building, it was and is impossible to get a sense of the building close-to because there is insufficient space to stand back and look up. Yama wanted people to be able to take in his towers at a glance, and to enjoy the spaces between them. This way a gargantuan complex is humanised. For very practical reasons he insisted the towers be virtually identical. When it came to letting office space real estate agents and tenants could not argue that one was superior to the other; there would be nothing to choose between them. In fact, there was a difference of about three feet. The North Tower would be that much taller than its twin in order to accommodate a desirable ceiling height in the Windows on the World restaurant, the tower reaching approximately 1,353 feet in total, thus making it then the tallest building in the world. (Those opposed to the plans included the owners of the Empire State who saw their building about to be relegated, for want of approximately 100 feet, to the second-tallest.)

To some extent record-breaking was foisted on Yamasaki by the Port Authority, whose public relations people believed that the world's tallest building would attract attention and tenants. Yama didn't much care about this, aware that the record would be his briefly. At a time when there was a vogue for raising up confidently gigantic blocks in America, two Chicago skyscrapers – the Amoco Building (1970–73) and Sears Tower (1970–74) – would both exceed the World Trade Center in height before long. Neither had the iconic quality of Yamasaki's towers, however. He had the benefit of a superb site, of course. Situated at the southern tip of Manhattan, the epicentre of America's greatest city, his towers were twin sentinels to travellers arriving from across the Atlantic, a symbol of the wealth and power of New York, and the United States. Great buildings are also sculpture, and the highly unusual double nature of the structure, though designed that way for pragmatic reasons, created a dramatic artistic effect. The towers also reflected the light wonderfully, due to the remarkable and innovative façades.

One of the inherent problems with Miesian high-rises is the need for bulky central cores which support the dead weight of the structure and give it the strength to resist lateral wind forces which, in a very tall building, are the main stress. Elevators, fire exits and the miles of conduit required for ventilation, plumbing and wiring are all typically slotted into cavities in the heavy core. But large cores consume floor space, and thus reduce the profit margin on a development. One of the themes of architecture in the 1970s was the freeing-up of space by moving some or all of these core elements to other parts of the building, the most celebrated solution being the Pompidou Centre (which we shall come to later, for it was only at competition stage in 1970). One of the most significant design innovations in the World Trade Center came when Yama, working with an engineer named John Skilling, devised a way of reducing the core size and keeping the floors clear of pillars by making the exterior walls part of the wind-resisting and load-bearing strength of the towers.

A high-strength steel skin was created from box columns, square and hollow, stout at the base (approximately three feet thick) where they were set 10 feet off-centre to allow easy access to the lobbies. Enclosed with glass, the lower part of the buildings would be transparent, allowing one to see through the lobbies, rather than being confronted with a wall of concrete, as well as lifting the towers on the lightest possible feet. At the third storey, these large columns divided into three slender tree-like branches 40 inches off-centre. (See picture 10.) As the columns curved outward and divided they formed arches that echoed those of the Doge's Palace. And, like that Renaissance building, the symmetry and rhythm of repetition was continued above by smaller columns. In the case of the World Trade Center these rose in parallel all the way to the roof – 35,000 columns in total. The columns gave Yama his Miesian simplicity, but the façade was also a structural wall that would absorb gravitational and wind forces. Welded to horizontal spandrel beams, the box columns formed a flexible but strong self-supporting mesh, known as a Vierendeel Truss, which could be prefabricated and erected in large sections (which became evident in the ruins of the building in 2001). It was a brilliant and innovative structural solution that gave rise to the aesthetic interest of the towers.

By cladding the steel columns in oversized aluminium covers Yama accentuated the bulk of the steel, giving the towers a corrugated or pleated appearance (as in Japanese paper-folding). The aluminium ribs protected the steel and the depth of the covers created shadow as the sun moved around the buildings, shading office workers inside and animating the exterior for the sake of beauty. Apart from making shadow patterns, the aluminium ribs also reflected light: the golden glow of the rising sun; the ruddy sunsets so glorious in the north-eastern United States burning through yellow, orange, and finally glowing purple. 'One day when the sun sets,' Yama predicted, 'this whole building will be illuminated with that beautiful reflection of the multi-coloured sky. What a beautiful ornamentation that will be.' And as the light of day was extinguished, electric light inside the buildings transformed them into something like giant Japanese lanterns.

It would have been cheaper to use less steel and aluminium, and more glass. The Vierendeel Truss would still have been strong enough for the safety regulations of the day.* Giving his reasons for the unusual density of the columns, Yama said that he was concerned about agoraphobic office workers. Up to 120,000 people would pass through these towers in a day, a significant proportion of whom would be uncomfortable with great heights. An irrational feeling that one might fall out of the building would be assuaged by the fact that the columns were only twenty inches apart, seeming to close one in. The architect added disarmingly that he sometimes felt uneasy in high buildings himself, a self-deprecating comment that led to the legend that the architect of the world's tallest building was scared of heights. In truth, Yama was almost certainly using his guile to get his way; he had never betrayed a fear of heights before. On the contrary, as Henry Guthard points out, 'he lived his life scampering around the tops of high-rise buildings like a squirrel'.

Like most great buildings, the World Trade Center was designed and constructed over several years, in this case spanning 1962–73,

---

*Nobody envisaged the terrorist attacks of 11 September 2001, of course, when fully-fuelled Boeing 767 jets were flown into the towers. Though even then, the towers stood a good hour before collapsing.

and controversy continued throughout. Naysayers argued that the complex was far too big, unbalancing the skyline of Manhattan; they said it was a monument to the ego of the Rockefellers (why not call the towers Nelson and David?); it would never be more than a white elephant in commercial terms; furthermore, migrating birds following the Hudson River had a dismaying habit of flying into the towers. For Yama and his team this was all highly disconcerting, the towers to them being nothing less than architecture as art. 'If we look at art and look at architecture we see that architecture is truly frozen art,' muses Henry Guthard. 'It's art that is crystallized into something that becomes very solid, and there's an obligation, I think, for architects to look at their work as something that will be there for a long time after they're gone, and I think that was something that Yama was concerned about.' The architect died in 1986, at age seventy-three, but his associates, who continue the firm that still bears his name, believe that Yama was vindicated. Certainly, the towers became in a short space of time an integral part of New York City and its skyline and to many eyes the towers were as beautiful as Yama predicted they would be. On Friday, 7 September 2001, Henry was reminded of this when he and a colleague flew into the city for a meeting. As they were driven past the East River into Manhattan they looked over at the twin towers, their solid forms glowing in the low autumnal sun, and were so enraptured that they decided that they had to have new photographs taken for the office in Detroit. 'Robert and I both said, *Yeah, we can't do it this time. But you know it'll always be there. It'll be there a long time after we're gone,*' recalls Henry. 'So you see there were a lot of hopes and aspirations, there were a lot of illusions, there were a lot of cruel realities that were revealed.'

Although work on the twin towers was undertaken simultaneously, the North Tower was constructed on a slightly advanced schedule. By October 1970, it had exceeded the height of the Empire State Building, and on the morning of Wednesday, 16 December, the first tenants moved into the lower floors. Margaret Siss, a secretary with the import-export company Irving R. Boody, was to be found hanging pictures in her new office on the eleventh floor that morning while her colleague Frank Ramirez dealt with a stack of invoices. However, Betty and Frank were obliged to work against a considerable background din, with thousands of construction men still on the job.

Later in December, Yama brought his team to New York for a board meeting followed by a celebratory meal with their wives at Chateau Richelieu on West 47th Street. When the coffee was being served Yama announced that to cap the evening, and the year, he had arranged a surprise private visit to the top of the North Tower. And so everybody went downtown where they were let on to the site, taking the partially enclosed construction elevator as far as they could – husbands and wives clinging to each other as they rose higher and higher in their rickety cage – then walking up the last few flights before emerging on the very top of the North Tower. 'We stepped gingerly out into the dark night, guided by fragile safety lines, to the edges where there lay before us the sparkling lights of the city below – like a blanket of stars, we thought,' recalls Henry Guthard. They all hugged their partners, said a prayer, and agreed the board meeting was thereby concluded.

It was bitter-cold that night, and bitter a couple of days later when Yama returned to the site for the traditional topping-out ceremony. The grey sky over New York was heavy with the threat of snow on 23 December 1970. A strong wind made it seem even colder, as well as making the North Tower sway more dramatically than usual. It was amazing that a structure so massive, made of steel and concrete, should bend like a tree, moving several feet from side to side at the top (as it had to do, if it was not to snap). Even more amazing was to stand 1,350 feet in the air, looking out over the wintry landscape of New York and the surrounding country. The men clustered under one of the 'jumping kangaroo' cranes, so-named because they had been made in Australia for the Sydney Opera House, then nearing completion. One of these cranes lifted the last section into place at eleven-thirty a.m., a Stars and Stripes attached to the steel. The workers cheered as the metal clanged into place. It was extraordinary to stand at the top of the tallest structure mankind had made, and they were the men who had built it, a proud moment indeed. For the architect there was also a deeper philosophical meaning. 'I feel this way about it. World trade means world peace,' said Yama. 'The World Trade Center is a living symbol to man's dedication to world peace.'

Tomorrow would be Christmas Eve, and snow was falling seasonally across the North-Eastern United States, faintly at first and then falling thicker and quicker as night closed in on the continent. Snow was also falling in London, where David Hockney put aside his paint brushes to enjoy the first white Christmas in years. Further east, snow drifted thickly on the roof of Slava Rostropovich's dacha in Moscow where, a couple of days later, on 30 December, Alexander Solzhenitsyn's first son was born. That night the author, now also a father, said a special prayer, wondering what the new year and the rest of the decade would bring for the world.

6

ADAPTED FROM THE NOVEL

*I knew that this book couldn't be successful [and] I was
convinced that nobody could ever make a movie out of it.*
PETER BENCHLEY, AUTHOR OF *JAWS*

In contrast to the seriousness and literary weight of Alexander
Solzhenitsyn's fiction, the 1970s saw the publication of many highly
entertaining blockbuster novels that became even more significant as
the basis of what are now regarded as classic films. Mario Puzo's *The
Godfather*, Frederick Forsyth's *The Day of the Jackal* and Peter
Benchley's *Jaws* all sold millions of copies in paperback during the
decade, despite the fact that their authors admitted the books were of
mediocre literary merit. '*The Godfather* is my least favourite novel,'
commented Mario Puzo, ranking the book that changed his life below
all his other works, though those are virtually unread. 'I like to think
[*Jaws*] was successful as a yarn,' offered Peter Benchley, with the modesty of a man still surprised by his stupendous luck. Frederick Forsyth
says that he wrote *The Day of the Jackal* purely to make money, having
failed in his chosen career as a foreign correspondent, and concedes
that some of the writing in his book is downright 'awful.'

Mafia saga, shark adventure and the tale of an assassination attempt
were all enhanced considerably by being transferred to the movies.
Fred Zinnemann's 1973 version of *The Day of the Jackal*, with Edward
Fox as the enigmatic killer tasked with eliminating President Charles
De Gaulle, is perhaps the most modest of the three adaptations. Still,

it is a superbly made and very exciting thriller, despite the fact that the outcome is a foregone conclusion (a quirk of the novel it is based on). Steven Spielberg's *Jaws* (1975) is a more significant cinematic achievement, not least for the fact that it is the picture that properly launched Spielberg's remarkable career, and because its stupendous box office success helped change the course of Hollywood filmmaking as surely as *Easy Rider* did. *The Godfather* (1972) is the picture that made the careers of both Francis Ford Coppola and the young Al Pacino, both of whom became giants of seventies cinema; it also resurrected the reputation of Marlon Brando and is, in short, one of the great dramatic cinema entertainments of modern times.

All three of these highly entertaining fictions started as ideas in the heads of hack writers down on their luck. None had a background in writing bestsellers, and two were in fact first-time novelists. Of our trio of writers, Mario Puzo was the oldest and most experienced, the author of literary novels such as *The Fortunate Pilgrim* (1965) that received decent reviews but did not sell very well. To eke out a living, Puzo wrote adventure stories and worked as a magazine editor in New York. Even so, his was a life of semi-permanent penury, partly because of a propensity for gambling. By 1965, when he was forty-five, Puzo was $20,000 (£11,000) in debt, with his family having little confidence that he would ever be able to write his way out of the hole he had dug for himself. However, in common with the other writers featured in this history, Puzo possessed prodigious self-belief. 'I never doubted I could write a best-selling commercial novel whenever I chose to do so,' he boasted in his 1972 memoir, *The Godfather Papers*, a bold claim considering the mysterious and quixotic tastes of the public. His opportunity to prove himself came in 1965 when the American publisher G.P. Putnam and Sons paid him the first portion of a $5,000 (£2,747) advance to write a Mafia novel. The cash was welcome, but Mario didn't really want to write the book, and three years slipped by, during which time he worked in a desultory fashion on various projects, including the Mafia story, before he forced himself to finish the manuscript in 1968. He only did so then because he needed the final portion of the Putnam advance (paid on delivery) to take his family on holiday. Mario's life changed when he got back from his vacation to discover that the paperback rights to his Mafia novel were selling for the hitherto unheard of sum of $410,000 (£320,000). 'Honey, we don't have to worry about money anymore,' he told his wife, returning home to Long Island after lunch with his publisher. So little regard did the Puzo family have for Mario's writing career by this stage that it took some time for everybody in the household to believe that the deal truly was worth $410,000. As with Minoru Yamasaki, the initial assumption was that a decimal point had been misplaced.

Puzo's tale concerns a Sicilian named Vito Corleone who migrated to America at the turn of the twentieth century to found a crime dynasty in New York's Little Italy. The book begins just after the Second World War when the Corleones are jostling with other crime families for power. Although Puzo wrote with a gloss of professionalism, the book is far from being accomplished in literary terms. The sex scenes for instance are lamentable, with such woeful erotica as: 'Her hand closed around an enormous, blood-gorged pole of muscle.' Puzo knew this was substandard. 'I wished like Hell I'd written it better,' he admitted later. 'I wrote below my gifts in that book.' He also felt guilty that he hadn't bothered to do in-depth research for the story. Mario was an Italian-American who had grown up in New York during the Depression, but he wasn't acquainted with Mafia people and didn't seek any out before embarking on the book. As a result, some readers who did have direct knowledge of this world felt that *The Godfather* lacked authenticity. '[It] was really terrible,' comments the screenwriter Mardik Martin, who at this time was working with his friend Martin Scorsese on *Mean Streets*, their naturalistic movie about the Italian-American criminal fraternity of New York. '[Marty] read it and he thought it was terrible, [too],' adds Mardik, 'because a lot of it seems made-up . . . Of course, there was a movie there, which in my opinion is one of the best movies ever made.'

When it came to selling the movie rights to his Mafia story, Puzo was a victim of his own financial ineptitude. Perpetually broke, he grasped at any money that was offered and when he was only a hundred pages into the manuscript he sold the movie rights to Paramount for a paltry $12,500 (rising to $50,000 [£39,000] if they made the picture). His agent told him to try and hold on for a better deal, but Mario was a hopeless case. 'That was like advising a guy under water to take a deep breath. I needed the cash and $12,500 looked like Fort Knox.' When the book became an international bestseller, Paramount – specifically its former B-movie-actor production chief, Robert Evans – were sitting on one of the bargain movie properties of the decade. To direct the film, Evans insisted on an Italian–American, wanting to 'smell the spaghetti' as he put it, and with few candidates available he offered the job to the young Francis Ford Coppola.

Since his apprenticeship with Roger Corman back in the early 1960s, assisting on movies such as *The Terror*, Coppola had enjoyed significant success in the film business. As a screenwriter he was responsible for the brilliant opening scene of the 1970 movie *Patton*, in which George C. Scott delivers a speech standing in front of a huge US flag. The screenplay won an Academy Award. Even more impressively, Coppola had established an independent film studio in San Francisco, American Zoetrope (named after a type of antique projector). Here, Francis and his friends, such as a quiet young man named George Lucas, could make pictures away from the studio system of Los Angeles, but with Hollywood financing. As early as 1970, Francis and George were planning a whole raft of extraordinary pictures including *American Graffiti*, *The Conversation* and *Apocalypse Now*. The ambition was impressive, but Coppola's skill and vision as a filmmaker were not matched by his business acumen, and poor management of American Zoetrope, combined with the failure of early pictures such as *The Rain People* (1969), put the company deep into debt. When Coppola read Puzo's novel, he didn't want to make the film, considering the book beneath him. He called it a 'hunk of trash.' But he needed money desperately, and it was for this reason that he reluctantly accepted Robert Evans' invitation to direct *The Godfather*.

Great books don't necessarily make brilliant films. Indeed, the poetry of a literary novel usually fails to translate into pictures on screen, whereas a hack work can become a wonderful cinema entertainment. This was the case with *The Godfather*. Although Coppola didn't think much of the book, he did appreciate that the essential ele-

ments were in place for a fine movie: strong characters involved in an
epic crime story set in colourful postwar America. In fact everything
that would be on the screen came directly from the book. However,
Coppola improved on Puzo's creation significantly, working with
remarkable intensity on the project once he had committed himself to
it. Coppola's dedication to the film and his all-important attention to
detail is symbolised by a fascinating document he created prior to
filming which he came to call his *Notebook*. When he read Mario's
novel, Francis wrote his first impressions into the margins of his edition of the book. Then he broke the book apart and pasted all 595
annotated pages into a large black ring-binder. In order to do so he
took pieces of paper, punched holes in them, cut out a square in the
middle, and mounted the printed pages on these paper frames in such
a way that he could read both sides of the book pages. Then he reinforced the holes and snapped the leaves into the binder. Next, Francis
hunched over his little Olivetti portable typewriter and pecked out a
synopsis of every scene, with sub-heads for notes about 'the core' of
the narrative; 'pitfalls' he wanted to avoid (such as employing cliché
Italian–American dialogue); notes about 'imagery and tone'; and
finally *aides-mémoire* about what was happening concurrently in the
real world in 1945. These were also clipped into the binder. As he
worked, he also underlined key passages in the text, and added a
plethora of footnotes about how he would approach each shot: *What
would Alfred Hitchcock do in this scene? How could he get the maximum
amount of tension?* Over a period of months, the *Notebook* swelled until
it was as fat and heavy as a bible. Coppola took it with him wherever
he went, adding to it constantly. A conventional screenplay was written as well, and re-written in collaboration with Mario Puzo, but
Coppola worked from his *Notebook* when he shot the picture.

Many of Coppola's annotations relate to capturing the period feel
of 1940s New York (also LA, Las Vegas and Sicily, where there were
additional scenes). The first of a series of confrontations with
Paramount came when the studio informed Coppola that they wanted
him to set the movie in the present day to save money. Francis resisted that idea and, moreover, insisted that the film should be shot on
location as much as possible, which made the film even more expen-

sive. Coppola had good fortune with his locations, and an excellent production designer in Dean Tavoularis who did a wonderful job of recreating the ambience of the period, including transforming a large section of modern-day (1971) Manhattan, between Avenues A and B, into how it would have looked just after the Second World War. In fact, Coppola was fortunate with all the principal people who worked on the production. *The Godfather* is a particularly handsome-looking film, for instance, partly thanks to cinematographer Gordon Willis who gave the picture its atmospheric old world gloom.

'The overall colour value of the *Godfather* films is yellow, kind of brassy yellow,' says Willis, explaining how he achieved that old-photographs look. 'Combined with the lighting and shot structure that were chosen you get retrospective or period visuals.' (For years afterwards, period movies would ape this yellowish look, as if it were the only way to indicate a bygone era.) Willis lit the film in unusual ways, often illuminating actors from above so that they were in shadow (adding to the enigmatic quality of Marlon Brando as the Don, for instance, as his eyes are frequently hidden under the shadow of his brow). Film was also left under-developed in order to induce a Stygian atmosphere, appropriate to the infernal work the Corleone menfolk are employed in. Most often, foul deeds are discussed in ill-lit, claustrophobic rooms. But when we move outside it is to a world – by contrast – of colour, light and life. This works particularly well in the opening sequence when the dark business conducted in the Don's study is juxtaposed with joyful scenes of the wedding party of his daughter in the garden.

Although taken directly from Mario's book, the wedding is much more effective on screen than on the page, partly because Coppola knew what to leave out, retaining only the most essential Puzo dialogue, and sharpening these sentences like knives. This is true of all the key scenes in the film including, for example, the sequence when Michael Corleone (Al Pacino) visits his father, the Don, in hospital after a botched assassination attempt on the old man, only to discover that nobody is guarding him. Michael convinces a nurse to help him move his father to safety before gunmen come to finish him off. In the book the scene reads in part:

Michael spoke very quickly. 'You've read about my father in the papers. You've seen that there's no one here tonight to guard him. Now I've just gotten word some men will come into the hospital to kill him. Please believe me and help me.' He could be extraordinarily persuasive when he wanted to be.

This is expressed with greater impact in the movie when Pacino speaks to the nurse in even shorter, sharper sentences:

'You know my father? Men are coming here to kill him. Do you understand? Now help me, please.'

The acting is one of the glories of the film. It is an extremely impressive cast, particularly in terms of the Corleone family, with James Caan, John Cazale, Robert Duvall and Al Pacino as the brothers (Duvall's character being an adopted son). Under the paternal leadership of Marlon Brando, these fine actors coalesce as a real family. It was Puzo who had the inspired idea of sending the book to Brando, asking him to consider playing the Don, and Coppola agreed that Marlon would be ideal as the paterfamilias. The actor is magnificent in the role, utterly convincing in every scene, so much so that one forgets it is Marlon Brando behind those distended cheeks. Yet Brando almost didn't get the part. Paramount hated the very idea of hiring an actor who was a pariah in Hollywood by 1971, having made a series of flops during the previous decade. 'People had this idea that he was extremely difficult to work with,' as Coppola recalls, 'and that his films would actually keep people away from the box office.' At one stage the President of Paramount, Stanley Jaffe, told Coppola bluntly (and absurdly in retrospect): 'Marlon Brando will *never* appear in this motion picture.'

Physically, it was true that Brando was past his best at forty-seven. It was also a fact that he could not be bothered to learn his lines anymore, insisting instead that they were written on boards so that he could read them. He argued that the public couldn't tell the difference. The man was contrary, certainly. But no other American film actor had achieved so much, in movies that included *A Streetcar Named*

Desire (1951) and *On the Waterfront* (1954). Despite the extra pounds he carried, Brando still possessed a remarkable physical presence, even heroic good looks, and when the mood struck him he was willing to lose himself in a part to a remarkable degree, as he had learned to do while studying with Stella Adler as a young man in New York. For all these reasons, there were few actors more interesting to watch on screen, and most young filmmakers still idolised the man. Jack Nicholson, for instance, who had recently bought a house with the proceeds of his new movie stardom, had chosen to live in a property adjacent to and just below Brando's estate on Mulholland Drive in the Hollywood Hills. Every day when he woke up Nicholson now looked up, physically and metaphorically, to the one actor he deferred to, the actor he saw as 'my only real competition . . . the guy on the hill.'

Late in 1970, Coppola and a cameraman were admitted to this compound on Mulholland, through the electric gates and up the drive past an avenue of bamboo and pepper trees, to Brando's whitewashed house with its terraces, swimming pool and Olympian views across the movie capital. Brando slept late habitually and came to meet his guests in a kimono, a heavy-set, unkempt middle-aged bohemian with long blond hair: nothing like the disciplined sexagenarian Don, who worked at crime in a suit and tie. One of the studio's concerns about casting Brando in *The Godfather* was that the actor was too young, in his forties, to play the gentleman Don. Coppola had arranged to film a screen test at Brando's home to remind the studio that Brando could play *any* character he put his mind to. As Coppola arranged props for the actor to work with, Marlon changed into a jacket and tie, darkened his hair with shoe polish, and pulled his hair behind his head out of sight. Then he stuffed Kleenex in his mouth to bulk his cheeks, muttering that his character should have the face 'of a bulldog.' Knowing that the Don sustained a wound to the throat in the story, when Brando began to speak he did so in a strained mumble, even answering the telephone in character. It was a brilliant transformation, and when the executives at Paramount saw the screen test there was no more argument. Brando had the job. He brings gravitas to every scene he appears in, and remarkably, considering the fact he is a gangster and a murderer, his Don is someone we grow to like, which is an essential part of why the film was so successful.

Just as nonsensical as Paramount's initial prejudice against Brando now seems, so does the studio's reluctance to countenance Al Pacino as Michael Corleone, complaining that Pacino, then a 31-year-old stage actor with negligible screen experience, was too obscure and too short for the role, and most absurdly of all objecting to the actor on the grounds that he was too Italian-looking. Robert Evans favoured casting Robert Redford, Ryan O'Neal or, best of all, Jack Nicholson in the part. The success of *Five Easy Pieces* had made Nicholson the most sought-after actor in Hollywood. The fact that Nicholson, O'Neal and Redford were all of Irish descent didn't seem to bother Evans. As a result, Coppola was obliged to audition many actors for Michael during long and expensive screen tests in New York, though his first choice was always Pacino. Martin Sheen came in to read. James Caan (whom Coppola wanted for Sonny) tested as Michael, while an unknown twenty-seven-year-old named Bobby De Niro tried out as Sonny. De Niro did so with the cocky aggression of the hoods he knew in Little Italy, where he had grown up. 'This was Sonny as a killer,' Coppola later said of De Niro's test. 'It wasn't anything you could sell. But I never forgot it, and when I did *Godfather II*, I thought [De Niro] could play the young Brando.' When work began on the picture in March 1971, Pacino *was* playing Michael, but on probation. The studio was still very unhappy with the casting, as the actor knew, and the executives were debating whether or not to fire him right up until they saw rushes of the restaurant scene in which Michael murders the gangster Sollozzo and the corrupt police chief McCluskey. In the scene Michael begins his transformation from relative innocent into the Angel of Death who, by the end of the picture, orders the simultaneous assassination of all the family's enemies. The intensity of Pacino's performance convinced Paramount that Al was not only a very fine actor, but also a natural movie star, as he would go on to prove in such seventies classics as *Serpico* (1973) and *Dog Day Afternoon* (1975). Another important *Godfather* discovery was Diane Keaton who played Michael's girlfriend, Kay, though it wasn't until Woody Allen cast Keaton in *Annie Hall* later in the decade that the actress came fully into her own.

Problems continued all through the filming, with Coppola fighting daily battles with the studio. At times he also clashed with members of his crew, many of whom were more experienced than himself. 'There's a certain amount of film student in Francis,' observes Gordon Willis, who became so exasperated with the director at one stage that he reportedly screamed at him: 'You don't know how to do anything right!' In return, Coppola yelled, 'Fuck this picture!' and went back to his office where he ripped the door off its hinges in frustration. The notoriously difficult Marlon Brando proved very easy to work with, however, amusing himself on set with practical jokes and entertaining cast and crew by staying in character when he wasn't acting, once hosting a communal dinner as the Don. The way in which Brando completely and naturally inhabited the part of Vito Corleone gave the project the extra ingredient that made it special. When *The Godfather* opened in March 1972 the film proved a huge success, deservedly winning multiple Oscars including Best Picture. Significantly, Brando also won as Actor in a Leading Role. 'That film made me,' says Coppola, who was now set on a path of glory that led him to direct a clutch of further very significant seventies pictures, 'and, largely, Marlon made that film.' And, of course, the pair would reunite to make *Apocalypse Now*.

Around the time that Francis Coppola was filming in New York, the telephone in Frederick Forsyth's London bed-sitter rang one morning at four a.m. Switching on the lamp, wondering who on Earth could be calling at such an hour, the author was reminded of the lowly conditions in which he was living. At thirty-two, when most of his contemporaries were married with children, living in comfortable homes mortgaged against secure jobs with Fleet Street newspapers or the BBC, Freddie was on his uppers. Without a steady job, he was living in a shabby single room, trying to turn his fortunes around by writing a novel, his first, to which he had given the peculiar title *The Day of the Jackal*. His journalist pals mocked him inordinately for this pretension, pointing out that first novels rarely work, and what was this one about, anyway, Freddie, an *animal*? To some extent Forsyth had already been vindicated. He had at least secured a modest British publishing deal for the book with Harold Harris of Hutchinson, and now here was Harold on the telephone at this unbusinesslike hour. It had to be something very important. 'Are you lying down?' asked the publisher, when they had exchanged greetings.

'Well, it's four in the morning, Harold.'

Harris apologised, explaining he was in the middle of selling the US paperback rights to *The Day of the Jackal*. Bantam was the front-runner. One of the directors was on the West Coast of the United States, another in Israel. Harold was in the middle of the time difference. Again, he asked if Freddie was lying down, which the author confirmed testily that he was. 'It's just as well, because I am going to give you a figure. I have just clinched the deal for $365,000.' The sterling equivalent of £200,000 was a life-changing sum in 1971 when a staff journalist in Fleet Street might earn £1,250-a-year. Finally, Freddie felt that he was on his way.

The idea for the book came to Forsyth in the early 1960s when he was working as a foreign correspondent in France. It was the time of the repeated assassination attempts on President Charles De Gaulle, attempts made by members of the Organisation de l'Armée Secrète (OAS), the terrorist group formed by disgruntled French army officers in angry and violent response to De Gaulle's decision to grant independence to the colony of Algeria. Because the OAS was thoroughly infiltrated by the French secret service, each assassination attempt was a fiasco. The idea occurred to Forsyth: *What if the OAS hired a foreign assassin of whom the French secret service knew nothing?* Freddie mulled this over for several years, until the winter of 1969 in fact, when, having resigned from the BBC after a disagreement about assignments, he found himself in London, broke, and dossing on a friend's sofa in a basement flat in Chelsea. Without a job or home, and despite having never written a novel (nor wanted to), he decided to turn his idea into a thriller and, in contrast to Mario Puzo, once he settled on his idea he went to work with zeal.

After getting over his New Year hangover, Forsyth opened his old Empire Aristocrat portable typewriter on the morning of 2 January

1970, set the machine up on his friend's kitchen table and began typing briskly, as if he was at the BBC with a report to file by lunch. He had the plot in his head, worked out in detail after seven years of rumination: an expert English assassin, code-named Jackal, hired by the OAS at considerable expense to kill De Gaulle, has a sniper rifle custom made so it can be disassembled and hidden under the chassis of his sports car. Assuming the persona of a tourist, he drives into France via a popular tourist crossing on the Riviera, heading for Paris where he plans to shoot De Gaulle as the President leads the annual Liberation Day celebrations. The drama of the story is that soon after the Jackal embarks on his mission the plot is rumbled by the French authorities who set their best detective on the case, a certain Claude Lebel. Although the Jackal soon learns that the French are on to him, he continues with his mission in the arrogant belief that he can outwit the government forces. Tapping out twelve pages a day, every day, between the hours of nine a.m. and three p.m., Forsyth finished his typescript in just over a month. Without making corrections, he then submitted *The Day of the Jackal* to publishers.

The recipients of the manuscript were nonplussed. For a start, it was almost unheard of for a political thriller to feature real-life personalities. Characters in the book included not only France's President, but the country's then Prime Minister, Georges Pompidou, and the British premier, Harold Macmillan. Apart from being unorthodox this created a problem of credibility, for it was self-evident that De Gaulle had *not* been assassinated. When Forsyth composed his novel, De Gaulle was living peacefully in retirement, and he died quietly in November 1970. Publishers asked themselves, reasonably, how there could be any suspense in a book about a plot to assassinate a real-life personality who readers would know had recently died of natural causes. The assassin himself, the Jackal, is a character so lightly drawn that the reader never learns his real full name, let alone anything about his personality other than the fact that he is evidently amoral and vicious. Who could empathise with such a hero? Most off-puttingly, Forsyth was a pedestrian writer to whom cliché was a first resort. A character's Welshnness, for instance, is established by his repeated use of 'boyo'; while Forsyth habitually used pet words such as *habitual*. He also wrote two 'extremely unconvincing sex scenes,' as he admits, 'presuming that there had to be a few purple passages, because otherwise you'd never get published.'

Three publishers rejected *The Day of the Jackal* out of hand and the manuscript was languishing at the offices of a fourth, Michael Joseph, when Forsyth decided to condense his story into a twenty-page synopsis which he presented to Harold Harris of Hutchinson, having finagled his way into Harris' office one Friday on the tenuous excuse of having met him briefly at a party. 'He had every right to take me by the scruff of the neck and throw me out.' Instead, Harris suggested that if Forsyth withdrew the book from Michael Joseph he would look at the synopsis over the weekend. Using his last shillings,★ Forsyth took a cab directly to Michael Joseph, extricated his manuscript, and cabbed back to Great Portland Street. Good as his word, Harris called Forsyth on Monday, saying: 'If you can be here by four o'clock with your agent we'll talk about a contract.'

Despite the book's faults, and eccentricities, Harris recognised *The Day of the Jackal* as being a book one feels compelled to read through to the end without a break, with characters that, though sketchily drawn, seem real. Claude Lebel is an engaging, terrier-like detective, actually the true hero of the book, as was Forsyth's intention, and his dogged hunt for the Jackal is exciting; postwar France is affectionately evoked; and the technical detail about forged identities, sniper rifles and so forth has a particular appeal, as does the Jackal himself. 'To my amazement, women liked him,' remarks Forsyth. 'A lot of people said they wanted to go to bed with the Jackal, despite the fact that the one woman in the book who did ended up getting strangled, because she saw too much in his suitcase.' Strangely enough, the fact that the tale would quite evidently have to end in the Jackal's failure didn't matter. Similarly, it doesn't spoil enjoyment of the film. Somehow, despite itself, the story is suspenseful. 'It still bewilders me to this day,' says the author, who began to see his life transformed from the moment Harris offered him a contract for the book, with an option

---

★This being shortly before the new decimal currency was introduced in the United Kingdom, in February 1971.

to write two more novels. The initial advance was £500 ($800). Not a fortune, but enough for Freddie to move from his friend's sofa to a bed-sitter and keep body and soul together for six months. Then, in November 1970, the film rights were sold for the seemingly astronomical sum of £30,000 ($47,000), enough for a new wardrobe, a car and a flat in Chalcot Square. Freddie was ecstatic. 'I sort of thought, *Wealth! Wealth! Wealth!* It's not retiring money, but it's living-pretty-nicely money.' Then came the dizzying US paperback sale. Still, the book was not yet published, and when it came out in England in June 1971, the omens were inauspicious

The launch party at Quaglino's restaurant was sparsely attended, and those critics who did show their faces exhibited little enthusiasm for the book. 'As far as the media were concerned, it was The Day of the What? by Frederick Who. They'd never heard of it or me. It was the name of an animal. It purported to be about the assassination of a man who [had just] died.' Scant reviews appeared in the national press, and critics were sniffy when they bothered to write about the book at all. But the novel started to sell by word of mouth. Reprints were ordered, and as *The Day of the Jackal* climbed the bestseller lists it was, belatedly, reviewed in many papers. It became a hit in translation in Europe, and did well in America. Before long, Fred Zinnemann was in France scouting locations for the movie, engaging a fine cast that included Derek Jacobi, Timothy West and Cyril Cusack in supporting roles, with the French actor Michel Lonsdale very good indeed as an understated Detective Lebel. Movie and paperback promoted one another and, eventually, *The Day of the Jackal* would sell an estimated ten million copies worldwide, utterly transforming Freddie Forsyth's life. From being an unemployed hack journalist with hardly two shillings to rub together he became a wealthy and internationally successful thriller writer, going on to publish *The Odessa File* in 1972 and many more thereafter.

Around the time of Forsyth's London launch party, our third writer embarked on a project which seemed the least likely to succeed, and yet spawned one of the most successful motion pictures in cinema history. By the summer of 1971, Peter Benchley was, by his own admission, a 30-year-old-failure, little better placed in life than Puzo or Forsyth before their breaks. After a spell in the 1960s as a junior speech writer for President Lyndon Baines Johnson ('very junior and quite incompetent,' Benchley notes) he was working at the start of the seventies as a freelance reporter ('quite an unsuccessful one'). His lacklustre career belied a famous name. Peter's father was the popular American writer Nathaniel Benchley, and his grandfather the still more notable Robert Benchley. Peter did at least have an agent, who occasionally fixed up lunches with publishers. During the summer of 1971, he went into Manhattan to have just such a lunch with Tom Congdon, an editor at Doubleday. Peter had two ideas to pitch to Congdon, a book about pirates, and another based on a newspaper story he had clipped from the *New York Daily News* back in 1964 and kept ever since because it intrigued him so. The story concerned a fisherman who caught a 4,550-pound great white shark off the beaches of Montauk, Long Island. One subject Peter knew about was the sea, and he was conversant with that part of the coast in particular. The idea of a huge predatory shark swimming into waters so popular with tourists was fascinating. 'I thought, *My God, what would happen if one of those things came in and wouldn't go away?*' Congdon had no interest in the pirate book, but said Doubleday would pay Benchley a thousand dollars to develop four chapters of the shark story, with more money to come if they published. Peter spent the advance almost as soon as it was paid to him. Then his agent rang to ask where the chapters were.

'Either give him the chapters or give him his money back.'

There was little choice but to write something. At the time Peter was living with his wife, Wendy, and their two young children, in a small house in Pennington, New Jersey. It was too crowded a home to work in. A mile down the road was a company that manufactured furnaces. If Peter could stand the noise of furnaces being built, he could rent an office there for fifty bucks a month. So he lugged his Royal typewriter down to the Pennington Furnace Supply Company and started to compose his shark story in, as he recalls it, 'a humorous way.' Perhaps influenced by the fact that his eminent grandfather had made such a success of funny stories, in *The New Yorker* and elsewhere,

Peter came up with the notion that this monster shark story should make people laugh as well as thrill them. And four comical chapters were duly delivered to Doubleday. 'You really can't do a funny thriller,' Congdon responded. 'Or at least *you* can't do that.' The inference was that a more skilful author might be able to pull off that trick, but Peter did not have that ability. Benchley was a hack writer, slightly below Forsyth's standard in fact, straining for effect with his similes, clumsy with the pace of his story, and prone to crass sex scenes (a failure both have in common with Mario Puzo). It wasn't all bad news though. On the plus side, Benchley had an exceptionally strong central idea — the giant, relentless shark terrorising a Long Island seaside community – and he knew enough about boats and the sea to make the nautical passages convincing. 'You've got to do it straight and you've got to do it as a thriller' was Congdon's sage advice, with which Benchley returned to Pennington.

While the furnace men banged and crashed next door, Benchley started all over again, hoping only to get Doubleday to part with $7,500 (£5,860) for a completed manuscript. He didn't expect anything more for reasons he explains: 'First of all I knew that this book couldn't be successful, because it was a first novel, and nobody reads first novels, and it was a first novel about a fish, so who the hell cared about that? And I was convinced that nobody could ever make a movie out of it, [because] I knew that nobody could catch and train a great white shark, and I thought that the Hollywood technology was nowhere near good enough to make one.' As we shall see, this was a significant misreading of future events.

7

WOMEN OF THE YEAR

If she'd have been a man, I'd have kicked her in the balls.

GERMAINE GREER ON DIANE ARBUS

The decade of the blockbuster novel was also the age of feminism, when remarkable women forged ahead in society and made a lasting impression on the world, often despite considerable opposition. The photographer Diane Arbus had a particularly difficult time working in the male-dominated magazine industry of New York. Her career might have gone more smoothly, it is true, had Arbus been a more conventional photo-journalist. The 1970s was in fact a boom time for magazine journalism, in the United States especially, with publications such as *Esquire*, *Harper's Bazaar* and *Rolling Stone* enjoying very large readerships in an era when print journalism commanded a much more significant place in public life, and editors spent freely on the best writers, illustrators and photographers. Arbus' photography was more art than journalism, however, her favoured subject matter – characterised as *freaks* – too strong for most editors. Although she produced some of her very best work in the first eighteen months of the 1970s, Arbus so despaired of her commercial career that she decided to crop herself by suicide out of the picture of her life in July 1971. Almost immediately thereafter she became a posthumous superstar of art photography, and a tragic feminist icon.

Diane – who pronounced her name Dee-Ann – was born in 1923

into a wealthy New York family. Her father, David Nemerov, owned Russek's, a department store on Fifth Avenue, and home was a fourteen-room apartment on the Upper West Side, where Diane's bedroom overlooked Central Park. When she was eighteen, Diane married Allan Arbus, with whom she had two daughters, Doon and Amy. The couple developed a shared fascination for photography: they studied art photography, and set up a commercial studio in New York after the war, shooting features for *Vogue* and other magazines. Allan was the principal photographer, the one who knew most about the mechanics and technicalities of using cameras, but Diane had the best ideas. Together they became part of the photographic community of the city, friends with the likes of Richard Avedon and the young Stanley Kubrick, then working as a photo-journalist. In the late 1950s, the Arbuses separated, later to divorce, though staying close friends, and Diane launched her own remarkable career.

There was a disquieting aspect to almost every photograph Diane took from then on, which grew out of her own personality. From early adulthood she had suffered from depression. Many people have dark moods, of course. Allan Arbus did himself. 'I would become discouraged, and feel blue, but with Diane it was something much more major.' He saw it as a chemical imbalance, a form of mental illness, and as the years went by Diane became an increasingly unhappy and, indeed, erratic person, quickly becoming elated, for example, typically about ideas for new projects, but then getting weighed down by depressions so severe she could not leave home. When she did summon the energy to get out of her apartment and take pictures, she chose subjects who appeared as strange as she felt inside, revealing an obsession with people she called *freaks*. It is a word associated in America with old-fashioned carnivals where giants, dwarfs, hermaphrodites and other human oddities – those dealt an unlucky hand by nature, and others who had turned themselves deliberately into curiosities by covering their bodies in tattoos, say, or festooning themselves with pins – were exhibited for the amusement of the public. Arbus maintained that, in her opinion, freaks possessed a special nobility. 'Most people go through life dreading they'll have a traumatic experience. Freaks were born with their trauma. They've passed their test in life. They're aristocrats,' she told *Newsweek* in 1967. However she also seems to have taken a prurient delight in her subjects.

Arbus invested considerable time in winning the trust and, indeed, friendship of her cherished freaks. She spent eight years in the company of Eddie Carmel, for instance, an eight foot-tall, 495-pound man mountain whom she ultimately made famous as her 'Jewish giant' (as she labelled him in her 1970 portrait 'A Jewish giant at home with his parents in the Bronx, NY'). In many ways, Eddie was an ordinary young man, with ambitions. In his case, he wanted to be an actor. But he was only ever hired on account of his bizarre size, performing for instance as a giant in the Ringling Brothers circus. There was additional pathos to Eddie's life in the fact that the condition that made him special would be the death of him. The giant suffered from bone disease and even as a young man he needed to support himself with a walking stick. Visiting Eddie at home in the Bronx, where he shared a tiny apartment with his parents, Diane saw the Carmel family as characters from a storybook: Eddie the fairy-tale giant who, with his arms around his little parent helpers, looked at times as though he might crush Ma and Pa Carmel to death.

There was a secret, or double, story to most of Arbus' best portraits. It was a quality she looked for in her subjects, and for this reason she was often drawn to photograph transvestites. Notable pictures include a portrait of a young man with his hair in curlers, eyebrows drawn on, holding a cigarette between fingers decorated with false nails; and a fey fellow posing nonchalantly in make-up, stockings and suspenders. Diane ingratiated herself into the circle of people who surrounded Andy Warhol's Factory studio in order to befriend such she-males, taking a close interest in the strange charisma of Warholian characters like Candy Darling and Holly Woodlawn before they achieved celebrity in the early 1970s by being name-checked by Lou Reed in 'Walk on the Wild Side'. Aside from the amount of time she invested in cultivating relationships with these people, part of Diane's success lay in being *stealthful*. Dennis Hopper, another visitor to the Factory who took photographs, spent a day shooting images with Arbus and recalls how, in contrast to his amateur handiwork, Diane was a wonderfully deft and always unobtrusive photographer: 'She'd just sort of glide in and take her picture [with] such grace and quietness.' As a result, her subjects barely noticed that they were being captured on film.

And so Diane's portfolio came to include images of drag queens, albino sword-swallowers, tattooed men, raving street people, human pin-cushions, strippers, midgets and giants. She was also quick to perceive the sinister side of apparently ordinary people: a baby contorted into a monster by its own tantrum; old-age pensioners with malevolent expressions; and all manner of alarming-looking children, including sinister twin girls, an image which inspired her friend Stanley Kubrick when he filmed The Shining (1980). Arbus trawled New York for such subjects, often taking a turn around Central Park, which she had known since childhood. One bright day an old acquaintance ran into her there and asked Diane cheerfully: 'What are you doing on such a beautiful day?'

'Trying to find some unhappy people.'

She found them sometimes taking part in political demonstrations: famously in 1967 she photographed a blank-faced youth attending a parade in support of the war in Vietnam, with two button badges on his jacket, one of which read GOD BLESS AMERICA and the other BOMB HANOI. For Allan Arbus, Diane could find 'beauty everywhere, in the most unexpected places,' and here was a textbook case. 'The pitiable delusion of that misguided innocent – the victim of some patriotic manure.' Allan adds: 'Empathy is the word. Diane said somewhere that there are things she sees which she believes no one else would see. She was very aware of the uniqueness of her vision. Her subjects moved her deeply and she treated them very nearly reverently. She was captivated by their self-images and the discrepancy between their view of themselves and the world's perception of them. She found them poignant.'

Sex was another area of fascination. Diane took pictures of dominatrices standing over submissive clients, middle-aged men cowering naked on the floor, vulnerable and flabby; couples fornicating, having apparently forgotten Diane was in the room with them. She gained remarkable access to these most intimate situations, partly because of her personal involvement in this twilight world. As she moved into middle age, Diane collected pornography, took partners of both sexes, and developed a taste for anonymous sex in public places. A scrappy little woman in appearance, with short dark hair, sad eyes, and wolfish, discoloured teeth, often dressed in black leather trousers, her unadulterated, essential femaleness and liberated lifestyle was the embodiment of the feminism being espoused by the likes of Germaine Greer at this time. Diane was not a woman who 'shaved and deodorised [herself] into complete tastelessness,' as Greer wrote in *The Female Eunuch*. She was elementally female, a woman who had sex with whomsoever she liked and didn't care who knew it; rather than conceal her periods, Diane *told* people when she was menstruating; she was also a single working mother, employed in a male-dominated industry where she insisted on being treated the same as men. 'I'm a photographer, not a woman photographer,' as she said.

Despite her apparent toughness, Arbus did not find it easy to make a living as a freelance photographer. Having grown up rich, she had never learned how to live on a budget and did not have the personality to deal effectively with editors, whereby one must win friends on one hand and extract money due on the other. Allan was a vital source of advice, practical assistance and moral support. But in the summer of 1969 he closed his New York studio and moved, with his second wife, to California to pursue his ambition to be an actor. (In the 1970s he became familiar to TV audiences as the psychiatrist Sidney Freedman in *M*A*S*H*.) Without Allan on hand, Diane found life increasingly difficult in New York. Her work was widely admired, and she was more and more noticed within the art community – her pictures acquired and exhibited by the Museum of Modern Art no less – but she found it grindingly difficult to earn a living. 'She had complete faith in what she was doing; she knew she had a unique talent and she had a great deal of enthusiastic support from people she admired [such as] Richard Avedon,' says Allan. 'But she found that the people who were in a position to give her work and *pay her for it* were often difficult, unfeeling, timid and ultimately discouraging . . . her reputation was soaring but her bank account was not.' Her ideas for magazine features tended not to be particularly commercial, featuring as they did the sort of people most of us look away from when they pass by. She was not averse to photographing celebrities, but wanted to subvert rather than celebrate their fame, which was an idea way ahead of its time. And her success with the famous was limited by the extent to which the personalities she met decided to co-operate with her. By and large they were not particularly accommodating. By contrast, Diane's retinue of freaks allowed her to photograph them again and again, uncomplainingly, thinking of Diane as a friend after so many years, and welcome company no doubt, until she got the image she was after. Then: *Eureka!*

Nearly all the images Diane had taken of the gigantic Eddie Carmel over the years had interest, but none were exceptional. Meanwhile, Eddie's health was deteriorating fast. The poor man was more bent over each time Diane visited him. After yet another session at his home in the Bronx in the summer of 1970, Diane had a roll of film developed (later identified as # 688), the first frame of which showed Eddie and his Ma and Pa in a composition that, rather like David Hockney's *Mr and Mrs Clark and Percy* (painted the same year), revealed the essence of a relationship, and hinted at more. Eddie leans on his stick, towering over his parents; Ma is looking up with an aghast expression, even a touch of disgust, with Pa almost hiding behind her. Eddie was their son, and they cared for him as such, loved him naturally, but he was also truly monstrous, and his freakish condition had been a blight on all their lives. All this information was in this one picture. Diane could barely conceal her jubilation. 'You know how every mother has nightmares when she's pregnant that her baby will be born a monster?' she burbled to friends. 'I think I got that in the mother's face as she glares up at Eddie, thinking, "OH MY GOD, NO!"'

The over-excited way she spoke about the picture – perhaps her most famous work – is at variance with her public comments about wanting to celebrate the nobility of freaks. In truth, Diane seems here to revel in Eddie's freakishness. Also, her method in taking hundreds of pictures of a person like Eddie over eight years, until she finally got *the* picture, is questionable. It could be argued that she was operating as a machine, pressing the button until she got lucky. Compared to the work of a painter like Hockney say, this seems to have less to do with artistry than persistence, the resulting classic image almost a matter of dumb luck. 'The photograph of the giant may have been an accident in the sense it wasn't planned,' concedes Allan. 'But she went back again and again looking for something. And finally found it.' Certainly, the end result is a fascinating picture, one of the greatest photographic portraits of the 1970s.

Diane did not enjoy New York in the summer. The oppressive heat, and the fact that so many friends left the city, increasing her sense of aloneness, aggravated her depressions, and those moods were made worse by the stress of the freelance life: trying to pitch feature ideas to indifferent picture editors, fighting for a decent fee when magazines did commission her, and trying to get paid in full on time. She did not have the temperament for such a life, breaking down in tears in late spring 1971 over a disputed expenses claim to *Harper's*. But unable throughout her career to establish financial independence, she was at the mercy of magazine editors and their whimsical commissioning – a miserable situation which meant that she often felt obliged to accept work she did not particularly want to do in order to make a living. Such was the case when, in the summer of 1971, Arbus was hired by *New Woman* to photograph Germaine Greer at the Chelsea Hotel. With little regard for the magazine, and enervated by the summer heat, the photographer trudged over to West 23rd Street to undertake a job she had minimal enthusiasm for, though one might think that Arbus and Greer would have been natural soulmates.

Dr Greer, a Shakespeare scholar and professional academic, with a Ph.D. from Cambridge University, had risen to fame in Britain the previous year with the publication of her first book, *The Female Eunuch*, in which she argues that women, who are naturally dynamic and creative creatures, have been 'feminised' (a pejorative term), turned into emotional and sexual eunuchs by men, who want them as passive concubines and reliable mothers to bear and bring up their children. In her book Greer urges women to rise up against this tyranny and declare, 'I am a woman, not a castrate,' to have sex when and how they like, to accept their bodies as nature intended them, body-hair and all, and demand an equal place in the world of work.

Much the same was argued by American feminists such as Kate Millett and Susan Sontag, but Greer had a particular charisma: a combination of a first-class brain, earthy humour and sex appeal. Australian by birth, resident in the United Kingdom, she was a six-foot Amazon with flowing dark hair and olive skin, her usual demeanour one of feisty good humour, though in anger she could be splendidly fierce. In her conversation and writing she combined erudition with a popular touch, juxtaposing references to Chaucer and Freud in *The Female Eunuch* with asides to Lucy Van Pelt, the irascible cartoon-girl in Charles Schulz's then highly popular comic strip *Peanuts*. (Lucy was apparently *crabby*, to use a Schulz word, because of the frustration of repressing her clever and lively true self in a society that required little girls to be merely passive and attractive.) In her book, Greer also lambasts famous men who were, to her and other feminists, archetypal chauvinists, notably the American writer Norman Mailer.

By 1971, the author of the celebrated Second World War novel *The Naked and the Dead* was a paunchy 48-year-old veteran of four marriages, infamous for stabbing his second wife during a drunken fight. The fact that he was a virtual slave to alimony may have had a bearing on his decision to largely abandon writing conventional novels in the late 1960s and early 1970s in favour of producing shorter, non-fiction books in the genre Tom Wolfe had recently labelled the New Journalism, mixing together all the techniques of novel-writing – the use of characters, dialogue, metaphor and so forth – to tell real-life stories. Often the author stepped into these books as a character, or in terms of making his personal feelings clear, which ran contrary to the objective tradition of journalism in the twentieth century. Some of Mailer's journalistic works were very slight indeed. Others, such as his 1968 book about taking part in a demonstration against the Vietnam War, *The Armies of the Night*, were more substantial, and indeed Mailer won his first Pulitzer Prize for that book. Despite this accolade, a cynic might say that books in which Mailer is usually a self-dramatising and often humourless central character (referred to disconcertingly in the third person in *The Armies of the Night*) fed the author's ego and his craving for publicity. Ever since he became famous at the age of twenty-five, having had the 'great good fortune to be shot out of a cannon' as he refers to the success of *The Naked and the Dead*, Mailer had liked to stay in the centre of public debate, and though he denies that he has been deliberately provocative he seemed to delight in raising hackles, for example describing women as 'low sloppy beasts' at the outset of the feminist movement, and remarking on a TV show in 1970 that women should be kept in cages! ('He grinned broadly as he said this, delighted with the gasp which came up from the audience,' Mailer later wrote of himself in regard to this episode, revelling in his mischief-making.)

Feminists rose to the bait, singling Mailer out for attacks in books such as Mary Ellmann's *Thinking About Women* (1969) and Kate Millett's *Sexual Politics* (1970). Mailer was tickled to count twenty-five pages devoted to himself in the latter volume and decided to write another quick non-fiction book in response. And so it was that over the winter of 1970 he produced *The Prisoner of Sex*, one of the most controversial works of his career. 'I must say I was staggered by the virulence with which so many women hated that book at that time,' says the author, looking back. 'I've run across young girls in college who won't read me because of *The Prisoner of Sex*.' In retrospect it was an insubstantial book, made slightly absurd by the author's pomposity – harking on his recent Pulitzer, and musing on whether he would get the Nobel next – padded out to 169 pages by means of voluminous quotes from Henry Miller, D.H. Lawrence, Kate Millett and even old interviews with himself. The essential argument can be reduced to a few words: women could be as free as they liked, but the ultimate point of a woman's life was to find a mate and reproduce. And if any woman expected Norman to put aside his pen and help wash the dishes she would be disappointed because his work was too important. Freud pronounced, 'Anatomy is destiny.' Mailer adapted and qualified this maxim as, 'Biology is half-destiny.' You didn't *have* to do what your chromosomes programme you to do. But the fundamentals are still important, and if you try to buck nature you pay for it in the long run. 'You know, if men are not macho . . . they pay a price for that,' he argues. 'If women don't have children, they pay a price for it. It seems to me that's just part of life.' When feminists read *The Prisoner of Sex*, firstly in *Harper's Bazaar* in March 1971, and took in all its points, including an apparent denunciation of birth control, they were scandalised. 'Do you have any idea of the trouble you are getting into?' the author was asked by a female friend. 'No, not really,' he replied, as he blundered on into a publicity stunt for the book at the Town Hall in New York.

Norman's idea was to stage a feminist debate, on 31 March 1971, with himself in the role of moderator, an event captured on film as *Town Bloody Hall* (1972), directed by D.A. Pennebaker. Kate Millett and several other leading feminists declined to appear with a man they considered the quintessential chauvinist, but with the forthcoming US edition of her own book to plug Dr Greer rose to the challenge. A striking figure, draped in fur, Greer charmed the audience at the Town Hall with her wit, eloquence and well-made points about ego-centric men, and she quite disarmed Mailer by flirting with him. Though he enjoyed Germaine's company, Norman Mailer admits that he has come to regret the evening, saying that he squirms in his seat whenever he catches *Town Bloody Hall* on television. 'I was sort of asinine, looking back on it . . . I was behind the wave, if you will, and since I'd always seen myself as being hip, and knowing what was going on, when I see that show I'm a little amazed at how backward I was,' he confesses. 'I didn't realise how passionate and how powerful the woman's movement was going to be. You know, I have many mixed feelings about the woman's movement, but what I don't forgive myself for is being so retrograde in understanding that this was truly a powerful movement starting, and it had immense momentum behind it.' He would make up for *The Prisoner of Sex* later in the decade, reviving his career with a factual work that for many was the best book he had written since *The Naked and the Dead*. The story of Norman Mailer in the 1970s does not end in 1971 by any means. In the meantime, he is generous enough to concede that on the matter of feminism he was outflanked and outgunned at New York's Town Hall in March 1971. 'Germaine was marvellous in that. I don't know if she's ever been better. That was her night.'*

*If this was one of Dr Greer's finest hours, her decision to take part in the Channel 4 television show *Celebrity Big Brother* in 2005 was surely her lowest point: a decision that undermined the moral authority she built up over her career, and leads one to wonder whether she was ever worthy of being taken as seriously as she was.

On a humid day a couple of weeks later, exhausted from her relentless book-plugging, Greer admitted Diane Arbus to her suite at the Chelsea Hotel. Although the photographer was a small woman of five foot six inches, and had originally won Dr Greer's sympathy by seeming too frail to heft her own camera equipment, Diane asserted herself during the shoot, ordering the feminist to lie on the bed, then straddling her and shooting down. 'It developed into a sort of duel between us, because I *resisted* being photographed like that – close up with all my pores and lines showing!' Greer told Arbus biographer Patricia Bosworth. 'She kept asking me all sorts of personal questions, and I became aware that she would only shoot when my face was showing tension or concern or boredom or annoyance (and there was plenty of *that*, let me tell you), but because she was a woman I didn't tell her to fuck off. If she'd been a man, I'd have kicked her in the balls.' Greer responded by adopting a stony expression. 'I decided, "Damn it, you're not going to do this to me, lady. I'm not going to be photographed like one of your grotesque freaks!" So I stiffened my face like a mask.'

In Greer's opinion, the battle of wills was a draw. The editors at *New Woman* evidently considered Greer *vs* Arbus had resulted in defeat for the photographer, for her pictures were never used in the magazine. In a letter to Allan, Diane discussed her attitude to the shoot, perhaps revealing her approach to her subjects generally. She wrote that she had liked Germaine Greer personally, considering her to be 'fun and terrific looking . . .' Nevertheless, she went out of her way to depict her in an unflattering light. As she said, 'I managed to make otherwise.' The picture from the session, printed posthumously as 'Feminist in her hotel room, NYC, 1971', is in fact fascinating, not least because in close-up, Greer's neatly plucked and re-applied eyebrows drawn into half moons over her dark, sardonic eyes, the feminist has more than a passing resemblance to the transvestite in curlers who Arbus photographed back in 1966.

May segued into June and Diane felt increasingly depressed. The hit album that summer was Carole King's *Tapestry*. Everywhere one went, King's sad ballads were floating in the air, most often her mournful number one single, 'It's Too Late', a theme for female depression with its lyrics about feeling too blue to even get out of bed in the morning. When Diane forced herself out of her own pit, she dragged her bones around Manhattan as per usual searching for unhappy subjects. Occasionally she took day-trips out to New Jersey where, for the past couple of years, she had been visiting institutions for mentally and physically retarded adults, becoming fascinated by these overgrown children. The contrast between their adult size, their sometimes alarmingly aged faces, and uncorrupted childhood innocence, was deeply affecting. Diane attended picnic outings, photographing the retardees holding one another's hands: docilely, obediently, lovingly. In her notebook, she recorded her impressions, describing how the retardees looked after each other as best childhood friends do, and how excited they became over small treats. Yet bitter tears came like summer tempests. 'They can cry over things like when their pinwheel stops turning.' Allan Arbus recalls that the project was a happy one for Diane, and the pictures she took at the New Jersey institutions are among her very best work, coming at the very end of her life: that summer the chemicals in her brain shifted again, finally, decisively, all happiness evaporated and she lost hope. On 10 July 1971, the photographer admitted to a friend, 'My work doesn't do it for me anymore.' This was fatal, because her work was all she had.

Diane's brother, Howard, came to visit that month. After they had dinner together he walked his sister back to her apartment, a cell-like space in a building near the Hudson River. Frankly, he found it a depressing flat and was glad to leave. Doon was in France, and Diane's other daughter, Amy, was at summer school in Massachusetts. Allan was filming in New Mexico, a movie entitled *Greaser's Palace*. So she was alone. On 26 July Diane ventured out to lunch with a friend at the Russian Tea Room on West 57th Street, a restaurant beloved of well-heeled New Yorkers and celebrities (Woody Allen was a regular customer, with his new girlfriend Diane Keaton). After lunch, Diane drifted back to her solitary apartment. It was the day of the Apollo 15 moon shot and the sound of the television coverage bled from the open windows of neighbouring apartments, though in truth America was already tiring of NASA's manned missions to the moon (of which there would only be two more before this historic series of voyages ended in 1972). Two days later, while astronauts David Scott and James Irwin were walking on the moon, having been unable to raise Diane on the telephone, a friend let himself into the apartment, where he found her body curled up in the bath, partly dressed. She had taken an overdose of barbiturates and cut both her wrists, repeatedly and deeply, and was stone cold dead at the age of forty-eight. While he was working that day in New Mexico, Allan had taken the time to look up at the sky. 'In Santa Fe, there are extraordinary clouds,' he says, 'and that day they were more extraordinary than anything I'd ever seen in my life. And [when] I got back to the hotel there were four or five calls for me and I knew something terrible had happened.' And, no, whatever any one might think, even considering the effects of the suicide on their two daughters, he says he was not angry with Diane. 'I don't know what outsiders assume [but] that's the truth,' he says, his voice made husky by the emotion even now. 'We were very close, long after the separation, *very* close.'

By killing herself, as perhaps she knew, the photographer of the dark and freakish added value to every picture she had taken. Not only had her subjects been peculiar, now the public knew that Diane Arbus herself had also been very strange. Suicide piqued the same voyeuristic curiosity that partly motivated Arbus' work, seeking out people as damaged as she knew herself to be. She had suffered depression all her adult life, and talked of suicide. It had been with her while she was taking those weird pictures and now suicide gave her whole body of work a mystique that made her, posthumously, one of the most famous photographers of modern times. When she was alive, precious few cared. A year after Arbus' death, in 1972, when the Museum of Modern Art mounted a one-woman retrospective of her work, a quarter of a million people came to see her pictures, demonstrating that the public's fascination with the weird is immense, exceeded perhaps only by its fixation with sex.

8

SEX AND FEAR AND LOATHING

. . . we're on our way to Las Vegas to find the American Dream.

HUNTER S. THOMPSON

Among Germaine Greer's gripes about men was the language they commonly used to describe sex. 'All the vulgar linguistic emphasis is placed upon the *poking* element,' she grumbled in *The Female Eunuch*, '*fucking, screwing, rooting, shagging* are all acts performed upon the passive female.' This was certainly true of male blockbuster novelists of the 1970s. The sex scenes in Frederick Forsyth's *The Day of the Jackal* are embarrassingly crass, as he admits with hindsight. 'They're awful . . . I just thought that it was a *sine qua non* for publication.' Other contemporary male writers made much better use of sex, however. In his so-called Rabbit books, for instance, the second of which was published in November 1971, John Updike gave a realistic and balanced account of modern sexual relationships.

For those who don't know the Rabbit stories, Updike offers a one-sentence summation of his most famous fictional character: 'A former athlete still looking for the bliss and fulfilment of his glory days.' Introduced in *Rabbit, Run* (1960), Harry 'Rabbit' Angstrom – the nickname derived from his upturned nose, the surname a play on his angst-ridden personality – was fleetingly, thrillingly a college basketball star in his hometown of Brewer, Pennsylvania. At the start of *Rabbit, Run*, set in 1959, Harry is recently and unhappily married to

Janice, has a son named Nelson, and lives in a dowdy apartment building, his halcyon days as a sports star recently put behind him, the grey highway of married life stretching ahead. Frustrated, he runs from the marriage and has a brief affair, the first bump on the road of adulthood. Despite this experience, Janice and Harry are back together at the start of the sequel, *Rabbit Redux*, ten years older and living in a more salubrious house in the suburbs of Brewer (reflecting the contemporaneous migration to the suburbs of America's white middle class). The year is 1969 and America is in bad shape, not least because of the war in Vietnam, and this second Rabbit book is as much about the state of the nation as what goes on inside Harry's house at the turn of the decade. 'It was a messy time of adjustment,' says Updike of the mood in the country, 'to the cultural revolution of the '60s and the failure of Vietnam.' As Harry worries over the war, his wife leaves him for a car dealer at her father's lot. In describing Janice's uncoupling from Harry and her coming together with her new lover, Updike employs the imagery of NASA's moonshots, partly as a timely metaphor, but also because he wanted to show in the book that there was at least this one great historical achievement to be proud of when so much else was going wrong with America.

Janice telephones Harry to explain why she has left him, her speech showing that the aftershocks of the social revolution of the mid-1960s are now reaching Brewer, as they rippled out to the Bakersfield home of Bobby and Rayette in *Five Easy Pieces*. 'Harry, I'm sorry for whatever pain this is causing you, truly sorry, but it's very important that at this point in our lives we don't let guilt feelings motivate us. I'm trying to look honestly into myself, to see who I am, and where I should be going . . . It's the year nineteen sixty-nine and there's no reason for two mature people to smother each other out of inertia. I'm searching for a valid identity and I suggest you do the same.' Although he shrugs off Janice's words as recycled TV psycho-babble, which he notes is increasingly prevalent these days, Harry soon experiences a delayed sexual liberation of his own, stumbling into an affair with a hippie drifter named Jill, and allowing her drug dealer pimp, a shamanistic black Vietnam veteran named Skeeter, to move in with them. In Janice's absence, Harry becomes entangled in

a boozy, druggy *ménage à trois* with his young companions, each getting something they need from the relationship: in Skeeter Harry has
a male friend with whom to chew over the war; Skeeter, in trouble
with the law, has a place to hide out; Jill obtains drugs from Skeeter
and Harry puts a roof over her head; in return, she makes herself sexually available to the men. Meanwhile, young Nelson Angstrom
watches the antics of the adults sharing his home with a mixture of
fear, loathing and fascination.

Jill is used roughly at times in *Rabbit Redux*, as a whore. Some of
these sex scenes make the reader wince, even now. 'I'm glad,' comments Updike. 'I meant my readers to be [disturbed].' Nevertheless,
sexual activity takes many forms in *Rabbit Redux*: it is also passionate,
casual, gentle, violent; it can be imbued with all the meaning in the
world and none. Sometimes Harry simply masturbates. In short, sex is
portrayed truthfully, as in the photographs Diane Arbus took. There
is none of the male-orientated poking about of Benchley, Forsyth and
Puzo, let alone the soft-core magazine pornography of the day, the
sort of stuff found in publications such as *Playboy*. Rather, Updike felt
that the sexuality of men and women, their *creatureliness* as he terms it,
had been hitherto under-represented in the literature of his country –
probably because of America's deep and strong puritan roots – and he
wanted to confront sex. It didn't have to be shut away as if it were
something shameful, or made into a lewd entertainment.

In fact, Updike had been gathering a reputation as an audacious
writer on the subject of sex for several years, especially for novels such
as *Couples* (1968). The author had been criticised for hitherto spending so much time in his characters' bedrooms, as though he was
exploring the boundaries of what could be decently published in
order to titillate his readers. But when *Rabbit Redux* was published in
1971 there was a feeling that Updike had been misjudged, and that he
had made powerful and justifiable use of the frank sexual material in
the book. 'Updike was always there – it's time we noticed' was the
headline in the *New York Times Book Review* when the novel came out,
with reviewer Richard Locke placing Updike among the very best
American novelists of the early '70s (along with Saul Bellow, Norman
Mailer, Bernard Malamud and Philip Roth).

In subsequent years the second of the Rabbit books has achieved the status of a modern classic, widely enjoyed by readers far too young to have lived through the time Updike was describing. More confident than the first novel in the series, also richer in metaphor, Updike presents characters that live in the mind, beyond the parameters of the books themselves. Beautifully and precisely written, with bone-true observations about the world and human behaviour, the book is also a time capsule from the perspective of Middle America in the months spanning the end of the 1960s and the beginning of the new decade: the excitement and glory of the Apollo programme, with Kubrick's *2001: A Space Odyssey* (1968) still playing at the cinema; the changing relationships between men and women, between black and white (Harry making black friends for the first time in his life); America's failure in Vietnam, and the first fuel-starved splutters of a faltering US economy. Updike closed the 1960s and introduced the 1970s brilliantly, as he would close the decade with *Rabbit is Rich*, set in the 1979 of Skylab, President Carter and jogging, by which time Harry and Janice were reunited, and had become wealthy during the intervening oil crisis as owners of a Toyota dealership, selling small economical automobiles made in Japan to their fellow Americans.

The month that *Rabbit Redux* was published a new comic masterpiece roared off the presses of *Rolling Stone* magazine: part one of an adventure by Hunter S. Thompson entitled *Fear and Loathing in Las Vegas*. The story made Thompson a star overnight, and was equally a triumph for one of the most significant magazines of the decade.

In common with Hugh Hefner's *Playboy*, *Rolling Stone* is one of those publications that is the manifestation of the tastes of one man: in this case its founder and publisher, Jann Wenner, a chubby, energetic Jewish New Yorker born in 1946. In common with many members of his generation, and people such as Hunter Thompson and Ossie Clark who were born approximately ten years earlier, rock music had a central place in Jann's life. To him it was not merely aural entertainment. Rock was a font of ideas for baby boomers such as himself as well as being a type of cultural glue for their lives, sticking to fashion, drug culture, sex and politics. The leading figures of popular music –

the likes of Bob Dylan and John Lennon – were regarded as philosopher-gurus, their albums studied, compared, rated and debated as previous generations worried over important new books. This was true for millions of young people in America and abroad, in the home and classroom, on college campuses, in bars and offices. Yet no one was covering the rock phenomenon, 'covering it in the sense of they understood all the cultural implications as well,' as Jann puts it. In 1967 he set out to rectify that situation by borrowing $7,500 (£5,800) with which to launch a bi-weekly rock newspaper, named after a Muddy Waters song and operating initially out of a San Francisco warehouse. Although amateurish in its early issues, *Rolling Stone* rapidly became established as *the* publication for the American music industry, the place for record companies to run ads for their acts, to get albums reviewed, and have their stars interviewed.

Moreover, *Rolling Stone* became one of the foremost publications of the literary genre which Tom Wolfe claimed would supersede the novel as the dominant form of the late twentieth century, leaving traditionalists such as John Updike behind. Wolfe was gratified to see eminent authors such as Norman Mailer joining him in the New Journalism, though Mailer rails against Wolfe's claim to have invented the movement. 'Tom Wolfe and I started around the same time. And Tom runs around claiming *he started* the New Journalism,' says Mailer hotly. 'My own feeling is: the Hell with that! That's not what's interesting. What's interesting is the degree to which techniques of a novelist can be used to improve journalism, and in which ways, and what are the pitfalls.' In the long run, much of the New Journalism hasn't stood the test of time, while traditional novels such as *Rabbit Redux* have. But Wolfe made a shrewd point when he argued that the best writing on the popular culture of the 1960s and 1970s wasn't to be found primarily in novels but in magazines, often in *Rolling Stone*. The magazine's coverage of the Charles Manson murder case and the disastrous Rolling Stones concert at the Altamont Raceway in California were two early journalistic triumphs, winning *Rolling Stone* the National Magazine Award in 1970, and this high standard was maintained well into the mid-1970s. 'Over the past three years no periodical has achieved a more spectacular success with the New

Journalism than Jann Wenner's *Rolling Stone*,' Wolfe asserted in 1973. 'One of Wenner's great strengths as an editor is that he insists on detailed reporting in a field – Rock, Pop, Hip, Underground – where many editors give in to writers who want to work strictly from off the top of their head. Wenner has discovered and encouraged many talented young writers.' There was some back-scratching here. Recently, Wenner had commissioned Wolfe to make a lengthy study of the lives of America's Pioneer astronauts, a project which resulted in a four-part article published in the magazine in 1973, appearing as the book *The Right Stuff* six years later. So Wolfe was in Wenner's debt. It was nonetheless true that, issue by issue, *Rolling Stone* was adding up to be a superlative history of the popular culture of the late 1960s and 1970s, with feature articles on a wide range of subjects beyond the realm of rock – but invariably touching on rock music in some way – written and illustrated by a remarkable roster of new talent.

In 1971 alone, reporter Joe Eszterhas, photographer Annie Leibovitz and Dr Hunter S. Thompson* joined *Rolling Stone*, the latter's work given additional impact by the illustrations of the British artist Ralph Steadman. At thirty-two, Thompson had already written one of the minor classics of the New Journalism, *Hell's Angels* (1966), for which he had ridden with the notorious motorcycle gang in San Francisco. Wenner was greatly impressed by the book and invited Thompson to come in for a meeting at *Rolling Stone*. The individual who entered his office was a tall, athletic-looking young man who walked stiffly due to an old football injury. From the ground up, he wore Converse baseball shoes, chino-shorts, a black leather jacket and motorcycle gloves. His head was set on an unusually elongated neck, eyes masked by aviator sunglasses, topped with a woman's blonde wig, which he put on and took off like a hat, revealing a shaven skull. He smoked English Dunhill cigarettes through a holder. His satchel contained cans of beer which he proceeded to drink during the interview, which lasted three hours, Thompson's speaking voice was a staccato stammer with the resonance of a Southern gentlemen, a

---

*Billing himself as a Doctor of Journalism, Thompson had in fact purchased a Doctor of Divinity by mail order.

combination of nervousness and authority which made him all the more intriguing. He was, as Jann says, 'quite the character.' When Hunter paused his discourse to visit the toilet, Wenner turned to his staff and said, 'Look, I know I'm supposed to be the spokesman for the youth generation and everything. But what was *that?*'

Strongly influenced early in life by reading Jack Kerouac, from whose books he says that he learned that 'writing could be fun . . . if you wrote about what you did,' Thompson had developed his own style of New Journalism (what he called gonzo journalism) in which he, Hunter, sometimes using the assumed identity of Raoul Duke, was the central character, a paradoxical hip-innocent who consumed absurdly large amounts of drugs and booze in order to cope with straight America, muttering all the while about the madness, *the bad craziness. Holy Jesus!* Stories which magazine editors sent him to cover became mere surfaces off which to glance into an exploration of his own feelings about the people around him, the state of American society, and life in general. Other practitioners of New Journalism inserted themselves in their stories: Eszterhas, Mailer habitually. But such were their egos, their sense of manly importance, they tended to be boorish. Thompson was no less self-indulgent but, starting from the relatively conventional, even sober, structure and tone of *Hell's Angels*, he evolved into a comically *fallible*, and therefore endearing, first-person narrator and frazzled hip hero of his 100 m.p.h. misadventures.

The first full-blown gonzo adventure had appeared not long before, in June 1970, in the radical magazine *Scanlon's*, which had commissioned Thompson to go back to his hometown of Louisville, Kentucky, to cover the annual Kentucky Derby horse race. *Louisville Redux*, so to speak, turned out to be an uproarious success, thanks partly to Hunter's good fortune in being paired on the assignment with the artist Ralph Steadman, a 34-year-old naïve on his first visit to the United States. 'It was,' says Ralph, shaking his head with wonder, 'the beginning of something which changed me forever.' Ralph's first marriage had recently failed. Melancholy by nature, the artist had fallen into a funk of depression at home alone in London, 'A bloody dreary time . . . a kind of painful time.' In an attempt to shake himself out of his malaise, he had accepted an invitation to visit an

American friend on Long Island, with the aim of having a vacation and maybe doing some work for American magazines. Over the past few years, Ralph had become established in London as a satirist specialising in grotesque caricatures of politicians and such like, drawings splattered with ink, as though the subject's brains had been dashed across the page. These distinctive drawings appeared regularly in *Private Eye* and elsewhere. One might say Ralph's was a unique style. However, another British artist was doing almost identical work at the same time. His name was Gerald Scarfe. He and Ralph had studied together in their youth, had been the very best of friends – until they discovered to their mutual dismay that they had started to draw in almost exactly the same style. 'It seemed as though both of us infected each other,' says Ralph, with a shudder of discomfort. So they parted, ever after wary of each other's company. The fact that Gerald's drawings were appearing in some of the same UK magazines, and that many readers couldn't tell the work apart, was another reason for Ralph to seek a change of scene. At any rate, he had been in Long Island only a short time when he received a telephone call from *Scanlon's*, saying that they had an ex-Hell's Angel reporter down at the Kentucky Derby who needed an illustrator. 'You wanna go to Kentucky?'

Hunter S. Thompson presented a natural subject to the artist. 'He is easy to draw in a way, because it's a specific . . . His bullet-head, you know, his particular sunglasses, his trademark cigarette holder and long neck,' explains Ralph who, upon arriving in the South, immediately began to sketch his reporter, which was appropriate because Hunter had little interest in the horse race they were attending. Rather, he was going to write about himself (and about Ralph as it turned out, though Ralph didn't know that yet), and their impressions of the people attending the Derby: the old-time Southern rich and the Southern poor, disporting themselves in holiday mood, often drunken, many racist. Despite the fact these were his people, they constituted an unappealing spectacle for Hunter. For his part Ralph was appalled. 'I was genuinely horrified,' he says. 'People were so unaware of their self-indulgence, that was the shock . . . they were the most awful people I could have imagined.' Ralph created grotesque drawings of racegoers, depicting them literally as monsters. Hunter affected to be revolted by the work. 'It's a filthy habit, Ralph, don't do that,' he growled while the artist sketched at the track, as though Ralph was picking his nose in public. And when Ralph whimsically gave some of these foul renderings as gifts to people they met, Hunter noted that the Kentuckians reeled back, regarding the artist with 'fear and loathing,' which was the birth of a catch-phrase that made the journalist's fortune. All of this was duly described in a comical short story, featuring Hunter and Ralph as the main protagonists, which *Scanlon's* ran in the summer of 1970 under the headline *The Kentucky Derby is Decadent and Depraved*. This 'gonzo' feature – Hunter later decided it was the first full-blown example of his hybrid form of New Journalism – concluded with Thompson unloading his Limey artist unceremoniously at the airport, and departing with these farewell words: 'We can do without your kind in Kentucky!'

In fact, Hunter and Ralph had forged a close and mutually beneficial working friendship in Louisville that would last for the rest of Hunter's life. Indeed he was collaborating with Ralph right up to his suicide in 2005. They were perfect for one another. Hunter's stories gave Ralph inspiring subjects for his art, not least Hunter himself, whose cartoonish profile would appear repeatedly in the feature articles they would create for magazines and, later, books. Steadman's freaked-out drawings and ink-splattered calligraphy became synonymous with Thompson's writing. They went together in the way of classic writer-illustrator partnerships of English children's literature: Lewis Carroll and John Tenniel, Kenneth Grahame and E.H. Shepard. Unlike those pairings, however, Steadman was also often a character in his author's stories, which were based on real, sometimes hair-raising experiences such as the time shortly after the Kentucky Derby when the two men went to Rhode Island to cover the America's Cup yacht race. Amidst scenes of everyday madness, Steadman noticed his friend gobbling pills. 'What are you taking?' he inquired of Hunter.

'Oh, these pills? They make me feel good.'

'Can I have one?'

'I never pushed anything like that on anyone, Ralph. But you can have one if you want.'

Ralph swallowed *one* pill. 'About ninety hours later I came down.'
It was psilocybin, an hallucinogenic. When the immediate effects
wore off, Ralph says that he felt like his insides had been gouged out,
and he vowed never to take another illicit drug in his life.

The artist was safely home in London when Thompson headed out
to Las Vegas for *Sports Illustrated* in April 1971, the notional story this
time being a cockamamie motorcycle race, the Mint 400. Hunter had
learned the value of travelling with a sidekick like Ralph: company for
the assignment, of course, and a useful foil to his own nature. Ralph
was unavailable this time, so Hunter took an attorney friend named
Oscar Zeta Acosta to Vegas. First they hired a red convertible in LA,
and collected a cache of drugs. Then they drove out across the Mojave
Desert, via the little town of Barstow, to the gambling capital of
Nevada. The assignment was, as ever, an excuse for Thompson to visit
a location and observe its inhabitants. He didn't give a damn for the
motorbike race. The twenty-four-hour energy and stupendous vulgarity of Vegas' casino-hotels provided an especially lurid backdrop for
gonzo journalism. In many ways, the city displayed Americans at
their worst: a people maddened with avarice and gluttony. Although
sickened by what he saw, Thompson and his friend made beasts of
themselves, too, following a dictum of Dr Samuel Johnson, 'He who
makes a beast of himself gets rid of the pain of being a man.'
Thompson would use that as the epigraph for *Fear and Loathing*.
When Thompson and his buddy had exhausted *Sports Illustrated*'s
expenses, drinking themselves sick, eating all their drugs and wreck-
ing their car and hotel suite, Hunter managed to stay on in Vegas for
a few more days courtesy of Jann Wenner, who suggested he take a
look at a convention of district attorneys for *Rolling Stone*. There was
indeed humour to be gained by observing the DAs' desperately unhip
attempts to understand drug culture, and Hunter had fun with the fact
that he, of all people, had got in amongst them. 'If the Pigs were gathering in Vegas for a top level Drug Conference,' he wrote, 'we felt the
drug culture should be represented.'

All the while he was in Vegas, Hunter made notes which constituted a stream of consciousness story in the style of *On the Road*.
Indeed, he felt that, strictly speaking, gonzo journalism had to be

written in the way that Kerouac had supposedly composed his classic novel, that is off the top of his head, without revising, letting the words pour forth. Unfortunately, it was almost impossible to produce good work with this method. *Fear and Loathing* succeeds because, after an initial burst of inspiration in Las Vegas, where he jotted down his impressions, the author spent six months crafting his notes, taking care not to lose the freshness of the original ideas, but reworking the material thoroughly so that the whole thing ran as smoothly as his Selectric typewriter. He began the work of typing up his notes shortly after leaving Vegas when he booked into the Ramada Inn in Arcadia, California. A few days later he called in at the Wenners' house in San Francisco, where he showed Jann the first twenty pages. 'He was up at my house and he showed me the stuff he had written about being in Vegas,' recalls Jann. 'And that was the beginning of that book, "We were somewhere [around] Barstow . . ." And he said, "I want to write this up as a piece." I said, "Absolutely, it's great. It's brilliant. Do it."'

After more work on the story at Wenner's house, Hunter went home to Woody Creek, a hamlet outside of Aspen, Colorado, where he, his wife Sandra and their son Juan lived in a large log cabin on a parcel of mountain land Thompson called Owl Farm. Hunter was a well-known local character, with many interesting friends including Aspen resident and film director Bob Rafelson. Later, Jack Nicholson bought a house in town and also became part of Hunter's social circle, Bob and Jack sharing many boozy nights with the charismatic *Rolling Stone* writer at his cabin home.

Rising every day in the middle of the afternoon, Hunter's work routine at Owl Farm began with a long sobering shower, followed by a hearty three p.m. breakfast after which he descended to his writing den which was a spacious wood-lined basement. With logs crackling on the fire, a favourite rock album revolving on the stereo deck and a Dunhill International smouldering in his cigarette-holder, he set to work. 'It was a very elegant room, a sanctuary, a beautiful cave,' recalls Sandra of the author's office, adding that Hunter consumed Dexedrine and bourbon as he wrote, and would take breaks from his work to have sex with her, outside in the snow when they'd taken LSD.

When the story was finished a copy was sent to Ralph Steadman in

London to illustrate. Not having been on the Vegas trip, but recalling his recent experiences with Hunter in Kentucky and Rhode Island – all that booze, the alarming people and his nightmarish drug experience – the artist produced a set of drawings that have become as indivisible from *Fear and Loathing in Las Vegas* as Ernest Shepard's pictures of Ratty, Mole, Badger and Toad are from *The Wind in the Willows*. Indeed, Ralph drew the attorney Oscar Acosta as a kind of Mr Toad. 'That was his character: out of control.' The famous large drawing he made of monstrous creatures lining a Las Vegas bar were in fact his recollection of the Rhode Island inn where he and Hunter had taken shelter after Ralph had swallowed *that pill*, the customers appearing to him as rabid red dogs. (See picture 11.) A fiend on a motorcycle, saucer-eyed DAs, a man ravishing an old hag as a drug dealer shoots up: all these pictures and more were dredged up from Ralph's memories of travelling with Hunter. 'It all poured out of me,' he says. 'Everything was pent-up.' When Ralph was finished, he rolled his drawings into a tube and air-mailed it to *Rolling Stone*, which ran the first instalment in the magazine's fourth anniversary issue on 11 November 1971: 'Fear and Loathing in Las Vegas: A Savage Journey to the Heart of the American Dream.' Part two next week.

The articles were such a popular success that it became clear they should also be published as a book, and Wenner wanted to publish *Fear and Loathing* under his own Straight Arrow Press imprint. After a disagreement over expenses on another story, Thompson sold the rights to Random House who put the book out in 1972, incorporating most of Ralph's illustrations (the originals of which Jann acquired for the bargain price of sixty bucks apiece – as Ralph now regrets – and they hang on the walls of his office and home still). Despite failing to secure the book rights, Wenner remained a staunch fan of Thompson, who had become the most famous of all *Rolling Stone's* correspondents. As such he was given *carte blanche* to write about whatever he pleased, and what tickled his fancy immediately was politics.

So it was that Thompson became National Affairs Editor of *Rolling Stone* and covered the 1972 Presidential election for the magazine, making plain from the outset his preference for the Democrat candidate George McGovern. The incumbent President, Richard Nixon, provided Hunter with an arch-villain, and Ralph found Tricky Dicky's baggy boozer's face ripe for caricature. Thompson attempted to bring the manic gonzo energy of *Fear and Loathing in Las Vegas* to his political reports, but at the end of the day he was just another hack on the campaign bus and the stories he filed from the campaign trail in 1972, and then later from Washington in 1973–75, as Nixon's second term was submerged in the effluent of Watergate, lacked the zest of the prototype. Also, there was an element of trying to repeat old tricks in articles with titles such as *Fear and Loathing in Washington*. Part of Thompson's problem was that, having created such a well-defined persona for himself, he became a prisoner of his image. Dr Thompson simply had to get drunk and stoned on every assignment and rage against the world. Eventually, he was reduced to a hopeless self-parody. But few journalists enjoyed such a ride as Hunter Stockton Thompson did in the early 1970s, and the mystique of gonzo journalism has proved remarkably durable, rediscovered by new generations of young readers – for it is entertainment primarily for the young, probably the young male predominantly – achieving the apotheosis of success when *Fear and Loathing* was turned into a movie in 1998 starring Johnny Depp. The director was *Monty Python* alumnus Terry Gilliam, who had forged a notable film career since his days working with cut-out animation for the BBC. Gilliam says that he sees Hunter's story as dealing with essentially the same subject John Updike tackled in *Rabbit Redux*: the aftermath of the 1960s. 'That's what *Fear and Loathing* was about: the sixties people who had all been changed, but reality had not changed [and] disillusion was creeping in.'

9

QUEER AS . . .

Viddy well, little brother, viddy well.
MALCOLM MCDOWELL AS ALEX, *A CLOCKWORK ORANGE*

By mid–afternoon such a large mob of people had congregated outside the New York gallery to see Gilbert and George that the fire department had been called to impose order on the crowd. It was Saturday, 25 September 1971, the opening day for a new gallery space at 420 West Broadway, a low–rent part of New York, south of Houston Street and north of Minoru Yamasaki's brand new World Trade Center, being reborn as SoHo (being an acronym of South of Houston). Four art dealers had bought a former warehouse in the neighbourhood, taking a floor each, with Illeana Sonnabend choosing to open hers with Gilbert and George's 'singing sculpture,' a thing so rare and strange that hundreds of people were pushing in from the street to see it. 'I'm not sure what a "singing sculpture" is supposed to mean,' confessed Mrs Leo Castelli, whose husband owned the gallery on the second floor where he was showing video–art, including work by Richard Serra, 'but don't miss it.' Since 'it' had started at one p.m., you could hardly get up the stairs for the crush of people. How could such a fuss be caused by new and experimental sculpture? As Serra complained, most people seemed content to ignore modern sculpture. Or they rejected it aggressively, as many did his large prop–pieces. Most unusually, the *avant-garde* sculpture on view on the floor above Serra's show was evidently extremely popular.

'At about four o'clock in the afternoon, we fought our way at last into the Sonnabend Gallery, and there were Gilbert and George, standing on a small table in the centre of a crowded room singing,' Douglas Davis reported in *The New Yorker*. (See picture 12.) The twosome, artists from London in their late twenties, known only by their first names, were dressed in grey worsted suits, old and not of the best quality but clean, with all the buttons done up; white nylon shirts; dark ties; brogues. George was a tall man, prematurely balding, and wearing thick National Health Service spectacles. Gilbert, slightly shorter and a year younger, with a fuller head of hair, had the appearance of a mischievous boy being led astray. Both their faces and hands were covered with metallic bronze paint, augmented with coloured blotches. Standing on a small, simple table, they moved together robotically like figures on a musical box, Gilbert holding a rubber glove and George twirling a gold-coloured walking cane with a green plastic stopper end that made a squeaking sound on the surface of the table, the men moving in a kind of slow dance as they sang along to a cassette-recording of the English music-hall song 'Underneath the Arches,' made famous in the 1930s by Bud Flanagan and Chesney Allen: a sentimentalised view of destitutes sleeping rough under London's railway viaducts:

Underneath the Arches I dream my dreams away
Underneath the Arches on cobblestones I lay.

When the recording came to an end, Gilbert and George swapped stick and glove. Gilbert climbed down, turned the tape over, and restarted it. Then he remounted the table, exchanged stick and glove, and the duo began again in exactly the same way. So it went on without variation, until the gallery closed at six p.m., neither man relaxing his implacably serious expression for a moment, nor so much as taking a break to visit the toilet. Although such an act, broadened for popular tastes, would become part of the repertoire of street entertainers, a common sight today wherever tourists congregate (Covent Garden in London, for example), it was a queer thing indeed in 1971, the very cutting edge of performance art, and New York was agog, eager to know what it *meant*. 'It's a completed work, like a painting,' explained George afterwards, speaking to the American press in the clipped tones of the English middle-class, but with a degree less emotion. Gilbert and George maintained the act, you see, even when not performing. George added that there was no satire intended. G&G didn't indulge in anything so sophisticated as satire. They liked simplicity, purity, sincerity. They wanted people to see the profundity in the lyrics of the old song, because the words were actually very good – 'I dream my dreams away' – and words were important to the art of Gilbert and George (perhaps because they couldn't draw very well, some might say). At the same time, this was not a concert but a sculpture, living sculpture: man as machine, man as statue, two men as one. 'Sometimes we think of ourselves as sculptors and sometimes as living sculptures,' George elucidated, his manner remote but obliging, deviant with a dash of innocence. Weird. 'We tend to slip from one to the other, so to speak. We feel very devoted to art, you see.'

'That's true,' Gilbert chimed in. 'Totally devoted.'

Who exactly were these oddballs? George, the tall bespectacled Englishman, was in full George Passmore, born in Plymouth, Devon, in 1942. His parents' marriage was an unhappy one and George took refuge in art, showing a precocious talent for making unusual things at the progressive Dartington Hall School, which was near his home, and later enrolling at St Martin's School of Art in London, on Charing Cross Road cheek-by-jowl with the National Gallery, book shops, the bohemian life of Soho and the music companies of Denmark Street. When George came up to St Martin's in 1965 it was a centre of experimental art in Britain, with no less a figure than Anthony Caro heading the advanced sculpture class, Caro being the sculptor whose decision not to set his work on a plinth influenced Richard Serra's art, while Caro had the same London dealer as David Hockney (Kasmin of Bond Street) – showing once again how many paths cross in the story of the arts during this period. Fellow students at St Martin's at this time included Barry Flanagan, later famed for his sculptures of leaping hares. And two years after George enrolled, a 24-year-old Italian student named Gilbert Proesch entered this august company. Gilbert was the son of a shoemaker from a village in the Dolomites and his meeting with George at St Martin's was, as he says 'love at first sight.' Henceforth Gilbert and George would be inseparable, in life and in art, which became one and the same thing in their case. Homosexuality became a motif of their work and one presumes they are a couple in that sense, too, but although Gilbert and George later became famous for their sexually explicit imagery they are remarkably coy about their own sex lives, a situation made more mysterious by the fact that shortly before their meeting George married, and fathered two children – a marriage he doesn't speak about in public. Gilbert and George are, however, intensely queer in the original sense of the word: odd, strange, peculiar, 'queer as a nine-bob note' as the expression is in the East End of London, where they were to make their home.

George was creating queer art before he met Gilbert. At St Martin's, George fried an egg one day and made a plaster cast of it. However outlandish his stunts, they had limited impact so long as he worked alone. When he joined forces with Gilbert, the two friends magnified one another greatly. Their grand idea, a life together as living sculpture, came about more or less by accident after they made a resin face mask and arranged for photographs to be taken of themselves posing with their work. It was then that they realised *they* were art, too – a breakthrough conceptual idea that would make them among the most notable artists of their generation. It was also a stupendously silly conceit, of course, deeply egocentric and very childish, but that was fine too because it was part of who they were. The teaching staff at St Martin's shook their heads at the sniggering pair, glad to see the back of them when they left in 1968. Anthony Caro sent the boys on their way with the heartfelt wish that they *wouldn't* be successful. When a would-be patron of the pair later wrote to the school for a reference, this splendid reply came from Frank Martin of the sculpture department:

Dear Madam,
Under no circumstances have anything to do with these people.

Regarded as charlatans, unloved by anybody but themselves, G&G set out into the world. They didn't go far. It is a walk of approximately half an hour from Charing Cross Road, through the City of London to Spitalfields, a then-slummy area on the threshold of the East End. At 12 Fournier Street, E1, Gilbert and George found a ground floor flat for rent in a large, dilapidated early eighteenth-century house. More than three decades on, they are still there, having bought the whole building and renovated it magnificently. Twelve Fournier Street, and every aspect of their lives there, became part of their art, which was a constant living conceptual performance, as was the fact that they ate their meals each day at the nearby Market Café, a place for workmen's fry-ups and mugs of tea. Dressed alike in suit and tie they walked about the neighbourhood like living statues, passive, fixed in gaze, polite when spoken to (unless they were drunk, when they behaved disgracefully★) and yet icily remote. *Extraordinary! Unbelievable!* as they would say. But in the early days, who cared?

They had to become famous or – even better – notorious, and set about this task with diligence and industry. Printed cards – bearing their slogan, *Art For All*, sometimes accompanied with a royal crest, conveying a bogus authority – were dispatched from 12 Fournier Street to the movers and shakers of the art world, inviting all to come view their Art. The duo's home address and telephone number were given clearly. 'So do contact us,' they wrote imploringly at the end of one early missive. At first it was a hard sell. In 1969 they failed to persuade Kasmin to show their 'magazine sculpture,' *George the Cunt & Gilbert the Shit*, at his gallery on Bond Street. The work consisted of photographs of the friends grinning for the camera, with the relevant obscenities attached to the front of their jackets, as if saying, *This is what people think of us*. Kasmin came to realise the duo weren't interested in him, anyway. 'It turned out they really wanted David to be part of one of their events.'

The pair pursued Kasmin's star client, David Hockney, relentlessly, hoping that an association with the most famous young British painter

---

★As the artists admit, early success went to their heads and as a result the duo embarked on 'an amazingly drunken period from 1971 to 1980' during which time they were both arrested for being drunk and disorderly, and became in their inebriation famously unpleasant dinner party guests: experiences which influenced mid-'70s artwork such as *Bloody Life No. 3* (1975) and *Cunt Scum* (1977).

of the day would somehow garner them attention, too. They invited themselves over to Hockney's flat at Powis Terrace, arriving together in character, dressed in their pin-neat suits, completing each others sentences, the whole *schtick*. 'They would come around when they were really unknown,' recalls Hockney's then boyfriend Peter Schlesinger. 'I think they liked coming around to see David because he would help them get known . . . they were quite calculating.' The good-natured Hockney was amused, and accepted an invitation to their very first art show, in an establishment called Frank's Sandwich Bar. This was not a trendy art space, but an actual sandwich bar. 'You had to go at a certain time and, when you went, they just bought you a cup of tea,' recalls Hockney with a laugh. The artists, who naturally dressed in suit and tie for the occasion, entertained their guests at a small Formica-topped table set out with the usual sandwich bar equipment of sugar bowl, condiments, ashtray and so forth, with a couple of drawings to look at if you cared to do so. All very childish and weird. 'I loved it. I thought, *Oh this is quite anarchistic* [sic],' says Hockney. The following year he agreed to take part in an elaborate G&G performance piece, *The Meal* (1969): a formal dinner party in suburban Bromley, with a butler who had apparently worked for Princess Margaret serving food prepared from *Mrs Beeton's Book of Cookery and Household Management*. Hockney was the guest of honour, and again he found the whole thing delightfully wacky. This sort of art – conceptual art, performance art, whatever you wanted to call it – was very different from his own more traditional work, his big naturalistic paintings and exquisite life drawings, but that was all right. 'You need all kinds of artists,' he says, good-humouredly. 'You shouldn't all be painting.'

Still, there was a silliness about Gilbert and George's early art that made one giggle, that is until *The Singing Sculpture*, which had a curious and compelling pathos. G&G had been developing the piece since 1969, with performances at various venues: at the National Jazz and Blues Festival in Sussex in the summer of that year, for example, where it failed to wow 20,000 music fans waiting for the Who, and underneath an actual railway arch in East London, where two genuine tramps in residence paid them not the blindest bit of attention. The mature *Singing Sculpture* was shown at the Nigel Greenwood Gallery in Chelsea in November 1970. 'There was something magical about it,' recalls Peter Schlesinger, who went along with Hockney. 'People were going because, you know, *You've got to see this* . . . People would stand there for hours watching it. It was sort of amazing.' The critic from the *Guardian* acknowledged in the paper's report that reading about the work might give the impression that it was utter nonsense, but 'I can assure you that seeing them perform was a riveting experience.' Children stood transfixed. Cynics turned away with a huff, but some sloped back later, if only to see whether they could catch the artists out. They couldn't. G&G kept going even when nobody was looking, as automatons would. It was hard not to have grudging respect for such dedication. The jazz singer and art collector George Melly persuaded the taxi driver who brought him to the show to come inside and have a look at these men standing on a table singing. 'They've got to be fucking barmy,' was the cabbie's reaction.

The following year Gilbert and George performed the piece in Belgium where they were seen by the renowned art dealer Illeana Sonnabend, who was about to return to New York after several years based in France to take a floor in the new co-op gallery on West Broadway. Not put off by the quintessential Englishness of the piece (despite Gilbert being born in Italy, there was a distinct element of *Monty Python* about it all), Sonnabend and her adopted son Antonio Homem decided to show the *Singing Sculpture* at the opening of their new gallery in Manhattan. 'The public in New York was as enthusiastic seeing it as we had been,' recalls Homem of the exciting day in September 1971 when New Yorkers flocked into the Sonnabend to see the duo perform on their table-top. 'Beyond being an eccentric English art performance, it seems clear that the *Singing Sculpture* touched deeply a very international crowd.' For some American critics, two young men from Britain in smart-but-worn suits, singing sadly of being down-and-out represented and emphasised the postwar decline of Great Britain as a world power, a diminution exacerbated in the 1970s with renewed sectarian violence in Northern Ireland, industrial disputes and worsening unemployment. Also, Gilbert and George came along at a time when the New York art world – from its new SoHo base – was about to expand and embrace conceptual art with enthusiasm, and here were two ready-made icons of the genre that became so important in the decade ahead.

The point of commercial art shows is to sell art, of course, and by its very nature *The Singing Sculpture* was not for sale. The only home in which Gilbert and George could be displayed was their own. They got around this problem by exhibiting drawings as well, naïve drawings of themselves (of course) often in pastoral settings, with ironic titles such as *There Were Two Young Men Who Did Laugh*. Despite being draughtsmen of limited ability – 'atrocious' was an adjective employed by one critic – the drawings sold in New York. In fact, Gilbert and George found they could get the largest amount of money they dared ask for: the equivalent of one thousand pounds per picture. Suddenly, they were rich, and would become still richer and more celebrated, soon replacing their charity-shop suits with bespoke apparel, but always retaining their spooky double act, their way of speaking blankly in agreement, without expression, and their ritualised life together in the house in Spitalfields. It has now been going on for decades, an impressive feat of endurance if nothing else. They even keep the same home telephone number, which was distributed so widely in their early, eager-to-please days. ('So do contact us.') It would be a repudiation if they were to change the number now they had made it big. Instead, they put an answer-machine on the line to screen calls, George saying in his imperious, robotic manner: 'Good morning. You have telephoned Gilbert and George. Sadly, we are not able to talk to you *just* at this moment. Therefore, kindly leave a brief message after the tone. Thank you. Goodbye. And good riddance.'

Gilbert and George were, and are, men mimicking machines in order to make art. In the 1970s, advances in electronics and computing meant the opposite was also happening. The synthesizer in particular helped define the music of the decade, in every genre from classical to funk, from the art-rock of *The Dark Side of the Moon* (1973) to Donna Summer's 1977 disco hit 'I Feel Love'. In many ways, the synthesizer was the sound of the '70s.

Of all the arts, music has always been made at the cutting edge of technology. Thus harpsichords gave way to pianos, acoustic guitars to electric. At times the transition has been like a revolution, as in the summer evening in 1965 when Bob Dylan played the Newport Folk Festival armed with a Fender Stratocaster. Dylan *going electric* caused a near riot.★ The next important step was the perfection of the synthesizer. Electric musical devices had in fact been around since the start of the twentieth century. A Russian, Leon Theremin, invented an instrument in the 1920s which consisted of electrically-charged rods that generated an eerie sound. The theremin was used for many years in movie soundtracks and taken up in the late 1960s by rock musicians such as Jimmy Page (for the freaky middle section of Led Zeppelin's 1968 song 'Whole Lotta Love'). Bob Moog, the inventor of the modern synthesizer, started his career in electronic music selling theremin kits by mail order while studying engineering and physics at Cornell University in America. He decided there were enough musicians with money, and a yen for new sounds, to justify setting up in business as a manufacturer of custom-made musical devices and began to develop a new generation of machines that created electronic monotonal noises, the timbre and pitch of which could be controlled by oscillators and filters, the resulting notes played on a keyboard as music. Thus the synthesizer was born. 'My company began designing, making and selling synthesizer components in 1964. We began calling the modular systems "synthesizers" in 1967,' explains Moog, whose Dutch name rhymes with *vogue*, though the onomatopoeic quality of the common mispronunciation *mooog* has done business no harm. An early client of the R.A. Moog Co. was an intense young musician named Walter Carlos who, in 1968, began to metamorphose into a woman named Wendy, cross-dressing initially, then receiving hormone treatment and finally, in 1972, having a sex change. There was a transgressive corollary between this sexual transformation and the music that Carlos made. Most remarkably, in 1968, he/she released the seminal electronic album *Switched on Bach*: a Moog synthesizer

---

★The musician Robbie Robertson who accompanied Dylan on his new adventures in amplified music told me: 'It seemed kind of a funny statement to me at the time, that somebody's *gone electric*. It was like, *Jeez, somebody's bought a television*.'

arrangement of J.S. Bach's Brandenburg Concertos. Electronic Baroque music was an astonishing concept that proved a surprise commercial hit, becoming the first classical album to sell more than a million units, and as a result Moog became synonymous with synthe- sizers, as Hoover is to vacuum. 'Once the recording of *Switched on Bach* was released, coverage of us in the press was much greater than any other electronic instrument builder,' as Dr Bob says.

Another important early Moog customer was musician Bob Margouleff who bought a Moog III and installed it in a New York recording studio where, with the help of a British-born engineer named Malcolm Cecil, he customised the instrument, adding com- ponents until they had built a contraption that measured 22 feet across, with control panels that resembled those of a jet airliner. A couple of unreconstructed pot-smoking hippies, Margouleff and Cecil named their beast The Original New Timbral Orchestra (TONTO for short). During the day this behemoth burped out electronic sounds for commercials, for everything from Ford Torino cars to Krazy-Daisy toilet paper. When their working day was done, Bob and Malcolm used TONTO to create radical new music, recording an album called *Zerotime* which, when released in March 1971, had an electrifying effect on young Stevie Wonder (as I describe in the next chapter). The synthesizer became ubiquitous in rock around this time. The Beatles used a Moog on their 1969 album *Abbey Road*. Mick Jagger also bought an early machine. And though some musicians decried the synthesizer as being inauthentic, as the 1970s got underway, techno- logically adept rock musicians such as Pete Townshend showed how electronic music and traditional rock 'n' roll could live together very happily. Working on songs for what became the Who's 1971 album *Who's Next*, Townshend played an organ through an EMS synthesizer (a rival product to Moog using similar electronics), coming up with a rhythmic fugue to underpin a new song, 'Won't Get Fooled Again'. The electronic figure takes centre-stage in the song when the band pause for breath before the climax. After a few moments of solo syn- thesizer – a bright, stabbing sound – vocalist Roger Daltrey lets rip a cathartic scream of 'YEAAAAAHHH!' before all four band members bring the number to its crescendo. The contrast between man and machine proves highly effective, and 'Won't Get Fooled Again' has been a highpoint of every Who show thereafter.

While the synthesizer was being taken up by the rock community, Wendy Carlos further explored its use in classical music, devoting herself to an electronic orchestration of the choral movement to Beethoven's Ninth Symphony. It was while she was engaged in this endeavour in 1971 that Carlos read Anthony Burgess' novel *A Clockwork Orange*, in which Beethoven's Ninth is a favourite of the teenaged delinquent hero, Alex. Carlos became fascinated with Burgess' novel and was very excited to discover that Stanley Kubrick was at that time directing a movie of the book in England. So it was that Carlos got involved in one of the most brilliant films of the 1970s, a *tour de force* of images, sounds, language and ideas that would have widespread influence on the culture of the decade.

In Burgess' *A Clockwork Orange*, first published in 1962, Alex together with a gang of friends – his droogs in the patois of the story – vandalise and terrorise a society of the future. A particularly vicious rape committed by Alex echoes an attack suffered by Burgess' first wife in London during the Second World War. The title of the book was inspired by a simile Burgess remembered as being in colloquial use in London at that time: 'He's as queer as a clockwork orange,' meaning strange rather than homosexual. Alex and his droogs were queer in their dress and speech, different from mainstream society, but conforming to a youth cult similar to the British fads for Teddy Boys and Mods: gangs of working-class boys who aligned in a uniform fashion and identified with particular music styles. In its early days the Who was the marching band of the Mods, a relationship commemorated in one of Pete Townshend's new synthesizer-based compositions, 'Baba O'Riley'. In a similar way Alex was obsessed with the music of Ludwig Van, as he referred to Beethoven. Teen gangs tend to have their own private language, each gang its distinctive slang. Based on his knowledge of Russian, Burgess invented 'nadsat' for his droogs, its vocabulary brilliantly evocative of hooligan attitudes. *Horrorshow*, for example, derived from the Russian *horosh* for good, conveys a strong sense of what droogs found fun. (Burgess spelled it out thus: 'Good to

Alex is tied up with performing horrors.') The story of *A Clockwork Orange* is narrated in nadsat in the first person by Alex who, after committing murder, is arrested and subjected to a form of aversion-therapy so radical that afterwards he vomits at the very thought of violence. 'The question was asked,' wrote Burgess, going to the philosophical nub of his book, 'is it permissible to kill free will in order to ensure the stability of society?'

Film rights were acquired by a New York attorney named Si Litvinoff, whose clients including the writer Terry Southern. Litvinoff's original plan was to produce the picture with Mick Jagger as Alex (having discovered that Jagger was a fan of the novel). Southern would write the screenplay, and hopefully Stanley Kubrick would direct. Southern had a working relationship with Kubrick, having collaborated with him on *Dr Strangelove* (1964), and the quirky brilliance of Burgess' book seemed perfect for such an individual filmmaker, a man who had by his achievements and strength of character managed to break away from the tyranny of Hollywood and set himself up on an estate in Hertfordshire, just north of London, where he made the films he wanted to, in his own time, with the financial backing of Warner Brothers. Unfortunately, Si Litvinoff sent Kubrick a US edition of Burgess' novel which, spuriously, had a motorcyclist on the cover, apparently on the basis that Americans would buy the book thinking it was a salacious biker story. For that very reason Kubrick ignored the book, didn't even open it.

So Litvinoff began working with the British cinematographer Nicolas Roeg, who was then starting his remarkable directing career after serving as a director of photography and second unit cameraman on such pictures as *Lawrence of Arabia* (1962). Roeg's debut as a director, *Performance* (1970), starred Edward Fox's younger brother, James, and Mick Jagger as a rock star recluse (seen playing his Moog in one sequence). Roeg is a remarkable filmmaker in his own right, steeped in literature, sharing with John Updike the desire to treat human sexuality directly, and fascinated by time. Characteristically, Roeg's pictures are not straightforward in the way the story is told. Time bends. He also looks for the unexpected in his actors. Roeg started work on a screenplay of *A Clockwork Orange* with the typically eccentric idea of making the droog characters old men, led by Lee Marvin as Alex. Before this scheme got off the ground another version of the book found its way to Kubrick. This time he read it, and made it known that he wanted to make the movie after all. Roeg was obliged to step away from the project, but with a consolation prize. Money raised for a Roeg production of *A Clockwork Orange* was diverted to fund a wonderful new Roeg picture, *Walkabout* (1971).

While it would have been fascinating to see Nic Roeg's *A Clockwork Orange*, Kubrick's version of the Burgess story turned out to be a masterpiece, as Roeg concedes: 'I enjoyed it tremendously.' For Alex, Kubrick cast not Lee Marvin (a truly weird idea) but the young Malcolm McDowell, who embodied Alex's priapic sexuality, his cleverness, youthful amorality and viciousness. Filmed on a modest budget in London and the Home Counties, Kubrick and his team created a visually stunning and entirely convincing future-world, partly by judicious choice of real-life locations. These included the new Thamesmead development in South East London. A classic example of the boldly modern architecture in vogue in Britain for major housing projects during the 1960s and early 1970s, Phase I of Thamesmead, known as Lakeside, is a vast futuristic residential council estate comprised of many different units, both high- and low-rise, though constructed predominantly from uniform grey concrete slabs. The design is heavily influenced by the ideas of the visionary Swiss architect Le Corbusier, with integrated shops, leisure facilities and raised walkways that are meant to separate pedestrians from motorised traffic. Although intended to make the life of residents civilised and enjoyable, the aesthetic of Lakeside (built around a shallow artificial lake, into which Alex pushes his rebellious droogs in Kubrick's film) was to many eyes both outlandish and bleakly depressing. It was, and remains, a commonly expressed sentiment that such modernist housing estates have a malign influence on the people who live in them, helping produce real hooligan characters such as Alex, and indeed parts of Thamesmead (Phase I of which was being completed when Kubrick shot his picture in 1971) soon degenerated into grim places to live, though it should be pointed out that a similar residential complex in the City of London, the Barbican, in construction throughout the 1970s, proved that a vast modernist concrete estate with integrated services could be a highly desirable environment.★

For the key scene in which Alex and his droogs burst in on the home of a writer and his wife, whom Alex beats and rapes while chirruping 'Singin' in the Rain', Kubrick chose another modernist British building: a house in Radlett, Hertfordshire, designed by Team 4, the leading partners of which were Norman Foster and Richard Rogers. Both men were soon to achieve international fame, the latter for co-designing the Pompidou Centre. Built on a plot of sloping land, its rooms stepping down with the incline of the terrain and sliding doors partitioning rooms for multiple use (a feature of Rogers' work), the so-called Jaffe House (Mr and Mrs Jaffe being the client) was a building of light, space and elegance. The rape was shot in its lounge at night under bright white light, making the attack particularly disturbing in its starkness. Alex first beats the couple, binds the wife, cuts off her dress and then, before committing the rape, directs the husband to look on: 'Viddy well, little brother, viddy well.'

In no other movie did actors talk like this, nor did any previous movie look or sound like this. Nadsat gave the film dialogue a unique quality. Wendy Carlos' music (she was billed as Walter) was not the normal nature sounds of movie soundtracks – wind over reeds, vibrating gut string – but an oscillating *brrrrrrrr* of electricity. As arranged by Carlos, Beethoven's Ninth took on an alarming new life, and Purcell's 'Music for the Funeral of Queen Mary' was wondrous strange indeed. From the pop-art opening titles, *A Clockwork Orange* was linguistically and sonically amazing, mind-expanding, eye-popping cinema, demonstrating that Kubrick was a superlative filmmaker not only of the 1960s, but as he moved into middle-age, also of the 1970s.

When the film opened in the USA in December 1971 American critics concurred that it was a masterwork, some perhaps making up for their less than enthusiastic reviews of *2001*, which they had belatedly come to fully appreciate. This time there was almost a rush to praise Kubrick. The New York Film Critics Circle awarded *A Clockwork Orange* the accolade of Best Picture, which had been

★I live in the Barbican myself, happy to be surrounded by fortress-like concrete walls.

bestowed the previous year upon *Five Easy Pieces*, and *A Clockwork Orange* did very well at the American box office. When the movie opened in Britain, however, the reception was unexpected and disturbing. Given an X-certificate for its scenes of sex and violence (toned down as they were compared to the book), the movie was not generally perceived as a black comedy or art film as it was abroad, but viewed in the popular press as an example of gratuitously explicit movie-making at a time when film censorship was being relaxed, the sort of picture that might deprave. And it did attract delinquents. In London, young men who followed Arsenal Football Club, partly as an excuse to engage in weekend wars with rival gangs of supporters, took to dressing in boiler suits, bovver boots and bowler hats like the droogs in the picture. 'Arsenal went *Clockwork*,' notes John Lydon, a North London teen soon to become famous as Johnny Rotten. So there was the disconcerting spectacle of droogs beating the shit out of rival hooligan gangs during the football season. But worse was to come.

In April 1972 a teenager named Richard Palmer beat a sixty-year-old Irish vagrant to death in Bletchley, Buckinghamshire, echoing a scene in *A Clockwork Orange* where Alex attacks a down-and-out. At his trial, Palmer's QC argued in his client's mitigation that the wretched youth had fallen under the spell of the movie. In another incident, a pensioner died of a heart attack after being beaten by a young man directly after he had watched the film. And in 1973 a teenage Dutch girl on a camping holiday in Lancashire was raped by a gang singing 'Singin' in the Rain'. Reports of similar *Clockwork*-style attacks on innocent people kept coming until, almost a year and a half after its release in Britain, Kubrick withdrew the picture from circulation in his adopted country. He refused permission for it to be shown again in Britain, *only* Britain mind, throughout the rest of his life, having wearied of the controversy he had created, and perhaps having become more than a little scared that he might be next in line for lashings of the old *ultraviolence*.

10

STEVIE AND THE STONES

That shit is just fantasticness!

STEVIE WONDER

Stevie Wonder came calling on a Saturday at the end of May 1971, the first day of the long Memorial Day weekend when the streets of Manhattan were relatively quiet and empty of traffic. At 310 West 57th Street, between Seventh and Eighth Avenues, was a church that had been converted into a recording studio named Media Sound, where Bob Margouleff and Malcolm Cecil worked on television commercials, with Cecil living in an apartment above the studio. When his bell rang that Saturday, Malcolm leaned out of his window to see his friend, the musician Ronnie Blanco, down below with a guy in a pistachio-green jump-suit clutching a copy of Bob and Malcolm's experimental album *Zerotime*. 'Come on down,' shouted Ronnie. 'I've got somebody here who wants to see TONTO.'

Installed in the basement, Bob and Malcolm's customised Moog synthesizer was an electronic monster, fitted into a series of overarching wooden cabinets, with keyboards arranged on what were essentially tea trolleys, a music system at once technologically advanced and curiously homemade. For instance, one of Cecil and Margouleff's innovations – now standard in synthesizers – was a joystick which they had cannibalised from model aeroplane controller, using a rubber band to return the stick to the zero setting. In order to 'see' this extraordinary creation, Stevie Wonder ran his hands back and forth over the innumerable buttons and switches, following the trail of gorgon-like cables as they patched one part of the system to another, twiddling the joystick and asking Malcolm questions all the while. 'This is the instrument that made all the sounds on your record?'

'Absolutely.'

'Made *all* of them?' insisted Wonder, whose previous Tamla-Motown recording career was characterised by working with a virtual army of producers and session musicians, a cumbersome arrangement which had become irksome to him. Now he wanted simplicity. When Cecil assured him that he and Bob created their entire album with this box of tricks, Stevie asked whether they also had a piano and drum-kit to hand, both of which he played with virtuoso and idiosyncratic skill, especially the drums which he played against the tempo in a distinctively funky style (though the term Funk was not yet widely used in pop music). Malcolm informed him that there was a Steinway grand and drums in the room. Having everything he needed to hand, Stevie asked if they could record. 'Yeah, I suppose so,' replied Cecil, who put in a quick, excited phone call to Bob Margouleff to tell him to get over right away because they had an important new client. When Bob showed up half an hour later, Stevie Wonder had already started playing and recording the funky, soulful, sexy, religious, polit-ical, *weird-sounding* music that constituted his classic 1970s albums: *Music of My Mind* and *Talking Book* (both 1972), *Innervisions* (1973) and *Fulfillingness' First Finale* (1974).

That first weekend, Stevie and Malcolm began by jamming together on conventional instruments. Malcolm set a microphone up at the Steinway, and accompanied Stevie on his acoustic bass guitar, following his distinguished guest by watching his hands for the chord-changes. The Englishman's background was as a professional bass player in London, primarily a jazz musician, doing sessions and work-ing at Ronnie Scott's club in Soho, and he soon realised that his acoustic bass was pulling Stevie's music in a jazz direction. So he sug-gested that it might be a better idea if they used TONTO to make a bass sound. If he and Bob programmed the synthesizer, Stevie could play the bass himself on the keyboard. 'He got really excited at that prospect. So that's when we started using the synth' . . . We started on the third song, which was "Evil", and it really made all the difference: the foreboding bass sound.' Stevie marvelled at the way TONTO's keyboards seemed to change under his fingertips; the mechanism was absolutely standard. Nothing magical about it. The usual number of black and white keys. But by Bob and Malcolm programming TONTO, the sounds that emerged in response to the pressure Stevie exerted on these keys were so varied in timbre and pitch, it was as if he was playing an endlessly changeable instrument, every sound of which was unique, which is really what a synthesizer is. And of course this was very exciting. The room resonated with extraordinary washes of sound as the trio worked on into the night, Stevie nodding his head happily as they continued making music – breaking only for food and sleep (on his own time clock which took no account of whether it was day or night, daylight meaning little to a blind man) – for three straight days, Monday being a public holiday: the start of a collaboration that resulted in amazing new music. 'First of all you immediately recognise[d] his genius,' recollects Bob Margouleff of his first weekend with Stevie. 'All you have to do is be in the studio with him for thirty minutes to understand his total genius. God just came down and put his thumbprint right on his forehead.'

The central fact of Stevie's blindness dates from his premature birth, in Saginaw, Michigan, in 1950, when too much oxygen was introduced to his incubator creating a condition that resulted in a permanent loss of sight. Wonder is of course a stage name. His mother was Lula Mae Hardaway and Stevie's natural father was a fellow named Judkins. The surname on the boy's birth certificate was, confusingly, Morris, being the name of the father of two elder brothers. The family was very poor, and in the early 1950s Lula Mae moved them all to Detroit to try and get a better life. Although he did not have any formal musical training, Stevie possessed perfect pitch and could sing, play drums, the piano and the harmonica all with exceptional skill. In 1961, when he was eleven, his mother signed him to a five-year contract with the local black music label Tamla-Motown, founded and owned by former Ford factory worker Berry Gordy. Under Gordy's direction, Motown had become a veritable music factory – run on the automotive model –

whereby factory marques were such artists as Smokey Robinson and the Miracles, the Supremes, and Marvin Gaye, and the product turned out in these names was solid, well-crafted R&B songs. Little Stevie Wonder was a new company line, packaged and promoted by Motown as a blind musical genius in the style of Ray Charles: led on to the stage at concerts just like Brother Ray to give similarly impassioned, improvisational performances. By 1964, 14-year-old Stevie was so successful that the Rolling Stones were his opening act.

As well as being an exciting live performer, Stevie was a songwriter from a young age, composing such hits as 'Uptight (Everything is Alright)', though he was not properly credited at first. As he grew older, he felt increasingly ill-used by Motown, regretting the restrictive contract he had been signed to as a child, which was extended for a further five years, and brooding on the money his records made, the bulk of his share being placed in a trust fund for when he was older. His primary complaint, however, was that he did not have artistic control over his music. Even when he wrote original material, his songs would be taken from him, like babes, and handed into the care of a musical director who wrote the arrangements and hired the musicians *he* decided should play on the recordings. 'Stevie would be called in to do the vocal, and be told how to do the vocal by the producer,' says Malcolm Cecil. 'He *hated* it.' As he approached his twenty-first birthday in 1971, Stevie began to plan for when he would be free of the contracts signed on his behalf by his family when he was a minor and able to record as an adult in the way he chose, and his musical ideas were by now much more wide-ranging than the formulaic R&B stylings of Motown. As he said, 'I wanted to do something else, go other places.'

On 13 May 1971, Berry Gordy hosted a twenty-first birthday party for Stevie in Detroit. The next day Gordy received a letter from Stevie's attorney informing Motown that contracts with Stevie were void. As soon as he had got his hands on his trust fund, the artist relocated to New York to embark on his new career, setting up home at the Holiday Inn on Eighth Avenue (always choosing to stay in a Holiday Inn because of the standard layout of the rooms). And after he had settled in, he set out to find the guys behind *Zerotime*.

In the later stages of his Motown contract, Stevie had not given the company his best songs, but held them in his mind for when he was at liberty to do with them as he pleased. He began to unload his music with Malcolm and Bob at Media Sound in 1971. 'And that's one of the reasons we called the [first] album *Music of My Mind*,' explains Malcolm Cecil. All the songs were composed, arranged and performed by Stevie. So in a sense it was the music of *one* mind, and the finished album was promoted as being very much that. But the vital programming was done by Margouleff and Cecil, so in effect all three would 'play' TONTO in a kind of electronic jam, Bob and Malcolm operating the controls in a fug of dope (Stevie declined to smoke along with them, saying it made his head feel *too tight*) and Stevie making the chord changes. 'One of us would work on the knobs, one of us – Stevie – would play the actual notes, and one of us would work on the keyboard,' recalls Malcolm. 'It was the three of us together doing it that made it happen.' The synthesizer keyboards and conventional instruments were arranged in a semi-circle in the basement studio so Stevie could move easily from one instrument to another, taking up the drums or playing the piano as the mood dictated. Only two session musicians were called in for that first LP, augmenting two numbers – a guitar solo on 'Superwoman' and a trombone part on 'Love Having You Around' – a remarkable fact in itself at a time when, in the main, the making of a rock album was becoming an increasingly baroque process. Although *Music of My Mind* was created simply with three men working a box of wires and switches (and rubber bands), the album pulsates with rich musical tones that were new in 1971 and still sound fresh today. When the track 'Keep on Running' was released as a single in 1972 it baffled the music press, who had nothing to compare it with. Now, it sounds remarkably like a track by Prince (aged thirteen when it was recorded, to put Stevie's achievement in perspective).

If Stevie Wonder had a weakness it was his lyrics which, initially at least, were only a slight advance on the dummy words musicians improvise when they begin constructing a new song. Mostly he sang about the travails of love, something that occupied a good portion of his life. His first marriage was already coming to an end, and he had many girlfriends. Sex was a subject journalists sometimes asked Stevie about, nervously, as though he would be different from sighted people. 'It's the same *thing*, Jack!' Stevie told Ben Fong-Torres of *Rolling Stone*, amused at the misconception. 'As a matter of fact it's probably even more exciting to the [blind] dude . . . That shit is just fantasticness!' (*fantasticness* being a Wonderism that could be applied to his new music). Stevie's Christian background led to some of his most exciting songs musically, gospel-inspired numbers such as 'Evil' and 'Heaven is 10 Zillion Light Years Away'. The lyrics are less digestible, however, ranging from soupy spirituality on the latter to judgementalism on 'They Won't Go', both of which appeared on *Fulfillingness' First Finale*, the last LP he made with Bob and Malcolm in 1974. Broadly speaking, Stevie's lyrics became more satisfying when he addressed political and social issues, which was a lead he took from his friend and fellow Motown star Marvin Gaye.

Eleven years Stevie's senior, Gaye was one of the most successful of all Motown artists, as well as enjoying added status within the organisation for being married to Berry Gordy's daughter, Anna. For years, the artist had been a reliable company man, turning out impeccable factory-made singles such as 'How Sweet It Is (To Be Loved By You)'. Concerned about the fact that many of his fellow African-Americans seemed to live as second-class citizens, and emboldened by the career independence shown by Stevie, Gaye set out in the early 1970s to take creative control of his work and to address social and political issues in his songs. The first album of his new career, *What's Going On*, is a mellifluous, socially aware song cycle, recorded with the help of some of the best session musicians in the business, such as Bobbye Hall whose insistent bongos can be heard on 'Inner City Blues (Make Me Wanna Holler)'.* This is perhaps the outstanding track on the album, both musically and lyrically, the well-chosen words contrasting the

---

*Bobbye Hall is one of a coterie of first-class US session musicians who appear on a remarkable number of classic albums in the 1970s, helping to give mid-'70s American rock its cohesive feel. Her distinctive pattering percussion can also be heard, for instance, on Randy Newman's *Good Old Boys* (1974), Joni Mitchell's *Hejira* (1976) and Bob Dylan's *Street-Legal* (1978), as well as Gaye's follow-up to *What's Going On*, the 1973 LP *Let's Get it On*.

astronomical expense of sending Apollo astronauts to the moon with the earthly reality of the Vietnam draft and the fact that many African-Americans were living on low incomes in squalid inner-city projects (many built, with the best of intentions, on the modernist principles of Le Corbusier). Little wonder there had been riots in the recent past, notably in Detroit in 1967. This was the tenor of *What's Going On* and Berry Gordy didn't *dig it at all*, didn't want to release his son-in-law's opus, only very reluctantly testing the market by putting out the eponymous title track as a single in 1971. The sinuous, insistently questioning 'What's Going On' proved to be one of the keynote sounds of that summer, a hit that convinced Berry to finally release the album, too. In the spring of 1972, having renegotiated its contract with Stevie Wonder, giving him ownership of his songs, artistic control over his releases and an enhanced royalty on sales, Motown also put out Stevie's *Music of My Mind*. With these two ground-breaking albums, Motown changed from being a font of immaculate pop singles to a purveyor of album-based African-American rock music.

Stevie enjoyed having people read to him, and during breaks in his work with Margouleff and Cecil – initially at Media Sound and then at Electric Ladyland, the studio Jimi Hendrix built in New York, later in LA and in London – he asked Malcolm in particular to read to him. The Englishman chose George Orwell, reading all of *Animal Farm* to Stevie and excerpts from *1984*, both of which Stevie became engrossed in, and which inspired songs. One day Stevie came in very excited about a new idea he had. 'Yeah, another bloody love song, right Stevie?' Cecil teased, having become accustomed to the singer's propensity for romantic ballads. 'And he [sang], "My name is Big Brother/ You say that you're watching me . . ." It was like a chill went down my spine. We recorded it that day.' The song 'Big Brother' would be one of the numbers on the new album, *Talking Book*, perhaps the best LP Stevie made in the early 1970s, featuring unforgettable songs such as 'Superstition' and 'Maybe Baby' that have terrific musical hooks and are also lyrically interesting, often expressing Stevie's growing interest in the ancestry of black Americans. For the album cover – in the days when gatefold sleeves were studied intensely as one sat listening to a new disc – Stevie was photographed with his hair in corn-rows, wearing an African robe and bangles, sitting contemplatively on a piece of arid ground that might have been in West Africa. (In fact, Margouleff took the photograph in a public park off Mulholland Drive in Hollywood, not far from the homes of Marlon Brando and Jack Nicholson, after a recording session in the neighbourhood.) Increasing social awareness also led Stevie to take account of fans who were unsighted. He insisted on Braille on the cover of *Talking Book*, which exasperated Motown because, with thicker cardboard sleeves, the same number of LPs would not fit in the standard box for shipment. However, Braille was very meaningful in terms of the album's title. 'What's a talking book, after all?' asks Margouleff. 'It's a book for unsighted people.'

Stevie was determined that his new adult music would not be stuck in a ghetto of R&B, as was the fate of most black artists in the early 1970s. 'That was something we discussed a great deal,' says Malcolm Cecil. *'This isn't black music. This is music for everybody. This is crossover music.* We were very conscious of that, and we pushed that the whole time.' So the decision was made to go out on tour with the Rolling Stones in the summer of 1972, showing a white rock music audience that Little Stevie Wonder had grown up into a remarkable adult rock artist.

For many music fans, the Rock Trinity of the 1960s was comprised of Bob Dylan, the Beatles and the Rolling Stones. By 1972, the Beatles were defunct; Dylan, now in his early thirties, had temporarily stepped away from the spotlight to be with his family and resolve some business problems; but the Stones were still working hard, and arguably they made their best music during their second decade. 'The Stones were brilliant in the '70s,' enthuses Jann Wenner, who as king-pin of *Rolling Stone* magazine was an invaluable booster of the British band in the United States. 'The fact that some of their greatest [music] was in the '60s doesn't mean they weren't pre-eminent artists of the '70s as well.'

It was a case of needs must. Due to mismanagement, the Stones entered the 1970s so broke they couldn't pay their UK income tax;

consequently, in the spring of 1971, the five band members, their partners, children and hangers-on, crossed the English Channel to live as tax exiles in France. Mick and Bianca Jagger, who had married in the South of France that May (Ossie Clark made Bianca's wedding outfit), were domiciled for most of the time in Paris, where they could hobnob with the jet-set. Meanwhile Keith Richard and his girlfriend Anita Pallenberg set up home in a magnificent mansion overlooking Villefranche on the Riviera, where they played host to visiting musicians such as the American country artist Gram Parsons, as well as the other Stones. Keith had a recording studio built in his wine cellar and, working closely with the young guitarist Mick Taylor (who had taken the place of the late Brian Jones in the band), he started to put down tracks late in 1971 for *Exile on Main Street*, a loose, boozy-sounding double album of blues-based, American-style rock 'n' roll made, incongruously, by five ex-patriot Englishmen in a villa in the South of France. Such is the paradox of the Rolling Stones: an ersatz American rock band that made better rock 'n' roll than almost any other contemporary group on either side of the Atlantic. And for many fans, *Exile on Main Street* is the best album they ever recorded.

Curiously, Mick Jagger doesn't agree with the consensus. 'The thing about *Exile* is that everyone loves it, but I don't really know why,' Jagger has commented. 'There aren't any real hits on it, apart from "Tumbling Dice". And although it's great to listen to, it isn't that great when you try and play songs from it. There are a lot of tracks on that double album, and only a handful of songs you can perform: "Tumbling Dice", "Happy", "All Down the Line" and "Sweet Virginia", which is a nice country tune. So there's a good four songs off it, but when you start to play the other nineteen, you can't, or they don't work . . .' Perhaps his feelings are a reflection of the fact that the album was more Keith's than his, the two friends being highly competitive. For most fans, Richard is the heart of the Stones, and when he is in control, as he very much was here despite his drug use, the music has a feeling which is authentic, funky, and slightly nefarious. Recorded in his basement with a mobile truck, *Exile on Main Street* also has an endearingly homemade and appropriately *stoned* feel that, to Jagger, sounds like shit. 'I'd love to remix the record,' he says, 'not just because of the vocals, but because generally I think it sounds lousy.' *Exile* is 'lousy' in the sense of sounding murky, blurred . . . whatever adjective one wants to employ. On that basis, so is Dylan's *Basement Tapes* (1975). Yet both are without doubt classics.* Rock music doesn't have to be well-recorded, or have lyrics that have literary merit, nor even lend itself to live performance in order to be effective. Jagger's lyrics on the album are his usual pastiche of the Americana that inspired him and Keith to take up music in their home town of Dartford, Kent, in the late 1950s: words that are essentially fake and mostly meaningless (compared, that is, to the poetry of Dylan, or the Beatles' brilliant vignettes of English life). By the standards of most pop, Jagger's words are merely par for the course. *Exile on Main Street* succeeds, despite the lame words, because it possesses a quality that is virtually impossible to describe – put most simply, a *feeling*, the credit for which goes to Keith Richard for following his own musical vision. 'The point is that the Stones had reached a point where we no longer had to do what we were told,' comments the guitarist, echoing the experience of Stevie Wonder. 'I was no longer interested in hitting number one in the charts every time. What I want to do is good shit . . . otherwise you're just trapped in that pop cycle.'

Still, when it came to the important business of filling their bank accounts, the band was fortunate indeed to have the level-headed former economics student Jagger at the helm of their ship. Although the Stones had made a hash of their business dealings in the 1960s (in common with Dylan and the Beatles), Jagger determined to steer the vessel straight in the 1970s, and by a combination of astute business decisions and hard work he put them on course to be one of the most enduringly successful and wealthiest acts in all showbusiness. Keith might not care about hit singles, but Jagger cared very much about keeping the Rolling Stones on top in terms of records sales, tour

*Both double albums of home recordings released in the 1970s, though the *Basement Tapes* was comprised of material recorded in the late 1960s. (Following on from Jagger's comment, Dylan seldom plays any of these songs either in his show, but they are wonderful nonetheless.)

revenue and hype as *the greatest rock and roll band in the world*. Having parted company with their manager, Allen Klein, and Decca Records, Jagger was the driving force behind the formation of Rolling Stones Records in 1971, the logo of which would be a pop art representation of his lolling tongue,★ the product distributed by Ahmet Ertegun's Atlantic Records. With the logistics in place, 1972 was the year the band would release a new album and promote it with their first US tour since 1969, marked and marred as it had been by the disaster of Altamont, where a fan was stabbed to death in front of the stage by Hell's Angels hired to provide security. Considering the unfortunate history, and the fact that three years had passed since they last went out on the road in the States, it was not clear how the band would be received. In fact, Jagger admitted he was 'scared shitless' the tour would be a flop.

In the months and weeks preceding the American tour, radio stations carpet-bombed the States with Stones hype. From his studio in Hollywood, disc jockey Wolfman Jack (who had a cameo role in George Lucas' new movie *American Graffiti*) reminded listeners at over a thousand AM radio stations that Mick and the boys were coming: 'They're Gods. They ain't even immortals anymore . . .' Wolfman piled hyperbole upon hyperbole. Jann Wenner's *Rolling Stone* further built expectations with the sort of advance coverage the British press reserves for forthcoming royal marriages. As a result, *Exile* stood at number one in the album charts when the band's Lockheed DC-7 aeroplane – the new lapping tongue logo decorating the fuselage – touched down at Vancouver for the Canadian warm-up show. There was a near riot the first night at the Pacific Coliseum as fans without tickets tried to join the 17,000 lucky people inside the arena, all eager to see a show which was in fact the state of the art for rock music in 1972: bigger, louder and much more extravagant visually than anything staged by contemporary American bands.

The 1970s was the decade in which the arena- and then stadium-

★Though widely supposed to have been designed by Mick's friend Andy Warhol, the famous lapping tongue logo was not a Warhol artwork, though the pop artist was among the Stones' entourage on tour in 1972, together with the likes of Truman Capote and Terry Southern.

rock show came into its own, and Jagger has argued that it was British bands such as the Stones, the Who, Pink Floyd and Led Zeppelin which pioneered the form, taking the trouble to make their shows visually and acoustically spectacular, however large or unsuitable the venue – partly, perhaps, because they felt they had to try harder to make an impact in a foreign land. By their example, these English groups changed the nature of the rock concert. In the old days, touring bands made do with the PA systems of the venues they visited, usually inadequate though they were with small speakers that sat on the stage and much of the sound being absorbed by the crowd, and in the case of the Beatles, completely overwhelmed by the noise of screaming fans. For a long time it was taken for granted that, in order to see a really big act, one had to put up with poor sound quality and lousy views.

Going out on tour in 1972, the Stones fed their sound through massive banks of speakers hoisted high above the stage so everybody could hear perfectly. Jagger made sure his customers had something to see, too, no matter how far back they were seated in the hockey stadiums and football arenas they were playing. The band had their stage custom-built and trucked it around the States with them. It was painted white and decorated with fire-breathing dragons. Overhead hung a mirror, measuring 16 by 40 feet, on to which were shone six 'Super Trooper' spotlights, thus reflecting light on to the stage and out into the audience at key moments in the show. As he was the focus of this extravaganza, Jagger commissioned his pal Ossie Clark to create special stage costumes for him to wear, white jump suits that were in the vanguard of the emerging glam-rock fashion, perforated with eyelets and lashed together with cord, which Jagger undid in the teasing style of a stripper as the show progressed. His accessories included heavy bracelets, a cross on a chain around his neck, and a pink sash which he whipped around his waist as he gyrated. To his side on the white stage, which was washed with a mixture of warm water and 7-Up each evening to make it more 'danceable,' Keith struck a more dignified guitar hero pose; Mick Taylor looked frightened and unhappy (he wouldn't last long in the band); lurking over on the far side of the stage, Bill Wyman eyed up the girls as he plucked his bass;

and at the back behind his drum kit Charlie Watts unobtrusively kept time, eyebrows raised sardonically as he watched Mick's antics. Blues singer, rock superstar, sophisticate, astute businessman, English gent, Mick was a brilliant showman, apparently fearless in his egoism, unabashedly playing the sleazy go-go dancer, and the American fans were loving it. *What a fuckin' larf!*

Stevie Wonder opened for the Stones each evening, with his eight-piece band, Wonderlove, plus singers. Malcolm Cecil and Bob Margouleff had programmed the synthesizers so that Stevie could generate on stage a fair approximation of the amazing sounds he made with TONTO in the studio, and Malcolm was at the soundboard to ensure the mix was right. Audiences were almost entirely white, middle-class, middle-Americans. Any scepticism they may have had about listening to a black Motown act, however, dissipated when Stevie performed his new music, with two songs from the forthcoming album *Talking Book*, 'Superstition' and 'Sunshine of My Life', getting audiences on their feet dancing night after night. 'It was stunning . . . very visceral and very compelling,' says Bob Margouleff of the concerts. 'He had a big standard Motown backline, but a lot of the show centred around electronic sounds, and people were immediately taken by its newness and its freshness.'

The tour is as legendary for the bacchanalian debauchery of the Stones and their entourage as the music made on stage: this was the tour of Robert Frank's vérité documentary *Cocksucker Blues*, commissioned but then denied general release by the Stones when they saw how footage of offstage sexual shenanigans, hooliganism and drug abuse made them all look bad. They visited thirty cities over two months that summer, culminating in a jamboree at Madison Square Garden on 26 July 1972, which happened to be Jagger's twenty-ninth birthday. Stevie joined the Stones on stage on the final evening for a romp through 'Uptight' followed by '(I Can't Get No) Satisfaction' and a custard-pie fight. The tour had been a major success, for Stevie and for the Stones, now back on top as the greatest rock band in the world. However, as Jagger knew, there was always somebody new on the scene, somebody younger and slightly different who might steal the limelight from them. Upon his return home to London, Jagger made a point of checking out the latest comer, a guy like himself from the hinterland of South East London, four years his junior, with a similarly shrewd business brain and, hard though it was to believe, an artist with an even more outrageous stage act. His name was David Bowie.

11

THE TRANSFORMERS

*'Everybody's bisexual' – that's a very popular thing to say
right now.*

LOU REED

The audience for David Bowie's big show was studded with celebrities: Mick Jagger, Elton John, Rod Stewart, Alice Cooper and Lou Reed were all seated in the front of the stalls, together with their entourages, lesser-known musicians, record producers, and music-press journalists. This concert, on the evening of Saturday, 19 August 1972, had been hyped for weeks in advance as one of *the* rock events of the year: the show where Bowie would perform in the persona of Ziggy Stardust in preparation for touring the United States. The venue was a North London cinema, the Astoria on the Seven Sisters Road, one of the largest movie theatres in the world when it was built in 1930 with seating for an audience of three thousand. With the decline of mass cinema attendance, the Astoria, known as the Rainbow, was being used as a rock venue these days, its escapist décor – Moorish foyer with fountain, Spanish-styled auditorium – lending a *faux* grandeur to any gig. Without the benefit of air-conditioning, the atmosphere inside the hall was hot and fetid, murky with the smoke of cigarettes and marijuana. The carpet was sticky with spilt beer and chewing gum. And at a time when it was fashionable for men *not* to bathe too frequently or use deodorant, there was a pervasive funk of body odour and unwashed denim. In short, it was a typical early '70s gig.

With tickets ranging from seventy-five pence to one pound-fifty, the show was outstanding value for money with two excellent support acts: a fine blues musician called Lloyd Watson followed by Roxy Music, a new band fronted by a 26-year-old art school graduate named Bryan Ferry. The latter had created a stage persona for himself that borrowed heavily from 1950s style as well as the emerging vogue for androgyny in rock – what American critics were calling 'pantomime rock,' later better known as glam-rock, short for *glamorous*, of course, which was what it was all about. Ferry came on stage like a matinée idol (appropriately for a show in a cinema), his hair dyed jet-black (by the fashionable hairdresser Smile) and lacquered into an exaggerated quiff. The band's clothing was mostly by designer Antony Price: metallic boots built up with platform soles, animal-print bomber jackets, and trousers cut from leather or satin. These extravagant outfits were accessorised with all that glittered and was colourful. Aside from Ferry, the Roxy drummer and the bass-player, there was a flamboyant lead guitarist named Phil Manzanera; Andy Mackay, another striking-looking man, blew oboe and saxophone, while a spindly keyboard freak called Eno made *wheeeoowww* sounds by twiddling the knobs on his VCS3 synthesizer (a cheap British answer to the Moog). Eno's synthesizer was the keynote to the band's debut single, 'Virginia Plain', booming out like a siren before the whole band came together for three minutes of monolithic rock 'n' roll, over which Ferry sang, in a highly mannered style, preposterous lyrics – of flying down to Rio, dancing the cha-cha till dawn, and so forth – that were nonetheless clever, fun, and certainly different.

'I *loved* Roxy Music's 'Virginia Plain'. *Worrr!* That was something you'd never heard the likes of. I don't know how these people put these things together, but they seemed to not care that it didn't fit into any format, and it worked a treat,' enthuses John Lydon, who was an early fan. Aged sixteen when 'Virginia Plain' came out, and living in a council flat just across the road from the Rainbow, John had a keen eye for anything different, and he had come over for the Ziggy Stardust show this evening. The fact that Bryan Ferry apparently wanted to inhabit the fantasy world of a 1950s movie star, later going so far as to wear a white tuxedo in publicity photos, struck John as *a right laugh.* 'They were wonderful,' he says of Roxy Music. 'They created a whole world of atmosphere and it was magic to watch.' He and his mates took to dressing up like Ferry to attend subsequent Roxy concerts, simultaneously enjoying and mocking the singer's pretentiousness: borrowing or buying second-hand dinner jackets, for example, and wearing them with a sense of irony, all of which was a precursor to punk rock.

Punk was still a little way off in 1972, however, when Roxy almost stole the show at the Rainbow, the power of 'Virginia Plain' making a big impression not only on the likes of the young John Lydon but also the music industry movers and shakers of the early 1970s, many of whom were seated in the stalls. 'Bryan was a total star,' recalls record producer Chris Thomas, who sat six rows from the front with Keith Reid of Procol Harum. 'It was brilliant.' Having learned his trade working under George Martin with the Beatles at Abbey Road, Thomas was currently in the studio with Pink Floyd making *The Dark Side of the Moon,* and he would soon produce Roxy Music, too, as well as a seminal '70s record that John Lydon had as yet no mental image of: *Never Mind the Bollocks, Here's The Sex Pistols.*

Backstage, Angie Bowie, a boyish young woman with cropped blonde hair, goaded her husband with the news that the support act had enjoyed a triumph. Despite the fact that they had been denied a sound check, there was a chance that Roxy Music might even upstage the headliner. 'You better watch out,' she warned David. 'They were *good.*' David Bowie looked up from under his haircut – a masterpiece of the hairdresser's art, long at the back, a puffball at the front, coloured with Hot Red hair dye – and smiled at his strident spouse. However good Bry had been, nobody out there in the audience had ever seen anything quite like what he had in store for them tonight: a concert that was more West End stage show than rock gig, with special lighting and back-projections, an elaborate set, mime artists, and costume changes. Appropriately, friends from the new musical *Jesus Christ Superstar* would be in later to give their verdict. He felt nervous, but nevertheless quietly confident that it would be a triumph.

How does me 'air look?

When the roadies had removed Roxy Music's equipment and re-set the stage, the house lights were dimmed, and Wendy/Walter Carlos' music from *A Clockwork Orange* began to play through the speakers. Bowie had latched on to Kubrick's movie for its look and the theatricality of the music, which he had arranged to continue live in the theatre. The recording duly segued into Beethoven's Ninth, played off-stage by the organist from Procol Harum and, as the audience gamely tried to clap along to Ludwig Van, the rock concert commenced: billowing dry ice, clouds of the stuff, rolled out through two scaffold towers which flanked the stage; then three musicians strode out on to the stage, three slightly self-conscious young men in drooglike bovver boots and silver jump-suits, the leader of the trio being the guitarist Mick Ronson. These were the Spiders from the Mars, the fictional band of a fictional rock idol, Ziggy Stardust, who was the star of the show, of course, but where was he? Out of the murky recesses of the stage another figure stalked forth, strumming an acoustic guitar, a slender young man of twenty-five, slightly above average height, wearing denim trousers tucked into silver boxer's boots, with a blue-green jacket open to reveal his bare chest. His face, pale and androgynous, with one blue eye and one green (the result of a childhood altercation) was accented with rouge and surmounted by a helmet of apricot-coloured hair. As the audience deduced that this was Ziggy, they applauded so enthusiastically that before he had sung a word of his first number, 'Lady Stardust', Bowie took a bow. And he hadn't done anything yet! 'It was ridiculous,' laughs Chris Thomas, recollecting the evening. 'And it was very clever.'

David Bowie's *Ziggy Stardust* concert at the Rainbow was the overture to one of the outstanding showbusiness careers of the 1970s. Not only did Bowie become a major rock star, he acted with distinction in movies and was, moreover, a sexual and fashion icon to millions of young people. In short, Bowie was one of the defining personalities of the decade. His success also represents a shift in the tastes of young music buyers away from the authentic and natural sounds that had characterised the rock scene of the late 1960s, music their older siblings adored (the Beatles, Dylan, the Band and so forth) to a slicker, superficially more glamorous era where narcissistic individualism was sexy, and selling oneself hard to the public was not seen by artists or their fans as being uncool. Interestingly, the New Hollywood was only now moving *into* naturalism, with pictures such as *Five Easy Pieces*. But rock – a younger, nimbler medium – was leaving authenticity behind and going all-out for glamour. Ahead was make-up, cocaine, glitter, disco, the whole delightfully gaudy shebang of mid-1970s pop.

Born illegitimately in London in 1947, Bowie's real name was David Jones, which he used until the mid-1960s when a more famous Davy Jones came along (he of Bob Rafelson's Monkees). The Jones family was eccentric. David's mother flirted with Fascism; his older half-brother, Terry Burns, suffered mental illness. Angie Bowie is one of those who believes that David developed a habit of adopting different personas in order to distance his conscious self from his deepest and darkest feelings for fear he too might go mad. This propensity for wearing masks made him a natural performer. He grew up in Bromley, a bourgeois suburb of South East London, not far from Mick Jagger's home patch, making his first foray into show business playing saxophone with an R&B group, then fronting a blues band. After school, David worked in an advertising agency for a short time and there is a good deal of the ad-man in his career: a delight in flashy ideas and slogans, always striving to make an impact, changing styles so often that one wonders whether he is ever serious about anything. David was a Mod when it was fashionable to be so, and he was a folk singer briefly. Adopting the stage name Bowie (from the knife), he signed to Pye Records in 1966 as a singer-song-writer, and had a novelty hit the following year with 'The Laughing Gnome' before cashing in on the space craze in 1969 with his best song to date, 'Space Oddity'. Bowie was by no means unique in tapping into the public interest in space exploration. It was a widely-used theme in the arts at the time of the Apollo missions (as we have seen with John Updike). But few made such a career motif of the subject, with Bowie coming to inhabit the image of a space traveller on a semi-permanent basis from 1969 onwards. The following year he married a brash American named Angela Barnett, who was openly and enthusiastically bisexual, not only taking partners of both sexes, but sometimes more than one at a time. David had similar proclivities and together they became, in Angie's words, '. . . the best-known bisexual couple ever. We were certainly the most famous couple ever to admit and celebrate our bisexuality so publicly.' In 1971 Angie gave birth to their only child, Zowie, and the family set up home in a substantial Victorian house in the Bromley area named Haddon Hall. Although married with a child, David increasingly made a feature of his feminine side, going so far as to wear what looked like a dress (but apparently wasn't exactly) for the cover of his 1971 album, *The Man Who Sold the World*, and striking an overtly camp pose for his next LP, *Hunky Dory*, the album with which he started to hit his stride, and where our interest in him begins.

Bowie's new record was made at Trident Studios, tucked away in the middle of the bohemian squalor of London's Soho. Despite the seedy surroundings, the studio was renowned for its distinctive sound, not least the tone of its famous piano which can be heard on many classic albums of the era such as *Elton John* (1970). The resident engineer was Ken Scott, another producer who learned his trade working with George Martin at Abbey Road. With Scott's expert help, and the close collaboration of Mick Ronson, Bowie recorded an album in *Hunky Dory* that remains one of the most charming of the decade, featuring notable songs such as 'Life on Mars' (the distinctively-resonant Trident piano played here by Rick Wakeman) and 'Changes', which Angie recalls her husband writing at Haddon Hall in the days when songs came easily, sitting cross-legged at the piano, absorbed and happy in his work. With young Zowie crawling about, one of his best *Hunky Dory* compositions was 'Kooks' in which David wrote and sang about two eccentrics bringing up a child in idiosyncratic style – if the kid didn't want to do his homework when he went to school (*if* he went to school) they'd throw the books on the fire, and so forth – that revealed a rare glimpse into the domestic life of Bowie as an apparently loving father. All the aforementioned songs appeared on Side One of *Hunky Dory*, back when albums had to be plucked from the turntable halfway through, checked for dust and turned over to be played in completion, quaint as this routine process now seems. Once the stylus had been put back into the crackling black vinyl groove, Side Two of *Hunky Dory* revealed Bowie paying tribute to his cultural heroes: 'Song for Bob Dylan', perhaps the weakest track on the album, showing in fact how far Bowie fell short of Dylan's facility with lyrics; 'Andy Warhol', for David was infatuated with the pop-art sophistication of New York; and 'Queen Bitch', a rocker inspired by, and dedicated with thanks on the sleeve to, Warhol's protégés, the Velvet Underground Band.

Seldom in the short history of rock has a group made such an impact with so few records in such a short time as the Velvet Underground did with the three studio albums they released between 1967 and 1969, when Lou Reed left the group,* records that were musically experimental – using unusual instrumentation, repetition, and feedback – and lyrically of the first order. The words were those of Lou Reed, brought up middle-class Jewish in suburban Long Island, where his behaviour became so wayward that when he was seventeen his parents consented to him receiving Electro-convulsive Therapy (ECT) at the local mental hospital. This searing experience served to further alienate Lou from his background, and as soon as he was able he moved into New York, writing songs about the drug users, dealers, pimps, madmen, drag queens and all-round bohemians who flitted through the bars, hotels and tenement buildings of Greenwich Village. Songs he wrote in the late 1960s are among the best in rock: 'I'm Waiting for My Man', 'Some Kinda Love', 'Heroin' and 'Pale Blue Eyes'. The list is long. And though the Velvet Underground sold few records during their brief association, it is a truism that they had a disproportionate influence on artists who came after them, especially those such as David Bowie who had literary pretensions. If Marlon Brando was the acting idol of Jack Nicholson's generation, Lou Reed was in many ways the musical idol of Bowie's (second only perhaps to Dylan). The fact that in both cases the relevant industries lost interest in Brando and Reed didn't matter. They were originators, heroes to their fellow artists. When Bowie signed with the American record company RCA in 1971, with *Hunky Dory*

*A fourth studio album, *Loaded*, was completed and released in 1970 after his departure.

the first album released under that deal, he was excited to find himself on the same label as Reed and in a position to work with him: something that would affect both their careers.

One of the remarkable aspects of rock in the early seventies is that artists recorded and released *so much* music. Only two months after *Hunky Dory* was finished, having been knocked out in a couple of weeks during April 1971, as was standard, and with RCA preparing its release, Bowie went back to Trident to make yet another LP. Having used the space theme several times since the late 1960s – 'Space Oddity', 'The Man Who Sold the World' and 'Life on Mars' – Bowie now decided to create a fully-fledged science fiction concept album about a pop star named Ziggy Stardust living at the end of Earth's history. In 1974, Bowie explained the Ziggy story in detail to the author William Burroughs for an article in *Rolling Stone*, at a time when Bowie was thinking of turning the record into a production for the musical theatre. 'The time is five years to go before the end of the Earth,' the singer told Burroughs, who had an interest in such ideas. 'It has been announced that the world will end because of lack of natural resources. Ziggy is in a position where all the kids have access to things that they thought they wanted. The older people have lost all touch with reality and the kids are left on their own to plunder anything. Ziggy was in a rock 'n' roll band and the kids no longer want rock 'n' roll. There's no electricity to play it. Ziggy's adviser tells him to collect news and sing it, because there is no news. So Ziggy does this and there is terrible news.' Bowie went on to say that Ziggy has a dream that Earth is going to be visited by aliens, and so sings of a 'Starman', who people think of as a saviour. Then Ziggy starts to believe *he* is the starman, and is torn to pieces finally on stage by the real aliens, the song 'Rock 'n' Roll Suicide'.

'It sounds good,' harrumphed Burroughs.

Having long been interested in acting, Bowie approached the making of this new record by inhabiting his character as if he were a method actor preparing for a role. 'Once he took on Ziggy Stardust, there was a distinct change in him,' recalls Ken Scott, who co-produced the album with Bowie. 'It was Ziggy sitting around having a cup of coffee. It wasn't David Bowie.' Angie had little time for her husband's affectations and believes he was no more serious about this new quasi-science fiction character than he had been about being a Mod or any of the other personas he had tried on and then discarded over the years: it was just, as she says, an excuse to dress in a new outfit. Nevertheless, Bowie returned to Trident with a solid collection of new songs which, with the help of Ronson and Scott, he made into a much rockier album than *Hunky Dory*. The lyrics were silly, but he belted them out with brio, and everybody involved in the LP had very high expectations of *The Rise and Fall of Ziggy Stardust and the Spiders from Mars*. Looking at each other in the control room during playback of the eleven tracks, the guys predicted, 'This is going to be *huge* in the States.'

David's US record company duly invited him and Angie over to New York in June 1972, putting them up at the Plaza Hotel where they received gift-wrapped presents of albums by fellow RCA artists, including notably Elvis Presley, whom they were taken to see perform at Madison Square Garden. It was the first time Elvis had ever played New York, surprisingly, and the shows were among the late triumphs of his historic career. At thirty-seven, Elvis was a good deal heavier than he had been in his prime, of course, but he was not yet the bloated wreck he would become over the next five years, his final years. Appearing on stage in a flamboyant white and gold cloak, backed by a large show band, performing big emotional ballads such as 'American Trilogy', here was a last glimpse of one of the key figures of pop music in the twentieth century. During the visit to New York, Bowie found time to see other iconic figures who were more germane to his own life and work, including making a pilgrimage downtown to 33 Union Square West to see Andy Warhol. This meeting was like that of two alien creatures equally outlandish to one another, with Bowie disconcerted by the 43-year-old artist's sallow skin, silvery wig and awkward manner. When David put out his hand in greeting, Warhol shrank from him, looking at the singer as if he was some kind of previously unknown life form, saying nothing, but taking pictures as though to gather evidence for private study later. Conversation finally commenced when Warhol noticed his visitor's yellow shoes. 'I adore those shoes, tell me, where did you get those shoes?' Warhol asked Bowie, who tried to ingratiate himself with the artist by presenting him with a copy of *Hunky Dory*, on which was the song 'Andy Warhol'. Flattering indeed, one might think, but Warhol didn't take it that way. 'Can he use my name without permission?' the artist asked his assistants peevishly after the singer had departed. 'Should he pay us royalties?'

More satisfactorily, Bowie was introduced to Lou Reed. It was not long after the release of Reed's first solo LP on RCA, a disappointing collection of weak, thinly-produced songs that had not done well. It was in fact amazing that the man who had written songs as powerful as 'White Light, White Heat' could turn out such dross as 'Walk and Talk It', but Reed was an extremely uneven artist. The first LP was such a stinker that RCA was all for dropping him from the label, until Bowie offered to produce a follow-up at Trident with his team. And so Reed came to make *Transformer* – an album specifically about New York City – in London. Furthermore, while making the record at Trident in the summer of 1972, Reed stayed in an apartment in the salubrious suburb of Wimbledon, thus being about as far removed from the milieu he was singing about as it was possible to get. From such a paradox came probably the best album of his erratic solo career, and the most deliciously decadent record of the glam-rock period. The songs are, of course, among Reed's most celebrated, including 'Perfect Day', 'Satellite of Love' and 'Vicious', each one of which has a story behind it, the latter coming from a suggestion by Warhol who asked Lou to write a song called 'Vicious'. 'It would be so *faahbulous*,' recalled Reed, imitating the effeminate languor of his mentor. When Lou asked Andy what he meant by *vicious*, the artist replied airily, 'Oh, vicious, you hit me with a flower.' In 'Walk on the Wild Side', Reed wrote about the drag queens, trans-sexuals and would-be movie stars who hung around the Factory. 'Wagon Wheel' was a Lou Reed pastiche written by Bowie, who was going through such a period of fecundity that he was giving songs to friends (notably 'All the Young Dudes', a hit for Mott the Hoople in 1972). *Transformer* was recorded quickly and cleanly by a team that knew each other well, and with the help of able session musicians, notably Herbie Flowers who devised the distinctive bass line for 'Walk on the Wild Side' and led the

Dixieland band on 'Goodnight Ladies', his jazz stylings suiting the sleazy late-night ambience of the album. Ken Scott recalls that Reed was 'stoned the entire time.' If true, this didn't prevent him achieving near-perfect results. Despite one or two spats in the studio, Lou and David also proved to be a very good team. They encouraged one another to do their best, and Bowie's soaring backing vocals complemented Reed's voice: the American being a limited singer who more-or-less spoke his lyrics in a smoker's croak. The combination of rough and smooth is particularly effective on 'Satellite of Love'.

Talking to the music press, the two stars flattered each other immoderately at this time, both having much to gain by the association. Lou was getting a leg-up from a younger more fashionable star, while Bowie's status was enhanced by working with an artist who had already laid down a stunning body of work, a man who commanded respect among those in the know – a relatively small group in London in 1972, but one that included the people David particularly wanted to impress. 'Lou's really got it together now,' Bowie told *Rolling Stone* in June. 'I like to think I'm playing my rock and roll in his tradition.' Meeting the press at the Dorchester Hotel in London, Lou lavished praise on Bowie in return and went so far as to kiss his producer very publicly on the lips, happy to play up to David's camp image shortly after Bowie had come out as a gay man.

The story broke in an interview with *Melody Maker* published on 22 January 1972. Bowie was quoted as stating plainly, 'I'm gay and always have been, even when I was David Jones.' Considering that he was married ('a good relationship,' Bowie said) with a child, he went on to qualify this statement by agreeing with the interviewer Michael Watts that he might more accurately be described as bisexual. Watts indicated that the revelations were made with a sense of playfulness, suggesting to readers that it might be a put-on. But there was very little room for misunderstanding. Aside from the central brief but unambiguous statement – 'I'm gay and always have been . . .' – everything in the article, from the studied effeminacy of the photographs, to Bowie's use of the homosexual patois, *polari*, served to show that he was part of the gay world, though he distanced himself in the interview from the so-called gay liberation movement, not wanting to be seen as part of a group. In this respect, he managed to offend campaigning homosexuals such as Graham Chapman of *Monty Python* who believed there was an onus on prominent gay men such as David to support a movement for social change. Nevertheless the statement was bravely honest: it was *brave* in as much as a revelation such as this might have been expected to scuttle a pop career in 1972; and it was honest by the account of both himself and his wife. In fact, Angie maintains that she was the one who convinced her husband to make a feature and virtue of his (and their) bisexuality. She had no embarrassment about this herself and figured that the publicity, which they gambled would be considerable, might outweigh any negative reaction. 'It seem[ed] like a perfectly strong, good platform with which to rally the troops,' she says. 'Not to be boring, not to be lackadaisical, but to come up to the plate and actually say something worthwhile.' Indeed, the statement to *Melody Maker* was part of what was essentially an orchestrated publicity campaign built on David's ambiguous sexuality. Around this time a picture story appeared in the national newspapers whereby the Bowies were photographed from the back pushing a pram, one parent with short boyish hair wearing a lumberjacket, the other a slight figure with longer hair. Pictures taken from another angle revealed the surprise: the butch figure was Mother and the long-haired creature Dad. A truly modern relationship, and an out-and-out publicity stunt, as Angie now concedes in her hard-faced manner, barking: 'Why would I bother to have my photograph taken with David and the child, if it wasn't for publicity purposes?' The surprising aspect to this whole coming-out episode is how tolerant the British media and public were to what was, after all, an unprecedented revelation for a pop star. The press continued to treat Bowie as a harmless curiosity, and among the young his popularity only rose.

From suburban sitting rooms to inner-city housing estates, Ziggy and his bisexual creator were regarded as cooler than ever. Moreover, John Lydon recalls that he and his teenage mates in Finsbury Park – tough, predominantly straight, inner-city lads who formed part of the hooligan army that followed Arsenal – admired Bowie's honesty:

'Around *Ziggy Stardust*, Dave Bowie was an absolute full-on "I'm a homosexual." That was his image. And it was as challenging to the world as you could ever hope to be at that point, and that was a damn brave statement to make. And yobs, hooligans, basically working-class [guys], really liked him for the bravery, for the front of it. It was taking on the world, going *That's what I am and fuck you!* A very, very good thing.' In fact, Ziggy was incorporated into the culture of the football terraces. Manchester United supporters in particular briefly adopted the Bowie look and so 'Ziggys' battled 'droogs', weirdly, in early '70s meetings between Arsenal and Man U. Angie Bowie argues that buying one of her husband's records in the early 1970s was 'an endorsement of a person's sexuality.' The truth was more remarkable: from football terraces to sixth-form common rooms, liking Bowie was totally acceptable and, indeed, fashionable for British teenagers in 1972. While some, like John Lydon, did admire the singer's individuality in coming out, many more thought it was all a bit of a laugh (Bowie was married after all, which was an apparent contradiction). There is also a British tradition of accepting and enjoying camp show-business folk. But the primary reason for Bowie's success in Britain in 1972 was surely that his music was exciting, and his image bold, original, and *sexy*. Despite his fey manner, he was a bantam-cock of a performer, whom girls found attractive and boys admired. 'He was always very much a *man*,' comments the actress and singer Dana Gillespie, a close friend of Angie and David. 'He wasn't a limp-wristed wooftery type.' (Indeed, by Angie's account, Dana slept with them both. So she should know.)*

Which is not to say that Bowie on stage at the Rainbow in August 1972 was not an outrageous spectacle. As he sang 'Lady Stardust', a photograph of pretty-boy pop star Marc Bolan was projected on to a screen to his left, giving the impression that Bolan was the Lady in question. At the same time, three dancers marshalled by David's mime-artist friend Lindsay Kemp, each dressed in spider-web body

---

*A recording artist in her own right, at this time Dana was appearing in London's West End as Mary Magdalene in the smash-hit Andrew Lloyd Webber–Tim Rice musical *Jesus Christ Superstar*.

stockings, strutted about wearing Bowie face masks. After 'Changes', the drummer Mick Woodmansey began rapping out the intro to 'Five Years', a key song in the story of *Ziggy*, giving Bowie time to change costume. He re-appeared high on the scaffolding in a skimpy V-neck body-suit, cut short at the crutch to reveal long white legs which he flexed narcissistically. ('Nice legs,' noted journalist Charles Shaar Murray sarcastically in the *New Musical Express*.) (See picture 13.) The show reached an apogee of camp during 'Starman', which had just been released as a single. As Lindsay Kemp pranced about, leering at the audience, Bowie improvised a lyric that incorporated '(Somewhere) Over the Rainbow':

There's a Starman
. . . over the rainbow

Music critics jotted down ironic *aides-mémoire*: 'Judy Garland hasn't left us!' Alexander Stuart wrote in *Plays and Players*. 'The entire evening seemed like a tribute to Judy. David Bowie, his delicate face made-up to look like hers, has the guts, the glitter, the charm [of] Garland and, yes, even the legs.' Almost to a man, the journalists in attendance made remarks about Bowie's legs in their reviews, but in a good-natured, typically British way. Despite the sound problems, and the sneaking feeling that Roxy Music had delivered the better set, Bowie's show was rated a success by the reporters. It was noted that Mick Jagger even got up and danced. Nobody seemed fazed by the gay content, bar Elton John strangely enough. He was a very big star by the summer of 1972, having scored hits with 'Your Song' (1970) and his own space fantasy, 'Rocket Man' (1972) – but Elton John was not yet openly homosexual, and he was sensitive on the subject. As far as Elton was concerned, his good friend David had just committed career suicide by prancing about in this queeny manner. Towards the end of the set, Elton was heard to announce, 'That's it! He's gone too far. He's through.' And having made his feelings clear, Elton flounced out of the theatre. Although this reaction seems absurd in retrospect, Elton John was in fact right to fear that Bowie's new image might be too rich for some audiences. Americans would *not* take to *Ziggy*

Stardust as British music journalists and fans had. It was too camp for them. It would be a while yet before Bowie became a truly international superstar. In the meantime, there would be more records, further changes of image, and the start of a movie career – which returns us to the story of seventies cinema.

12

DOWN THE MEAN STREETS

You see, Mr Gittes, most people never have to face the fact that at the right time, and right place, they're capable of anything.

NOAH CROSS IN *CHINATOWN*

In order to raise the money to make *Mean Streets*, Martin Scorsese went to a neophyte producer closely tied to the rock business. At twenty-six, Jonathan Taplin had worked for Bob Dylan and the Band, and was interviewed by Mick Jagger for the job of road-managing the Rolling Stones' recent US tour. Having decided to make a new career in the film business, he had recently relocated from the East Coast to Los Angeles and had thrown himself into the industry with great confidence. 'I figured if I could produce 150 concerts for Dylan and the Band I could produce a movie.' Two years his senior, Scorsese was also new in the City of Angels, though he was finding it harder to adjust than Taplin. Marty, still dressed as though he was back in New York, turned up at Taplin's house in warm, fragrant Laurel Canyon (just down the street from where Joni Mitchell was living), wearing a full-length leather coat, the kind the SS wear in movies, as Taplin recalls with amusement: 'And there we were sitting out by the pool and Marty didn't even take off his black leather coat, and he was sweating. It was really kind of bizarre.' The diminutive, saturnine New Yorker seemed further distracted by Taplin's girlfriend who was sunbathing topless nearby. Perspiring freely, glancing over to the girl, and taking frequent hits on his asthma inhaler, Scorsese delivered his pitch for *Mean Streets* at machine-gun speed, aided by three storyboard books. 'He had wanted to make the movie for so long that he had literally drawn out every single shot,' says Taplin. 'He had really dreamed the whole movie up.' As Marty told it, the essential story concerned a group of young guys scuffling around on the edges of the criminal world in Little Italy, not the romantic Little Italy of *The Godfather*, but the real place, in the modern day. As he explained, Marty came from the neighbourhood himself, so he knew what he was talking about.

Born in 1942 to parents whose family had emigrated to the US from Sicily, Martin grew up largely in a tenement on Elizabeth Street in Little Italy. Because of his asthma, he spent much of his childhood at home watching old films on television. His father, Charles Scorsese, was a movie fan and the family were among the first in the neighbourhood to have a TV, on which old films were repeated so frequently in the 1950s that Marty got to know the classics like well-thumbed storybooks. The other defining influence in Marty's early life was the Roman Catholic Church. He attended seminary school with a mind to becoming a priest, but the pull of cinema was too strong and in 1960 he enrolled at New York University to study film, thereby meeting some of the key characters in his life. These included a stocky young court stenographer named Harvey Keitel, who had ambitions to be a film actor, and a fellow film student named Mardik Martin, who spoke English with such a thick accent hardly anybody in class could be bothered to talk to him. In fact, Mardik's story was remarkable. He was from Baghdad, where he had worked for the local distribution arm of MGM, learning English by watching American pictures and thereby falling in love with what seemed to be a verdant Heaven on Earth populated by such goddesses as Betty Grable. Mardik worked his way from Iraq to the promised land, intending to take a business degree in the USA, but when he found out that it was possible to study film in America he changed courses, and when Marty got talking to him he met a student as passionate about movies as he was himself. Together, they set out to view every picture they could, every picture ever made if possible, later calculating that they sat through 50,000 flicks in the early years of their friendship: everything from Fellini's *8½* to *Abbott and Costello Meet Frankenstein*. 'There was a book that had all the lists of movies you should see and those you shouldn't,' reminisces Mardik. 'We saw both.'

Marty and Mardik had a dream to make pictures of their own and spent their free time talking about this, often sitting in Mardik's parked car (in order to get away from their wives who wanted them to put aside their movie-making ambitions and get regular jobs). The friends had a grand plan for a trilogy of movies about Little Italy, where Italian-Americans were born into petty crime as they were born into the Catholic Church, the temporal business of hustling a living at odds with their faith and mortal fear of sin. Marty would direct, Mardik would write the screenplays. Although the first movie in this notional trilogy was never made, the second picture became Marty's NYU thesis, shot over four years in dribs and drabs when he could scrape together the cash, and finally finished in 1968 thanks to a gift of money from his tutor. It was called *Who's That Knocking at My Door?* Although essentially Scorsese's film, Mardik helped out with the screenplay, and the lead actor was their stenographer pal Harvey, who aged visibly between scenes because the whole thing took so long to finish.

Harvey would also fill the central part in the third movie in the trilogy, *Mean Streets*, playing Charlie, the guilt-ridden nephew of a Mafia boss who buddies around with a likeable fool named Johnny Boy, and Johnny's epileptic sister, Teresa, who in this tight-knit community is also Charlie's cousin. As he becomes drawn into a life of petty crime, and succumbs to his lust for Teresa – both sinful acts in the eyes of the church – Charlie is tormented with Catholic guilt. This is the essential story of *Mean Streets*, the title of which comes from Raymond Chandler: 'Down these mean streets a man must go who is not himself mean.' The screenplay evolved over several years as Marty and Mardik talked it over between them, with Marty telling stories about Little Italy and Mardik working the best of these into the script. For instance, one time Marty mentioned a local character named Solly who went crazy when somebody called him a *mook*, though nobody knew what mook meant. Realising how funny this was, Mardik put it in *Mean Streets* and the mook scene became a highlight of the picture. It didn't add to the story, but it was an authentic slice of local life. By 1970, when Marty moved to Los Angeles to pursue his career, every set-up was planned, the very camera angles decided in Marty's storyboard books, but raising the money to get *Mean Streets* made was another matter entirely.

Relocating to California was a severe culture shock to Martin Scorsese, who disliked almost every aspect of life out west, finding the climate particularly oppressive. LA was, however, the centre of the film industry and he made many important contacts at this time, working initially for Roger Corman like so many fledgeling filmmakers before him, and becoming friendly with Corman alumnus Francis Coppola and his friend George Lucas. Other West Coast buddies included directors Brian De Palma and Steven Spielberg, the latter an intensely shy young man then making television films for Universal. All were movie nerds whose favourite activity was watching pictures and then discussing what they had seen, though there was a social life, too, albeit limited, and even occasional forays to the beach. One time, Spielberg tried to convince Scorsese to join him for a dip in the ocean. 'No, no, no,' shuddered the leather-clad New Yorker, 'there's things out there you don't even want to know about.'

'You afraid of jellyfish? There's no jellyfish there.'

'No, no, no, things with teeth.'

Life began to turn around for Scorsese in the summer of 1971 when his new contact, Jonathan Taplin, succeeded in raising the minimal half million dollars required to make *Mean Streets*, investing his own cash and money from a wealthy friend, naïvely confident that they would earn it back. Scorsese lost no time getting to work. In Hollywood, he called upon an acting group that met in a little theatre off Vine Street, a group that included Richard Dreyfuss, Teri Garr and Jon Voight who had starred in *Midnight Cowboy* (1969) and *Deliverance* (1972). Voight turned down the chance to play Charlie, but suggested two members of the acting group for supporting parts. So David Proval became the barkeeper Tony, and Richard Romanus played the money-lender Michael. Scorsese eventually gave the part of Charlie to Harvey Keitel, while Johnny Boy fell to an actor almost nobody had heard of called Robert De Niro.

Although he was another Italian-American from Greenwich Village, growing up within walking distance of Elizabeth Street, De Niro's background was very different from Scorsese's. His parents were bohemians, his father, also named Robert De Niro, was a well-connected artist who counted Tennessee Williams and Jackson Pollock among his friends. Although predominantly homosexual, De Niro senior married a girl named Virginia Admiral, and they had one child, born in 1943, a boy named after his dad but known to family and friends as Bobby. Growing up in his parents' loft apartment in Greenwich Village, Bobby De Niro developed into an introverted young man, in love with film, whose aspiration was to be a movie actor like Lon Chaney or Marlon Brando, an actor who remade himself for each role, as opposed to a personality actor such as Humphrey Bogart, who was essentially himself in every movie. Following in Brando's footsteps, Bobby studied with Stella Adler at the Actors Studio in New York and, possessing a fierce ambition – belied by his inarticulate, withdrawn manner – he forged his way into stage and film work. His main competitor in New York in the early days was another Italian-American, Al Pacino, who leapfrogged Bobby's career when he secured a part in *The Godfather*. Via Brian De Palma, who cast him in a couple of relatively small pictures, De Niro then met Scorsese, which proved the vital connection in both careers. 'We were both brought up in the same area, and we see things the same way,' says Scorsese, explaining why the young men hit it off so well. 'I think, also, we both had the sense of being outsiders.'

In the autumn of 1972, Scorsese met with his leading actors in a two-room suite at New York's Gramercy Park Hotel for ten days of rehearsal prior to location work on *Mean Streets*. Time was short, money tight, and *Mean Streets* was going to be unconventional. Richard Romanus for one was not impressed by what he saw and heard. He disliked Mardik's script, which seemed weighed down with religious references – *'a lot more'* than are in the finished movie he says with emphasis – and was taken aback by the way Bobby and Harvey jabbered back and forth in New York street talk that was almost incomprehensible to an outsider such as Richard who, despite being cast as an Italian-American, and being of an appropriately swarthy hue, was raised in Vermont of Lebanese descent. He was amazed that his fellow actors intended to talk this way in the picture, and that they meant to use such obscene language. In the climactic confrontation between Bobby's character and Romanus', for instance, Bobby intended to spew forth every obscenity he could think of: 'You're a fuckin' jerk-off! I'll tell ya something else, Mikey: I fuck you right where you breathe . . . Fuck face! Motherfucker . . .' No picture had language like this in 1972!

Once the camera started rolling, Scorsese shot at a furious pace, up to thirty-six set-ups each day, using available light and a hand-held camera. If passers-by got in the way, likely as not they would be on screen. Everything was dictated by the budget, but the cost-cutting method also had the positive effect of lending the movie a 'sense of anxiety and urgency,' as Scorsese says, as well as a documentary feel. Despite the frantic pace, Scorsese retained a keen eye for detail. He brought the film to its conclusion during the three days of the annual San Gennaro religious festival in Little Italy, for example, symbolising how his characters, while living in go-ahead modern-day New York, were still anchored to the superstitions of the old country. Shooting footage at the festival, Scorsese was careful to work in glimpses of the newly finished World Trade Center: not far away in terms of distance, but another world symbolically to the small community inhabited by Charlie and Johnny Boy in the ghetto, and showing how these young men were caught between two cultures.

There were numerous problems on location. Locals who saw that a film called *Mean Streets* was being made in their neighbourhood complained that Little Italy wasn't *that* bad – and this was a part of town where you took care who you offended. The Mafia were all over. Indeed, the Mob stole the wardrobe truck. The whole shoot was such a stressful experience that Marty wore white gloves to stop himself biting his fingernails bloody. With all the actors crammed together in one Winnebago, there was the additional problem of personality clashes. 'De Niro tended to stay in character off the screen,' recalls Jonathan Taplin with a smile. '[He] intimidated Richard Romanus all the time.' Towards the end of the film Michael confronts Johnny Boy in the neighbourhood bar with a $2,000 debt, a scene that ends in a scuffle between the men with Johnny Boy pulling a pistol on Michael and unloading his most obscene invective. This results in Michael hiring a hit-man to murder Johnny, gunning him down in the movie's climax. The animosity between De Niro and Romanus was real by this stage in the shoot. 'I played on it,' Scorsese has commented. 'They had got on each other's nerves to the point where they really wanted to kill each other.' De Niro thought Romanus should be angry in the bar scene, for instance, rather than laughing, and told him so. Romanus bridled at the advice, asking Scorsese pointedly, 'Marty, who's directing this picture, you or him?'

Fuck face. Motherfucker. Jerk-off . . .

To Romanus, Little Italy and these Neanderthal Italians were a mystery, and he still sees De Niro as being essentially the man he played on screen. 'Johnny Boy is Bobby's basic character,' he observes, 'sort of lower-class, New York Lower East Side character. I mean, it's a character that he does over and over again, and has been doing it for years. It's his basic character, and if you know Bobby – or at least back then – that's who he was.' Whatever sort of man he was in everyday life, De Niro proved himself, at age thirty, to be a brilliant film actor in *Mean Streets*. He is truly and literally explosive in the role of Johnny Boy, right from when he struts around a street corner in his first scene and, just for the hell of it, drops a cherry bomb in a mail box. From here on in, Bobby is completely convincing as this irresponsible, irrepressible young guy who gets by – just and for a short time – on charm and luck. *Mean Streets* is a very significant 1970s movie for many reasons, not least because it introduced the cinema-going world properly to De Niro. In everyday life, he was an unprepossessing, mumbling introvert. With the camera on him, he became fascinating. 'Suddenly he was like [150] pounds of energy right in front of you saying the words so crisply and nicely,' as Mardik Martin expresses the change. 'It was quite a contrast.'

If the movie has a weakness it is the pervasiveness of Catholicism. For Scorsese and his characters, sin and redemption, God and the Devil, Heaven and Hell, are all very real. 'You don't make up for your sins in church, you do it in the streets, in your home. All the rest is bullshit and you know it,' Scorsese spits out in the preface to the picture, words that Charlie hears as the voice of his conscience. The words disturb Charlie, and meant much to the director, but to a secular audience the idea of 'sin' carries less meaning, if any. Nevertheless, *Mean Streets* is a marvellously rich entertainment, so full of ingredients that it is impossible to take it all in at one viewing. The use of slow-motion subsequently became a Scorsese trademark, as did innovative camera shots such as the one in which Harvey Keitel reels drunkenly around Tony's bar, an effect achieved by strapping a camera to the actor's body. Symbolism is everywhere. Tony's bar is always lit red, a hellish colour for a place where sinful acts are performed. When Charlie puts his hand over a glass he does so with his fingers arranged as a priest holds the sacramental chalice. It helped to be a Catholic to notice that nuance, but everybody could appreciate the soundtrack.

Ever since he had seen Kenneth Anger's *Scorpio Rising* (1964) as a film student, Scorsese had been enthused with the idea of using pop-ular music to add a dramatic dimension to movies. He did so first with *Who's That Knocking at My Door?*, but he realised the concept fully with *Mean Streets*, a film set in a crowded urban environment where music of all sorts plays constantly from diverse sources and seeps nat-urally from one space to another, dramatising ideas and actions. At the start of the picture, Charlie wakes from a nightmare, featuring Scorsese's doom-laden message about sin, to consciousness in cacoph-onous Manhattan, gets up, looks at himself in the mirror, and lies back down. As soon as his head hits the pillow – BAM! – 'Be My Baby' by the Ronettes begins playing. This forges a connection between the audience and the character, a young guy probably of their age group, with sex on the brain. Music could be used ironically, too: when Charlie goes to see his Mafiosi uncle, he passes a street band playing 'The Star-Spangled Banner'. Songs serve as heralds: when Johnny Boy swaggers into Tony's bar with two girls he does so to 'Jumping Jack Flash'. This is who he is. And so it goes on. Now, around the same time, George Lucas was using a pop music soundtrack to enhance *American Graffiti,* in which Richard Dreyfuss, Candy Clark and others played small-town teenagers whiling away a summer night in the early 1960s. 'George Lucas used rock 'n' roll because so much of *American Graffiti* is in cars, it's always on the radio, but Marty used music so dramatically,' argues Jonathan Taplin, who used his rock 'n' roll connections to secure permission for two Stones' songs in the movie. 'When the Rolling Stones hit when Bobby De Niro is coming into the bar for the first time and everything slows down into slow-motion with this amazing Stones track, it was a piece of art, different to anything I'd ever seen . . . And that really started something that hasn't stopped.'

Nineteen seventy-three turned out to be a fascinating year for movies. In the spring, as Scorsese edited *Mean Streets*, Bernardo Bertolucci released his brilliant *Last Tango in Paris*, starring Marlon Brando as a French-speaking middle-aged American named Paul, emotionally adrift in Paris after the suicide of his wife. Meeting a 20-year-old girl called Jeanne (played by Maria Schneider), Paul embarks on a cathartic, anonymous affair in an empty apartment. When Jeanne insists he tells her his name, Paul groans: 'A name? Oh Jesus Christ. Oh God, I've been called by a million names all my life. I don't want a name.' Who but an actor has a 'million names'? In this and so much else in *Last Tango in Paris*, Brando was speaking of his own life. As Jeanne and Paul lie in bed together, Brando improvises a remarkable scene for which he drew deeply on his unhappy childhood in Omaha with alcoholic parents, talking to the girl essentially about himself. The scene is riveting to watch, but was emotionally exhausting for Brando to do, so much so that when it was over he decided he would never reveal himself in such a naked way again. 'I felt I had violated my innermost self and didn't want to suffer like that anymore,' he wrote in his autobiography, adding, 'when I've played parts that required me to suffer, I had to experience the suffering. You can't fake it. You have to find something within yourself that makes you feel pain . . . It takes an enormous toll.' In 1973, *Last Tango in Paris* was an international sensation because of its sex scenes, specifically the (faked) anal sex where Paul appears to lubricate Jeanne with butter before penetrating her. In retrospect, it is not so much the sex (which is pertinent to the story) as Brando's performance that is sensational. He made *Last Tango in Paris* directly after completing work on *The Godfather*, giving two of his best-ever performances in succession, proving that he had lost none of his talent. However, that didn't mean he chose to continue to exercise it fully. Unfortunately, *Last Tango* stands as one of the last great performances Brando gave. 'In subsequent pictures I stopped trying to experience the emotions of my characters,' he wrote, adding cynically that audiences don't know the difference when actors fake it. Audiences *do* know when they are being sold short, and it was a tragedy for Brando's career that he decided to sell himself short for most of the rest of his career. It was not until 1976, when Francis Coppola persuaded him to appear in *Apocalypse Now*, that Brando came close to doing work of such quality again.

In the spring of 1973, Coppola saw *The Godfather* bedecked with Academy Awards (including Best Actor for Brando) and he began filming the brilliant sequel with Robert De Niro as the young Vito Corleone, casting him partly on the strength of his performance in *Mean Streets*. Not that Paramount appreciated what a discovery De Niro was. When Coppola told the studio that he wanted to use the actor, the same executives who had looked askance at Al Pacino refused initially to countenance this newcomer, showing yet again what lamentable judgement they had. In his entertaining but self-serving memoir *The Kid Stays in the Picture*, studio boss Robert Evans gives his readers the impression that he played a very significant part in creating a golden age of cinema in America in the 1970s by presiding over such notable Paramount pictures as *Chinatown* (1974), *The Godfather* (1972) and its sequel. From Coppola's point of view 'the mountain,' as Paramount was known, after its logo, was not populated by people of discernment, but by executive philistines, the most egregious of whom was Evans himself. In Coppola's view, almost every decision Evans made on the *Godfather* films turned out to be wrong.

Coppola offered invaluable support to his friend and protégé George Lucas when George's new picture *American Graffiti* was previewed to similarly asinine studio executives at a screening early in 1973. Universal hated the picture, telling Lucas after the screening to go back to the editing room and, indeed, to come up with another title, suggesting that *Rock Around The Block* would be an improvement, because Bill Haley's '(We're Gonna) Rock Around the Clock' was the first song to be heard on the soundtrack. Maybe then the studio might release it. Coppola, who was present, roared at the executives: 'You'll see if you can *release* it?' He had invested his own money in *American Graffiti*, and having watched the same film they had, he felt confident that his friend George had created an excellent movie that would earn them all a handsome return. He continued to berate the men from Universal: 'You should go down on your knees and thank George for saving your job.' After some relatively minor modifications, *American Graffiti* was released to great commercial success in August 1973, making more money than even Lucas and Coppola could have dreamed, its pre-Vietnam innocence offering welcome escapism in the year that the US signed the cease-fire agreement in Paris, effectively admitting defeat in the Far East; also, coming out at a time when an embargo by oil-producing countries in the Middle East meant Americans were being forced to think about driving smaller, more fuel-efficient cars for the first time. *American Graffiti* helped create nostalgia for the gas-guzzling automobiles of the past and the apparently better world that represented. 'It kind of revived the whole scene,' comments Candy Clark, who played good-time girl Debbie in the movie and, along with others, did very nicely out of the 0.1 percent share of the profits Lucas generously gave his actors as a thank-you for sticking with him when the studio suits thought the movie unreleasable.

Martin Scorsese had a similar problem with Universal, and other studios, when he finished *Mean Streets* and, along with Jonathan Taplin, shopped it around Hollywood in the summer of 1973, literally carrying the movie in cans between studios. First stop was Universal, where Scorsese and Taplin were told bluntly 'This is not for Hollywood', which was the moment that it began to dawn on Taplin that it was possible he might not recoup his investment. At Paramount, Robert Evans' right-hand man, Peter Bart, stood up halfway into the 130-minute picture and announced 'This is not a Paramount film.' It was only thanks to John Calley, the Warner Brothers executive who showed so much vision in supporting Stanley Kubrick's unique operation in England, that *Mean Streets* got a studio release. Meanwhile, flush with the success of *The Godfather*,

Paramount was pouring its money into another picture that dealt with crime and punishment and borrowed from Raymond Chandler. The studio had persuaded the great Polish filmmaker Roman Polanski to return to Los Angeles – four years after his wife, Sharon Tate, had been murdered in the city by Charles Manson's gang – to direct a remarkable private-eye picture starring the new king of Hollywood, Jack Nicholson.

Chinatown was tailor-made for Nicholson by his screenwriter friend Robert Towne, who created private eye Jake Gittes in Jack's image, taking account of the charismatic actor's 'temperament, his manner and the way he uses language.' As Towne explains, 'All of it was part of the inspiration.' Since his breakthrough in *Five Easy Pieces*, Nicholson's career had been uneven in terms of success, even a tad eccentric at times, including his taking a turn behind the camera to direct *Drive, He Said* (1971), which flopped. *Carnal Knowledge*, also released in 1971, had not been the major success many expected. Neither had a second Bob Rafelson movie, *The King of Marvin Gardens* (1972), a study of a relationship between brothers (played by Jack and Bruce Dern), despite its excellence in many respects. *The Last Detail* (1973) was more successful commercially, the story of two sailors who escort a prisoner to jail, directed by Hal Ashby whose previous release was the marvellous *Harold and Maude* (1971), and who would end the decade with the wonderful *Being There* (1979). It was with *Chinatown*, however, that Nicholson's career took its next leap forward.

The project came to life when Robert Towne was having dinner with the ubiquitous Robert Evans at Dominic's restaurant in Los Angeles. Evans wanted Towne to work with the studio on adapting *The Great Gatsby*, which Paramount was preparing to film. Towne said he was more interested in making a picture with Nicholson, which is when Evans' ears pricked up. Recently, Evans had convinced the owner of Paramount to let him produce one film a year independently while retaining his executive position with the company. If Evans chose wisely, this was his chance to make a fortune for himself. For all his faults, Evans intuitively understood Nicholson's appeal. If Jack wanted to make a private-eye flick with Towne, Evans wanted to be in on the deal, a hundred percent, as studio boss *and* producer. Only he didn't understand Towne's screenplay or his title: *Chinatown*. 'What's that got to do with it?' he asked Towne over dinner. 'You mean it's set in Chinatown?'

'No. *Chinatown* is a state of mind.'

To Evans this explanation was 'pure Chinese,' and when Roman Polanski signed up to direct the picture he agreed that it made no sense at all. Indeed, the title has almost nothing to do with the complex plot of the movie. Loosely based on a real-life scandal in the pre-war history of Los Angeles, the film starts with a scam involving the city's water supply, taxpayers' money and land purchases. The mastermind of this villainy is a corrupt multi-millionaire named Noah Cross (John Huston) whose daughter, Evelyn Mulwray (Faye Dunaway), is married to Hollis Mulwray, the bureaucrat in charge of the city's water and power. Jake Gittes (Nicholson) is hired ostensibly to investigate an allegation that Mulwray is having an affair. In fact, this is an attempt to blacken his name after he refuses to go along with his father-in-law's nefarious plans. Mulwray winds up dead, drowned, ironically, during a drought, murdered by Cross for his intransigence, and Gittes finds himself drawn into a story of murder, government corruption and parallel moral degeneracy. For it turns out that Cross has fathered a child incestuously with his daughter, Evelyn, and is now pursuing the granddaughter. The only link with LA's Chinatown is that the film reaches its climax in the Chinese district of downtown LA, and in writing the screenplay Towne had in mind a comment he once heard from a police officer who worked the Chinatown beat. Asked what he did in the neighbourhood, the cop retorted 'as little as possible,' because it was hard to get to grips with who the criminals were in such an exotic, closed community. Thus *Chinatown* is meant as a metaphor for the murky situation Gittes finds himself in. However, the success of the movie has less to do with its metaphorical title and knotty plot than the morally ambiguous characters, the fine acting and the atmosphere of a vanished world.

Enough pre-war architecture was still extant in Los Angeles in 1973 for Roman Polanski to shoot the picture on location there, and it is partly for this reason that *Chinatown* is so evocative of the often under-appreciated romance of this great (both in size and cultural importance) city. There was an early suggestion that the film should be made in black and white, but Polanski thought that unnecessary and shot in Technicolor. 'Unlike Bob Evans I saw *Chinatown* not as a "retro" piece or conscious imitation of classic movies shot in black and white, but as a film about the thirties seen through the camera eye of the seventies.' While using the latest cinema techniques, Polanski found subtle ways in which to give the movie a period feel. He decided not to have blue in the film, because blue indicates water, and this is a movie about a drought in a city built on desert. Also blue tends to 'pop' out on screen, attracting the eye of the viewer. Without blue, the film looks parched, older. For the same reasons, the characters are dressed primarily in subdued colours, with Faye Dunaway, who plays a widow for much of the story, mostly wearing black. The combined effect is to create a colour picture with a *noir* feel. Art Deco titles and the laconic jazz theme music further help audiences refer back to old black and white private-eye movies such as Howard Hawks' 1946 version of *The Big Sleep*, of which it is highly reminiscent.

Filming commenced on 28 September 1973, the day 'World War Three started,' as Robert Evans has remarked wryly. A furious little man, marked by his experiences of the Holocaust (when his mother was killed in the camps) and his wife's more recent murder in this very city, Polanski was a terror on set, rasping that if he had his way he would make movies with *puppets*, not actors. He was exasperated by his leading lady, the *Dreaded Dunaway* as Faye became known, driven half-mad by the amount of time she took in make-up, contemptuous of her apparent inability to learn her lines and dismissive of her constant requests for motivation. Polanski exploded that the pile of money she was being paid should be motivation enough! Actress and director fell out spectacularly when Polanski yanked a hair out of the actress' head because it was catching the light. 'I don't believe it!' Dunaway shrieked. 'That motherfucker pulled my hair out!' Filming was suspended while a crisis meeting was held in Robert Evans' office, during which Polanski informed Dunaway undiplomatically that she was merely a pawn in his game. They barely spoke afterwards.

By contrast, Polanski lavished praise on his leading man, noting that despite his penchant for staying up half the night disporting himself, Jack was always on set on time, knowing his lines, and everybody else's, 'and he's such an exceptionally fine actor that the worst piece of Hollywood dialogue would sound crisp when he delivers it.' Nevertheless, star and director rubbed each other the wrong way, too. One Friday afternoon, Nicholson was distracted by a basketball game on TV. His beloved LA Lakers were playing and he wanted to stay in his dressing room to watch. There was a scene to do, but a simple one from the point of view of the actor: Gittes looking at photographs on a wall at the Department of Water and Power. Polanski became obsessive about getting the light right, calling Jack back repeatedly. Nicholson grumbled that he knew they'd never finish on time. 'OK, it's a wrap,' said Polanski, assuming Jack would say, *No, it's OK, let's finish it.* Instead, the star went back to his dressing room. Polanski followed and smashed Nicholson's TV to pieces, screaming, 'Know what you are? You're a fucking asshole.'

There was further tension for Nicholson when he filmed with John Huston, who was playing the sinister Noah Cross. Apart from being the director of one of the classic private-eye movies of the 1940s, *The Maltese Falcon*, and a formidable figure in all respects at sixty-seven, Huston was the father of Jack's new girlfriend, Anjelica, who was on the set when her father, as Cross, asks Gittes whether he is sleeping with his daughter – a *double-entendre* that caused them all discomfort. 'One of the secrets of *Chinatown*,' recalled Nicholson, 'is that there was a kind of triangular offstage situation . . . it actually fed the moment-to-moment reality of my scene with John.'

When Gittes confronts Cross with murder, and worse, the old man defends himself and his black deeds shamelessly: 'I don't blame myself. You see, Mr Gittes, most people never have to face the fact that at the right time, and right place, they're capable of *anything*.' This speech goes to the heart of the film. On the face of it a man like Noah Cross is a monster – to have sex with one's child under any circumstance is surely the most heinous of actions – but nothing is quite that simple in *Chinatown*. Indeed, it seems that perhaps Evelyn did not go to bed with her father unwillingly; Polanski is careful to leave that sensitive matter ambiguous, introducing a smidgen of doubt as to whether Noah Cross is indeed irredeemably wicked. The old man is also central to the ambivalent climax, which is perhaps the chief interest of the film and a cause of more problems on set. In his original screenplay, Robert Towne wanted Jake Gittes to rescue Evelyn and her daughter from Cross and take them to Mexico to start a new life. He wrote a happy ending in other words. Polanski was against this, insisting that the film was a tragedy and as such *Evelyn must die*. So much animosity had built up between director and leading lady by this stage that it almost seemed as if Polanski wanted to see Dunaway play dead. The disagreement became so heated that the screenwriter was barred from the set, and Polanski wrote the final scene himself: a confrontation between the protagonists in Chinatown, as Jake attempts to help Evelyn and her daughter, Katherine, to escape to Mexico. In the confusion of the final meeting Noah Cross steps forward and tries to claim his granddaughter. Evelyn swears he will never touch her, and when he continues to advance towards the girl, Evelyn shoots her father, then makes off in a car with Katherine. When the police fire warning shots after the automobile, Evelyn is hit and killed. As everybody gathers around the dead woman, Cross hustles Katherine away. Gittes rails against this, and all the injustice and wickedness he has become privy to, but the cops advise him to shut up and leave before he is arrested. There's nothing for it, his friends tell him, as they lead him from the scene: 'Forget it, Jake – it's Chinatown.' So Cross gets away with murder and incest, as well as a multi-million dollar fraud.

The ending of *Chinatown* is wonderfully dark, so much so that Polanski has questioned whether it was the last time in mainstream American cinema that a director could get such a black ending past studio executives. It certainly didn't leave the audience with a happy feeling. At the same time, the film was a significant box office success when it was released in the summer of 1974 (the same summer that *Time* magazine unearthed the truth of Jack Nicholson's complicated parentage, to his astonishment). To some degree the picture tapped a cynical mood abroad in society. The optimism of the sixties had finally evaporated and a more realistic seventies sensibility was emerging in popular culture, especially in the United States, which was a country shaken by the failure of the war in Vietnam and the disgrace of President Nixon, who resigned from office in August 1974 over the Watergate affair. Many of the most interesting Americans films of the 1970s have ambiguous endings where the wicked are not necessarily punished for their crimes, and it is not clear who the evil-doers are: *Mean Streets*; *The Godfather* (and most particularly its sequel, concluding with Michael Corleone sitting alone in the fastness of his estate contemplating the murder of his brother Fredo); and the killing of Colonel Walter E. Kurtz at the end of *Apocalypse Now* in which Kurtz himself is part monster, part sympathetic character, while the apparent hero of the film, Willard, is a paid assassin, a murderer in other words. Recall also how Bobby Dupea abandons Rayette at the end of *Five Easy Pieces*. The leading characters of all these important '70s films are morally ambiguous. Certainly, the 'right thing' is not done. Good does not triumph. Endings are not happy or simple. For filmmakers of the 1970s, and cinemagoers who came of age at this time, this was the way of the world now. Idealism and hope had been tarnished. Right and wrong were increasingly difficult to define. In common with Charlie from *Mean Streets*, and J.J. Gittes, almost everybody in society had been plunged into a metaphorical Chinatown, a confusing, shadowy place where good and evil, even if they can be so identified, are inextricably entwined.

13

THE SYDNEY OPERA HOUSE

I like to be absolutely modern and work at the edge of the possible.

JØRN UTZON

While Roman Polanski worked to finish *Chinatown*, a grand opening ceremony was held on a hot, windy day in Sydney, Australia. On the afternoon of Saturday, 20 October 1973, around and upon the deeply-dark waters of Sydney Harbour, thousands of Australians gathered to watch Queen Elizabeth II, 47-year-old monarch of Great Britain and head of state to this Commonwealth land, open the city's new opera house. 'Controversy of the most extreme kind attended the building of the pyramids, yet they stand today – 4,000 years later – acknowledged as one of the wonders of the world. So I hope and believe it will be with the Sydney Opera House,' Her Majesty enunciated in her characteristically high-pitched, crisp and emotionless tones, such an un-Australian way of speaking. (Her composure was particularly admirable considering two hat pins were all that prevented her bonnet flying into the harbour this blustery day.) 'I have much pleasure in declaring the Sydney Opera House open.' The talking over, RAAF fighter bombers streaked overhead; 60,000 balloons flooded the sky; ships sounded their sirens; yachtsmen and motorists blared their horns; and thousands upon thousands cheered for Australia fair and this fabulous building, an edifice of such beauty and imagination you might call its architect, a Dane named Jørn Utzon, a genius.

But where was Utzon? Most of those involved in this enormous project were gathered around the Queen, including the distinguished engineer Ove Arup, whose firm had done so much to help build it. But the man who dreamed up this remarkable design was not present. Neither had he been thanked by name in the Queen's speech, when one came to think of it, but was alluded to only when Her Majesty mentioned the *controversy*. In truth it was a tragedy. Utzon, until recently seen as the golden boy of international architecture, once feted like a movie star in Australia, had fallen out so badly with his client and colleagues that he had long since resigned from the building of his Opera House and fled Australia to live as a recluse in Europe, abjuring responsibility for how his great building was finished and vowing that he would not come back to see it. He declined an invitation to attend this opening ceremony, and in the decades that followed he showed, by his resolute absence, that he intended *never* to return to Australia. The story of the Sydney Opera house is one of the most remarkable in the history of modern architecture, and it is also a torrid human story.

Upon its opening in 1973, the Sydney Opera House became one of the foremost symbols of Australia, joining the kangaroo, Ayers Rock and the Great Barrier Reef as international trademarks of the nation. Moreover, this spectacular building engenders national pride, encouraging Australians to look beyond their colonial past. After all, this remote and sparsely-populated land has given the world one of its most sublime public buildings, maybe *the* outstanding public building of the twentieth century. Certainly, the Sydney Opera House is one of the most beloved of all public structures. Relatively few visitors to Sydney venture *inside* of course. Fewer attend one of the diverse cultural events held here, and to see an opera in the Sydney Opera House is an uncommon experience indeed. But since 1973, it has been unthinkable to visit Sydney and not stroll around the promenade that surrounds the Opera House, basking in its splendid profile, made still more lovely by being surrounded on three sides by Sydney Harbour. The Opera House is that rarest of edifices: a monolithic modernist building – built of concrete with public money, if you please – that the public actually *likes*. Indeed, most people love it. For the men who built it, feelings run deeper still.

Great buildings are not constructed quickly. As we have seen, Minoru Yamasaki started work on the World Trade Center in 1962, topping out the North Tower eight years later, and that project was not properly finished until 1973: fast work compared to the Sydney Opera House, which was sixteen years from drawing board to opening day. By virtue of being finished and opened in 1973 it can be claimed as a great 1970s structure, attracting world-wide attention at that time, and influencing the subsequent development of international design. The story began, however, way back in the mid-1950s when the governing politicians of New South Wales decided to grace their state capital with a music hall. They had a spectacular site available in Bennelong Point, which juts into Sydney Harbour between the Botanical Gardens and Circular Quay, where ferries and liners disgorge passengers into downtown. The Harbour Bridge, itself a fine piece of engineering, flanks the Point to the west; opposite, on the North Shore, crowd the homes of Sydney's prosperous middle classes. All look in at Bennelong Point, upon which stood nothing more than a tram shed. The plan was to tear down the horrible shed and erect in its place a magnificent building, an opera house by name, though misleadingly so because it would be a multi-use complex, ill-suited in fact to the staging of opera.

An international competition was organised to find a design. The brief called for two main auditoria on the site, a large one seating about 3,500 people and a smaller hall of approximately 1,200 seats, both suitable to staging a range of performances. There was a cash prize and, more importantly, the winner would have his design made real, paid for out of money raised by public lottery. By the closing date in December 1956, there had been more than two hundred entries from architects all over the world. All but one of these suggested erecting conventional rectilinear buildings, whereby the box-like auditoria would sit one behind the other on the promontory. Having fully grasped the essential fact that whatever was built on Bennelong Point would be displayed in the round, one exceptional contestant set his auditoria uniquely side-by-side at the far end of the finger of land,

and covered the halls over with a dynamic roof system of shell-like structures that could be seen to advantage from north, south, east and west – and, additionally, from above (from an aeroplane, say, or indeed from the lofty highway of the Harbour Bridge). Although the competition specified that architects should submit detailed drawings, this singular entrant hadn't bothered with specifics. His submission consisted of a Big Idea, illustrated with a series of *magnificent doodles*, as the Australian art critic Robert Hughes later remarked. Despite breaking this rule, and others (the proposed building was too big for the site, for example), he was declared the winner.

Because the competition was judged blind, the government of NSW had no knowledge of the identity of the winning architect until his design had been chosen and the winner turned out to be an unexpected fellow indeed. Rather than one of the titanic figures of modern design (and many competed), he was an obscure young Danish architect named Jørn Utzon, from the small town of Hellebæk, near Elsinore, of *Hamlet* fame. Aged only thirty-eight, Utzon had never worked on anything approaching the scale of the Opera House. He mostly designed houses. He had entered the competition as a long-range intellectual challenge, little thinking he could win, and had never in his life so much as visited Australia. In order to visualise the site for his entry, he bought nautical maps of Sydney and spent time sailing around the point of land at Elsinore upon which sits Kronborg Castle, imagining this as Bennelong Point (which in many ways made his plan even more impressive). As Utzon had not submitted perspective plans of his design, the competition team were obliged to get an architect at the University of Sydney to draw a hasty impression of what the opera house would look like for the benefit of the Australian public, and thus a dramatic impression of Utzon's proposed Opera House – its shell-roofs much slinkier than the finished article – appeared in newspapers on 30 January 1957.

Reaction was not entirely positive. Functionalists, who then held the high ground in architecture, noted that the size and shape of the shells had little relation to what would go inside these extravagant structures: the stages, flys, acoustic lining and public seating of the halls. For optimum acoustics, the ideal shape for a concert hall is a large shoe-box. In Utzon's plan, it seemed likely that there would be gaps between the ceiling and the fanciful roof vaults. Taking the golden rule of modernism that form should follow function, this was wrong and it led to pertinent questions such as: how much attention had Utzon paid to the acoustics? (Very little, it turned out.) Meanwhile, Utzon's fragmentary shell roofs, unlike complete domes, would have no inherent geometric strength. In short, Utzon's shells might look impressive, but they were neither practical nor functional. Frank Lloyd Wright condemned the design: 'This circus tent is not architecture.' Mies Van der Rohe also disparaged it. In Australia, the mocking press likened the shells to copulating armadillos.

When, however, Utzon arrived in Sydney in July 1957, he won over all his critics, and moreover he made a friend of the Australian people. Utzon was a tall, handsome man slightly reminiscent of the actor Gary Cooper. He spoke only broken English but was nonetheless eloquent, evidently intelligent and very *charismatic*, which was the adjective most often used about him. He charmed the Australian media, the public and his client (the government of New South Wales). As importantly, on a visit to London *en route* to Sydney, he had won the friendship of 62-year-old engineer Ove Arup who would play a vital part in the project. Born in Britain of Danish descent (his father was a Dane, he was educated in Denmark and spoke the language), Arup had built an international reputation as a brilliant structural engineer with a specialist interest in modern architecture. He had already had a hand in the design of many important *avant-garde* structures, including the delightful Penguin Pool at London Zoo. As soon as he saw who had won the Sydney competition, Arup wrote to congratulate Utzon and offered the architect his firm's services. Meanwhile, behind the scenes the government of NSW was anxious that Arup team up with the relatively inexperienced Utzon to ensure that this ambitious design came to something. Fortunately for all concerned, Arup and Utzon took to each other when they met in England, and agreed to collaborate on the job, the older man being thrilled to find a young architect and fellow Dane who shared so many of his ideas about design. '[Jørn] was probably the architect [Ove] had wanted to meet all his working life,' comments Jack Zunz, one of the senior men at Ove Arup & Partners. 'He was very articulate, immensely creative, visionary [and] he was Danish. They used to gabble away in Danish.'

With the competition won and the team in place, construction started. In fact, it started too quickly, the NSW government wanting the public to see them getting on with the job, even though detailed plans for the building were nowhere near ready. ('It's always a disaster,' sighs Jack Zunz, regretting the premature start.) Essentially, the job was split at the outset into three phases, the first of which would be the construction of a massive concrete base that would be both foundations for the shell roof, and also provide the voids for the auditoria. Essentially, Bennelong Point was going to be encased in concrete which in turn would be partly clad in pink granite, forming a platform inspired by the architecture of ancient civilisations. Although Jørn Utzon was an architect in the European modernist tradition, all his design ideas were heavily influenced by the antique world, particularly traditional Chinese and South American architecture. One of his best ideas in designing the Opera House was that it should be set upon a podium, like a temple of old, which was appropriate considering that Bennelong Point was not only a very dramatic site but one of great history, having been inhabited by Aboriginal Australians for thousands of years before the British sailed into Sydney Cove. '[Jørn] was the first modern architect to really take the ancient world as a serious starting point of departure in architecture,' comments Peter Myers, who joined Utzon's team as a graduate student from the University of New South Wales. Because of dramatic ideas like the podium, Utzon had a strong following among Australian architectural students. 'As a young person, every one wanted to work with Utzon,' as Myers says.

The practical problem caused by starting the platform hastily was that the footprint of the building was set in concrete before Utzon and the engineers at Ove Arup had worked out how to build the shells. And this was all before anybody had paid much mind to what should go inside the building: a topsy-turvy way of constructing an opera house which should, in fact, be designed from the conductor's podium out. As with the platform, Utzon's inspiration for the roof vaults was poetic, ancient and modern: poetic in that Utzon said he envisaged the roofs as clouds reflected in water; ancient in that they had similarities to traditional floating Chinese pagoda roofs; and modern in the tradition of pre-cast concrete structures such as Minoru Yamasaki's St Louis Airport Terminal, which was part of Jørn's inspiration for the Opera House. The practical problems were immense, however. In the freehand doodles Utzon had done for the competition, his roof-vaults were irregular shapes, which proved almost impossible to work out mathematically. Engineers at Arup in London spent *years* on the problem, turning to new computer technology to try and solve the geometric puzzle posed by these wild shapes.* As legend has it, Utzon then experienced a Eureka moment at home in Denmark. Peeling an orange for his son Kim, he saw that the segments of the spherical orange might be the shells of the Opera House. Telephoning Ove Arup he exclaimed, 'I've solved it! I've created a sphere.' In fact, the spheroid solution had already been suggested to Utzon by Jack Zunz at a meeting in London in August 1961. Zunz had explained to Utzon that if the shells were all cut from one giant theoretical ball, as it were, the components would be geometrically the same and sections could be rolled out without too much difficulty on a production line on site. 'It was Arup's who said, *Why don't you have spherical geometry?*' states Mick Lewis, another senior man at Arup who worked on the job. 'When [Utzon] saw this marvellous idea, that you could have a sphere, and you could carve ribs out of it, it became his [idea].' Indeed, Utzon went on television in Australia to explain *his* breakthrough, using a ball to demonstrate how the geometry worked. No matter who thought of it first, the solution came at a considerable cost: years of work by Arup's on the irregular shells was wasted; the new geometry meant the auditorium would be 141,000 cubic feet smaller than previously thought, which meant reduced seating capacity; and the exciting flowing shape of Utzon's competition doodle – the very thing that had won him the commission – changed into a much chunkier series of structures. Still, the roofs could now be built

---

*The Sydney Opera House was one of the first buildings designed with the aid of computers.

and, even though the shells as we see them are not as dramatic as in the competition entry, they are still majestic. Indeed, *they are the building*. In architectural jargon, the Opera House is an *expressed structure*. 'It is what it is,' as Peter Myers puts it most simply. 'That's why the building is so powerful.' Monumentally solid and self-weathering, the shells should last as long as the Great Pyramids (another expressed structure). And they are beautiful. Concrete can be beautiful, as is demonstrated by several of the great buildings in this history. Utzon certainly proved as much in Sydney, demanding a flawlessly smooth finish to the concrete areas exposed to view, and on one occasion being moved to tears by the perfection of a concrete section as he watched it being uncovered by workmen.

Erection of the 2,400 shell ribs began in 1963, a year after Utzon had originally suggested the building might be finished, at a cost of five million Australian pounds. The estimated cost was now eighteen million pounds, and it would take until 1967 to crane all the lids in place, which meant that the roof would be up *ten years* into the project. The lids are chevron-shaped and covered with tiles finished with an off-white glaze deriving from an eleventh-century Chinese formula Utzon had re-discovered. Most of the tiles are glossy, with those around the edges of the chevrons in a contrasting matt finish, creating a two-tone quality. The fact that the shell tiles are white, or off-white, is important. First and foremost, white is the colour of modernistic architecture (though as any school pupil knows white is not really a colour at all), from the masters of the Bauhaus to a new generation of American architects coming to the fore in the 1970s, such as Richard Meier and his friends 'the whites' – so-named because of their conviction that white is the ideal finish for reflecting light. 'White has always been a source of tranquillity,' argues Meier. '[It] reflects the changing light of the day.' This was particularly relevant to building under Australian skies. In the morning light, the roofs of the Opera House appear luminously white like sails against a blue or leaden sky (contrary to popular belief, Sydney receives heavy and frequent rainfall). Sunsets over Sydney are often dramatic, a conflagration in red and orange which is reflected in the tiled lids. Then, as the sun smoulders into the ocean, the shells seem to cool like steel in 'the pale violet glow of a Sydney night,' as the architectural writer Françoise Fromonot has described it poetically.

Despite all the many pressures and problems of the job, Utzon took a remarkably relaxed attitude to this gargantuan project. He would, for instance, disappear on holiday for a month or more, during which time he was essentially incommunicado. This was a cause of dismay to senior engineer Mick Lewis, who came out to Sydney in 1963 to set up a permanent Arup office (heading a team of engineers that included a young man named Peter Rice who would later play a key role in the building of the Pompidou Centre). Lewis was in charge of the technical side of the third and most troublesome part of the project: the design and construction of the glass walls and fitting-out of the inside of the halls. In trying to get this work done Lewis became exasperated with his architect. When Utzon eventually returned from his holidays, a long list of questions was always waiting to be answered and Lewis had an over-arching anxiety, that became ever more acute as time passed, about the lack of detailed drawings. Utzon's response was to complain that he was being bothered too much, and in order to stop this he had the connecting door between his and Lewis' on-site huts *bricked up*. When Mick Lewis wanted to see Utzon in future he had to make an appointment. When Utzon felt he still wasn't getting the privacy he needed, he moved his drawing office to a houseboat next to where he and his family were living at Palm Beach, 25 miles away. He did not like answering the telephone when he was there, and would come to the site only twice a week.

Meanwhile, the press and opposition politicians were grumbling about the increasing cost of the Opera House, and the inordinate time it was taking to finish. For many Australians outside Sydney, the idea of an Opera House for the city had always been an extravagance. Any delay or problem became a news story and made the job more difficult. And plenty did go wrong, with Utzon creating many of the problems himself. He had for instance become enamoured of using plywood – of all materials – for Stage Three of the build, arguing that everything from the acoustic ceilings to the mullions in the huge windows could be fabricated from plywood. This was a highly unconventional idea, raising questions about durability, weight, manufacture and cost. When Utzon was questioned about such details by the technical panel advising the state government, he assured them expansively that everything would turn out beautifully so long as they trusted him. That was the key. Utzon's charisma had got him through situations like this in the past, but panel members were now becoming more demanding. They wanted firm answers to important questions such as would there be sufficient seats? One of the few specifications in the competition brief had been seat numbers. The Major Hall should hold between 3,000 and 3,500 people, for instance. This expectation had been downgraded to a capacity of 3,200, and now Utzon announced that he believed he could fit in no more than 2,900 seats, but *he* considered this sufficient. Mick Lewis then took the trouble to silently count the seats on Utzon's sketches and quickly discovered that the architect had room in the hall for even less than 2,900 seats. 'There were about 1,700 [seats],' recalls Lewis. 'And you know he got up in front of the committee and he said, 'I can't give you the 3,200, but this will give you 2,900.' And it was absolutely incorrect. I just goggled at this. I mean, they all had the sketch. They could have done the count, just as I had done, but they didn't do it.'

Lewis kept quiet during the meeting, confronting the architect in private when they both emerged. 'Jørn, I counted the seats. There's 1,700 there,' he said, when they were alone.

'It doesn't matter, Mick,' replied Utzon, with a flourish, 'it doesn't matter how many seats we put in there. It'll be so beautiful everybody will be delighted.'

Unlike many people who came into contact with Jørn Utzon in Sydney, Mick Lewis was not dazzled by the Dane. In fact, the engineer had a low opinion of Jørn's abilities. 'I didn't think Utzon was really much good,' Lewis says bluntly. Still, he believed that they both had a duty to work together to get the job finished. To expedite matters he suggested to Utzon that he now appoint another firm of architects to work under him and produce the detailed drawings which he and his team seemingly couldn't. 'Oh no, that wouldn't work,' the architect replied loftily. 'Le Corbusier tried it . . . Frank Lloyd Wright tried it and it didn't work. Can't do that. I must do everything myself.' Lewis came away shaking his head at such conceit, asking himself: *How do you deal with a person like this?*

So long as the Labour government was in power, Utzon could just about get away with this egocentric behaviour. A Labour premier initiated the Opera House project and Labour intended to carry it to completion, though they were no longer so enamoured of their dashing architect. When Labour lost the 1965 state election, Utzon found himself in an exposed position. The incoming Liberal coalition had been elected partly on a platform of getting to grips with the spiralling cost of the Opera House – a daily scandal in the popular press – and the new Premier appointed a tough character named Davis Hughes from the Country Party (whose constituents were most distrustful of fancy Sydney ways), as Minister for Works, with special responsibility for bringing spending under control. Hughes told Utzon sternly that from now on government money would only be released to him when he reached certain stages in the project. Previously, and somewhat unconventionally, New South Wales had essentially bankrolled Utzon's office. With Hughes' hand on the purse-strings, Utzon began to experience acute cash-flow problems. Meanwhile, relations between Utzon and Ove Arup & Partners deteriorated, with Utzon feeling that Mick Lewis and the other Arup engineers were going behind his back as well as taking credit for what he felt was his work. Utzon was prone to wild talk about resigning if things weren't done his way, which was a wholly unnecessary stance since his status as the architect on the job was enshrined in law – literally – in the Sydney Opera House Act, which the Labour government had passed to ensure their grand project was completed as envisaged. In effect, Utzon could only be sacked by himself, which foolhardily he proceeded to do.

When Hughes insisted on a detailed estimate for the cost of the glass walls, as he was perfectly entitled to do, Utzon failed to provide one, and informed the government in a meeting that unless he was paid some more money immediately he would have to close his office and resign. He reiterated as much in a letter which he sent to Hughes on 15 February 1966. Utzon probably didn't mean to hand in his resignation. Rather he was trying to coerce the government into doing things his way. The letter was clumsily worded, however, and Hughes was happy to interpret it to mean that the bothersome Dane had quit. He lost no time in telling the press as much. UTZON RESIGNS, shouted the *Sydney Morning Herald* on 1 March. Even at this stage, Utzon could have saved himself. There were opportunities for him to come back on the job in a managerial capacity, with exec-utive architects appointed under him to produce the detailed drawings that were essential to get the building finished; this would involve only a modest loss of face. Utzon did meet with the government to discuss a way forward, but he seemed to think that he was negotiating from a position of strength, declaring that they could not finish the job without him. Meanwhile, his young fans – and such a charismatic figure inspired many – launched a campaign to reinstate him, culmi-nating in a public meeting at Sydney Town Hall. This fed Utzon's ego at a time when, as Mick Lewis remarks wisely, 'a grain of humility might have saved the whole situation.' Utzon then retreated into him-self, and perhaps fell into a depression. Revealingly, Utzon's wife pleaded with his supporters, '. . . please do not try to keep Jørn here, he is not a well man.' Colleagues later wondered about Jørn's mental health. He certainly started to behave oddly. When Ove Arup and Jack Zunz flew from Europe to Sydney to try and strike an eleventh-hour compromise with their architect, Utzon refused even to meet them. And four days later Jørn gathered up his family and left Australia. The architect sent Ove Arup a postcard from Hawaii, com-plaining bitterly that the old man – to whom he had been like a son – had failed to understand him and his work, adding with a touch of megalomania 'the Sydney Opera House will be destroyed com-pletely if I am not fully in charge.'

There was no 'if' about it, he wasn't in charge any more. Hughes quickly replaced Utzon with a team of three architects led by an Australian named Peter Hall, to whom fell the almost thankless task of finishing Utzon's half-built Opera House. It emerged from what sketches were left behind that there were a host of problems to deal with, including some that were hitherto unknown: not only was there insufficient space for seating, but the proposed air-conditioning, drainage and power cabling were all inadequate for requirements;

there had not been proper consultation with the Fire Brigade; and ten years into the job nobody knew how to build the glass walls. Hall and his colleagues, David Littlemore and Lionel Todd, had little choice but to treat the concrete platform and shells as a found object and create the interiors from scratch. For staunch supporters of Utzon, such as Peter Myers, the third phase of the build was a disaster. And by accepting the commission Hall and his colleagues betrayed a fellow architect. 'All the architects had to do was say: *Utzon finishes this building and that's it*, and Hughes' hand would have been stayed,' says Myers fiercely. 'But of course they couldn't help themselves, you see. Power corrupts . . . It corrupted Hall so fast. He was not an unintelligent person, Hall, but he ended up an idiot, just being kicked around by Davis Hughes.'

In very recent years, the elderly Jørn Utzon has been persuaded to work with the administrators of the Opera House on a series of renovations and improvements to the building, and as a result the Reception Hall has been extensively remodelled and renamed the Utzon Room in his honour. Other changes are planned. Nevertheless almost everything inside the shells of the Opera House was designed not by Jørn Utzon, but by Peter Hall's team, and for the most part it is the work of the late Peter Hall that we see today when we visit the building. There is both good and bad design in Stage Three. The glazing of the shells was a mammoth and technically difficult task, not least because the shapes to be filled are massive and irregular. The solution is only partly successful, with a particularly awkward-looking detail where the glass bulges out of the sides of the building like the ends of a walrus moustache. When all the glass was finally in place, in 1971, the building was at least weatherproof and the inside could be finished. In the foyers and passageways, wooden screens were, unfortunately, poorly designed, making an awkward connection with the concrete vaults. Plywood *was* used in the Major Hall (concert hall), though not to Utzon's designs and in a way that lacked his panache. Stepping into the Major Hall is like entering an ornate wood-lined box, certainly not unpleasant, but not what one expects considering the brilliant exterior. 'Everybody says the inside is not nearly as dramatic as the outside,' admits Lewis. 'Nobody can make it as dramatic as the outside.'

In truth, the Opera House was finished neither perfectly, quickly nor cheaply. By the time the Queen arrived in Sydney in October 1973, a building originally costed at five million Australian pounds had ballooned to a hundred million Australian dollars (the dollar system having been introduced during the build). Originally intended to accommodate 3,500 concertgoers, the main hall only had seats for 2,679, and many of these were tucked away behind the stage; the Opera Theatre wasn't finished, and was not big enough to be of international standard when it was; there was no provision for parking, insufficient access for disabled patrons, and the organ wouldn't be ready until 1979. Finally, everybody sat down with Her Majesty to listen to an opening performance of Beethoven's Ninth Symphony. Settling in his seat to listen, Mick Lewis reflected on the whole saga, and a truly Scandinavian saga it had been: the technical problems had been immense; Utzon himself had behaved stupidly at times, and in many ways he had let people down, not least Ove Arup who was shattered by the experience. But even Lewis conceded that it took somebody as individual as Jørn to dream up such a fantastic concept in the first place.

When his brilliant competition entry was revealed in the 1950s, Jørn Utzon was hailed as one of the important new figures in world architecture. And his building, as opened in 1973, was a popular triumph. Moreover, it has inspired generations of younger architects to break from the modernistic tyranny of rectilinear design, reintroducing the curve – and thereby the *fun* – to building. Frank Gehry, for instance, has acknowledged the debt owed by his multi-faceted Guggenheim Museum in Bilbao to the Opera House, and one can see the similarities between these two delightfully curvaceous structures. However, Utzon himself built relatively little after Sydney, his reputation having been both made and broken by a sublime but notoriously troublesome project. Over the next few decades he designed a bank in Tehran, a church in Denmark, an assembly building for Kuwait and a house for himself on a cliff on the island of Majorca. Not very much. As younger men such as Richard Meier, Renzo Piano and Richard Rogers emerged as the leading figures in architecture in the 1970s, designing many buildings of world renown, less and less was heard from the genius behind what may be the most beautiful structure of the twentieth century. In fact, Utzon largely withdrew from society, abjuring his magic like Prospero to live as an ageing hermit in his island home on Majorca, becoming so inconspicuous there that one might be forgiven for not knowing whether he was dead or alive – until 1999 that is, when the by then octogenarian architect agreed, surprisingly, to assist with renovations to the Opera House. Still, he kept his distance, communicating his ideas to colleagues in Sydney by telephone and fax, declining all offers to come back to Australia in person, and it is unlikely now that Jørn will ever return to see his great building. He says he is too frail to make the journey and friends believe he is too hurt by what happened to him all those years ago. As a result, the architect has never seen his completed masterpiece and probably never will.

'It's very tragic,' comments Peter Myers, of the fate of his erstwhile boss. 'One of the reasons that Jørn lives as a recluse is because he is not unaware of how tragic it is himself.' Jack Zunz, who *thought* he got to know Utzon well during the long years of the Opera House project, travelling frequently with him, even having fun at times, now says that he has come to realise that he never fathomed the man. 'He's seemingly outgoing, *very* engaging . . . But then the curtain came down. And he became very reclusive,' remarks Zunz thoughtfully, pondering Utzon's complex character. 'I think he probably suffers from depression . . . In hindsight there were one or two signs I should have recognised.' Certainly, Jørn Utzon was never an ordinary or easy man. Like so many of the great figures in the arts in the 1970s he was fiercely individualistic, egocentric and uncompromising. But it is such people who make history.

14

EXILE

Go away! You are worse than the KGB!

ALEXANDER SOLZHENITSYN

F ar away to the north the writer Alexander Solzhenitsyn, another complex and wilful genius of the age, was entering the most per-ilous stage of his career. After being awarded the Nobel Prize for Literature in 1970, the novelist had remained in the Soviet Union, working clandestinely on the last and most important books of his his-tory of the prison camps: that great project he planned while a zek in Stalin's gulags. These volumes were now starting to come to comple-tion. In the summer of 1971, *August 1914* was published in the West, the book in which Solzhenitsyn showed how Russia's ill-fated clash with Germany in the early stages of the Great War ushered in the Communist era, with the author making clear for the first time his abhorrence of Marxism. In response to this heresy, the leaders of the Soviet Union and their KGB henchmen became so concerned about what they were now calling the 'Solzhenitsyn problem' that, it seems, an attempt was made to have him assassinated.

A bizarre Cold War operation code-named 'spider' went into effect on 8 August 1971, when Solzhenitsyn was visiting the town of Novocherkassk for research. According to one former KGB man, whose story was published in the 1990s, a number of secret police fol-lowed the author into a local shop where they appeared to inject him surreptitiously with poison, probably ricin, which the KGB favoured as a method of bumping off its victims at this time. The poison would have been expected to induce a heart attack. Solzhenitsyn was not aware of what was happening, but quickly became seriously ill and had to curtail his work in Novocherkassk, taking the train to Moscow where he arrived in a state of intense pain, his body covered with blisters. He was taken to the home of the Rostropoviches, where friends and doctors gathered around to see what could be done for the writer, and though the medical advice was for Solzhenitsyn to go to hospital, he preferred to suffer in the privacy of Slava's dacha. Although he did not die, he was laid low for months.

Solzhenitsyn had a home of his own, a flat on Gorky Street in Moscow, where he kept the curtains closed so that the KGB could not spy on him through the windows. Once recovered from his mysterious illness, the author returned to this dingy apartment and resumed work on *The Gulag Archipelago*, as well as his memoir, *The Oak and the Calf*, both of which were written furtively in instalments that were then copied and smuggled out to the West with the help of a network of supporters. If the writing was perilous, the secret copying and dissemination was no less so – as was demonstrated by the fate of 67-year-old Elizaveta Voronyanskaya, one of Sanya's volunteer typists. Like all Solzhenitsyn's friends and helpers, Voronyanskaya took great pride in the part she played in his work, and though he did not give her permission to do so, she kept copies of the pages she typed for the author, hiding one set in her attic, and burying another at the home of a friend. They were her secret treasure, and possibly she felt she was doing Solzhenitsyn a service by preserving duplicates. Unfortunately, Voronyanskaya was betrayed to the KGB, who raided her home in August 1973 and, under interrogation, elicited from her the secret of her hiding places. In her shame, she then apparently hanged herself. *Apparently*, because Solzhenitsyn asserted in *The Oak and the Calf* that it was murder. There was blood on her body, he reported, which did not fit with the official cause of death. Also, suspiciously, her family were not permitted to see the corpse.

Almost as curious at the death of Voronyanskaya was Solzhenitsyn's reaction to it. Primarily, he was mortified at the loss of his work, stating that Voronyanskaya had no right to keep copies of his pages,

writing angrily in *The Oak and the Calf* that, 'it was only this deception of hers that enabled the KGB to seize the book.' He asserted that
the loss of the manuscript was an unparalleled calamity in *his* life –
'The disaster seemed bottomless, irreparable' – which seems an over-
statement considering what he had previously been through, not to
mention the terrible fate of Voronyanskaya herself. But Solzhenitsyn
had a weakness for hyperbole, and no doubt his nerves had been
rubbed raw by the long years of secret industry, and the constant
stress of possible arrest. In the wake of the Voronyanskaya tragedy,
Solzhenitsyn made a pact with his second wife, the young mathematician Alya Svetlova, who had given him three sons in the past three
years. They would work together to finish and publish *The Gulag
Archipelago* and his remaining books in the West as soon as possible, no
matter what happened to them or the people around them, finishing
the task even if – they contemplated the very worst scenario – the
KGB took their children from them. '[We] made a superhuman decision,' the author wrote, 'our children were no dearer to us than the
memory of the millions done to death.' It is because of statements
such as this that one wonders at the state of Solzhenitsyn's mind as his
life's work reached its climax. To believe so fiercely in the rightness of
a course of action teeters on fanaticism.

It was at this time that Solzhenitsyn had a dramatic meeting with
his first wife, Natalya, with whom he had a delicate and melancholy
relationship, knowing that she had betrayed him to the KGB in the
past; he even suspected it was she who led the police to Elizaveta
Voronyanskaya, yet wanted to stay in touch with her if only to try and
prevent her causing further damage. Inevitably, Natalya still had
ammunition with which to do him harm: the innumerable shared
secrets of a married couple. To make matters more complex, she had
never got over her feelings for Sanya and was bitter about the fact that,
having told her for years he didn't want a family and thereby denying
her motherhood, he had now become a father thrice over with
another woman. Meeting at Kazan train station on 24 September
1973, as KGB functionaries watched and took photographs of them,
Natalya spoke to Sanya as a hard-faced emissary of the secret police (as
he later characterised her), urging him not to publish any more books

for twenty years. Solzhenitsyn jotted down a contemporaneous note of the discussion, which he reproduced in *The Oak and the Calf*: 'In general, if you just keep quiet a bit, it will be *better for everybody*,' he recalled his ex-wife as saying to him.

'Yes, but I'm not the aggressor; *they* are forcing me into it . . .'

'You're a fanatic,' she shot back, 'you have no thought for your own children.'

This accusation was hurled at Solzhenitsyn by an unhappy woman who had been deceived, and was now herself steeped in deceit. (Secretly, Natalya had become involved with a KGB man, whom she married in 1974, a fact she kept dark until the end of her life when she defended herself pitifully: 'I was never a KGB agent, I swear it!') Natalya had fallen low, but she was right; Solzhenitsyn *was* fanatical about his task. 'Who did kill sixty million people?' he demanded of Natalya on the train platform, with characteristic intensity, raising yet again the injustice that burned in his mind like religion. It was the ghosts of the dead, some he had known personally, the other millions extrapolated from what he had found out by research, that drove him on: their memory and, yes, God Himself, whom Solzhenitsyn believed was guiding his work.

Shortly after the meeting with his ex-wife, the first volume of *The Gulag Archipelago* (one of a trilogy) was published in Russian in the West. This was part one of the complete story of the gulags, stretching back to the Great War, based on Solzhenitsyn's experiences, plus those of 277 witnesses who had shared their knowledge with him. The title of the book referred metaphorically to the way the prison camps existed as a chain of islands in the sea of the Soviet empire. Although non-fiction, the book is written in the same brisk style as Solzhenitsyn's novels, a style born out of necessity, as he wrote: 'The jerkiness of the book, its imperfections, are the true mark of our persecuted literature. Take the book for what it is.' The style also came from a feverish conviction that he *must* impart these stories: 'I am writing this book solely from a sense of obligation – because too many stories and recollections have accumulated in my hands and I can not allow them to perish.' The killing of sixty million wasn't done with gas in factory conditions as with the Nazis, he wrote in the book, but mostly by working zeks to death on building projects carried out in barbaric conditions. Furthermore, Solzhenitsyn argued that the system had not been dismantled with Stalin's death in 1953, but had continued, quietly, under Nikita Khrushchev. So it was that in *The Gulag Archipelago* the author accused the state of a crime which, if true, was numerically the greatest in history.

The Politburo had long been exasperated by Solzhenitsyn. At a meeting in April 1972, Premier Brezhnev voiced the frustration of the power elite when he was recorded as saying, darkly: 'Solzhenitsyn is becoming more impudent. We should take the most resolute steps to deal with him.' It seems they had already tried and failed to murder him. Now, as he committed the greatest outrage of his literary career (by their lights), they took another tack. In February 1974, the author was ordered to appear at the Public Prosecutor's office in Moscow. Solzhenitsyn refused, questioning by reply the legality of the whole Soviet system. Simultaneously, he alerted the BBC and the *New York Times* to a sinister development in his case, and talked with his wife about what he would do if arrested. At the age of fifty-five, Sanya doubted he could survive more than two years in the camps. Nevertheless, he found himself preparing for arrest, putting together a kit of clothes and simple items he knew would be useful in custody. The following afternoon – 12 February 1974 – eight men burst into the Gorky Street apartment. 'So that's your game!' exclaimed the writer, surprised despite expectation by the sudden rush of men into his hall, with police packing the cramped apartment like commuters on a bus. Kissing Alya goodbye, not knowing whether he would see her again, Solzhenitsyn put on his old sheepskin coat and fur hat, picked up his prison kit, and allowed himself to be taken downstairs and driven through the snowy streets of Moscow to Lefortovo Maximum Security Prison where he was charged with treason. Potentially, it meant fifteen years in prison. He might even be executed.

Locked in a cell with two other men, Solzhenitsyn noticed that he was not being treated as harshly as in the past. The food was basic, but palatable. Out of habit he put aside a hunk of prison bread in case they tried to starve him later. But this began to seem unnecessary. Rather than treating him brutally, his jailers took a benevolent interest in his wellbeing, becoming concerned when a medical examination revealed that the author suffered (unsurprisingly) from high blood pressure. Then, before too many hours had passed, he was hauled before an official and told that he was to be stripped of his citizenship and expelled from the USSR as a traitor. Shocked and confused, the author thought first of his wife and children. 'I can only go with my family,' he protested.

'Your family will follow you.'

And so he was bundled into a car and driven to the airport. In all his life, Solzhenitsyn had only left the Soviet Union once – with the Red Army advancing into Germany during the Second World War – and he had never flown. A scheduled commercial plane was waiting for him at Moscow airport, the passengers having taken their seats three hours earlier. Finally, Solzhenitsyn was escorted aboard by seven KGB men and a doctor. The doors closed and they took off. So it was that with a lump of black prison bread bulging in the pocket of his shabby coat, Solzhenitsyn found himself lifted out of the grey world of the Soviet Union to a dazzling altitude – new to him, of course – where the sun shines without interruption during the day like a vision of Heaven. Wondering at this glory, Sanya envisaged himself as a character in a folk story, but also began to fear that the KGB might be taking him abroad in order to murder him. Before he could brood on this unhappy thought, the plane came down to land at Frankfurt (he had not known what country he was going to). When the jet had taxied to a stop, Solzhenitsyn was ordered roughly to put on his hat and coat and then taken to the door where, to his astonishment, one of the KGB thrust some Deutschmarks into his hand so he would not arrive penniless in what was then West Germany. The USSR wanted the world to see that, though they had expelled their most famous living writer, Solzhenitsyn left them in good health, even with money. Then he was urged to go. Walking down the steps, Sanya could not help but glance back to verify that the KGB were no longer pressing around him. He was indeed alone, the other passengers being held back while he was welcomed with a diplomatic hug by a representative of the Federal government, and presented with a bouquet of daffodils.

Shown to a police car, the author was then chauffeured on to the autobahn, bound for the country home of the Nobel laureate Heinrich Böll, who was to be his host in these initial days of freedom. As with anybody who crossed from East to West during the Cold War, and for Solzhenitsyn in particular who had not been outside the USSR since the Second World War, the cultural and technological contrast was dramatic and astonishing. Having emerged from a drab, grey land, he was driven past a succession of brilliantly-lit service stations and inviting-looking restaurants, all colourful and exuberant in their advertising, totally different from the world he had left behind. All around him on the immaculate highway West German citizens powered their expensively sleek Mercedes, Audis and VW automobiles to their various destinations, seemingly oblivious to their comfort. The wheels of the cars created an alternating Moog-like hum on the tarmac (the sound of wealth, as well as the sound of the new German band Kraftwerk and their song 'Autobahn'.) The prosperity and quality of life (at least what he could see of it) was impressive. Yet Solzhenitsyn was not seduced by the West.

In the morning, Solzhenitsyn awoke to find that the press had gathered outside Böll's house in the eager expectation of pictures and interviews. He was advised that they would not go away until he went out to them. The Western press worked differently from the journalists of the USSR, he was told: they were constantly, impertinently inquisitive and demanding like children. Emerging in his shirt sleeves, Solzhenitsyn posed grumpily and briefly for the excitable photographers before telling the reporters curtly that, no, he would not give them an interview. 'I will not answer a single question. I will not give a single interview. I have said enough in Moscow,' he snapped. Like Jørn Utzon, Alexander Isayevich apparently wanted to be alone. And when the press pursued him to Zurich a little later, he became very ratty indeed. 'Go away!' he snarled, adding with unintentional comedy: 'You are worse than the KGB!'

No doubt, Solzhenitsyn's refusal to speak to the press at this time was partly because he was mindful of his wife and children held behind in Moscow (though they followed him into exile soon). Nevertheless, Solzhenitsyn's brusque encounters with reporters set the tone for the next twenty years he lived in exile. Other cultural superstars who left the Soviet Union around this time tended to ingratiate themselves with their host nations, appearing immensely grateful for their new lives. The 26-year-old ballet star Mikhail Baryshnikov, who literally ran for freedom while on tour in Toronto in June 1974, went so far as to become a Hollywood actor with all the *schmoozing* that entails. Solzhenitsyn's great friend, Rostropovich, who also left the USSR in 1974, became a busy and popular figure in exile in the West. Unlike a dancer or musician, an author does not have to appear in public, of course. The work lends itself to the insular personality. Even so, rather than embracing the West, Solzhenitsyn became a near recluse during his exile. Wealthy, thanks to the considerable sales of his works and his Nobel Prize, which he collected belatedly in December 1974, he retreated with his wife and three sons to an estate near Cavendish, Vermont, to live as closely as possible to a traditional Russian life, speaking Russian and practising the Russian Orthodox faith. Curiously, for a man defined by his experience in prison camps, he chose to enclose his US property with a barbed wire fence, which was only one of the ways in which he offended his American hosts. In his rare public appearances, he made it plain that he considered the West pampered and weak, abhorring its popular culture, and while he was anti-Communist, it became evident that he was no democrat, describing democracy as 'the surrogate faith of intellectuals deprived of religion.' Moving into old age, Solzhenitsyn was increasingly perceived, especially in the USA, as a cantankerous and ungrateful old man (though who among his critics had lived such a life?), and fewer readers were willing to tackle his books. The first volume of *The Gulag Archipelago* was a great bestseller when it was published in translation in 1974 – two million copies sold in the USA alone put the book alongside such contemporary blockbusters as *All the President's Men* (1974) and *Watership Down* (1972) – but subsequent volumes and other books received diminishing attention. Lengthy and severe in tone, they were not an easy read, and then came questions about how good the history was.

After the disintegration of the Soviet empire in the late 1980s, academics gained access to official archives and thereby discovered that

Solzhenitsyn's totemic figure of sixty million dead was very wide of the truth. 'Solzhenitsyn's numbers are a wild exaggeration,' states Professor Ronald Grigor Suny of the University of Chicago, a leading historian on the Soviet period. Other experts agree. Professor Stephen G. Wheatcroft of the University of Melbourne elaborates: 'We now have detailed evidence from a whole network of archives that the maximum number of prisoners in the Gulag was 1.7 million in 1953,★ and that mortality levels were normally well below ten percent.' Adding together inmates of normal prisons, prisoners of war and those sent into exile, and multiplying this figure by the number of years from the 1917 Revolution to Stalin's death, Wheatcroft arrives at a figure for the *maximum possible* death total in the Soviet penal system in the Stalin era. It is approximately 38 million. He adds a very important caveat: 'In reality I think that the correct figure would be less than a tenth of this.' The true number of people who died in the gulags is therefore probably considerably less than the victims of the Holocaust, and to compare the two is problematic for other reasons. '[It] is wrong to take the Gulag to be the symbol of the worst aspects of Stalinist repression and to equate it with Auschwitz,' argues Professor Wheatcroft. 'The Gulag was not an extermination camp, even though Solzhenitsyn has argued powerfully on both these cases. Solzhenitsyn was making a powerful political case on the basis of the evidence that he had before him, and he described his work as a lit-erary exploration rather than a history. His style was blatantly and brilliantly provocative . . . I have no objection to that. The only mate-rials available to him at the time were survivor reminiscences, including of course those of his own. Furthermore the state was not just refusing to acknowledge the scale of repression, but was con-sciously disseminating false information.'

That Solzhenitsyn got his figures wrong does slightly lessen the impact of his books, though he never claimed to be using anything other than anecdotal evidence. Combined with the fact that the Soviet Union crumbled sooner than anybody might have guessed (though, again, Solzhenitsyn predicted it wouldn't last), his books are inevitably

★The year Stalin died.

less relevant today than in the 1970s, when they offered fascinating insight into a closed world. But as accounts of the human spirit in adversity, his books remain monumental and timeless works of literature. If Solzhenitsyn had published only *One Day in the Life of Ivan Denisovich*, his place in history would be assured. Although sixty million dead was an exaggeration, the important point is that the *spirit* of what he wrote in his subsequent books was true, and the specific details of his personal ordeal are unimpeachable. As such, his books shamed the Soviet Union in the 1970s, when the USSR deserved to be exposed for what it was, and just as importantly the books remind us today of the nightmare society that existed behind the Iron Curtain (once so solid, now almost forgotten) in very recent history. In writing and publishing in the way he did Solzhenitsyn also showed outstanding personal courage. There are few more inspiring stories in the literature of the twentieth century.

Both raised without a father by a strong and devoted mother, intensely serious from a young age and, in adult life, becoming a religious zealot: there are remarkable similarities between the life of Alexander Solzhenitsyn and that of Bob Marley, the Jamaican musician who brought reggae music to the world at the same time that the Russian writer was cast into exile. That is precisely where Marley believed he was, too: a soul in exile, in *Babylon*, as he would say.

The story of popular music in the 1970s is so dominated by American and British artists that it is refreshing to turn to an example of a major figure from a totally different culture, from the Third World indeed. Bob Marley was born in Jamaica in 1945, when the island was still a British colony. His mother was a poor rural teenager, his father a white plantation overseer who took no part in his upbringing. Like Solzhenitsyn, and indeed Jack Nicholson, Bob didn't appear to suffer from not having a father figure in his life, but rather flourished under exclusively maternal care. When he was still a boy, Bob and his mother moved from their country home to Trench Town, a ghetto of Kingston, capital of Jamaica, where Marley became immersed in the local music scene, forming a close-harmony group with two other boys, Bunny Livingstone and Peter McIntosh (later known as Bunny Wailer and Pete Tosh). The trio became the Wailers, so-named as Marley later claimed because they were bewailing the fate of an exiled Rasta people (though he did not come to hold Rastafarian ideas until much later). The music they made and listened to was *ska* (its onomatopoeic name invoking a guitar sound), a melding of calypso and other Caribbean music with American rhythm and blues. By the late 1960s, the Wailers were one of a number of local groups who developed a hybrid form of ska that had more emphasis in the back beat, usually with heavy bass and drum. The Wailers weren't the first group to make and release 'rock steady' or reggae records (Toots and the Maytals beat them to it in 1968 with 'Do the Reggay' [*sic*]) but they brought this music to an international audience and helped overcome its initial novelty-song image.

Like all performers who enjoy great success, there was a felicitous coming together of factors in Bob's career. Firstly, he had a profound sense from an early age of knowing that his destiny was in music. 'There is something in me, and when I am singing with everything in me I feel it,' he wrote to his mother as a young man. As he grew up he became a very intense character who said little and noticed much, a man who commanded attention and ultimately respect, a natural band leader and somebody who mesmerised audiences. Women in particular always found him attractive. In his short life, which ended at the age of thirty-six in 1981, Bob fathered eleven children by eight women, including Rita Marley, whom he married in 1966, the year that Haile Selassie came to Jamaica.

Bob and Rita were both already young devotees of Rastafarianism, the cult religion built around the African leader Haile Selassie, which is in itself another reason for Bob Marley's great success in the 1970s. It is a truly weird belief system, but one founded in circumstances of injustice: essentially the feeling that black citizens of the European colonies were a dispossessed people, treated as second-class even after the abolition of slavery. In the early years of the twentieth century, a black Jamaican named Marcus Garvey lectured his people about being part of an international black brotherhood whose ancestral roots were in Africa, specifically in the land now known as Ethiopia, adding that one day a black king would come and gather them all together again in Africa, giving them back their pride. Then, in 1930 a 38-year-old black man named Ras Tafari Makonnen was instated as Emperor of Abyssinia (as Ethiopia then was). As such, Ras Tafari was renamed Emperor Haile Selassie, also known as the Conquering Lion of the Tribe of Judah, among other high-flown appellations. For many Caribbean blacks, here was the fulfilment of Garvey's prophecy: the coronation of a black African king who would 'deliver us from our situation as a colonised people,' as Rita Marley says. And so the cult of Rastafarianism was born, the name of the religion derived from the Emperor's original name.

Taking Selassie as their God, Rastas constructed an eccentric religion around the new Abyssinian king, one based on scripture mixed in with Caribbean custom and a good deal of chauvinism. It is ironic that in the decade of feminism, one of the fastest-growing religions in the world confined women to the role of wife and mother. Rasta women may not wear make-up or use birth control, and the menfolk make all the major decisions. Aside from this primitive division of the sexes, various types of food are forbidden, as is alcohol. However, smoking marijuana – a popular pastime in the islands – is almost mandatory. From their own eccentric interpretation of the eighth verse of Psalm 18 in the Old Testament – 'There went up a smoke out of his nostrils, and fire out of his mouth . . .' – Rastas deduced that God Himself smoked ganja, and thus it was right and proper for them to smoke the herb, too. In fact, getting high had a spiritual dimension. 'When you smoke herb,' Bob Marley would say, 'herb reveal yourself to you.' Apart from these customs, Rastafarianism also has its own vocabulary. It is a Biblical language mixed with Jamaican patois. Thus 'Jehovah' becomes 'Jah,' or God, and Babylon is a general term for the purgatory Rastas are living in before the return to Ethiopia, where everything will be 'irie,' or perfect. One of the most obvious manifestations of this faith is that Rasta men do not cut their hair, but train it into matted plaits or dreadlocks, which tend to become fusty with the smell of ganja.

When Haile Selassie made his one and only visit to Jamaica in 1966, he was evidently astounded by the reception he received. Despite heavy rain, one hundred thousand ecstatic Rastas gathered to welcome him at Kingston airport: trembling, praying, wailing and holding up signs such as 'Behold the Lamb of God'. So unnerved was the Emperor (whose views on being worshipped as a God in Jamaica were never entirely clear, though it must have been disconcerting for him to say the least) that he turned and hid in his aircraft until he was assured the worshipping crowd was under control. Coaxed from the plane into a car, his motorcade then swept out of the airport past throngs of sodden but jubilant Jamaicans, including Rita Marley who locked eyes with Selassie momentarily, fancying that she saw stigmata on his raised hand. Although she and Bob were recently married, Bob was in the USA visiting his mother, so he missed out on this rare opportunity to witness God on Earth. For Rita it was an almost over-powering experience. 'I yelled, "Oh my God" and went home screaming and cheering,' recalls Rita in her memoirs. 'And Aunty said, "Lord have mercy, there she goes! Now she's truly mad!" It had been raining and I was soaked, but I didn't care . . .' Rita wrote to Bob with a fulsome account of this holy experience and thereafter the Marleys became ever more involved in the Rasta cult, with Bob making it part and parcel of his musical persona. In the 1970s, a pic-ture of Haile Selassie would hang behind the Wailers on stage, with the Lion of Judah being used as a logo for the band, while the lan-guage and credo of the Rasta cult became integral to their songs. Bob also referred to his faith constantly in interviews, which read some-thing like Rasta sermons. 'War and peace, right and wrong. Heaven and Hell. You know, people are get ready to go to Mount Zion,' he told *Rolling Stone* typically in 1975, speaking in the Jamaican patois that most Westerners found only semi-coherent, but which was nev-ertheless intriguing and indeed poetic. As was Marley's religion, which at root is as nonsensical as any other if not more so, but by virtue of its exoticism, language and drug culture, Rastafarianism was intriguing and attractive to many young (mostly male) music fans in the '70s. In fact, Rastafarianism served to lend Marley's songs a special mystery and weight, while Marley himself came to be seen by believers as a Rasta prophet.

At the start of the decade, however, Marley was virtually unknown outside Jamaica – or only known at all inasmuch as he was one member of the Wailers, who were struggling to expand their career beyond the Caribbean. Several forays were made into the wider world, not all of them successful. In 1972 the Wailers found themselves in London, virtually broke, and so turned to record label boss Chris Blackwell for help. A wealthy Anglo-Jamaican whose family fortune was based in sugar plantations and the Crosse & Blackwell food company, Blackwell was a suave, Harrow-educated entrepreneur who had built up a record company named Island on the success of rock bands such as Jethro Tull. Recently, Island had also signed Roxy Music. With close personal ties to Jamaica, Blackwell knew reggae music well and had long seen its potential for crossing over into mainstream album charts, if only the right act could be found. Island had distributed Wailers' records in the UK in the past but Blackwell had never met the band, and now here came Bob, Bunny and Peter trooping into his office, in dire need of his financial help but retaining their dignity. Chris was impressed by how self-possessed they were considering their situation. Also, they were obviously very bright people, with Pete displaying a particularly sharp wit. Bob was the easiest to get along with, though, and the most charismatic. Like that other famous musical Bob, he was a close-mouthed watchful little man, wiry of build with intense eyes. The Wailers needed money in a hurry, they explained, in order to get home. But more than that they were looking for a record company to help them break into the American market in the long term. They told Chris Blackwell their ambition was to have a single in the R&B charts, competing with mainstream American black artists. Blackwell considered this a misconceived plan. 'I felt there was never a chance of them getting a single in the R&B charts, because at that time black America couldn't have been less interested in anything coming from Jamaica,' he says. 'However, I felt that Bob could be a rock star. Because, remember, Hendrix had been around a couple of years before. I felt that one could make [Bob] a rock star, in a sense, initially referencing Hendrix.' Blackwell decided that the way to win the trust of the Wailers was to advance them the money to fly back to Jamaica and record an album for Island. How much did they need? The answer was four grand. So he gave them a cheque for that amount and waved them goodbye, wondering whether he would ever see them again. Indeed, colleagues at Island told Chris that he was mad to trust these rude boys.

In fact, the Wailers seized this opportunity to prove themselves to be a professional and disciplined musical unit. Returning to Kingston, the band went directly into Dynamic Sounds and worked quickly to record an album-worth of original songs, such as 'Stir it Up' and 'Concrete Jungle', which described life in the ghetto. The music as originally laid down was, as Bunny says, 'a hard driving rhythm that suggests the basic reggae principles.' At the end of the year, Bob brought the master tapes to Britain for Chris Blackwell to remix. Though Chris loved the Wailers' 'hard-driving rhythm,' to break the Wailers as a rock band he decided the songs had to have a more commercial sound, and so he hired two American session musicians, John 'Rabbit' Bundrick on keyboards and guitarist Wayne Perkins, to over-dub rock 'n' roll licks on the songs. As a result the album *Catch a Fire* (1973) is reggae sweetened for a white audience. Marley didn't mind. In fact, he was delighted with the result, describing Chris Blackwell as his *translator*, rather than his record producer – the man who had helped him speak to the world.

The Wailers toured extensively supporting their first album, sharing a bill with a young Bruce Springsteen in New York, and upstaging Sly Stone so comprehensively at a concert in Las Vegas that he fired them from his tour. But Island shipped only 14,000 copies of *Catch a Fire* in the first year. 'It was a very hard sell,' as Blackwell says. Still, he kept faith, and a second Island LP, *Burnin'*, was released later in 1973. This was more authentic reggae, featuring such songs as 'Get up, Stand up' and 'Burnin' and Lootin' that referred to the unhappy political situation in Jamaica. It sold better than *Catch a Fire* and, very significantly, Eric Clapton chose to cover one of the *Burnin'* songs for his excellent new album, *461 Ocean Boulevard*. Clapton's version of 'I Shot the Sheriff' became a top ten hit in both Britain and the USA in the summer of 1974, which for Chris Blackwell was one of the key factors in making Bob Marley a superstar. 'Because Eric Clapton at that time was god,' as Blackwell says. 'He was virtually worshipped, and the fact that Eric Clapton had gone to Bob Marley for material suddenly put the focus on Bob Marley.' Other artists followed Clapton's lead, seeking out Marley and making reggae music part of their repertoire. In 1974, Stevie Wonder created the infectious 'Boogie on Reggae Woman' for his album *Fulfillingness' First Finale* (the fat *burrump* sound made using a new Moog synthesizer). And in 1975 Stevie came down to Jamaica to perform a concert with Bob, jamming together on songs including 'Boogie On' and 'I Shot the Sheriff.'

Peter Tosh and Bunny Livingstone had quit the Wailers by this time. Bunny had been a problem from the start, by Chris Blackwell's estimation, because he didn't like to fly so couldn't leave Jamaica to tour, while Blackwell found Pete, though clever and witty, to be unreliable and uncompromising to the point of being impossible to work with. Bunny and Pete were also jealous that Bob was receiving the lion's share of Blackwell's attention, being presented increasingly as the star of a band which they had created as three equal partners. Now all that had changed. In future, Bob Marley and the Wailers would mean Bob himself and anybody hired to play with him. To add an extra dimension to the new Wailers' show, Bob's wife Rita formed a group of backing vocalists with two other women, calling themselves the I-Threes. This was the line-up with which Bob Marley proceeded to conquer the world, his success as a live act and recording artist confounding those who predicted that reggae would never break through in the West. After all, here was an intensely foreign act, introduced each night as coming 'all the way from Trench Town, Jamaica.' The Wailers' stage was draped with images of Haile Selassie and the Lion of Judah, ganja was thick in the air as the band performed, and the musicians looked and sounded like no rock band working in Britain or the USA. But the music was powerful and Marley himself was fascinating to watch. The insistent rhythm of bass and drum, in counterpoint with the exquisite harmonies of the I-Threes and impassioned lead vocals from a man who, at the centre of it all, was on a mission from Jah, eyes shut tight in concentration, his small body convulsed with the spirit of his message, rarely failed to rock a concert hall. As he enunciated short bursts of ghetto patois about the Exodus of his people, of crime and punishment, death and rebirth, Marley occasionally broke into an insistent jogging-on-the-spot dance as if he were possessed. Strange but mighty entertainment.

Over two hot, sticky evenings in July 1975, Bob Marley and the Wailers gave two of their most outstanding concerts at the Lyceum theatre in London's West End, shows that were recorded and released as one of the essential live albums of the decade and named simply *Bob Marley and the Wailers Live!* The capacity audience was fired up with enthusiasm for the concerts, and Bob and his musicians felt inspired to excel. The performance of the ghetto lament 'No Woman, No Cry' is one of the great moments in '70s music, touching the sublime when the band changes tempo for the cantering bridge and Bob, backed by Rita and the other singers – all eyes on the little man hopping about with the spirit – call out repeatedly that *everything is going to be alright*. If the Lyceum hadn't had a panel in the roof that opened to the sky, allowing the ganja to funnel up and away over the city, the London crowd would have lifted the roof off with its lion roar.

15

GOOD GRIEF!

Watergate! Watergate! . . . What is this senseless orgy of recrimination week after week?

DOONESBURY

In contrast to the likes of a music star such as Bob Marley, who was worshipped like a god in his lifetime, the comic-strip artist plies his trade with little if any public recognition, let alone adulation. His drawings are regarded for the most part as being as disposable as the newspapers they appear in. The cartoonist's name, if known at all, is little more than a tag to the title of his creation – *Peanuts* by Schulz, *Doonesbury* by G.B. Trudeau. Yet this work can be fascinating, and the two aforementioned artists were among the most successful exponents of the trade in the twentieth century, coming head-to-head in the mid-1970s.

By the start of the decade, Charles M. Schulz was well-established as the king of strip cartooning, *Peanuts* having been a popular feature of American newspapers since the 1950s. Most unusually for the genre, Schulz's cartoon characters – notably Charlie Brown, his pet dog Snoopy, their neighbour Lucy Van Pelt and her kid brother Linus – had found favour with generations of readers, also becoming a truly international phenomenon in the 1970s. The longevity of the strip and its worldwide appeal are especially remarkable considering how deep-rooted the strip was in Schulz's narrowly defined life as a Midwestern American. Born in 1922, Charles Monroe Schulz,

Sparky to his friends, was the only child of an unassuming couple named Carl and Dena Schulz. Carl was a barber by trade and the family lived in St Paul, Minnesota. Father and son shared a love of cartoons, which Schulz started to draw at a young age, using the family's lively pet dog, a black and white mongrel named Spike, as a model for an early canine character. The family's quiet but happy life was shattered in 1943, when Schulz's mother died of cancer and Charles was almost simultaneously drafted into the army. Although he didn't see combat, the three years Sparky spent in the service during and just after the Second World War were immensely traumatic for an unworldly, innocent and clean-living young man. The strongest language Sparky used were quaint phrases such as 'good grief' or 'rats,' and he didn't smoke or drink. Apart from which, he was a very gentle sort of person, easily hurt. 'He was ultra-sensitive [and was] thrown in with a lot of people who smoked and cursed,' says his second wife and widow, Jean Schulz, of Sparky's war. 'So it was a very difficult experience.'

When he returned home to St Paul after the war, Schulz took a job at a correspondence art school, marking artwork submitted by students. In his free time, he taught Sunday School and created gag cartoons, featuring child characters, one of whom had a dog like his old pet Spike. In 1947, Schulz's drawings began to run weekly in St Paul's *Pioneer Press*, under the heading *Li'l Folks*. Three years later a New York syndication agency expressed interest in Schulz's cartoons, though he was told that *Li'l Folks* was not an acceptable name, being too similar to the already nationally popular strip *Li'l Abner*. Instead, it was suggested that Schulz should put his characters into a strip cartoon and call it *Peanuts* because it was about little kids, and the strip would be very small on the page. Schulz always disliked this title, believing that it diminished his characters. Nevertheless, he was now in a position to launch a career as a professional cartoonist, and with the swelling of his fortunes he found the courage to ask a pretty red-haired girl he had recently started dating to be his wife. Her name was Donna Mae Johnson and she was a student of Sparky's correspondence school. Although Schulz had reached the relatively mature age of twenty-seven this was the first serious romantic relationship of his life, and when Donna Mae rejected his offer of marriage it was truly the shock of his life. 'I can think of no more emotionally damaging loss than to be turned down by someone whom you love very much,' said Schulz, whose misery was doubled when Donna quickly married a rival suitor. 'A person who not only turns you down, but almost immediately will marry the victor. What a bitter blow that is. It is a blow to everything you are. Your appearance. Your personality.' Schulz found an expression for this profound and enduring sense of personal failure in *Peanuts*, specifically in the character of Charlie Brown.

The full title of Schulz's strip, only given in the larger Sunday panels, was *Peanuts Featuring Good ol' Charlie Brown*, indicating who in Schulz's mind was his star character. Charlie Brown is a round-faced kid who is neither personable, popular or successful nor possessed of any particular talent. Other *Peanuts* characters have some skill or charm: Schroeder plays his toy piano like a prodigy; Lucy is smart, if crabby; Linus is loveable. Charlie Brown's defining characteristic is that he's a loser, a little boy defeated and humiliated at every turn. One of his torments is that he harbours an unrequited crush on a little, red-haired girl, a story Schulz took directly from his own life. Failure in love, and other slights and embarrassments cause Charlie Brown's face to crumple, and his cartoon mouth to balloon into a wail of despair. 'The initial theme of *Peanuts* was based on the cruelty that exists among children,' Schulz reflected in the mid-1970s. 'I recall all too vividly the struggle that takes place out on the playground.'

Although the children in *Peanuts* could behave horribly to one another, the world they inhabited was (or should one say *is*, as old strips continue to be recycled in newspapers years after Schulz's death in 2000) a cosy place to escape into for a few seconds each day. Aside from the fact that there are no visible adults in the strip, no reminders of the workaday world at all in fact, *Peanutsville*, USA, looks like an ideal place to live. It is very clean and totally unblighted by crime, traffic, graffiti or litter. The characters inhabit comfortable detached homes, surrounded by large yards and picket fences. In summer, the children play Little League baseball. When autumn leaves fall, they carve pumpkins into Hallowe'en faces, and come winter there is the innocent fun of ice-skating and sledding. It is 'an idealised . . . very contained world,' observes Jean Schulz. Her husband was essentially drawing the Middle America he remembered nostalgically from his boyhood and youth. Charlie Brown's home town certainly bears little resemblance to contemporary America in the 1970s. There was only one black character in *Peanuts*, for instance, Franklin, who was introduced by Schulz in 1968, but little-used thereafter. 'I've never done much with Franklin, because I don't do race things. I am not an expert on race,' the artist explained, rather feebly. 'I don't know what it's like to grow up as a little black boy . . .'

While storylines featuring Franklin were as rare as hen's teeth, hardly a week passed without Snoopy making an appearance, for Charlie Brown's dog was really the star of *Peanuts*. While the child characters behave in a more or less realistic way, Schulz allowed himself to indulge in the fanciful when it came to Snoopy, a dog whose thought bubbles betray a personality far more sophisticated than the young human beings who surround him. Certainly, he's the intellectual superior of his nominal owner, in whom Snoopy is interested only inasmuch as Charlie Brown is the kid who brings him his supper dish each day. Like real dogs, Snoopy is ruled by his stomach. He is a glutton who spends most of his time lying, improbably, on the apex of his dog house, digesting his last meal and wondering how long it will be until Charlie Brown delivers the next. As he waits to be fed, he indulges in a fantasy life. In his dreams, Snoopy is a Casanova, a wooer of females both canine and human; he is a dog of the arts, a music lover and literary animal who sometimes taps out stories on a typewriter, and is apparently employed part-time as an Agony Uncle. His other fantasies, or alter egos, include attorney, tennis champ, ice skater, and, most improbably, First World War air ace. Snoopy is a dog of contradictions. He can be brave, but timorous (scared of the cat next door); amorous, yet innocent (Schulz once summed-up Snoopy's character as a 'combination of innocence and egotism.') Above all, the dog is and was *cool*, in the particular early 1970s meaning of that word. Like the Fonz in the TV comedy show *Happy Days* (which began its run in 1974), Snoopy is cool in that he is very relaxed about life and yet keenly aware of his own dignity. One of the alter egos Schulz gave Snoopy was the character Joe Cool, whereby the dog wears a turtleneck sweater and shades: the very image of Jack Nicholson in *Five Easy Pieces*. And like Jack and the Fonz, Snoopy became an iconic character of the laid-back 1970s. His familiar rounded outline, with huge banana nose, floppy black ears and pot belly, was worn on T-shirts and printed on to posters that hung in innumerable bedrooms, offices and school rooms.

Although *Peanuts* sold strongly in the USA throughout the 1950s and 1960s, it was in the new decade that Snoopy and his friends reached a global audience, partly due to the increased syndication of the strips to newspapers such as Britain's *Daily Mail*; also because of the popularity of *Peanuts* books and feature-length animated films, a long series of which began in 1969 with *A Boy Named Charlie Brown*. But the licensing of the characters was perhaps the most significant factor. In 1970, Schulz formed a management company, Creative Associates, which exploited the *Peanuts* characters with phenomenal international success. Charlie Brown and his friends came to endorse a vast number of products and services ranging from Ford motor cars to medical insurance, and their friendly images were used to sell bushels of stationery, calendars and greetings cards. Snoopy in particular lent himself ably to the merchandising business, with Schulz giving the go-ahead for Snoopy mugs, Snoopy money boxes, lunch boxes, even wrist watches. Stuffed Snoopy toys proved hugely popular, beloved not only of children but collected by young women, who often received them as love tokens from their soppy boyfriends. When Schulz created a cartoon bird named Woodstock as a friend for Snoopy in 1970, a whole new line of toys and gifts appeared in the shops.

Most unusually, Schulz personally drew all the characters featured in these items whereas most famous cartoonists hire assistants to do the donkey work of merchandising for them. For instance, Sparky drew every one of the *Peanuts* greetings cards marketed by Hallmark. No other popular cartoonist would take this much trouble, but then Sparky always retained a rare dedication to his characters and to his craft. The artwork was in fact very good for what it was. Charlie

Brown may only have had funny, stubby little hands, for instance, but as Schulz knew, in order to draw a cartoon character's hand well, one had to know how to draw a human hand realistically in the first place and Schulz's life drawings in his Second World War journal prove that he was indeed a fine draughtsman. When he drew rain, as he often did in the strip, for he took pleasure and pride in his technique, he said that he *felt* rain. This conviction comes through to the reader. Yet Schulz was always modest about his drawings. 'I do not regard what I am doing as Great Art,' he said, explaining that strip cartooning was first and foremost a commercial product, always compromised by the size the strip is reproduced in the newspapers, the quality of newsprint, and many other factors beyond the cartoonist's control.

Peanuts travelled in the 1970s partly for the same reason that so much American culture was exported successfully at this time: the American way of life, even reduced to a cartoon, appeared luscious and expansive compared to life in most other countries. Certainly that was true in Britain, which seemed a distinctly narrower, poorer place than the USA during the decade, as indeed it was in many ways. (Very few cartoons created by European artists succeeded in return in the United States.) *Peanuts* also sold around the world because the characters' small problems were universal: Charlie Brown's hopeless adoration of the little red-haired girl, for instance, was understandable on every continent. In some respects, by contrast, the strip was very much *of its time*. Naturally introspective in his own life, Schulz created a long-running story in which Lucy Van Pelt dispensed pithy psychiatric advice for five cents from a stall, her most frequent customer being the hapless Charlie Brown. In the age of analysis, this resonated with many readers. Apart from all these factors, Schulz believed that the phenomenal and enduring success of *Peanuts* was due to his abiding by a golden rule of cartooning never to stray into political or otherwise controversial topics. Comic-strips were not the place for comment or satire, in his opinion. Rather, as he said, 'The idea of a comic-strip is to be funny and sell newspapers.' But then, in 1970, a new cartoon strip came along that broke his golden rule, and was wildly successful nonetheless. Indeed, it threatened to eclipse *Peanuts* as the world's number one cartoon strip. This was *Doonesbury* by a young man named G.B. Trudeau.

There was a gulf between Schulz and Trudeau that was in part a generation gap as well as a chasm of class and background. Sparky was from lower middle-class Midwestern stock, raised during the Depression, after which he went straight into army service during the Second World War. He never attended college, and made his way in the world by choosing a trade and excelling at it. Success made him rich. By the 1970s he was living in a large house in the country outside Santa Rosa, California, a pleasant town north of San Francisco, indulging his love of ice skating by owning and operating the town's ice rink (at a loss), and taking delight in buying himself luxury automobiles. Early each morning he drove his Jaguar – or whatever fancy car he had at the time – to a purpose-built studio at 1 Snoopy Place, where he drew his characters while a team of assistants ran the busy and lucrative *Peanuts* industry. When he had to fly down to Los Angeles for meetings about the *Peanuts* movies, Schulz did so by private jet. Despite the affluence he had achieved, Schulz was still a Midwesterner at heart: a quiet, cautious, conservative man who went to bed every night at ten p.m.; still disapproved of drinking, smoking and cursing; voted Republican; and reread his Bible for moral guidance, humming hymns to himself while he worked at Snoopy Place. By the start of the 1970s, Sparky was also approaching fifty years of age.

By contrast, G.B. Trudeau was a young East Coast sophisticate, a baby-boomer from a liberal, privileged background. In full, he was Garretson Beekman Trudeau, Garry for short, born to a doctor and his wife in New York in 1948, the family being related to Canada's Prime Minister Pierre Trudeau. Raised in upstate New York, Trudeau suffered a life-changing trauma in 1960 when his parents divorced and he was sent to a prep school where he was very unhappy. Physically small, and shy, Trudeau felt out of place in the company of more outgoing kids at an institution where sports were prized highly, and he retreated into art. It is often the case that cartoonists begin obsessional drawing as a way of escaping the real world, finding a fantasy outlet from loneliness, isolation and pain. Schulz, for whom the world had always been overwhelming, worked out his neurosis in a kind of kindergarten group therapy with *Peanuts*. Another example of an unhappy kid who escaped into cartoon fantasy was Robert Crumb, who grew up in a highly dysfunctional home in the 1950s. He became the king of underground comix, venting his feelings by drawing grotesque and outlandish characters, and satirising America itself. In a sense, Garry Trudeau's escapist cartooning falls between these two stools.

Trudeau went up to Yale in 1966 and it was here as a student that he created *Bull Tales*, a weekly strip that ran in the *New York Daily News* from 1968. His characters were a group of college students living in a commune, the humour resting in satire on campus life, with college types such as the football jocks singled out as figures of fun. A syndication agency noticed *Bull Tales* and convinced Trudeau to turn it into a daily strip renamed *Doonesbury*, after Trudeau's central student character, Mike Doonesbury, a character similar to Charlie Brown in that he is a pliable naïve around whom events revolve. The strip debuted in twenty-eight newspapers in October 1970. Trudeau was not much of a draughtsman, compared with Schulz (or a brilliant talent such as Robert Crumb, whose work is really fine art). Early *Doonesbury* strips were very crude indeed, the lines becoming cleaner after Trudeau engaged the services of an 'inking assistant,' a fellow named Don Carlton, to translate his pencil sketches into published drawings. The other commonplace reaction to first seeing *Doonesbury* is that the black-and-white drawings in the four boxes of the daily strip (a larger colour panel on Sunday, in common with *Peanuts*) often look almost identical. This is a stylistic device Trudeau took to its extreme when he turned his attention to national politics, typically filling each of his four boxes with a drawing of the south façade of the White House, with dialogue emanating from unseen characters within. One had to look closely to see that each drawing was in fact different. The reaction of established cartoonists to this audacious yet primitive new style was one of bemusement. 'Anybody who can draw bad pictures of the White House four times in a row and succeed knows something I don't,' commented Al Capp, the creator of *Li'l*

Abner. Schulz concurred wholeheartedly with Capp, as well as being very surprised by the satirical content of the *Doonesbury* strips, which were printed alongside *Peanuts* in the section of newspapers hitherto reserved for cartoons that were traditionally cute and funny in a non-controversial way.

There has been a long history of satirical cartooning, of course, from James Gillray in the eighteenth century to Ralph Steadman and Gerald Scarfe. But this type of work doesn't usually cross over into what Americans call the funny pages – the section at the back of the paper where one goes to do the crossword, check the TV listings and have a laugh. Satirical cartooning traditionally stands alone on an editorial page towards the front of a publication. Trudeau broke this rule. Looking back, it was inevitable that *Doonesbury* would be drawn into political and social issues. Trudeau was, after all, a sixties' student, of an age with the civil rights protestors and those opposed to the Vietnam War, and his cartoon characters were similar young adults. So of course they smoked pot, listened to rock music, had sex outside marriage and engaged in the great debates of the day. In 1972, Trudeau became the first syndicated American cartoonist to make direct reference to the Vietnam War in his strip (a subject which the likes of Schulz usually ignored). One of Trudeau's main characters was a football jock named BD, modelled on a football player back at Yale. Like many college ball players, BD is politically conservative and none too bright. In the strip, BD volunteers for service in Vietnam, partly as an excuse to get out of doing his term paper – a good joke in itself. Better still, in Vietnam BD is thrown together with a Viet Cong named Phred (freedom fighter, or terrorist depending on your point of view) who is portrayed as a thoroughly decent human being, concerned about the fate of his country and his people. The two become firm friends. One of the most telling strips in their story comes when Phred and BD are sheltering under a USAF air strike. 'I hope you can live with all the destruction and carnage you've brought to my little country!!' shouts Phred in the third panel, shaking his fist at the bombers in the sky. The last panel shows two US pilots immured in their cockpit high above the clouds, oblivious to the mayhem they have wreaked on *terra firma*, chatting about sports. (See picture 19.)

As well as the Vietnam War, Trudeau also tackled many domestic issues of the day such as feminism, introducing a character named *Ms* Joanie Caucus, a middle-aged woman who had become so disillusioned with her life as a wife and mother that she simply walked out on her family and enrolled in college to study to become a lawyer. Explaining to Mike Doonesbury and fellow student Mark Slackmeyer why she left her husband, Joanie recalls an evening when her old man brought his bowling buddies home for dinner. 'At the end of the meal, one of his friends complimented me on my french fries. Clinton leaned back in his chair and said with a big, stupid grin, "My wife, I think I'll keep her!"' In the final panel, Joanie says: 'I broke his nose.'

Above all else, Watergate was the making of *Doonesbury*. The story started in the real world in June 1972, as the presidential election campaign of that year built towards its climax. Five men linked with the Republican campaign to re-elect Richard Nixon were arrested breaking into the headquarters of the opposition Democratic party at the Watergate building in Washington, with the intention of planting surveillance equipment. As the burglars were prosecuted, and a Senate hearing was instigated into the affair and its attempted cover-up, it became increasingly clear that President Nixon (re-elected in November 1972) was implicated. Nixon had never been popular with the characters in *Doonesbury*, the students being, like their creator, liberal in outlook. In the strip, Mike Doonesbury campaigned for Democrat challenger George McGovern during the '72 campaign. It was therefore delicious retribution for the artist and his characters that Tricky Dicky was receiving his comeuppance. Trudeau relished the opportunity for satire afforded by the scandal, lampooning not only Nixon but all the participants in the drama, which unfolded over a two-year period. One of his targets was US Attorney General John Mitchell, later sentenced to a prison term for his part in the Watergate cover-up. In May, 1973, long before Mitchell was convicted, Trudeau had Mark Slackmeyer yelling, with typical cartoonish over-emphasis, that Mitchell was 'Guilty! Guilty! Guilty! Guilty!' the *Washington Post*, whose reporters Carl Bernstein and Bob Woodward did so much to expose Watergate, refused to run this strip. 'If any one is going to find any defendant guilty, it's going to be the due process of justice, not a

David Hockney's double portrait *Mr and Mrs Clark and Percy* (1970–71) captures for posterity the look of a fashionable young couple in their stylish London apartment at the start of the new decade. The models were his close friends Celia Birtwell and Ossie Clark.

Celia Birtwell and David Hockney are seen here in a recent picture at the artist's London home.

Jan van Eyck's *Arnolfini Portrait* of 1434 was part of the inspiration for David Hockney's portrait of Mr and Mrs Clark.

Although seldom seen on screen, the American artist Terry Gilliam was a vital member of the Monty Python team, working behind the scenes to create the brilliant credit sequences and surreal collages (such as the two examples here) which helped give *Monty Python's Flying Circus* its unique character.

In June 1970, the Pythons posed for this publicity photo for the forthcoming second series of *Monty Python's Flying Circus*. Left to right (back row) are: Graham Chapman, Eric Idle and Terry Gilliam. Front row: Terry Jones, John Cleese and Michael Palin.

Richard Serra's massive metal sculptures were among the boldest and most challenging new works of art in the seventies. This is *Strike* (1969–71), a slab of steel approximately 8 feet tall and 24 feet in length.

Feminist author Germaine Greer is seen
here outside the Hotel Chelsea in New York
in 1971, around the time of her encounter
with Diane Arbus.

Minoru Yamasaki, architect of the World
Trade Center (1962–73).

The graceful branching ribs of the World Trade Center,
seen here in detail, were part of the innovative design of
New York's twin towers.

This drawing – *Lizard Lounge* – is one of the splendid illustrations the British artist Ralph Steadman created for Hunter S. Thompson's 1971 story *Fear and Loathing in Las Vegas*. Ralph didn't go on the trip to Vegas with Hunter, but made his drawings at home in London, recalling previous alarming experiences in the US with the American writer.

Two young art school graduates from London, calling themselves simply Gilbert and George, achieved international fame in September 1971, when they performed their *Singing Sculpture* at the Sonnabend Gallery in New York.

When David Bowie debuted on stage as Ziggy Stardust in 1972 (this photo was taken the following year), he treated his audience to an audacious costume change. 'Nice legs,' remarked the writer Charles Shaar Murray in the *New Musical Express*.

Lou Reed is seen here on stage around the time of his 1972 LP *Transformer*.

Jack Nicholson in *Five Easy Pieces* (1970): the film that made him a star.

Martin Scorsese directs Robert De Niro (left) and Harvey Keitel (right) in their breakthrough movie *Mean Streets* (1973).

Francis Ford Coppola is seen here directing Marlon Brando in the wedding scene at the start of *The Godfather* (1971).

In this 1970 *Peanuts* strip, Charles M. Schulz makes a rare, oblique reference to the Vietnam War.

Although the drawings in *Doonesbury* were crude, G.B. Trudeau used his cartoon strip to make sharp political points.

Architect Jørn Utzon (left) smiles broadly as he looks at plans for his Sydney Opera House, with engineer Jack Zunz (middle) and Professor Harry Ashworth (right), one of the competition judges.

My own snapshot of the Sydney Opera House, taken from the back (south), isn't the most flattering picture of this magnificent building (opened in 1973), but the shells are stunning from any angle, especially against a perfect blue sky.

The cast of *Jaws* (1975): Richard Dreyfuss (left) played the ichthyologist Hooper, Roy Scheider (middle) was police chief Brody, and Robert Shaw (right) stole the show as Quint.

Bob Marley delivers a passionate performance in front of a portrait of Haile Selassie.

One of the foremost singer-songwriters of the seventies, Joni Mitchell is seen here at home in Laurel Canyon, California, shortly before the release of her wonderful 1971 album *Blue*.

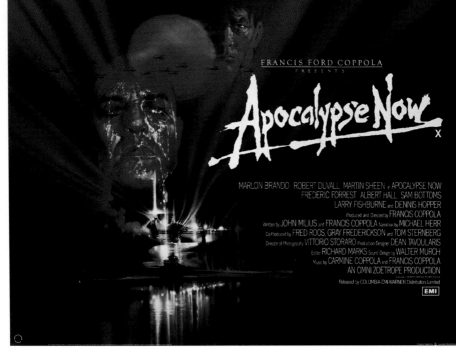

Apocalypse Now was in production such a long time that when these posters finally went up outside cinemas in 1979 the film was already a legend.

A Clockwork Orange (1971) was mind-expanding, eye-popping cinema, demonstrating that Stanley Kubrick was a superlative filmmaker not only of the 1960s, but also of the 1970s.

Misbehaving in London in December 1976, here is the original line-up of the Sex Pistols (clockwise): Steve Jones, Glen Matlock, Paul Cook and John Lydon.

Of the many rock star deaths in the 1970s, the demise of Sid Vicious was perhaps the most pathetic. 'My Way' was his swan-song.

One of the most accomplished architects at work in the 1970s Richard Meier was a leading member of the so-called 'whites' – a school of American architects who took their lead from the masters of European modernism.

Richard Meier's Douglas House (1971–73) is positioned spectacularly on a wooded incline overlooking Lake Michigan.

Designed by Richard Rogers and Renzo Piano, much that is normally found inside a building is displayed on the outside of the Pompidou Centre (1971–77). Here we see colour-co-ordinated conduit on the rear (eastern) façade.

After giving Paris its iconic inside-out shed (above), Richard Rogers designed an amazing new headquarters for Lloyd's of London.

Richard Rogers poses with a model of his Lloyd's building, during the planning stage in the late 1970s.

Andy Warhol's *Skull* pictures were a powerful counterpoint to the commissioned portraits he spent so much time creating during the 1970s, reminding himself and those interested in his work of the transience of human life.

David Hockney's 1978 Glyndebourne production of *The Magic Flute* concluded with this spectacular sunburst set.

Iris Murdoch's 1978 book *The Sea, The Sea* was one of the most enjoyable and thought-provoking novels of the decade.

Annie Hall (1977) was Woody Allen's most popular movie. Here he is in a scene with his co-star Diane Keaton, whose eccentric dress sense created a new seventies fashion.

Woody Allen closed the decade with a star-studded party in New York on 31 December 1979. Guests included (from left): Norman Mailer and his partner Norris Church; Andy Warhol; Mick Jagger and Jerry Hall.

comic-strip artist,' the paper editorialised sternly, explaining why the strip had been pulled. As Trudeau returned time and again to Watergate (and other controversial issues such as Vietnam, and drug use), editors frequently refused to run the offending sequences in their newspapers. Alternatively, they moved the strip to their editorial pages, arguing that Trudeau had crossed the line from comic artist to political commentator.

Still, as Schulz would say, the principal job of a strip cartoon is to entertain and sell papers, and Trudeau never lost sight of that. As light relief from the war and the crisis in Washington, he introduced a new character in 1974 who became *Doonesbury's* Snoopy: a character so charismatic that he threatened to take over the feature. One of the stalwarts of the strip, the dope-smoking layabout Zonker Harris, announced one day that he had to pay a call on his Uncle Duke, about whom *Doonesbury* readers had as yet heard nothing. 'What's he like?' asks Joan Caucus. 'Quite nice,' replies the freak, 'but a little strange – he's incredibly reckless with drugs . . .' *Doonesbury* readers met Duke in the offices of *Rolling Stone*, where he worked as a journalist. Actually, Duke was absent from the first two panels of his debut strip because he was under his desk when Zonker came by, stoned, 'killing bats with my ruler,' he explains when he emerges: a bald-headed cove wearing sunglasses and smoking through a cigarette holder.

Duke was of course modelled on the now-famous gonzo journalist Dr Hunter S. Thompson, who uses Duke as his pseudonym in *Fear and Loathing in Las Vegas*. By 1974, Thompson was a figure ripe for caricature. Having reported the 1972 presidential campaign for *Rolling Stone*, the writer had recently returned to Washington to cover the Watergate scandal, setting up the magazine's National Affairs desk at a downtown hotel, and attending the Senate Watergate hearings. He soon realised he was too much of an outsider to do much but spectate, however. The likes of Woodward and Bernstein were breaking all the Watergate stories; Thompson didn't have the contacts to rival them. 'There was not a hell of a lot of room for a gonzo journalist to operate in that high-tuned atmosphere,' as he conceded. In his Watergate reports, Hunter wrote instead about drinking beer by his hotel pool and then gave up covering the story on the ground and went home to

Woody Creek to watch it on television. Without any direct contact
with the action, Thompson wrote a daily precis of the news reports
and commented on these in an outrageous and provocative way: going
so far as to compare Nixon and his cronies to Hitler and his henchmen during the last days of the Third Reich. He also meandered off
the subject into accounts of the further adventures of that old double
act, Hunter and Ralph, throwing in stories about boozy evenings and
smashed-up rental cars: *Fear and Loathing*-style stories that seemed
trivial and irrelevant considering the grave matters at hand, which in
fact Hunter misread. He was convinced, for instance, that Nixon
would be prosecuted (and had a long piece going to press with *Rolling
Stone* on that very subject when Gerald Ford pardoned Nixon). In
short, Thompson lost his way during Watergate. The moment he
realised he had in fact crossed into a gonzo caricature – in *Doonesbury*
and life – came one day when he was leaving the Supreme Court
building in Washington DC and noticed a group of people looking at
him and giggling. '. . . I heard them saying, "Uncle Duke." I looked
around, and I recognised people who were total strangers pointing at
me and laughing,' he recalled. 'It was a weird experience, and as it
happened I was sort of by myself up there on the stairs, and I thought:
*What in the fuck madness is going on? Why am I being mocked by a gang of
strangers and friends on the steps of the Supreme Court?*'

As the Watergate story neared its crisis point in the summer of
1974, Trudeau increasingly turned the strip over to the façade of the
White House. He refrained from showing Nixon's face in his cartoons, but had the President's speech – or, rather, what Trudeau
fancied Dick might be saying – emerging from the building: the paranoid utterances of a man clinging to power. As the situation became
increasingly desperate, Trudeau constructed a brick wall around the
White House, an illustration of the siege mentality within. Then, in
August 1974, facing impeachment, Nixon resigned from office.
Unlike most cartoonists who strive to build up a long lead-time, so
that they have two or even three months' worth of strips waiting to go
to press if they fall ill, or want a break, Trudeau worked close to publication date so he could remain topical. As a result, he was able to
comment on the momentous news from Washington with a strip that

showed the imaginary wall he had built around the White House being torn down, the neo-classical building revealed once more, gleaming as new in the summer sunshine.

This sort of work made *Doonesbury* the most talked-about cartoon strip in America in the mid-1970s, a claim that Charles Schulz used to be able to make for *Peanuts*. Everybody seemed to be reading *Doonesbury* and talking about *Doonesbury*. 'There are only three major vehicles to keep us informed as to what is going on in Washington,' said President Ford, not long after taking over power from Nixon, to whom he had been vice-president briefly, 'the electronic media, the print media, and *Doonesbury*, not necessarily in that order.' When reporters interviewed Schulz at that time, they often asked why he didn't tackle big issues like *Doonesbury*. This exasperated Schulz, and prompted the angry retort, 'I deal in more social issues in one month than *Doonesbury* deals in all year. I deal in issues that are much more important than drawing four pictures of the White House.' In this outburst, Sparky was expressing his belief that the children in *Peanuts* wrestled with the elemental questions of life, not political ephemera. Trudeau gave few interviews, and was reluctant to reply directly to Schulz's criticism, but friends retaliated for him. '[*Peanuts*] is a play-ground uncontaminated by adults,' wrote the author Garry Wills in his preface to *The Doonesbury Chronicles*, a paperback compilation of strips published to great success in 1975. 'The strip says that we are all chil-dren; there are no adults. That view has just enough truth in it to get by, but the strip does so by a drastic narrowing. The fantasy-for-its-own-sake ends up logically in a dog's dream of being a German air-ace. This is [a] way of escaping the world.'

Comments such as this cut the sensitive Charles Schulz deeply, and though he had the comfort that *Peanuts* was still the number one strip cartoon in the world in syndication terms, *Doonesbury* was gaining ground, being picked up by more and more newspapers in North America and abroad. Then, when the judges of the Pulitzer Prize gathered to consider which American journalists should be honoured for their work in the tumultuous year of 1974, they decided, for the first time in the history of the Pulitzer, to give the prize for editorial cartooning to a comic-strip: *Doonesbury*. It was the ultimate acknowledgement of the triumph of Garry Trudeau's satirical style of strip-cartooning over the old-fashioned, homespun folksiness of *Peanuts*, and enough to make Charlie Brown bury his round head in his stubby little hands and utter the strongest exclamation of disappointment permissible in Schulz's universe: 'Good Grief!'

16

WATERSHED

See it – before you go swimming.

CINEMA TRAILER FOR *JAWS*

The movie *Jaws* premiered in the USA in June 1975, when Americans were still reeling from Watergate. The release of the film also came just a couple of months after the country's final defeat in Vietnam, with the fall of Saigon having occurred in April. Here then was a fine opportunity for escapism and the American public seized that offer with both hands, flocking to the cinema to scream at a monstrous great white shark and cheer on the brave men who fought it to the death. After its hugely successful American launch, *Jaws* became a massive international hit, too, and its commercial success changed the course of Hollywood for a generation. For that alone it is important. But *Jaws* is also an excellent movie in terms of script, acting and direction, a triumph of popular cinema in fact, perhaps surprisingly so considering its origin.

As we have seen, the self-deprecating Peter Benchley never expected his shark story would make it to the cinema at all because of the technical problem of representing the shark on screen. Neither did he have high hopes for his novel. After his first, comical version had been rejected by his editor, Tom Congdon, in 1971, Benchley had returned to his rented office in Pennington, New Jersey, to try again, hoping merely to turn out a book that Doubleday would accept for publication, and thus release the full advance of $7,500 (£4,120), a modest sum but money he very much needed. Working through most of 1972, Peter rewrote the basic story of a rogue great white shark attacking a Long Island resort town called Amity. Deciding that the shark story alone made for a thin book, he padded the novel with two subplots: one about Ellen Brody, wife of the police chief, becoming romantically involved with a handsome shark expert (Hooper); the second concerning the Mafia. The author became so involved in these secondary stories that the actual shark hunt became squeezed into the final third of the novel, beginning belatedly when Amity hires a fisherman named Quint to kill the beast. At any rate, Doubleday accepted the revised manuscript for publication, though up until the last minute it lacked a satisfactory title. In April 1973, Benchley had lunch with Tom Congdon at the Dallas Cowboy restaurant in New York to make a crunch decision as to what the book should be called. Peter's title contenders at this late stage included *A Stillness in the Water* and *Silence in the Deep*. Congdon wasn't impressed by either. Other suggestions were *The Jaws of Death* and *The Jaws of Leviathan*. Neither were right, but they contained a common word that both men considered to be evocative. 'Look, the only [word] we agree on is *jaws*,' said Benchley. 'Why don't we call the bloody thing *Jaws*?'

'What does it mean?' queried Congdon.

'I have no idea what it means, but it's short.'

The sales people at Doubleday loved the title, as did the art director: *Jaws* was short and simple and would look striking in red letters on the cover. Still, Peter had misgivings about the name, as did his agent and his famous writer-father, Nathaniel Benchley, when he told them. All in all, *Jaws* did not seem destined for greatness. And with only three hundred dollars of his Doubleday advance left in his bank account, Peter decided that he had no future as an author. In fact, he was just about to go out and post a job application to the *National Geographic* when he received a telephone call to inform him that the paperback rights to *Jaws* had sold for over half a million dollars: a life-changing moment for the author, as the paperback sale of *The Day of the Jackal* had been to Frederick Forsyth and, likewise, to Mario Puzo with *The Godfather*. When Peter put down the telephone and told his wife the good news, she burst into tears. 'What's wrong with you? It's great, isn't it?' he asked, to which Wendy Benchley replied emotionally that their life would never be the same again.

Film producer David Brown heard about *Jaws* via his contacts in the publishing world, his wife being the editor of *Cosmopolitan*. Brown was an urbane 57-year-old veteran of the movie industry who had recently set up in business with Richard D. Zanuck, the son of the founder of Twentieth Century-Fox. Their first picture, *The Sting*, a period caper starring Robert Redford and Paul Newman, was one of the hits of 1973. Looking around for another money-maker, Brown and Zanuck obtained galley proofs of *Jaws* and read the story simultaneously, Zanuck in California and Brown at home in New York. 'We both read it overnight, and got on the phone to each other the next morning and said, *Look, we don't know how we can possibly do it, but [we] must have this,*' recalls Zanuck, referring to the problem of showing the shark on screen. 'This is the most exciting thing we've ever read.' Prior to publication, the Zanuck-Brown company snapped up the movie rights for $150,000 (£82,400), paying Benchley an additional $25,000 (£13,700) to write a screenplay. Peter had no experience of this sort of writing, but with a Writers Guild strike looming Brown and Zanuck thought it prudent to get something on paper. From the start it was clear that there would have to be radical changes to Peter's story. 'The first thing that is going to go is that so-called romance,' Zanuck told Benchley when he came to California for a meeting, meaning the adulterous affair between Ellen Brody and Hooper. Zanuck also ordered Benchley to dispense with the Mafia story. 'This is an A-to-Z adventure story, and I don't want any subplot.'

Zanuck and Brown had a distribution deal with Universal and one of the young directors under contract to the studio was 26-year-old Steven Spielberg, whose two credits of significance were a TV thriller called *Duel* (1971), about a petrol tanker possessed of a demonic spirit, and a forthcoming feature movie titled *The Sugarland Express* (1974), with Goldie Hawn and William Atherton as a couple of petty criminals who kidnap a policeman and his patrol car. Though not yet released, *The Sugarland Express* showed Spielberg to be a gifted storyteller whose artistic vision was influenced strongly by 1950s and

1960s television. Characters in the serial stories Spielberg grew up watching were broadly-drawn types – good, bad or charmingly eccentric – with strongly-plotted scripts. These were all characteristics of Spielberg films and part of the reason for the enormous popularity of his work. Passing through the Zanuck-Brown offices one day, Steven's gaze fell on Peter Benchley's recently submitted screenplay, a block of pages with *Jaws* typed on the cover sheet. 'I didn't know what that meant. *Jaws*? Is it about a dentist?' Reading the script over the weekend, the young director decided he wanted to make this movie, the great white shark reminding him of the monstrous truck in *Duel*, though he also saw the potential problems of the project – not only the technical difficulty, but in terms of what it meant for his career. At this stage, Spielberg was unsure of what sort of pictures he wanted to make in the long term, and was wary of limiting himself as a director. Looking at the pictures friends such as Martin Scorsese were working on (he who had warned Spielberg about 'things with teeth' that live in the ocean), Spielberg asked himself whether *he* shouldn't also be making personal, naturalistic movies: 'I didn't know who I was. I wanted to make a movie that left its mark, not at the box office, but on people's consciousness. I wanted to be Antonioni, Bob Rafelson, Hal Ashby, Martin Scorsese.' Also, it was evident that Benchley's script needed much work.

After Spielberg attempted a redraft, the still-unsatisfactory pages passed into the hands of Pulitzer Prize-winning playwright Howard Sackler. He only had a short time available to work on the project but gave the film of *Jaws* its essential and unusual structure. Unlike the novel (or most films), the movie plays out over two rather than three acts. Act One is everything that happens on land: the reaction to the initial shark attacks; the closing of Amity's beaches; and the town leaders engaging Quint to catch the monster. The second act is a sea adventure, with Brody, Hooper and Quint hunting the shark from the deck of Quint's boat, the *Orca*. For the entire second half of the film, these three men are the only human characters. It is therefore imperative that the audience cares about them all. Brody and Hooper are already well established by the time the *Orca* leaves harbour, but Quint is an enigma, having joined the narrative late with no back story provided by Benchley. To make Quint sympathetic, Sackler made the fisherman a survivor of a notorious naval disaster of the Second World War: the sinking by a Japanese submarine of the USS *Indianapolis* in the Pacific. Of the eleven hundred men on board the vessel, approximately four hundred died in the torpedo attack and seven hundred more were cast into the ocean. In the six days it took to effect a rescue, approximately half of the shipwrecked sailors were eaten by sharks. By having Quint as a survivor of the *Indianapolis*, one could quite believe how he might have both respect and loathing for sharks. In casting this key role, Spielberg was fortunate to hire the roguish English actor Robert Shaw.

Spielberg insisted *Jaws* should be filmed at sea rather than in a water tank in Los Angeles, which would have been much cheaper, and work began in May 1974 on Martha's Vineyard, the island off the coast of Massachusetts. Spielberg chose the location because one can sail a long way off the coast and still be in shallow waters with a flat, level seabed. This meant he could photograph the *Orca* in the round without the audience seeing land, thus giving the sense that the men on board were beyond help; and the director should also be able to operate a mechanical shark in the shallow water. For close-ups of the shark underwater, Spielberg commissioned a diver-cameraman to shoot footage of real great whites off the coast of Australia. These are the sharks seen in sequences such as the one where Hooper's shark cage is attacked. Spielberg was insistent, however, that when the fish breaks the surface, the men on board the *Orca* must be in the same frame with the creature. Without using animation, and in the days before computer-aided visual manipulation, the only way to do this was to build a mechanical shark on a submerged tracking system whereby the beast would appear to swim near the boat and could be made to rear up out of the water and snap at the actors on command. Nicknamed Bruce by cast and crew, the mechanical shark worked well in dry tests, but rarely performed at all when submerged in the salty sea water of Nantucket Sound, its failure pushing *Jaws* months over schedule, and millions of dollars over budget. When David Brown and Richard Zanuck came to the Vineyard to check on progress, only to see the shark sink before their eyes, they felt their careers and fortunes sink with it. 'Everything that could go wrong with the shark went wrong,' laments Brown.

Technical problems did at least allow Spielberg time to perfect the screenplay, which he did in conjunction with actor-writer Carl Gottlieb, a personal friend who had signed on to play the editor of Amity's newspaper but also found himself deeply involved in rewriting scenes. The men worked together on the screenplay at a house they shared on location in Edgartown: a superior log cabin overlooking the water with several bedrooms, a handsome living area with an open fire, and staff to cook and clean for them. In the lengthy process of rewriting, which carried on right up to the last minute, the screenplay of *Jaws* was given a very different tone from that of the book it was based on. Shocking though it seemed when first released in 1975, the movie of *Jaws* is essentially family entertainment, which is certainly not true of Peter Benchley's novel. In the book, Benchley lingers over the carnage the great white shark causes, relishing descriptions of every mangled limb. In contrast, Spielberg is sparing in his use of violence and the depiction of its aftermath. He actually cut some of the scenes he shot because he considered them to be too strong for his audience. In the novel, apart from masses of blood and guts, there is a salaciousness that is absent from the film. The opening sequence of the movie shows a young woman taking off her clothes and going for a skinny-dip in the ocean, granted, but Spielberg shot this in such as way as to be almost entirely innocent, and despite the fact that there are several subsequent beach scenes, his camera never lingers in a prurient way on the bathers, whereas there is a distinctly prurient tone to the book. Ellen Brody, a wanton adulteress in the novel, becomes in the movie a loving and loyal wife to her police chief husband (Roy Scheider), who himself is transformed from cuckolded small-town boor in Benchley's story to solid-gold hero. Meanwhile, Peter Benchley's seducer-ichthyologist Hooper becomes an unthreatening bearded nebbish played by Richard Dreyfuss. None of the movie characters even swear (remarkable considering the trying circumstances). In short, *Jaws* the movie is imbued with the innocence of the early American television that Spielberg was raised on, as well as reflecting the personality and lifestyle of a young man who, unlike so many of the directors in Hollywood at this time, did not debauch himself, but worked at his trade like a schoolboy absorbed innocently in an all-consuming hobby.

Aside from sweetening the characters in the story and taking out much of the nastiness of the novel, Spielberg and Gottlieb worked intensively in their cabin quarters on rewriting one very important scene in particular, the sequence preceding the final confrontation with the shark: what Steven and Carl came to think of in terms of the type of scene commonplace in war films when the characters sit around a camp fire talking before the carnage of battle. The purpose is to establish the characters as people the audience care about before they fight for their lives. In *Jaws*, this takes place in the cabin of the *Orca* at night, after Brody, Hooper and Quint have had their first encounter with the shark, which has escaped despite being harpooned. Over drinks, the men regale each other with tall tales, culminating in Quint's story about the USS *Indianapolis*. Although this device had been Howard Sackler's invention, Sackler only had time to sketch in the details. To develop the scene into the superb sequence it is (one of the finest speeches in any popular movie of the decade), Spielberg consulted widely among screenwriters he knew, making long-distance calls to friends in LA such as Paul Schrader and John Milius. Gottlieb listened in on an extension during these conversations, making notes, and then incorporated the best suggestions in the screenplay. It was Milius who proposed that Brody, Hooper and Quint might compare scars while drinking, which is the comical episode of macho bluster that precedes Quint's monologue. When Brody asks Quint about a mark on his arm, Quint replies that it was a tattoo for the *Indianapolis*, and so relates the grim story of that disaster, creating an atmosphere of intimacy and comradeship between the men, and lending Quint a humanity lacking in Benchley's novel. Still, nobody could quite get the speech right until Robert Shaw took it in hand.

Apart from his career as an actor, Shaw was a published novelist and playwright, and after working on the scene he brought the revised lines over to Spielberg's log cabin one night as the director, Carl Gottlieb, film editor Verna Fields and Richard Dreyfuss were finishing dinner. When everyone had settled for coffee in front of the fire and the housekeeper had dimmed the lights for atmosphere, Shaw, in character as Quint, read his 400-word monologue (unusually lengthy for a popular movie), telling how he and his shipmates had been plunged into the ocean in June 1945 after the sinking of the *Indianapolis*. 'Eleven hundred men went into the water. Vessel went down in twelve minutes. Didn't see the first shark for about a half an hour,' intoned the actor, going on to relate how the tiger sharks came swarming at dawn. Recalling what it was like to be in the water with these man-eaters, Quint said: 'You know the thing about a shark, he's got lifeless eyes, black eyes, like a doll's eyes. When he comes at you, he doesn't seem to be livin'. Until he bites you, and those black eyes roll over white. And then, ah then, you hear that terrible high-pitch screamin' and the ocean turns red.' The lines were terrific, with some brilliant images, and Spielberg announced they would shoot it.

An attempt to do so was made on the afternoon of 11 June 1974. Unfortunately, Shaw started boozing at lunch and became so befuddled that he couldn't follow his own script. 'As the scene progressed he got more and more under the influence and towards the end he got absolutely wild,' recalls Carl Gottlieb. Realising he was letting everybody down, Shaw apologised and did it again the following day. In fact, parts of both the drunk and sober speeches are edited together in the movie. The scene concludes with Quint singing a sea song, followed by all three men joining together in an uproarious 'Show Me the Way to Go Home,' becoming louder and louder, slapping the table and hollering until – *thwuumpp!* – the boat reverberates with the impact of the returning shark. Now we are into the final thrilling part of the picture.

By this stage in filming, Peter Benchley's novel was a major bestseller. Reviews were poor when *Jaws* was published in America in February 1974, but like *The Day of the Jackal* the book sold by word-of-mouth, sales fuelling interest in the making of the film and, likewise, the moviemaking boosting interest in the book, until *Jaws* was such a phenomenon that *Time* devoted a cover story to it. The headline read: 'Super Shark – *Jaws* on Film, and other Summer Thrillers.' Buoyed up with his success, Benchley came to Martha's Vineyard to play a cameo in the movie, as a TV reporter covering the re-opening of the beaches on the Fourth of July. Although flattered to be given a screen appearance, the author was increasingly disgruntled about the many changes Spielberg had made to his book. Peter was especially riled about an interview Spielberg had given to *Newsweek* in which he was quoted as saying that Benchley's original characters were so unpleasant that cinema audiences would never have cared about them. Spielberg joked that they would *want* the shark to eat them, 'in alphabetical order.' In response, Peter complained to an *LA Times* reporter on location that Spielberg was too young to understand his characters. Indeed, he had a low opinion of Mr Spielberg generally, going so far as to predict, absurdly, that Steven hadn't much future in Hollywood.

In truth, Spielberg had improved Benchley's story greatly and was also coping manfully with all sorts of problems on set, not least of which was the day that the *Orca* sank, almost drowning his actors. In the fleeting moments when Bruce deigned to work, Spielberg snatched the vital scenes he needed with the shark, notably when Brody is shovelling chum into the water from the back of the boat, and the monster rears up to bite at him. This is the first dramatic encounter with the fish, after which Brody tells Quint, 'You're gonna need a bigger boat.' Despite the technical problems, the out-of-control schedule and mounting costs, and although he was a shy and gauche young man who had to deal with strong personalities on set – notably a drunken Shaw and a rambunctious Dreyfuss, who thought so little of the picture that he predicted to *Time* that it would be a 'turkey' – Steven Spielberg proved himself to be a masterful filmmaker on *Jaws*. 'He knew how to budget his time. He knew how to talk to actors,' recalls Carl Gottlieb. 'He was always in charge. You never thought of his age.' Zanuck and Brown recognised these qualities and, as the budget doubled to $7 million (£3.8 million), and the location shoot expanded from thirty-five days to more than five *months*, the producers did not fire him, as Spielberg feared they might. Even though he was only shooting a tiny amount of film each day, Spielberg's rushes looked promising.

Finally, they wrapped location work in September 1974, and Spielberg flew back to Los Angeles. In editing the movie, the decision was made to postpone the moment when the audience sees the shark as late as possible. This was partly pragmatic. Bruce had been so unreliable that Spielberg didn't have all the shots he had hoped for, and if you look closely the shark is obviously fake. The trick was to get the audience so involved in the story that they would be willing to suspend disbelief. Spielberg establishes the dread presence of the creature in the first eighty minutes of the picture by showing some evidence of its appetites and giving glimpses of fins slicing through water. With precious few effects he nevertheless succeeds in building a powerful feeling of suspense and expectation, so much so that by the time the shark does break the surface the audience is yearning to scream at *something*. Similarly, audiences developed such a liking for the three men on the boat that there was an emotional need at the end for them to triumph over their adversary. Benchley's novel ends on a sombre note: Quint harpoons the shark and is dragged down to the deep with its body. Hooper also perishes, leaving Brody the sole survivor. Spielberg wanted a more exciting, indeed euphoric ending. His solution was to make the audience first *think* Hooper has been killed when diving down in his shark cage. Then Quint's worst nightmare becomes real as he is devoured by the shark. Finally, as the *Orca* goes down and the shark closes in for the kill, Brody resourcefully jams an oxygen cylinder in its gaping maw and then shoots the canister, which explodes, blowing the shark to smithereens. 'Steven, it couldn't happen that way. It's not possible,' complained Benchley, considering this ending too far-fetched. The director replied that he didn't care. He was confident that he would have such a grip on the audience by this stage that they would believe anything for the last three minutes. His final touch was to have Hooper pop-up as a surprise survivor. The shark expert and the policeman then paddle into shore together: a companionable feel-good ending that, more than anything, showed *Jaws* to be a return to traditional Hollywood filmmaking, eschewing realism in favour of crowd-pleasing. Another vital late ingredient in the success of the picture was John Williams' score, of course: the low, thumping signature sound of the approaching shark, like the increasing beat of an excited heart. It is hard now to think of the picture, or pick up Benchley's novel, without hearing the music in one's mind.

The first test-screening was in a shopping mall in Dallas, where *Jaws* was paired with *The Towering Inferno* (1974), Old Hollywood's idea of a blockbuster. Brown and Zanuck feared that the audience would laugh at their fake shark, but the Texans loved *Jaws*; bereft though it was of big names (in contrast to *The Towering Inferno*), and despite the fact that, for a monster movie, there were long periods of inaction. Indeed there is almost as much talking in *Jaws* as in a Woody Allen picture. The audience became so wrapped up in the story that they didn't seem to notice that the shark was a rubber model, and they screamed and cheered themselves hoarse in all the right places. Because of this success, Spielberg won the time – though not the extra money (he had to pay the $3,000 [£1,648] bill himself) – to insert one extra screamer, as he called those moments when the audience jump out of their seats in fright. This is the scene in which Hooper dives down to investigate the wreck of a fishing boat and finds a hole in the side where the shark has taken a bite out of it. As he feels around the jagged edges, the severed head of the late owner Ben Gardner floats out to meet him. Complete with this bonus shocker, the second preview in Long Beach, California – where Spielberg had attended film school – was even more of a sensation, convincing the producers that they had a major hit on their hands.

The hype for *Jaws* was immoderate. 'None of man's fantasies of evil can compare with the reality of *Jaws*,' boasted the trailers. 'See it – *before* you go swimming.' Opening in America in June 1975, *Jaws* soon surpassed the record $86 million (£47 million) that *The Godfather* had taken at the box office, and then it broke the $100-million barrier. First and foremost, Spielberg's *Jaws* worked because it is a terrific movie. It looks great. The photography is imaginative and creative. After so much rewriting, the screenplay was superb, with Quint's *Indianapolis* speech especially fine. All the performances are good, with Shaw all but stealing the picture. As noted, the movie was welcome escapism for Americans in the summer of 1975, coming just after Watergate and the fall of Saigon, and it was a picture that crossed all barriers, entertaining men and women, young and old alike, its charms and thrills as effective with suburban teenagers as metropolitan sophisticates. Andy Warhol was one of those who jumped out of his skin that summer when Ben Gardner's head rolled out of the boat. ('Why didn't you *warn* me?' he asked his companion, who had seen the film before.) In order to savour the success, Spielberg took to driving over to the cinema in Hollywood where the picture was showing so he would be standing at the back of the stalls to see the reaction when Dreyfuss encounters the severed head. Every night the surprised Angelenos lifted up *en masse* in their seats and shrieked. This pleasing reaction was replicated in theatres around the world in 1975–76. One small-town beach resort is much the same as another, and Europeans, Australians, Asians and Latin Americans could all imagine a shark swimming into their favourite cove. Suddenly, everybody everywhere was talking about *Jaws* and looking out for great white sharks (who had heard of them before?). The strength of the basic story is of course to the eternal credit of Peter Benchley. But, as with *The Godfather*, Peter's book was improved immeasurably by being transferred to the screen, as he conceded: 'I like to think the book was successful as a yarn, and as a story, but I don't think it broke any literary ground. I think the movie did break a lot [of cinematic ground], and it had a huge effect cinematically. It created the blockbuster. It did all sorts of things financially and artistically to the movie business.' And he had to recant his impetuous criticism of the young director who seemed, during filming, to Peter's eyes, to have little future in Hollywood, but turned out to be, as he says, 'one of the great geniuses . . . in the history of the motion picture business.'

With the success of *Jaws*, Spielberg went on to make a long-cherished science fiction project, *Close Encounters of the Third Kind*, released in 1977, and by the end of the 1970s he was established as one of the most significant directors in the history of cinema, a status that he built on in the eighties and nineties. Back in 1975, however, he received relatively little kudos among his fellow directors and film buffs for *Jaws*, which was seen as being low entertainment for the masses, rather than art. To his surprise and dismay, Spielberg was not nominated for an Academy Award for his direction. In 1976, the Oscars for best movie, script, director, star and supporting actress all went to *One Flew Over the Cuckoo's Nest*. In a sense, this fine Jack Nicholson picture was the last gasp for small naturalistic pictures about real people, pictures that ended ambiguously, or downright tragically. Hollywood executives looked at the stupendous financial return of *Jaws* and saw the future in terms of massive summer blockbusters, films that could be opened with a major advertising campaign, and inordinate hype. And if the picture works, repeat the trick with a 2, 3 or 4 after the title. Although superior to most of the films it spawned, a classic of cinema indeed, and highpoint of popular movie-making in the decade, *Jaws* was the watershed.

17

CENTREPIECE

Who's this guy, Springfield?

BOB DYLAN

The pop culture of the seventies started to change midway through the decade. The old-fashioned got junked, and in rushed the new-fashioned, like a line of cocaine: blockbuster movies, disco, punk. The first five years of the seventies were, in many ways, an extension of the sixties, particularly in movies and rock music. It was metaphorically, and often literally, the age of marijuana: of mellow, hophead introspection. Filmmakers looked within themselves in order to create movies that explained the human condition, as novelists and poets always had. Then came *Jaws*, and Hollywood remembered it was in business to make money. Music was about to change, too, just as radically, but before it did so there was another flowering of the singer-songwriters, especially those great North American artists who had come to prominence in the previous decade.

After his motorcycle accident in 1966, Bob Dylan had changed the priorities of his life, eschewing constant touring and spending less time recording in favour of being a family man, living quietly with his wife Sara and their five children, initially in a large house near Woodstock, upstate New York. 'I'm gonna move up to Woodstock. I'm gonna live in the county. I'm just gonna paint,' Dylan confided to his friend the folk singer Ramblin' Jack Elliott, shortly before entering into semi-seclusion. 'I gotta get out of this

business. It's a bad business.' Dylan didn't forsake showbusiness altogether during his years in Woodstock. He recorded and played live
sporadically, and went to Mexico in 1972 to act in and record the
soundtrack for Sam Peckinpah's western, *Pat Garrett & Billy the Kid*,
which yielded a rare hit single for Dylan in 'Knockin' on Heaven's
Door'. But as he passed from his twenties into his thirties, Dylan
spent most of his time with his family, learning to paint for recre-
ation, and generally taking life at a slower pace than he had during
the dangerously excessive years of the mid-1960s. He was eventually
lured back into the full glare of the spotlight in 1974 for an arena
tour with his old backing group, the Band. The money on offer was
considerable, and there is a part of Dylan that craves attention. One
of the musicians who worked with him closely in the mid-'70s,
David Mansfield, puts it very well when he says that Dylan has a
'voracious, although completely veiled, appetite for celebrity.'
Another aspect of the man is his love of women, and fleshy temptations abound for a rock star on the road, some of which he found
impossible to resist. As a result, when Tour '74 concluded, Bob and
Sara Dylan effectively separated, with Sara and the children staying
at their new home in California, and Bob retreating to a farm he had
recently purchased in his home state of Minnesota, not far from St
Paul (where Charles Schulz hailed from).

It was on his Minnesota farm that Dylan started writing the songs
that became *Blood on the Tracks*, songs that in their structure were
influenced by his interest in modernist art in the sense that he decided
to create narratives that are not necessarily straightforward. Elements
of the story are often jumbled up, notably on 'Tangled Up in Blue', so
the full picture emerges gradually, as in cubist painting. One has to
step back, as it were, to comprehend what is going on. Thematically,
the songs are mostly about lost love, with a good deal of bitterness
mixed in, especially on tracks such as 'Idiot Wind', an emotional epic
replete with rhymes that attracted the admiration of Dylan's friend the
poet Allen Ginsberg among others. (Rhyming *skull* with *Capitol*, as in
the Capitol building in Washington, particularly impressed Ginsberg.)
'Idiot Wind' is typical of the album in that Dylan is pointing the finger
of suspicion at his erstwhile partner (one must assume he was thinking

of Sara), though he concludes the song by admitting his own culpability in what went wrong in the relationship, stating in the final verse that they are as bad as one another ('We're idiots, babe . . .'). Although it was Dylan who had betrayed Sara on the road in 1974, by the testament of friends and lovers, Dylan seems to accuse his spouse again in 'You're a Big Girl Now', his voice dripping sarcasm as he sings that he knows he will always be able to find his love when he needs her: she'll be in another man's room, which is the price he has to pay, because she's a big girl *all the way*. Snidely nasty though this is, the song is also remorseful, with Dylan speaking of the pain of separation, and lamenting how sad it is that love did not last. Above and beyond anger and bitterness, *regret* is the keynote emotion of *Blood on the Tracks*, with Dylan capturing that feeling better than any rock star had done in the past, as he had shown a rare ability to express so many feelings and ideas in song. The 25-year-old Bob Dylan who reached the peak of his creative youth with *Blonde on Blonde* in 1966 could not have written *Blood on the Tracks*. It is infused with the maturity of a man approaching middle-life who has come to realise that, despite his talents and accomplishments, he is in some respects — as a husband at least — a failure.

In order to record these powerful new songs, Dylan went into a studio in New York in September 1974, working with musicians including Eric Weissberg and his band Deliverance (named after the 1972 John Boorman movie of the same name for which Weissberg created the 'Duelling Banjos' music). Dylan wasn't entirely happy with the results, however, and chopped and changed musicians during the New York sessions. Then he went home to Minnesota for Christmas and played a test-pressing of the album for his brother, David Zimmerman, who persuaded Bob that it might be wise to re-record some of the tracks. They did so in a little local studio in Minneapolis during the holidays. In the process, Dylan excised some of the bitterness and the most obviously autobiographical references from songs such as 'Idiot Wind'. The result is still an emotionally charged record, but not so much of an open wound.

Despite the fact that so many musicians worked on *Blood on the Tracks*, the finished album has a remarkably cohesive and satisfying sound. It is acoustic music, the predominant sound that of string instruments, recorded live in the studio with very few overdubs, which made *Blood on the Tracks* unusual in 1975. Most rock artists were availing themselves fully of synthesizers and multi-track recording by this time in order to build towers of sound. 10cc's 1975 album *The Original Soundtrack* is a typical record of the period, an LP more or less composed of sound effects. Dylan was one of the few rock artists who resisted new technology. He preferred traditional instruments, and insisted on recording live with his musicians gathered around him in one room taking a run at a song. If it worked, fine. If there were mistakes, he didn't much care, being more concerned about capturing the spontaneity and truth of live music. As a result, *Blood on the Tracks* had a somewhat old-fashioned feel when it was released in February 1975. Writing in *Rolling Stone*, the critic Jon Landau went so far as to condemn the album as *shoddy*-sounding. The truth is it didn't have the fashionable gloss of 1975, the state-of-the-art production of an album like *The Original Soundtrack* or David Bowie's *Young Americans*, both of which sound smooth as a rhapsody (to borrow a simile from Dylan). Nevertheless, *Blood on the Tracks* was a very big hit, reaching number one in the US album charts, and going on to become Dylan's biggest-selling studio album. Furthermore, we can now look back and say that *Blood on the Tracks* stands alongside *The Freewheelin' Bob Dylan* and *Blonde on Blonde* as one of the best albums Dylan ever made. Which is to say that it is perhaps the masterpiece of his many masterpieces.

With Sara and the children in California, Dylan found himself spending time alone in New York after *Blood on the Tracks* was released, hanging out in the clubs on and around Bleecker Street in Greenwich Village where he had started his professional career in the early 1960s, and where he still had friends. Walking through SoHo one day he ran into an acquaintance named Jacques Levy, a playwright who also co-wrote songs with Dylan's buddy Roger McGuinn (of the Byrds). This chance meeting led to Levy and Dylan collaborating – very unusually for such a self-sufficient artist – on several new songs, which were also atypical for Dylan in their structure and subject matter. One of the earliest and most notable collaborations was 'Hurricane', a saga about prizefighter Rubin 'Hurricane' Carter, then in jail for a double-murder he claimed he did not commit. There was a campaign afoot to get Carter a retrial, and Dylan was one of many celebrities won over to what had become a fashionable cause, writing this lengthy, topical protest song with Levy as a plea for Carter to be granted another hearing. In its structure, the song is highly theatrical – it opens with a burst of gun shots for instance – showing the influence of Levy the dramatist. It also reports Carter's story in detail, employing an almost journalistic realism not common in Dylan's work. Though unusual, the result was very successful. Indeed, Dylan was so pleased with 'Hurricane' that he suggested to Jacques that they spend some more time writing together, preferably away from the distractions of Greenwich Village. And so, in the early summer of 1975 when Americans were screaming at *Jaws*, Bob and Jacques drove to Dylan's beach house in the Hamptons on Long Island.

The two men lived a kind of *Odd Couple* existence in Dylan's holiday home, as Jacques recalls, shopping for themselves at the local supermarket, warming up tins of soup for lunch most days, and going out to local restaurants and bars in the evening. Dylan was missing his wife greatly, and shared a new song with Jacques called 'Sara', recalling the happy days of his marriage, describing time spent with their children, and pleading with Sara to return to him. Dylan had rarely exposed himself so autobiographically in song, and was ambivalent about whether he should finish and record the number. 'He was a little hesitant to do that,' says Jacques. '[But] I encouraged him to continue with it, and he did, and I think it's a beautiful song.' Songs the friends wrote together at the beach house included 'Black Diamond Bay', inspired by the stories of Joseph Conrad, and 'Joey', a long narrative about a New York Mafia figure.

Returning to New York City after his writing sojourn, Dylan surprised his record company CBS by going back into the studio so soon after the release of *Blood on the Tracks* and recording another album of original material. Sara showed up unexpectedly during the sessions, and Levy and the musicians watched in fascination as Dylan sang 'Sara' directly to her – the very take that is preserved for posterity on the LP *Desire*. Although CBS would delay the release of *Desire* until 1976, not wanting to flood the market with Dylan material,* Bob was itching to play his new songs for an audience. He had already done so informally for friends, including one special evening at the New York loft studio of the abstract artist Larry Poons. Numerous musicians were invited for the occasion, some of whom Bob knew very well, and younger people he hadn't yet become close to: Patti Smith, soon to release her debut album *Horses* (1975), was there; so was Mick Ronson, who had recently left David Bowie's band to launch a solo career; also present was a Texan guitarist named Henry 'T-Bone' Burnett, and another up-and-coming guitarist named Steven Soles. Accompanying himself on guitar, Dylan treated them all to a remarkable private concert in Larry's loft that included renditions of new songs such as 'One More Cup of Coffee' and the lengthy, mystical, part-humorous 'Isis', which was the first song that Bob had written with Jacques' help. '[Patti Smith] was dumb struck. We all were,' recalls Poons. 'If you had any ear, it was just fucking wonderful.' This gathering was the genesis for one of the most remarkable concert tours of the 1970s: a gypsy caravan of a tour Dylan called the Rolling Thunder Revue.

For years, Dylan had been talking to friends about travelling across the country with a backing group and guest artists, a troupe of singers and poets: rolling into town by train maybe, setting up for one night in a small local theatre, and then packing up and moving on in the morning, like a circus. It was a romantic idea that tapped into his infatuation with the life of the travelling minstrel, going back to his adolescent devotion to Woody Guthrie. Popular success meant that Dylan could go around the country playing arenas if he wanted to, like the Rolling Stones. That was what Tour '74 had been. But while he liked the money a big tour generated, that sort of showbusiness was not Dylan's taste. His ideal tour was a smaller and more eccentric setup where he was free to experiment and, in the tradition of the coffee houses where he had started his career, share the spotlight with his

---

*Like *Blood on the Tracks*, *Desire* also went to number one in the USA, making 1975–76 the peak of Dylan's commercial success as a recording artist.

friends. The Rolling Thunder Revue was created with all this in mind. To accompany himself and his guests on stage, Dylan assembled a house band featuring several of the musicians he had met at Larry Poons' loft, including T-Bone Burnett and Steven Soles. Then he drew up a list of guest artists, an eclectic mix of friends including Roger McGuinn, Allen Ginsberg, Ramblin' Jack Elliott, and Bob's former lover Joan Baez. Also brought into the fold were new faces like Mick Ronson and the actress and singer Ronee Blakley, who had recently delivered a riveting performance as a country music star in Robert Altman's brilliant movie *Nashville* (1975). Dylan decided to film the perambulations and performances of this ensemble as a concert film-cum-road movie in which the Revue members would act out improvisational scenes. The young playwright Sam Shepard was hired by Bob to write the script, though Sam soon discovered that the movie – released in 1977 to near-universal bafflement under the title *Renaldo & Clara* – was far too free-form a project for anybody to stick to any lines he wrote, and simply went along for the ride. All these disparate characters convened in New York in the autumn of 1975, at the Gramercy Park Hotel (where Martin Scorsese had rehearsed *Mean Streets*), and then headed out to New England to begin the tour.

Initially, the Revue played small halls with little or no advance publicity, partly in the romantic spirit of an old-time travelling revue, but also to build a sense of excitement among Dylan fans. The first show, on 30 October 1975, was in the War Memorial Auditorium in the Massachusetts town of Plymouth, where the Pilgrim Fathers landed in the *Mayflower*. Plymouth is not a traditional stop on rock tours, but this was an uncommon tour, with a Fellini-esque cast of characters: a beat poet (Ginsberg); a movie actress (Ronee Blakley); a former member of the Spiders from Mars, and Dylan and Baez, the golden couple of the folk revival reunited, one might think romantically too by their flirtatious manner. But there in the front row each evening was also Mrs Sara Dylan, this being the first and last time that Bob's wife took a public stance in his career. (She would also act in the movie.) Bringing up the rear was the tour clown, a scruffy reporter from *Rolling Stone* named Larry Sloman, whom Baez nicknamed

'Ratso' after Dustin Hoffman's disreputable character in *Midnight Cowboy*.

The show was intimate and deliberately old-fashioned, markedly so compared with the voguish music of 1975. 'The Hustle' and 'Jive Talkin'' were among the hits of that summer; David Bowie's disco-slick 'Fame' was at number one in the US in September. Meanwhile, many American college kids were getting into New Wave groups that embraced anarchy and rebellion, such as the Tubes, a wild-looking band from Arizona (by way of San Francisco) whose stomping, nihilistic debut single, 'White Punks on Dope', was getting a lot of radio play, and whose provocative stage show was part glam-rock concert, part proto-punk shocker. By chance, the Tubes were playing Boston the same night the Revue hit town and Larry Sloman and Sam Shepard went to check out the opposition. Shepard was aghast at what he saw, as he later wrote in his *Rolling Thunder Logbook* (1978): 'TV sets flashing all over the place, violent distorted feedback that sounds like a cow stepping on her afterbirth and not knowing what hit her. An eight-foot transvestite in stilted platform heels, silver skin-tight jump-suit, teased blond hair, and the drummer behind slashing away at his kit as though he was caught in his own mosquito netting. If this is supposed to be satire, I don't get it.' The playwright couldn't believe that anybody would prefer *this noise* to the music – the art! – of Bob Dylan and his distinguished friends. But then Sam came to realise that, at age 32, he was experiencing a generation gap. The generation that grew up with Dylan in the 1960s, Sam's generation, was moving into middle age in the mid-1970s, and a new stratum of youth was pushing up beneath them to re-shape the cultural landscape. This was borne out by the fact that some of the younger members of the Revue audience evidently came to see Bob Dylan in 1975 not quite knowing who he was, but feeling that he was a famous older guy they should experience. 'One impression that I'll never forget,' says Sam Shepard of his days with the Rolling Thunder Revue, 'was this sense that there was this huge sudden generation gap between the kids who were coming to these concerts and the sixties, when I grew up with Dylan . . . They'd heard about him, through their brother or their older sister, or someone who happened to have some old Dylan albums around, but they really didn't know him, or relate to him, and they'd come more out of curiosity.' Jacques Levy confirms Sam's recollection, noting that at one show the Revue did at Brandeis University in Massachusetts, the students (in their very early twenties) sat in awed silence before Dylan (now in his mid-thirties): 'If anybody would even whisper anything, they would go *shussssh*. They didn't want to miss a syllable! It was very funny and sweet . . . as if the Budapest String Quartet had come to play.'

The twenty-somethings who did come to see the Revue may have expected a history lesson in folk-rock, but they found themselves lifted out of their seats each night by the sheer sonic power of Dylan and his cohorts. This was probably Dylan's most dynamic tour since 1966, a mature artist performing high-energy, richly varied sets that featured songs both old and new, often reinterpreting his most well-known tunes in a radical way. For instance the romantic song 'Tonight I'll Be Staying Here With You', from Dylan's mellow 1969 country album *Nashville Skyline*, became lusty and raucous. With appropriate rage, but making room for regret and sadness, Dylan also tore through the best songs on *Blood on the Tracks*, as well as a selection of tunes from the not-yet released *Desire*. Brand new songs such as 'Isis' were essentially unknown to concert audiences in the autumn of 1975, yet Dylan invested such passion in his performances – taking care to enunciate the words clearly – that they became highlights of the shows. What was most striking perhaps was that passion, and the speed and volume at which songs were delivered. From Dylan on down, every member of the Revue seemed wired, and indeed many were hyped-up on cocaine, which was consumed liberally backstage. The Tubes might be singing about 'White Punks on Dope', but these elegant Greenwich Village hipsters were often high as kites when they performed. Coke made the music and the words roar out in a torrent. Dylan almost bellowed his lyrics at times. Taking coke was not concealed on tour (so long as the police weren't alerted). On the contrary, it had become a normal way of life in the upper echelons of the rock business by 1975. Rob Stoner, the bass player in the Revue band, says: 'You were suspicious of anybody who *didn't* do drugs back then.'

★

Although it is true that Dylan and his guests on the Rolling Thunder Revue were no longer *the very latest thing* in 1975, in the sense that this was not the kind of music teenagers necessarily flocked to, it is important to remember that Dylan (like the Stones) was at the top of his game in the mid-1970s, and the shows that the Rolling Thunder Revue staged were widely regarded as supremely hip and sophisticated entertainment. The concerts were in fact stupendously good, musically vital and exciting events, as is proven by the clips in *Renaldo & Clara*, and the recordings released by CBS.★ Certainly the Rolling Thunder Revue is a rock legend, long after the Tubes have been forgotten. Indeed, such an aura developed around these shows that many major artists who had not been invited in the first place petitioned to join in the fun, including, most interestingly, Joni Mitchell. She flew in from California, on 13 November 1973, to take part in the show that night in New Haven, Connecticut, and stayed with the tour until its first leg culminated on the evening of 9 December with a fundraiser for Rubin Carter at Madison Square Garden.

Joni Mitchell was one of those artists who had been inspired by Dylan's example in the 1960s to put aside folk standards and other cover-songs and write personal narrative songs concerning her own feelings and the world as she saw it. Countless musicians had followed Dylan's lead in this way, of course, but along with her fellow Canadian Leonard Cohen, Mitchell was one of those who came closest to matching Dylan's facility for storytelling and language, composing lyrics that are original, poetic and true. Playfulness and humour are always present in her work (as is true of Dylan and Cohen), but so is seriousness and melancholy. Indeed, sadness suffuses the Joni Mitchell songbook. Since the start of her career, Joni's *music* had been firmly in the folk idiom, defined by the sound of her acoustic guitar and piano, segueing into the folk-rock of her 1971 album *Blue*, songs from which she performed with great success at

---

★The double CD set *The Bootleg Series Vol. 5: Bob Dylan Live 1975: The Rolling Thunder Revue* is recommended. Even more so, *Hard Rain*, which captures Dylan and the Revue members at the ragged end of their glory in 1976.

the Isle of Wight Pop Festival in 1970. Following the release of that
superb LP she took a sabbatical, living in seclusion in a cabin in
Canada for several months. When she re-emerged, Mitchell moved
her lyric-writing and music-making far ahead of what she had done
in the past. Settling again in Los Angeles, where she started working
with a dynamic jazz-rock band named the LA Express, and embarked
on a love affair with the band's drummer, John Guerin, Joni cut her
1974 album *Court and Spark*, the first of her records to make the lis-
tener want to move as well as think. In her adoption of strongly
rhythmic amplified rock music on *Court and Spark*, Mitchell was
rediscovering her first musical love. In common with Dylan, she had
been a rock fan before she became interested in folk music, the folk
revival coming after the heyday of rock 'n' roll. With its bright,
lively sound and Joni's wonderful lyrics and vocals, *Court and Spark*
proved a considerable commercial success. Mitchell even scored a hit
single with the song 'Help Me'. Just when she seemed to have found
the key to mainstream popularity, Mitchell released a follow-up LP
that to many was a grave disappointment: an overly arty, not to say
pretentious, album of weird-sounding music. In retrospect, however,
The Hissing of Summer Lawns may be Mitchell's finest album, an LP to
stand alongside *Blood on the Tracks* as one of the masterpieces of mid-
'70s rock.

Musically, *The Hissing of Summer Lawns* is a highly experimental
record. Apart from the jazz-rock inflections contributed by members
of the LA Express, including Joni's lover John Guerin who drums on
almost every track, *Summer Lawns* also features elements of world
music and washes of synthesizer ambience. She mixes synthesizer with
Burundi drums, for instance, on the track 'The Jungle Line'. This
sophisticated and unexpected blend of musical tones was highly
unusual and ahead of its time in 1975; Dylan had never been so
experimental with his music, by contrast, and in years to come Prince
would cite *Summer Lawns* as an influence on *his* career. The album
didn't find favour with critics in 1975, however. Writing in *Rolling
Stone*, Stephen Holden admitted that the lyrics on *Summer Lawns* are
'substantial literature' (as indeed they are), but added that they were set
against 'insubstantial music,' and went so far as to ridicule Joni's

atmospheric playing of the Arp synthesizer on 'Shadows and Light' as sounding like a 'long, solemn fart.' This is nonsense.

The rich and unexpected mixture of musical styles and surprising instrumentation was in fact a perfect setting for the song stories on *Summer Lawns*, which have even more depth and diversity than anything Mitchell had recorded before. As in the past, there was a strong autobiographical element to the lyrics, but the artist seemed a much older and wiser soul than on previous releases. Indeed, she had been on a formidable, character-forming journey in life. From her obscure background in rural Canada and her miserable experience as a single mother and unhappy young wife, she had forged a very successful career in the highly competitive, male-dominated rock business in the late 1960s and early '70s. And although she didn't much care to associate herself with the feminist movement, Joni Mitchell was a *de facto* feminist figure. As Mitchell reminded her listeners on the song 'Don't Interrupt the Sorrow', since she reached the age of seventeen 'I've had no one over me.' Meaning no man and no boss. There was a steely pride in that. In another song she referred to a time in her youth when she was 'working cheap,' but those days were long gone, too. Entering middle age, Joni, like many rock stars of her generation, was independent and rich. Most of her contemporaries (Dylan for one) shied away from writing about their wealth. But Joni seemed proud of her financial status – as well she might be, for she had achieved it all on her own – and she made affluence part of her subject matter on this new record. Like Dylan, Mitchell is an amateur painter (both of them quite bad, in fact) and the cover of *Summer Lawns* features one of her (better) artworks, a detail of which is a small study of her handsome Bel Air home. One could almost call it a mansion. Inside the original gatefold sleeve of the LP, the singer is photographed floating sensuously on her back, in a bikini, in the pool at the house. There is a corresponding wealth and *sensuality* to the music on the LP, with lyrics that evoke a world of money and comfort, but not necessarily happiness, and not restricted to the singer's personal experience. The songs on *Summer Lawns* include many characters. In the title song, for instance, Joni sings about a woman living in a gilded cage of a marriage, the view from her window that of a landscape studded with swimming pools. The central image of the song, and album, 'the hissing of summer lawns,' recalls of course the automatic sprinkler systems commonplace in the richer parts of LA. David Hockney was so struck by the aesthetic of this during his early visits to California that he painted pictures of the sprinklers: *A Lawn Sprinkler*, and *A Lawn Being Sprinkled* (both 1967). It took a foreigner perhaps to be impressed by everyday Southern Californian wealth. Like Hockney, Mitchell was from a sufficiently remote and working-class background to be struck by it, too, and to comment on it in her work.

Perhaps the stand-out track on *The Hissing of Summer Lawns* is 'Harry's House – Centrepiece', which tells the story of a man named Harry on a business trip to New York, during which we learn something about his tired marriage. The song begins with a vivid vignette of Harry arriving in Manhattan: his cab journey from the airport to his mid-town hotel, his taxi one of the schools of checker cabs swimming like yellow fishes between the buildings, as Joni sings in metaphor; Harry looking about in an idle way as he travels into town, gazing at the pretty girls outside Bloomingdale's, watching a helicopter land on the roof of (what was then) the Pan Am building 'like a dragonfly on a tomb.' Gradually, Harry drifts off into a reverie of his life back home, and how he and his wife have little in common any more. Midway through the song, Mitchell and the LA Express segue into a slinky cover of the Harry Edison–Jon Hendricks jazz classic 'Centrepiece', a supremely romantic number that invokes the happier early days of Harry's marriage. As this interlude ends and we are returned to the main song, we hear Mitchell playing the part of Harry's nagging wife back in the suburbs, yelling at the kids and pestering Harry on the telephone. Mitchell concludes the track by noting, in character, that she is not the girl Harry fell in love with all those years ago at the public swimming pool. Although it is difficult to paraphrase a song such as this and communicate its essence in a few words, in short there is a great deal of poetry and art to 'Harry's House – Centrepiece'. It is almost novelistic in detail and characterisation, reminding one in many ways of John Updike's characters Harry and Janice Angstrom, and their troubles in mid-life, in middle-class, mid-'70s America.

Although Dylan eschewed writing songs about the bourgeoisie, or indeed his own considerable wealth, persisting in his romantic dream life as gypsy poet, to whom money is apparently of little importance, Joni Mitchell was not the only singer-songwriter of this generation of American rock stars to address the fact that they had reached a new stage in life's journey. By the mid-1970s, *Rolling Stone* magazine increasingly read like a rock 'n' roll *House & Garden*, with celebrities showing off their new-found wealth in feature articles replete with photographs that were as much about the millionaire lifestyle as music: Elton John in his vast suite at the Sherry-Netherland Hotel; Paul Simon talking at home in his Manhattan duplex, furnished with Bauhaus chairs, an Art Deco piano and Helen Frankenthaler painting (all of which the reporter dutifully described). In common with Mitchell, Simon referenced this plush new life in his work. The characters in his 1975 album *Still Crazy After All These Years* are far from the beatniks who inhabit *Bookends* (1968) and *Bridge Over Troubled Water* (1970). But then, by 1975 Simon was a very different person from the boy he describes hitchhiking on the New Jersey Turnpike in 'America'. Once he had been that character. Now he was living on Central Park West, venturing out by limousine for dinner at Elaine's, comparing therapists with his friend and fellow diner Woody Allen. The wealth and sophistication seeped into the music, as it did with Joni Mitchell. Still, comfort is mixed with melancholy and the regret that comes with age, as is well-expressed in the title song on *Still Crazy After All These Years*. Simon's first marriage was ending in divorce at this time. Mitchell was a divorcee of long-standing. And though Bob and Sara Dylan were briefly reunited during the Rolling Thunder Revue, their marriage would also soon end unhappily.

Another music star attracted to the Rolling Thunder Revue in 1975 was the up-and-comer Bruce Springsteen, who came by the Veterans' Memorial Coliseum in New Haven to say hello to everybody in the show, though he didn't perform on stage. Dylan affected not to have heard of the singer, when he was told he was coming to meet him. 'Who's this guy, *Springfield?*' Bob asked his bass player Rob Stoner, no doubt having a joke, but one underpinned with a touch of professional rivalry. Both Dylan and Springsteen were CBS artists, both signed to the label by the legendary record executive John Hammond, though a decade apart. A singer-songwriter of traditional-sounding music, with a leaning towards narrative songs, coming up in Dylan's shadow, CBS promoted Springsteen initially as *the new Dylan*: an impossible billing to live up to, and one that did Bruce little good in the first couple of years of his career, when he released two mediocre albums.

Bruce Springsteen and his E-Street Band were, however, a barnstorming live act, and their fortunes began to turn around in April 1974 after they played an uproarious show at the Harvard Square Theatre in Cambridge, Massachusetts. In the audience that night was Jon Landau of *Rolling Stone*, the critic who thought *Blood on the Tracks* shoddy-sounding. Springsteen's show was a revelation to Landau, who responded with an effusive article published not in *Rolling Stone*, but a small magazine he also wrote for, the *Boston Real Paper*, gushing that he had witnessed the future of rock 'n' roll at the Harvard Square Theatre 'and its name is Bruce Springsteen,' a priceless endorsement which CBS was quick to quote in promotional material. As a result, Landau and Springsteen became friendly and were soon working together. Apart from being a music writer, Landau was an aspiring record producer and, when he heard that Bruce was struggling to complete his third album, not knowing quite what direction he should be going in, Landau persuaded Springsteen to switch to a first-class New York studio, the Record Plant, where he began to work with a talented young engineer named Jimmy Iovine. Landau got involved as a co-producer on the record, deciding with Bruce that what they really wanted to do was make a '*great* rock 'n' roll record,' as Landau recalls, 'something very focussed, and very exciting. Which I think we did.' In Bruce's mind, it would be an album like a supercharged automobile with fuel injection and chrome wheels. It was *Born to Run*.

In contrast to the new albums by Joni Mitchell and Paul Simon – established artists in their thirties, living moneyed, sophisticated lives – Springsteen was still a young man in 1974. He was from a blue-collar background in New Jersey (he grew up just down the road from Jack Nicholson), and he wrote and sang about the world he knew, romanticising it inordinately. The Romeos and Juliets who rode through the songs of *Born to Run* didn't have much but their wheels, their youth and their love, and were portrayed most often by Springsteen as being in a state of crisis, on the verge of taking flight: *born to run*. With the help of Jimmy Iovine, Jon Landau and Springsteen's wonderfully tight E-Street Band, featuring saxophonist Clarence Clemons, these new songs were set to operatic rock 'n' roll that didn't quite topple over into bombast. From 'Thunder Road' to 'Jungleland', the eight tracks that make up *Born to Run* roared out into the world in the autumn of 1975, Bruce Springsteen's heart and lungs apparently on the point of bursting as he bellowed, growled, beseeched and wailed about the broken-hearted, misunderstood, young and restless reckless drivers of New Jersey.

Like Steven Spielberg's *Jaws*, *Born to Run* was a triumph of marketing as much as art. Certainly, it is a very good rock 'n' roll record, but there were many of those in 1975. The difference with *Born to Run* is that CBS got behind the product, pushed it hard – much harder than they had ever promoted any record by Bob Dylan, a prestige Columbia artist. *Time* and *Newsweek* were persuaded to give Springsteen a cover story (not long after the *Jaws* cover, appropriately). Columbia reps made sure stores ordered in bulk and that tracks from *Born to Run* were played heavily on the radio. At the end of November, with *Born to Run* already a gold record in the USA – meaning that the Recording Industry Association of America (RIAA) had certified over half a million copies sold – CBS ran a full-page ad in *Rolling Stone* telling its readers, '1976 is the year of Bruce Springsteen. Why wait?' As with a blockbuster movie, the marketing strategy was to make the public believe something exceptional was happening. You were going to buy *Born to Run* eventually, just as you went to see *Jaws*, so why not do so before your friends?

The sales of rock albums were booming in the United States in the mid-70s, so much so that in 1976 the RIAA announced a new level of achievement in the metallic scale which had been in operation since the late 1950s. A platinum record would now be awarded to artists who shifted over one million copies of a record. The first album to be certified Platinum was the Eagles' compilation, *Their Greatest Hits 1971–1975*. Bands such as Fleetwood Mac and Led Zeppelin were soon similarly honoured, and in time *Born to Run* would go Platinum, too, and indeed multi-Platinum, selling over six million copies in the US alone. It took a while, however. After the excitement of the initial release of *Born to Run*, the remaining years of the decade were difficult ones for Bruce Springsteen. Having fallen out with his manager, Mike Appel, the artist became embroiled in legal problems, much delaying his follow-up LP, *Darkness on the Edge of Town* (1978). It would not be until the early 1980s, with the erstwhile *Rolling Stone* writer Jon Landau now ensconced as his manager, that he came into his own with the release of *The River* (1980) and *Born in the USA* (1984), and the lengthy world tours he undertook to promote them. As Springsteen trod water in 1976, and the great singer-songwriters such as Dylan and Mitchell relaxed into the background after their recent exertions, popular music turned out to be defined more by the sound of disco, with the rumble of punk like thunder in the distance. In Britain, the Sex Pistols were giving their first gigs, a band unknown outside their own small world, but soon to be infamous. And David Bowie entered his golden years.

18

SPACED-OUT

There is only the moment . . . There is no future.

Almost four years since his appearance as Ziggy Stardust at the Rainbow in London, David Bowie sauntered on to the stage of the Los Angeles Forum to be greeted by 17,000 American fans: the first of three shows at the start of a major tour of North America and Europe. Dressed in white shirt, black trousers and waistcoat, his hair dyed copper-red and swept back from his pale forehead, Bowie began to sway with the train rhythm of the opening number 'Station to Station' from his eponymous new album. With this song, Bowie introduced his mid-'70s persona, that of the Thin White Duke: a narcissistic *faux* aristocrat inspired by his interest in the chillier reaches of German culture, from Nietzsche to Nazism. The music as well as the image had changed a good deal since 1972. In Mick Ronson's place as his band leader, Bowie had hired a young New Yorker named Carlos Alomar, whose funky rhythm guitar was the keynote of the singer's mid-'70s albums, starting with *Young Americans* which had yielded his first US number one. A new single, 'Golden Years', from *Station to Station*, was high in the charts as Bowie took the stage in Los Angeles in February 1976. His face was on the cover of *Rolling Stone*, and the glitterati had come to the Forum to pay him court. Sitting in the front rows were a host of celebrities, including Carole King, Elton John and Rod Stewart; also Henry Winkler (aka the Fonz) and the

President's son, Steven Ford. Also there were David Hockney and his friend Christopher Isherwood, whose stories about pre-war Berlin conjured up a world that fascinated Bowie. The singer seemed much preoccupied with Hitler, in particular, going so far as to compare himself with the Führer in the latest edition of *Rolling Stone*. 'I think I might have been a bloody good Hitler,' he told the publication, ridiculously. 'I'd be an excellent dictator . . . I *do* want to rule the world.' On stage, dressed in black and white, spot-lit as he struck a series of arrogant poses, Bowie seemed only a step away from leading a Nazi rally. Indeed, when he brought his show to London in May, his stiff-armed wave to fans at Victoria Station was interpreted by some as a Nazi salute.

More than anything in 1976, Bowie looked like an actor playing a part on stage and, fittingly, his first motion picture was released during the tour. It was *The Man Who Fell to Earth*, a still from which adorns the cover of *Station to Station*. The director was the British filmmaker Nicolas Roeg, who had cast Mick Jagger in *Performance* (1970). Later in the decade he would make *Bad Timing* (1980) with Art Garfunkel. 'Everything was changing in terms of acting,' says Roeg, reflecting on a time when rock stars began to feel that they could be movie actors, too. Dylan was another example, appearing in *Pat Garrett & Billy the Kid*. For the most part rock stars proved themselves to be bad actors, but Roeg considered it a perfectly valid aspiration for musicians to want to cross over into the medium of film. It was all a *performance*, after all, which is why he named his first movie exactly that. To his mind, a rock show was no less a performance than a production of a Shakespeare play, say. It was just *different*, and maybe even *more*, because of the size of the audiences. As Roeg points out, Laurence Olivier never played to crowds as large as the 17,000 people who filled the Forum night after night to see Bowie: '[David] drew them there. A single performance.'

Nic Roeg is one of the most interesting directors of the 1970s, though also one of the most neglected. His stories are rarely straightforward in the telling: Roeg likes to manipulate time, to create narrative puzzles – and he has made some eccentric career choices. As a result, he has become a marginal figure in film, certainly in America. Nevertheless, having missed out on the chance to make *A Clockwork Orange*, Roeg contributed three classic movies to 1970s cinema. The first of these, *Walkabout* (1971), is a minimalist fairy story in which two innocents – an English schoolgirl and her kid brother – are stranded in the Australian Outback after their father goes insane and kills himself. Just as their situation seems hopeless, the children are rescued by an Aboriginal youth who befriends them and tries to win the girl for his bride. When she ignores his advances, affecting not to understand him, he too kills himself. *Walkabout* is a film about sex and death, and about the modern world versus the natural world. Like all Roeg's films, it is beautifully photographed; the action takes place in the iron-red centre of Australia, with its amazing flora and fauna, under azure-blue cathedral skies. Roeg's second masterpiece of the decade was his 1973 picture *Don't Look Now*, adapted from a ghost story by Daphne Du Maurier. Again red plays an important part. It is the colour – unforgettably – of the raincoat worn by the little girl who drowns accidentally in the first scene of the film, the tragedy that sets the story in motion, red being used thereafter to signal terror. After the drowning, the child's grieving parents (played convincingly by Donald Sutherland and Julie Christie) travel to Venice where the husband is employed in restoring a church during the quiet winter months. As Roeg had captured the colour and feel of the Australian Outback better than any previous filmmaker in *Walkabout*, so did he find a distinctive watery-grey melancholy in off-season Venice. At the centre of the picture is a scene when the husband and wife make love in their hotel, tentatively and then passionately, for the first time in a long while, rediscovering themselves as a couple after the tragedy. It is a bedroom sequence so sexually truthful that Roeg had to battle with censors to get any of it on screen, and when the film was released in 1973 the explicit nature of the sex caused a furore. Roeg is unapologetic. Like John Updike, he is mindful that sex is a fundamental part of life, believing therefore that it *must* be prominent in his work. 'I wouldn't like to make a film that isn't sexy, because sex is a truth, isn't it?' he asks, quietly, an understated man. 'That's who we are. Without sex none of us would exist . . . The only thing common to all life is sex.'

The next project for this singular director, the one that brings his story into confluence with that of David Bowie, was based on an obscure science fiction novel by an American named Walter Tevis, whose first novel, *The Hustler*, was made into the film of the same name in 1961. Encouraged by that success, Tevis went to Mexico in 1960–61 to write his second novel, but lost himself in the life of a barfly (the writer was a chronic alcoholic), sobering up enough to dash off one story in the last weeks of his trip. The result was *The Man Who Fell to Earth*, a long (and wonderful) title for a short novel about an alien from a planet named Anthea that has been ravaged by five years of war, with the result that vital natural resources such as water are virtually exhausted. Marshalling what energy they have left, the Antheans send one of their kind to Earth, which the Antheans have seen is mostly comprised of water. Their spaceman's mission is to build a larger space ship to ferry them all to safety. Falling to Earth in rural Kentucky, the alien assumes the appearance of a human being, based on television transmissions the Antheans have intercepted. He poses specifically as an Englishman, an interpreter at the United Nations named Thomas Newton. But the Anthean has his references slightly skew-whiff. He appears unusually tall, at six-and-a-half feet; he is very pale; extremely thin, with the persona of a man but the bone structure of a woman. He doesn't cope well with Earthly forces, such as gravity and the speed of travel, and easily becomes ill. Despite these handicaps, Newton builds a mighty corporation specialising in photographic equipment, though the secret purpose of his World Enterprises is to construct and send a rescue ship to his home planet. Newton is assisted in his work by a brilliant patent lawyer named Farnsworth and a scientist called Bryce, and is also befriended by a hotel chambermaid.

Although it sold respectably well in its day, Tevis' novel was largely forgotten by the mid-1970s and, indeed, science fiction was in the doldrums at the start of the decade. Certainly as far as the movies were concerned, the genre had become associated primarily with the sort of cheap, exploitation films made by Roger Corman and his ilk. There were exceptions, of course: Stanley Kubrick's glorious 1969 picture *2001: A Space Odyssey*; also *Silent Running* (1971), an engaging low-budget picture that expressed the fears of the growing ecology movement, with Bruce Dern as a green-fingered astronaut attempting to save Earth's plants and wildlife. But science fiction films were not regarded as natural money-makers, and wouldn't become so until after the success of *Star Wars*. So when Nic Roeg decided that he wanted to make a movie based on Walter Tevis' novel, he was not swimming in the mainstream. But then he never had. Anyway, he wasn't interested in Tevis' story *because* it was science fiction in the conventional sense, concerned as the genre mostly is with space ships, time travel and monsters. It wasn't that kind of book at all, in fact. 'What I liked about it very much was this human quality,' explains the director. Newton was an alien so similar to a human being that he could pass as one of us, and during his time on Earth he shows himself to be vulnerable to human temptations. This was a fascinating concept to Roeg, especially if he could cast the lead role cleverly, which he certainly did.

Nic began by going to tall, thin actors, thinking initially of Peter O'Toole as Newton. Then his executive producer Si Litvinoff, the attorney who brought *A Clockwork Orange* to Stanley Kubrick's door, heard that David Bowie might be interested, and Bowie's agent arranged for Nic and Si to see a recent BBC documentary about the singer, a film called *Cracked Actor*, that showed Bowie on tour in America. The singer was thin, pale and androgynous, almost exactly as Tevis describes Newton in the novel: 'He was not a man; yet he was very much like a man . . . His frame was improbably slight, his features delicate, his fingers long, thin, and the skin almost translucent, hairless.' Watching *Cracked Actor*, Roeg saw that this young rock star might be very good indeed as *The Man Who Fell to Earth*.

When the *Cracked Actor* documentary was made Bowie was still working to establish himself in the United States, a campaign started in 1972 with the release of *The Rise and Fall of Ziggy Stardust and the Spiders from Mars*. Despite the great success of the LP in Britain, and although Bowie toured widely to promote the record in the US, *Ziggy* reached no higher than number 75 in the American album charts, and the singles RCA released from the record did nothing in the States. The Ziggy image was too exotic for mainstream American tastes, as *Rolling Stone* publisher Jann Wenner believes. 'He had a very campy, gay sensibility,' says Wenner of Bowie, 'which has always been part of the English popular culture, and not so here, not as ingrained.' British bands that prospered in the States in the early to mid-'70s – the likes of Led Zeppelin, the Who and Fleetwood Mac – tended to conform to the macho rock uniform of long hair, jeans and leather. British glam rock bands such as Roxy Music never achieved wide-spread popularity in the USA, while *outré* homegrown stars like Lou Reed were always a minority interest. David Bowie, specifically, was 'a little too precious for the American audience,' as Wenner sees it. US radio stations were noticeably slow to play Bowie's singles, even ones as catchy as 'The Jean Genie' and 'Rebel Rebel' from his post-*Ziggy* albums *Aladdin Sane* (1973) and *Diamond Dogs* (1974). But Bowie persisted. He toured, he did call-in shows, and appeared on American television, promoting himself tirelessly. The breakthrough came when he went into Sigma Sound in Philadelphia in 1974 to make the disco-soul crossover LP *Young Americans*. With this slickly produced album, Bowie created a sound and image that was broad enough to appeal to mainstream America, and album and singles went to the top of the charts in 1975. 'But that's a long time from when we started,' observes Angie Bowie, who still had a hand in her husband's career, though their marriage had all but fallen apart. 'Everyone imagines it was this big, immediate hit. Well, it wasn't.'

It is also worth observing that by the mid-1970s Bowie's ambivalent sexuality was no longer such a hindrance to his career in America as it had been in 1972. As Lou Reed noted, it seemed that everybody was going around saying they were bisexual these days. A sign of the changing times in the USA was the recent proliferation of bisexual bath houses in the major cities, formerly gay saunas where men *and* women now had sex in bewildering permutations, defying the categories Gay or Straight, or indeed Bisexual. The Hugh Hefner of what was being called *pansexuality* was a businessman named Stephen Ostrow. Despite being married with two children (and a dog named Snoopy), and spending part of his time as a conventional family man in suburban New Jersey, Ostrow was one of those men who, not unlike Ossie Clark and David Bowie, believed that it was possible to have a wife and yet also enjoy a parallel gay life. For some time, Ostrow was a regular patron of the gay bath houses of New York. Seeing how much money was to be made in this world, he then opened his own establishment, the Continental Baths, in the basement of the Ansonia Hotel on West 74th Street, a place where men and women were welcome to have sex in any combination they liked, right in front of everybody if they wanted, or in the privacy of a ten-dollar room. To further enliven the evenings, Ostrow hired entertainers to perform at the club. Notably, he gave a break to a wait-ress named Bette Midler, whose pianist was one Barry Manilow. By 1976, the Continental Baths was one of the hippest venues in all New York, with similar sex clubs opening on the West Coast.

Cocaine was part of the hedonistic bath-house scene, as it was part of club culture generally. In fact, coke was becoming a commonplace recreational drug for millions of Americans by 1976, with *The Cocaine Consumer's Handbook* a minor bestseller in the US. Certainly the drug had become all-pervasive in the rock music industry, where it had a reputation for being a healthy high. 'Everybody thought it was safe and easy fun, and it was cheap,' recalls Jann Wenner, a heavy user at this time. As we have seen with the Rolling Thunder Revue, there was no embarrassment within the business about using cocaine. But, as Wenner concedes, cocaine proved to have a dark side. 'People got diverted by a lot of drug use. And people became very *unpleasant*.' Perhaps Bowie's cocaine habit was part of the explanation for some of *his* more unpleasant and preposterous press statements (likening him-self to Hitler for example); he was using a lot of cocaine by 1976. The artist was so stoned during the recording of *Station to Station*, as he later admitted, that he could remember hardly a thing about it. And when he wasn't working, he seemed to need to recover from this drug-fuelled lifestyle by hiding away from the world in his New York town house, on West 17th Street, what Angie Bowie described as 'a dark, horrible house.' The Bowies were estranged by now, with Angie spending most of her time in London, where she had her own drug issues. Husband and wife spoke sporadically, often antagonistically, on the telephone, and it was during one of these ratty, druggy conversations that Angie informed David that he had an offer to make a film, which had long been an ambition. 'Finally, I got him on the phone. He was obviously stoned out of his brains. And I said, "You wanted to do a film . . . I got you a film. Why don't you see the director?" So then he started making whining [noises]. I said, "You know, actually, it's not a good idea; don't bother to do it . . . thinking about it, the condition you're in, you'll just humiliate yourself." Then of course he called me back for the whole plan.'

Bowie didn't audition for film. Rather, the director was summoned to meet the rock star at his New York home to answer David's questions about the project – at least that's why Roeg thought he was going to New York. But when he arrived at David's house, the singer wasn't in. Although they had an appointment for nine p.m., Bowie had simply forgotten about the arrangement. Not wanting to lose his opportunity, Roeg sat and waited in David's kitchen, and waited, until midnight when Bowie rolled home from a recording studio and told the director that he was far too tired to talk about the movie at this late hour, but that he would do the picture, saying 'Let me know when you want me.' And that was that. With Bowie on board, though in rather unorthodox circumstances, Nic and his executive producer Si Litvinoff quickly cast the other parts in *The Man Who Fell to Earth*. Rip Torn, the actor originally set to play Jack Nicholson's part in *Easy Rider*, would be the scientist Dr Nathan Bryce. Buck Henry became the lawyer Oliver Farnsworth. When it came to casting the waitress, named Marylou in the film (Betty Jo in the book), Litvinoff suggested Candy Clark, the vivacious actress who played Debbie in *American Graffiti*. One of the ways in which the movie of *The Man* differs from Tevis' novel is that the part of the waitress is enlarged significantly, and she becomes Newton's lover. As Marylou, Candy Clark would have almost as much time on screen as David Bowie himself, making the picture as much about their relationship as anything else, again emphasising the humanity of this very unusual sci-fi story.

Tevis had written a very good novel in *The Man Who Fell to Earth*, creating a highly original and intriguing story. But as with the other movie adaptations we have looked at, the story was enhanced by being brought to the screen. In casting Bowie, Roeg was able to explore thoroughly the idea of *being an alien*, not only because of Bowie's spacey stage image (though that helped). More significantly, as an Englishman in America – where the story was set and filmed – Bowie *was* an alien. Yet because of the common language his foreignness was accepted. This was perfect for the film. 'Your foreignness is never challenged in America, if you're English,' as Roeg observes. 'So, it's a marvellous disguise.' Clever use of the Englishman–abroad motif was made both in the dialogue of the picture and in creating Bowie's wardrobe. For instance, when Newton first appears, stumbling into a small town in Kentucky, he is wearing a duffel coat, a commonplace garment in Britain and one the alien might well have seen on TV, but an item not much worn in the United States. So the alien doesn't look normal in the American idiom, yet he is not completely outlandish. This was far more interesting than if Newton had appeared in a space suit, or indeed jeans and a T-shirt. When Bowie drops the hood of the duffel coat, he is revealed as having bright red hair, with a streak. In the novel, Newton has curly white hair. This red wedge was Bowie's stage image at the time, and he didn't want to change it, but in fact it worked well in the picture. Again, it would be uncommon indeed for a young American in the South in the mid-1970s to dye his hair red and have it cut in such a radical style. Most American youths preferred long shaggy locks at this time. But on an English visitor, such a modish hairstyle passed as foreign eccentricity.

As with many of Roeg's films, *The Man Who Fell to Earth* is told in a non-linear way, switching back and forth in time, partly because of Roeg's interest in the manipulation of time – and time is the essence of what concerns this alien visitor for whose planet time is running out. Newton also came from a past that was technologically ahead of the present he was in. These Einsteinian gymnastics fascinated Roeg. 'There is only the moment. Otherwise, it's all the past. There is no *future*,' muses the director. 'It's a word.' For Newton, the future will be a return to Anthea to rescue his people. Or so he *hopes*. It doesn't turn out that way. Newton becomes stuck in the present day, in developing his business empire, in his dealings with his lawyer and Dr Bryce. Most of all, Newton is grounded by a woman.

In her role as the fluffy, tipsy innocent Marylou, Candy Clark is one of the delights of *The Man Who Fell to Earth* and her scenes with Bowie are both touching and convincing, as realistic in their domestic detail as those between Jack Nicholson and Karen Black in *Five Easy Pieces*. Similarly, Marylou and Tommy (as she calls Newton) are young lovers in a small town, getting drunk, getting laid, trying to understand each other, and ultimately there is betrayal and disillusion. These are all commonplace themes for a regular drama, of course, but very unusual for science fiction. As one had come to expect from a Roeg film, there is plenty of sex: between Dr Bryce and a string of girls, and between Marylou and Tommy. At the time, Candy was dating Roeg and she found the experience of having her boyfriend directing her in bedroom scenes with Bowie extremely embarrassing. 'I hated doing those . . . I am very self-conscious about my body. And so was David. I could tell he hated doing them.' Still, it is a rare movie in which extra-terrestrials are seen making love. There are also many humorous moments which add depth to the characters: when, for instance, Marylou talks about how when you look at the sky you just *know* that there has to be a God up there. As the space traveller Newton, Bowie raises his eyebrows sardonically, showing his character to be bemused by such an earthly observation; by this subtly comic gesture Bowie also proves himself to be a natural screen actor.

Although much of the picture is concerned with personal relationships conducted in small rooms, a domestic story in fact, Newton's visit to Earth also has an epic dimension, and it gradually becomes evident to the viewer that *years* are passing. Newton does not age physically, but Marylou, Farnsworth and Bryce all become old. (Emerging from make-up one day, 28-year-old Candy looked at herself in a mirror and, seeing a woman who resembled her mother, burst into tears. 'I suddenly saw how I would look in the future.') For the most part, however, Roeg keeps make-up and special effects to a minimum. Rather, the story is made as ordinary as possible and the epic nature of the film is indicated in the most simple ways. For instance, when Dr Bryce summons the courage to ask Newton directly where he is from, confronting him outside a shack in a desert, Bowie answers by looking down a highway that extends to the horizon and saying casually, 'somewhere down there.' Looking at the majesty of the view, our imagination makes the awesome leap into space.

Newton builds World Enterprises with advanced technology brought from his planet, but these innovations are not so very far-fetched, rather developments on commonplace items such as cameras, and televisions. 'He was not a genius,' says Roeg of Thomas Newton. 'He was an ordinary person in another culture . . . We thought they'd be maybe just twenty years ahead of us.' In short, the subject matter, by definition fantastical, didn't have to be treated in such a way as to be beyond belief. This approach helps make the ending of the movie especially moving. When the authorities become suspicious about the activities of World Enterprises, Farnsworth is murdered and Newton is abducted by the American secret service and imprisoned in a labyrinthine apartment complex where he is interrogated, but also indulged with anything that an eccentric billionaire might want. After years of confinement in this luxury maze-jail, Newton is allowed a visit by Marylou. She is in her late middle age now, and after the excitement of their reunion both realise that they no longer have the same feelings for one another. More time passes and we next see Marylou at Christmas, buying a bottle of booze, and taking it home to the apartment she now shares with Dr Bryce, the pair living out a sozzled retirement on the money Newton paid them. The movie ends with Bryce tracking Newton down in a bar. Having finally got free of his prison-apartment, Newton looks the same as always, but has evidently been ruined by his time on Earth. With no hope of seeing his planet again, he spends his days getting drunk. The picture ends with the alien knocking over his glass. The waiter says to Bryce, 'I think Mr Newton has had enough now, don't you?' Bryce replies sadly that he thinks maybe he has. As Newton's head drops to the table, we hear Artie Shaw's clarinet rendition of 'Stardust': a musical pun, and an elegant punctuation to this most stylish and unusual spaceman-movie.

The soundtrack to *The Man Who Fell to Earth* is both one of its strengths and part of the reason for the failure of the film commercially. Originally, Si Litvinoff cut a deal with RCA whereby Bowie would receive $250,000 (£137,000) for his work on the picture, and in return he would also record a soundtrack. His fame as a music star had helped make the movie possible, of course, and a Bowie soundtrack, hopefully yielding a hit single, would naturally be a boon. Bowie did record music for the film, fragments of which appear on his albums *Station to Station* and *Low* (1977), the latter being the first of a series of LPs he made with the collaboration of Roxy Music veteran Eno. One of the tracks on *Low* intended for the movie was the instrumental 'Subterraneans'. Other songs, specially 'TVC15' on *Station to Station*, seem inspired by the characters in the film. But then the film producers unwisely tried to renegotiate Bowie's fee for the project. 'David said, *Go fuck yourself*,' recalls Litvinoff. 'And that's how we lost the soundtrack.' Obliged to find alternative music, Roeg attempted to obtain rights to Pink Floyd's new record *The Dark Side of the Moon* which fitted perfectly, but it was too expensive. So he called on John Phillips of the Mamas and the Papas to assemble a soundtrack comprised of source music: guitar riffs and ticking clocks in a cheeky pastiche of *The Dark Side of the Moon*, also effective snatches of symphonic music from Gustav Holst's *Planets Suite*, as well as country, jazz and rock 'n' roll covers, a couple of the tunes recorded especially with Mick Taylor, who had recently quit the Rolling Stones.* The resulting soundtrack is an eclectic montage of music that serves the story well. But the loss of Bowie's music rendered the movie much less marketable.

The US distributor was also alarmed by the non-linear structure of the film, the length of the movie at over two hours and the *dollops of good sex* (as Buck Henry refers to Roeg's trademark bedroom scenes). Other graphic sequences, such as Marylou pissing herself with fear when Newton reveals his alien form to her, caused the censor additional concern. As a result, the film was cut severely for American distribution, losing much of its sense. When it was released in May 1976 during Bowie's tour, it flopped in America (though it did somewhat better in Britain). 'Oh, it crushed us all,' laments Candy Clark of the failure of the project. 'It just knocked the wind out of everyone's sails.' For Buck Henry, with his considerable experience of the

*Taylor was replaced by Ron Wood at this time.

American film industry and cinema-going public, there was an inevitability about the fate of the picture. Roeg's perverse approach to narrative means his audience has to invest more than the usual amount of effort in his films to get something back from the experience of watching them, and ordinary American audiences 'don't want to be working,' as Henry observes. Si Litvinoff agrees with Henry, saying that Roeg was his own worst enemy in this respect. Still, in Britain the film attracted an appreciative if small audience, and for those who watch attentively, *The Man Who Fell to Earth*, now restored to its full splendour for DVD, is still a highly unusual and thought-provoking picture, a shining example of how delightfully eccentric and experimental seventies' cinema could be at its best. Certainly, there is no '70s movie in which a rock star is better cast, or gives a more convincing performance.

The month that the bowdlerised version of Nic Roeg's film was released, to perplexed reviews and small audiences, George Lucas was in London making a very different science-fiction film, one of the most significant in the history of cinema (though perhaps not as brilliant as *The Man Who Fell to Earth*). After *American Graffiti* had turned out to be a commercial success, despite the fears of the executives at Universal, Lucas looked forward to directing a project he had long been contemplating: the Vietnam movie *Apocalypse Now*, written by John Milius, with their mutual friend Francis Coppola pencilled in as producer. Lucas' vision was to make an anti-war film, ideally shooting in Vietnam with character actors rather than big stars, and hopefully with the co-operation of the United States military. But history got in the way. As defeat for South Vietnam became inevitable, there was no prospect that the US Army would assist with such a movie, and with the fall of Saigon in April 1975 it became practically impossible to shoot on location under any circumstances. So Lucas turned to another idea. He wanted to make a movie of the comic-strip story *Flash Gordon*, the television serial of which was a favourite of the director's when he was growing up in the small town of Modesto, California, in the 1950s. When he failed to obtain the rights to the serial, Lucas invented his own science fiction epic, modelled primarily on *Flash Gordon*, but borrowing ideas from Frank Herbert's *Dune* stories and taking visual cues from the samurai films of Akira Kurosawa. Having been frustrated in his attempt to make *Apocalypse Now*, Lucas also wanted to incorporate some spectacular battle scenes and to have a Manichaean clash between good and evil. The resulting concoction is *Star Wars*, another science fiction film dreamt up when sci-fi was very much out of fashion, with little prospect of making a lot of money. Indeed, two studios turned down Lucas' project before Twentieth Century-Fox ventured a modest $10 million (£5.5 million) – at a time when major movies were costing twice as much – to bankroll the project.

Star Wars was shot mostly in England, at Elstree Studios to the north of London, where Stanley Kubrick made *2001*, because there were several large sound stages available there as well as skilled British technicians who, by Hollywood standards, were relatively cheap. For Kubrick's story, British carpenters and model-makers had created gleaming-white space ships that seemed to redefine the look of science fiction. Watching these dazzling models spin through space to the waltz music of Johann Strauss was an aesthetic triumph. In contrast to the pristine look of Kubrick's future-world, one of George's clever innovations – perhaps the *most* immediately arresting aspect of *Star Wars* when it was released in 1977 – was that life in space might not always be so shiny new. One of the key characters in *Star Wars* is pilot-for-hire Han Solo, his space ship, the *Millennium Falcon*, as battered as a second-hand Ford, 'a piece of junk!' as Luke Skywalker exclaims when he first sees it. To be fair, *Star Wars* was innovative and inventive in other ways, too: the battle scenes were state of the art; in creating the aliens and droids, Lucas brought a surprising amount of humour to the film; the androgynous gold-plated C-3PO and its dustbin-like companion R2-D2 make an amusing double act, as they must because they carry the movie for the first few scenes. The human characters are less successful. The principals – Luke (Mark Hamill), Han Solo (Harrison Ford) and Princess Leia (Carrie Fisher) – behave as children in what is essentially a Saturday morning television serial brought to the big screen. Their dialogue is apparently assembled from every cliché George Lucas could remember from years of watching such TV shows. (At one point, Han Solo announces: 'I've got a bad feeling about this!') The young cast found *Star Wars* a tiresome picture to make, something of an embarrassment in fact in the age of New Hollywood. Having struggled with his lines, Ford told Lucas at one point, 'You can *type* this shit, but you can't *say* it.' Feisty Carrie Fisher found her token girl character such an anachronistic stereotype in the (Earthly) age of feminism that she asked Lucas sarcastically whether she shouldn't have a scene cooking for the boys.

While the cast made fun of the movie, the British crew were equally as irreverent, irritated by a relatively inexperienced and uncommunicative American director, and contemptuous of a low-budget, low-brow and apparently very silly science fiction flick. (Famously, the crew mocked Chewbacca, the hairy bear-like creature whose dialogue is limited to growling, as *the dog*.) Without the special effects that would bring the battle scenes to life and lend verve to the climactic last few minutes of the movie, the rushes were unimpressive and the executives at Twentieth Century-Fox began to worry about their investment. Shooting also went over schedule. Having started work at Elstree in March 1976, George was still in London in mid-summer, an unusually hot and humid summer that made life even more stressful. Depressed and worried, the director developed such severe chest pains that he feared he was going to have a heart attack. And what made the process all the more painful was the knowledge that his erstwhile mentor, Francis Ford Coppola, was now in the Philippines shooting the film that Lucas had really wanted to make – *Apocalypse Now.*

19

APOCALYPSE NOW

Art is long and life is short, and success is very far off.
JOSEPH CONRAD

When Francis Ford Coppola and his family arrived in the Philippines in March 1976, they found the heat and humidity almost overwhelming. The country felt as though it were being smothered like a feverish patient under suffocating blankets, the temperature rising daily ahead of the rainy season. Then there was the culture shock. The Coppolas – Francis, the great film director, big as a wrestler as he approached his thirty-eighth birthday; his petite wife, Eleanor; their two sons, 12-year-old Gio and Roman, ten; and their 4-year-old daughter Sofia* – gazed in fascination at peasants labouring in rice paddies alongside lugubrious water buffalo, while whole families lived together in mud huts, a green swathe of wilderness hemming in their villages. Sofia commented brightly: 'It looks like the Disneyland Jungle Cruise.' For her father, this was the start of a much more rigorous journey, one that would take him into what Joseph Conrad called the 'heart of darkness.'

Having looked at a number of seventies films adapted from mediocre, even hack, works of fiction, we now turn to a movie based on a work of great literature. In Conrad's novella *Heart of Darkness*,

---

*Sofia was a babe in arms when *The Godfather* was filmed, actually *the* baby in the climactic baptism scene; in adult life she directed *Lost in Translation* (2003).

written in 1899, and published just after the turn of the century, a seaman named Marlow relates how, as a young man in the late nineteenth century, he piloted a steamboat up the River Congo into the West African jungle, a land then being plundered by European ivory traders. Marlow's destination was an ivory post run by a man named simply Mr Kurtz – a polyglot European of French ancestry, with a German name, raised in England. Kurtz was a legend in the ivory trade for his outstanding success at the business, and because of his remarkable bearing and mind. He was physically impressive: tall, strong and fearless. He was also an intellectual. With his stature, portentous speaking voice, intellect and European authority, Africans at his trading post worshipped Kurtz as a demi-god and Kurtz allowed himself to become a kind of chief to them. In Conrad's tale, Marlow is travelling to find Kurtz because the trader has fallen ill and his company wants him and his ivory rescued. As Marlow sails from London to Africa, then makes his way slowly up the Congo, he hears more stories about this singular man, who begins to fill his thoughts and those of the reader. (What will Kurtz be like when we encounter him?) When Marlow arrives at the trading post, the scene is a dismal one. Kurtz is on his deathbed. His mud house is surrounded by African followers, and evidence of their savagery, including human heads impaled on stakes. Kurtz is brought on to the steamboat and borne away, too sick and mad to hold much conversation, uttering only a few enigmatic words in justification of what he has done and what he has become. Yet Marlow develops an admiration for Kurtz, and in the few words he hears him speak he believes he catches 'a glimpsed truth' of what it truly is to be a man.

Conrad's book bewitched readers throughout the twentieth century, being much more than an adventure story – rather an exploration of metaphysics – and many filmmakers aspired to bring Mr Kurtz to the screen. Orson Welles got close in the 1930s, but abandoned his *Heart of Darkness* due to inadequate funds. At film school in California in the 1960s, John Milius became similarly fascinated with the story and wrote a screenplay that combined elements of Conrad's book with the Vietnam War, seeing parallels between America's actions in South East Asia and the way in which Europeans behaved in West Africa in the late 1800s. In Milius' screenplay of *Apocalypse Now*, Kurtz the ivory trader becomes Colonel Walter E. Kurtz of the US Army's Special Forces, an exceptional officer corrupted by war. Kurtz sets aside his training and his American values and acts in the field instinctively as a warrior-king, a ruthless and terrible king who leads a native army over the border into Cambodia, without authority, to prosecute the war as he sees fit. He is brilliantly successful in his renegade campaign, embarrassingly so for the desk generals at HQ who decide that Kurtz must be eliminated, i.e. assassinated. Captain Willard is a young soldier sent to find the Colonel and terminate his command. Other characters in the screenplay include a charismatic air cavalry officer named Kilgore, whom Willard meets on his journey. In writing the screenplay, Milius incorporated the psychedelic nature of the Vietnam War: the drugs that soldiers used and the rock music they listened to, drawing inspiration from the war reports of Michael Herr, stories collected in his powerful 1977 book *Dispatches*.

This Milius-scripted movie was one of many projects that Francis Coppola and his friends had worked on in the early days of American Zoetrope, with the plan that George Lucas would direct, possibly shooting in 16 mm, documentary-style, on location in Vietnam. When Zoetrope floundered in 1970, owing money to Warner Brothers, the rights to *Apocalypse Now* passed to the studio. After Francis' success with *The Godfather*, he bought the film back. Lucas was still hoping to direct, and indeed planned to make *Apocalypse* his next picture after *American Graffiti*, as we have seen, but it became apparent that Francis now wanted to direct the movie himself. So it was that Lucas went to London to make *Star Wars* and Coppola travelled to the Philippines to shoot *Apocalypse Now*, both directors commencing filming at approximately the same time in the spring of 1976, with Lucas feeling that his old friend and mentor had, to a degree, betrayed him. There was to be poetic justice, however. Making *Apocalypse Now* became a nightmarish experience. Though the original plan was to release the picture in July 1976, the month the United States celebrated its bicentennial year, to make a timely comment on America and its foreign policy, *Apocalypse Now* became so mired in problems that it did not reach cinemas until 1979. This painfully protracted project almost broke Coppola financially, and mentally.

The trouble began when Francis tried to cast the picture. Despite having achieved extraordinary success with his two *Godfather* films, and having commented perspicaciously on Watergate with his excellent 1974 surveillance movie *The Conversation* (one of many minor cinematic gems of this brilliant decade), none of the big-name actors he approached wanted to star in *Apocalypse Now*. Partly the problem was that the Vietnam War movie genre was not yet established. By the end of the seventies, there would be a surfeit of such pictures, but when Coppola began casting *Apocalypse* in 1975, Vietnam was a very recent, very bad experience that few Americans wanted to reflect upon. Also, to shoot in the Philippines meant American actors leaving their comfortable US homes for long periods of time in Asia, which they were loath to do. As a result, Coppola suffered a series of frustrating rejections. To play the enigma that is Kurtz, only the greatest screen actor would do, and Coppola went directly to Marlon Brando, whose career he had done so much to revive. But Brando wouldn't return Coppola's phone calls. Robert Redford and Jack Nicholson then turned down Kurtz. Al Pacino, who one might think owed Coppola a very big favour for casting him as Michael Corleone, passed on Willard. So did James Caan and Steve McQueen. One day Coppola snapped. His wife Eleanor describes the moment in her memoir of the making of *Apocalypse Now*, the fascinating and revealing book *Notes*. 'Francis feels frustrated,' she reports. 'He gathers up his Oscars and throws them out the window. The children pick up the pieces in the backyard. Four of the five are broken.' Indeed, Coppola might have been wise to give up on the project at this stage. But he carried on.

Brando relented and said he would appear in the picture, for a fabulously high fee of $3.5 million (£1.92 million). He also wanted one million paid in advance. Coppola wrote the cheque without hesitation, literally wrote the cheque himself because – most unusually – the director had decided to finance *Apocalypse Now* personally. Coppola used the fortune he had made from the *Godfather* films, borrowing the balance of the $13 million (£7.14 million) budget from Warner Brothers, with his property as collateral. This way he felt he would have greater control over the movie, which was to be an immensely personal, even perhaps self-indulgent project. Aside from Brando as Kurtz, other key parts went to first-class character actors: Robert Duvall became Lieutenant Colonel Bill Kilgore; Martin Scorsese's friend Harvey Keitel was cast as Captain Willard. Much of the action would take place on a patrol boat (PBR) that takes Willard up river to Kurtz's compound. The role of the boat chief went to Albert Hall; the mustachioed Jay 'Chef' Hicks was played by Frederic Forrest (who was also in *The Conversation*); Sam Bottoms became the surfer Lance, and 14-year-old Larry Fishburne played the young soldier nicknamed Clean.

Coppola chose to film in the Philippines because the country looked so much like Vietnam, which was now effectively closed to Westerners. Also, the Filipino government offered to lend the director US-made military hardware. The country was essentially a dictatorship at the time, run by President Ferdinand Marcos, whose air force included American Bell HU-1 helicopters, known as Hueys, the ubiquitous 'chopper' of the Vietnam War. One of the first scenes to be filmed was the classic battle in which Robert Duvall as Kilgore leads a squadron of Hueys in an attack on a Vietcong village, to the sound of Richard Wagner's 'Ride of the Valkyries'. Part of Coppola's vision of *Apocalypse Now* was that all human life should be in the film because war is the biggest hold-all of human experience, and this sequence provided the requisite big battle, with all the excitement that entails: war machines, fighting, loud noises and pyrotechnics. It didn't quite go to plan. Two houses containing stunt equipment were blown up accidentally, causing $50,000 worth of damage to materials. Even more troublesome, the Filipino Air Force kept flying away to fight real rebels in the south of the country, which wasted days that became weeks. Then, when he sat down to look at his rushes, Coppola realised that Harvey Keitel was miscast as Willard. Keitel had proved a fine actor in *Mean Streets*, and had given an interesting cameo in Scorsese's new picture *Taxi Driver* (a movie that deals with the story of a damaged Vietnam veteran, of course). But he looked uncomfortable in battle fatigues. When Coppola told him he was out of the film, the actor seemed almost relieved, though it was a body blow to his career, and potentially to the film itself. Francis had to hire a replacement Willard fast, before Hollywood trade journalists got wind that the production was in trouble. Martin Sheen swiftly took the part and was soon aboard the PBR on its voyage up river to Kurtz, a journey every bit as ponderous as that described in Conrad's novel, with the added element that the actors in the boat were becoming like a real company of soldiers. '[Coppola] created a war within the movie,' comments the actor Frederic Forrest. 'You just lived the part.'

There were many strange, and indeed comical, experiences during the filming of *Apocalypse Now*, including the episode of the tiger. In the story Willard (Sheen) gets off the boat to investigate a disturbance in the jungle, taking a reluctant Chef (Forrest) with him, only to come face-to-face with a tiger. The animal represents the elemental nature of Vietnam and the impossibility of American forces taming it. To film the scene, a tiger was flown in from Los Angeles with its handler, a fellow named Monty Cox, whose face bore the scars of his trade. The tiger was named Gambi, and Monty told the actors that Gambi had appeared in several movies. He was 'a Hollywood tiger.' But Monty cautioned them not to forget that Gambi was also *an animal*. When they heard that, Fred and Marty looked at each other nervously. The tiger caused consternation all around from the moment it arrived in the Philippines. Its crate was too big to get into the little plane that was to fly it up to the location, so Monty Cox walked it on like a passenger, freaking out the human beings who had already boarded. They fled to the back of the plane, while the pilot climbed on to a wing, refusing to take off. When Gambi was finally delivered to the jungle, Monty had to lure it into shot by tempting it with a live pig on a rope. Hopefully, the tiger would pounce into frame with the actors, in order to swipe the pig for its supper. Before shooting, Francis asked Fred what he thought Chef would do before getting off the boat and going on this dangerous foray into the jungle – maybe smoke a joint to give him courage? 'Yeah, probably,' agreed Forrest. 'Go and smoke a J,' suggested Coppola, and Fred did so. Many of the actors were using drugs on the movie, often just before filming, figuring that this is what it was like for the real soldiers in Vietnam. Actor Sam Bottoms has spoken frankly of consuming a whole array of drugs during the making of *Apocalypse Now*, including marijuana, LSD and speed.

As they were making final preparations for the scene, Monty Cox told the actors: 'Gambi is very hungry today. I haven't fed him for two days.' Meanwhile Coppola was concerned that everybody was in shot, and kept telling his actors to get closer to the tiger. 'You get closer, Francis,' muttered Fred in return, wired as he was on dope, and fearful that when they started running Gambi would ignore the pig and go after *them*, bringing literal meaning to Marlon Brando's cynical observation to Freddie that the movie business was a 'meat rack.' When the tiger leapt, Fred and Marty fled for their lives, zigzagging every which way through the jungle trying to lose the cat, which they were convinced was right behind them. 'The look in his eyes to me was the essence of that war,' comments Forrest. 'It was just madness. There was no reasoning. If that tiger wanted to eat you, he could have.' When they clambered back on the PBR, Forrest's memorable breakdown scene where he screams and yells about never getting out of the boat, and never wanting to have anything do with this fucking war in the first place, was less acting than sheer terror.

A week later it started to rain. At first the rain was a welcome break in the humidity. Sofia Coppola danced about in the garden of the family's rented house in Manila, luxuriating in the downpour. There was a holiday mood. Francis came home from work early and played opera on the hi-fi as he cooked pasta for the family. But as the rain persisted for days without end, stories began to reach them of a typhoon, escalating into the full fury of Hurricane Olga. Up country, an elaborate set built for the scene where *Playboy* bunnies come to entertain the troops was wrecked. Set designer Dean Tavoularis found himself in the unusual, though perhaps not altogether unpleasant, position of being holed up in a house with a terrified Playmate of the Year. 'We sat around, and it started raining harder and harder until finally it was literally *white* outside, and all the trees were bent at forty-five degrees,' as he recalls. Helicopters were tossed off their landing pads, the PBR was blown out of the water as if it were a plastic toy. When the set for Kurtz's jungle headquarters was washed away, Coppola had little choice but to send the cast home while the Filipino labourers rebuilt everything.

By the time of the rain-enforced hiatus, *Apocalypse Now* was already six weeks over schedule and $3 million (£1.64 million) over budget, with the sickening thought for Coppola that he might lose his homes if the picture collapsed. And he was very worried about the script, especially the ending which had to be filmed when they returned to location.

In Milius' version, *Apocalypse Now* ends with Captain Willard falling under the spell of the charismatic Kurtz, and Kurtz bringing the might of the US military down on the heads of the enemy in a cataclysmic battle scene, raining fire and napalm from the sky. The problem was that there were already two big battles in the picture, and Coppola knew he couldn't top Kilgore's 'Ride of the Valkyries' scene, ending with Robert Duvall giving his wonderfully mad speech about nothing being quite like the smell of napalm in the morning. So Coppola returned to *Heart of Darkness*, which ends with Marlow metaphorically probing the rotten core of mankind, like a man sticking his finger gingerly into a mouldering cadaver. Coppola was still trying to resolve exactly how this intriguing but nebulous idea might be conveyed in words and pictures on the screen when he returned to the Philippines in August 1976.

With no sign of Marlon Brando, who was finishing a long, languid summer holiday on his private island in the Pacific, Coppola made use of the time he had by shooting one of Willard's key scenes, in his Saigon hotel before going on his fateful assignment. This comes right at the start of the picture, establishing Willard's back story and his mentality. The scene was shot on 3 August 1976, which happened to be Martin Sheen's thirty-sixth birthday. Although he looked very well, Sheen was not a healthy man, either physically or mentally. He drank. He smoked three packs of cigarettes a day. And, as Americans say, he had unresolved personal issues. As he puts it, 'I was in a chaotic spiritual state inside.' In preparation for playing the scene, Sheen deliberately became drunk, thinking this would help him loosen up enough to get to the root of who Willard was. As he drank, Francis explained to him that Special Forces men like Willard were often vain. So Martin should admire his reflection in the mirror and, as he did so, try to face up to who he was and what he was doing with his life, which was essentially killing people. Good and drunk, dressed only in his underpants, Sheen followed the direction dutifully, admiring his reflection in a full-length mirror, then deciding to practise his karate moves. 'I was so intoxicated, I didn't realise how close to the mirror I was. So when I struck it, I ended up catching my thumb in the mirror . . .' Blood spurted forth and Coppola called for shooting to stop. 'I said, *No. Let it go. I want to have this out right here and now,*' says Sheen. 'It had to do with facing my worst enemy: myself.' Bloody and drunk, Sheen proceeded to plumb the depths of himself, weeping and wailing about his own personal misery, ultimately rolling around on the floor of the hotel room in anguish, rambling about God, singing snatches of 'Amazing Grace', and beseeching those nearby to pray with him – much of which can be seen on the film.

As if the atmosphere wasn't heady enough, Dennis Hopper then arrived on set, lending his own unique personality to proceedings. After the triumph of *Easy Rider*, Dennis' brilliant career had gone badly wrong. He had followed his 1969 hit by writing, directing and co-starring in *The Last Movie*, a remarkable picture about the making of a Western, shot in Peru in 1971. Although *The Last Movie* won the Critic's Prize at the Venice Film Festival, mainstream reviews were extremely hostile and Universal Pictures let the picture die. Indeed, it became one of the most notorious flops of the decade and as a result Hopper didn't get another directing opportunity until 1980. He left Hollywood to live in New Mexico, working on his painting and photography and appearing only sporadically on screen, mostly in small and often foreign productions. He drank heavily and used drugs to excess, becoming a notable early victim of the cocaine culture of the time: an unpredictable and sometimes irascible wild man with manic eyes, fluttering hands and machine-gun speech. 'Oh, I was nuts. I was definitely crazy,' he admits now, lucid and eloquent after many years of sobriety. 'Creative, but nuts. I was doing a lot of coke, and drinking.' Although many directors were wary of Dennis, Francis was an old buddy and was willing to take a chance. Dennis and Francis had hit it off years ago when they discovered that they had a mutual friend in the artist Larry Poons (he who hosted the jam session in New York, described in Chapter 17, that led to Bob Dylan's Rolling Thunder Revue). Small world that it is, Larry and Francis went to high school together in New York and Dennis was friendly with Larry because of his connections in the art world. At any rate, Francis decided his old pal Dennis would be just right for the cameo role of a CIA operative who joins Kurtz's renegade army and Dennis accepted, partly because he wanted very much to work with Brando. He had known Marlon since the 1950s – Dennis knew virtually everybody – but they had never acted together, 'and I wanted to have a scene with him.' Brando still hadn't shown up when Dennis arrived in the Philippines, so Hopper chose his uniform and amused himself playing war with the other actors and the former Green Berets who had been hired as advisors. 'We had these war games at night [with] flares,' recalls the actor with boyish relish. 'It was really incredible. They would attack by canoes on the beach and we'd try to hold this bridge . . . It was great. We played these real war games with over two hundred, three hundred people, firing howitzers with powder balls, and if you got hit with the powder you were dead. It was great stuff. And then Marlon arrived.'

In Conrad's story, Kurtz is skeletal. In Milius' screenplay he is a soldier in peak physical condition. Brando weighed seventeen stones when he showed up in the Philippines. This was a considerable shock to Coppola, to whom Brando had promised that he would get into shape for his role. Despite Brando's gross appearance, there was great excitement that he was there at last. Dennis Hopper and the other actors put on a mock parade for the man who would be their commanding officer, giving him a display of their fighting prowess. 'We shot the howitzers and we had guys climbing trees and doing jujitsu, and running and falling and firing their guns, and there I was in my neat uniform,' recalls Hopper. *'These are your soldiers!'* All the actors on set admired Marlon enormously, to the extent that some were too much in awe to speak to him naturally. Even though Frederic Forrest had been in a previous movie with Brando – *The Missouri Breaks*

(1976) – he was one of those thespians on set who found normal conversation with Marlon almost impossible 'because he was my hero . . .
He was the greatest actor of the century.' Strong character that he is,
Dennis did not share this particular hang-up. He chattered away to
Marlon in his normal garrulous fashion. But this caused problems of its
own. After the welcome parade there was a dinner for Brando during
which Dennis asked if he had read 'the book' yet, referring to a little
book about covert operations that the actors had been given by their
Green Beret advisors. The little red book had become indispensable to
the actors as they played war games, and Dennis kept his copy tucked
into one of his boots. He was just about to lean down and extract the
book for Marlon, when Brando threw a tantrum. 'Read the book?
Read the book?' he raged. Then he got up and stomped out of dinner.
'Shit, what have I done?' asked Hopper. It turned out that Brando had
assumed Hopper was asking him about *Heart of Darkness*. Way back
when Marlon first spoke to Coppola about the movie, the director had
gained the impression that the actor had read Conrad's novel. Coppola
requested reasonably that the actor *re-read* the text before they began
work in order to refresh his memory. When Brando arrived on set, it
became apparent not only that he had not re-read the book, *he had
never read the book*. 'I lied,' he confessed to the director. So this was a
very sensitive subject. In the end Francis was obliged to read the book
to Brando, which meant shooting had to be put on hold for many days.

In his memoir, *Songs My Mother Taught Me*, Brando claims he did
know *Heart of Darkness* when he came to the Philippines. Brando
writes that he was dismayed by how far Coppola had strayed from
Conrad's story, creating a script that in his words 'simply didn't make
dramatic sense.' So *he* advised Francis to return to the book. Whether
there is any truth in this version of events is hard to say, but in his
memoir Brando makes some observations which show that, at some
stage at least, he came to know Conrad's novel very well. He points
out astutely, for instance, that Conrad builds Kurtz up in the book by
referring to him constantly in the first two chapters, but withholds the
man in the flesh until the third and final chapter, in which Kurtz
appears, first distantly and then at close quarters only fleetingly, saying
little. As Brando observes, Kurtz is an enigma, and the enigma loses its

power if the character is fully present in the story for too long. Brando argued that for these reasons, in portraying Kurtz he should be filmed in semi-darkness. (Coppola says the truth is the actor wanted to hide his obesity.) Brando further claims in his memoir that he took his cue directly from *Heart of Darkness* when he decided, without telling Francis, to shave his head like a billiard ball (as Kurtz's head is described by Conrad, billiard balls being made of ivory, of course). So here was another shock for the director: a fat, *bald* leading man. Little wonder Coppola felt himself suffering a kind of nervous breakdown, convinced that the movie he was making was going to be his last. 'This film is a twenty million-dollar disaster,' he wailed to Eleanor. 'Why won't anybody believe me?'

Partly because Brando didn't want to learn lines, his dialogue would be improvised, with Brando bouncing off his fellow actors, principally Martin Sheen and Dennis Hopper. Coppola now re-cast Dennis in a much more substantial role, based on the Russian whom Marlow meets in *Heart of Darkness* when his steamboat arrives at Kurtz's ivory post. The character is described by Conrad as an 'enthusiastic, fabulous' madman in harlequin rags who immediately seizes Marlow and tells him feverishly how Kurtz has enlarged his mind. Conrad writes: 'He opened his arms wide, staring at me with his little blue eyes that were perfectly round.' This *was* Dennis in all his manic intensity back in the days when he was drinking and using cocaine. In the movie, the Russian becomes a photojournalist. Dennis wore a bandanna and festooned himself with cameras to look the part, the crazy eyes being his own natural and unique accessory. As this philosopher character (he has no name), Hopper delivers some of the best lines in the film, many taken straight from Conrad: telling Willard and the rest of the PBR crew not only how Kurtz is a great man who has enlarged his mind (Hopper's hands fluttering by his face as he says so), but also that Kurtz is sensitive enough to read poetry out loud. Yet he forgets himself at times. Indicating the carnage all around – decapitated heads, bodies hanging from trees – Hopper's character echoes the Russian when he says, in pained apology, that Kurtz *hated* all this. 'Sometimes he goes too far,' the journalist tells Willard as he comes ashore. 'He's the first one to admit it.'

Coppola drew on other source material for the key scenes with Brando, Hopper and Sheen, such as the work of T.S. Eliot who borrowed a phrase from *Heart of Darkness* as an epigram for his 1925 poem *The Hollow Men*. In fact, the whole poem echoes *Heart of Darkness* in that Conrad writes of Kurtz in the book that, having given himself over to the jungle and its ways, Kurtz became 'hollow at the core' – that is, he lost his moral values. This is the essence of Conrad's novel, and some literary critics have argued that the author never quite conquered the central idea of Kurtz's hollow soul, or the evil into which he plunges.* It is the same ineffable subject matter that Eliot grapples with in his poem. Expressing these ideas in movie dialogue proved exasperatingly difficult. There was an attempt to type up lines for Brando, Hopper and Sheen to use as a starting point as they tried to get at the heart of the matter, with snatches of Conrad and Eliot thrown in, but chaotic and sometimes comical improvisation was the order of the day. (As Dennis recalls, Francis would typically yell, 'Just say the words, just say the words!' To which Hopper would reply, 'What fucking words are you talking about, Francis?')

The set for Kurtz's compound was littered with severed heads: some fake, others those of extras buried up to their necks in the dirt. (It is with black humour that Hopper quotes in character from Kipling: 'If you can keep your head when all about you/ Are losing theirs . . .') To create an authentic feeling of corruption, wax cadavers and stage blood were mixed with animal carcasses, bones and kitchen waste. The rotting material attracted flies and rats. 'It was the grimmest set,' recalls Frederic Forrest, whose last scene was as a decapitated head tossed into Willard's lap by Kurtz. 'It was death . . . it was just horrible.' And there was more. At the culmination to the film, a water buffalo was led down the steps of the compound, slowly in the driving rain, and sacrificed for real in front of almost a thousand cast, extras and crew. When cut together with the Doors' song 'The End', this would be the last big scene in *Apocalypse Now* before the dying

*James Guetti in his essay 'Heart of Darkness: The Failure of Imagination' wrote of the book: 'At the end of the search we encounter a darkness, and it is no more defined than at the beginning of the journey . . . it continues to exist only as something unapproachable.'

Kurtz exclaims with his final breath: 'The horror! The horror!' (a line taken directly from Conrad).

As mentioned, Dennis Hopper had signed on to the movie because he wanted to act with Brando, and he was delighted when Coppola recast him to give him more screen time with Marlon. But then Brando refused to work with Dennis. Relations between the actors had been testy since the incident of the little red book, and trouble flared again over some remarks Brando made about Dennis' late friend James Dean. Intemperate words were spoken and the next thing Dennis knew Marlon was refusing to be in the same room as him. For the three-way scene inside Kurtz's cave-like quarters – featuring Brando, Hopper and Sheen – Marlon would do his side of the improvisation on his own. The next night Dennis would come in to say *his* lines. Crew kept the actors informed of what their opposite number had said the night before, so they could react accordingly. This led to some bizarre evenings, as Hopper recalls: 'One night I came in – we did those for about two weeks – and one night I came in and they said, "Marlon called you a whimpering dog and threw bananas at you last night."' As a result, that evening a prop man tossed bananas at Dennis while he acted. 'Because we were never on the set together which, very honestly, at the time, I thought, *Motherfucker!*' Out of this insane working situation came some of the most compelling dialogue in all of seventies' cinema, with Brando reading aloud from *The Hollow Men*, and Hopper paraphrasing the Eliot poem when he tells Willard: 'This is the way the fucking world ends – Look at this fuckin' shit we're in, man! – not with a bang, with a whimper, and with a whimper I'm fucking splitting, Jack.'

In his final speech, Brando talks about what it means to be a soldier, and how he had learned that the North Vietnamese were stronger than the Americans because they were ruthless, giving an example of how the Viet Cong had come to a village where the Americans had inoculated children and hacked off all the children's arms as a lesson to them not to trust the enemy. 'I made it all up extemporaneously,' the actor wrote in his memoirs, 'I was hysterical; I cried and laughed, and it was a wonderful scene.' Indeed it is, having the same quality of truth and fascination as the very personal scene Brando played in *Last Tango in Paris*, when he talked about his childhood. In *Apocalypse Now*, the themes are larger. The picture starts as an action adventure, but widens like a river as the journey progresses, becoming broader and deeper. It is a film about the biggest philosophical ideas, about life and death, about the savagery within man, and the rights and wrongs of pursuing political ends to their ultimate conclusions, which was after all the crux of the Vietnam War.

And then, as suddenly as he had arrived on set, Brando departed at the start of October 1976, disappearing back into his private world of wealth, gluttony and self-loathing. The actor would never give another performance to equal his portrayal of Walter E. Kurtz. It was his final triumph, a character to rank alongside Stanley Kowalski, Vito Corleone and Paul in *Last Tango in Paris*, and he knew it. 'It was probably the closest I've ever come to getting lost in a part,' he wrote. But while this was an ending of a kind for Brando, the story of *Apocalypse Now* was far from over.

20

THE FILTH AND THE FURY

We hate everything.

SEX PISTOLS PRESS RELEASE

Back in London, where George Lucas was struggling to finish filming *Star Wars*, over budget and over schedule, though not quite so mired in trouble as *Apocalypse Now*, a transmogrification was taking place. From June until late August 1976, Britain experienced an extraordinary heatwave, one so freakishly long, hot and dry that it would never fade from the memory of those who lived through it. It began with a succession of unusually warm and sunny early summer days, a welcome distraction from a worsening economic situation. Under the Labour government of James Callaghan – who had recently taken over as Prime Minister following the surprise resignation of Harold Wilson – the pound was falling in value, inflation was rising, as was the rate of bankruptcies, and there was a postwar record number of one and a half million unemployed. At a time when much of British industry and services were run by central government, daily life was interrupted by frequent industrial action that affected everything from car production to the collection of refuse. As the summer of '76 wore on, getting hotter and drier, the shabbiness and relative poverty of the United Kingdom became glaringly apparent, particularly in London where the unclouded sun starkly revealed the dilapidation of many parts of the capital: the scabs of wasteland in and around the redundant docks, and numerous derelict properties, many of which were infested with squatters. The parks faded to dust-brown as the worst drought for 250 years was declared. Tempers frayed in the heat: prisoners rioted in Hull, causing a million pounds' worth of damage; the Notting Hill Carnival degenerated into a bloody battle with the police. Starved of water, factories worked short time, and forest fires destroyed hundreds of acres of historic woodland.

Out of this landscape of ruination, despair and decay came the punks: a musical movement and fashion style that was confrontational and provocative. Punks dyed their hair in strange colours and wore it in weird styles; they pierced their tender skin with safety pins; cut and slashed their clothes, and donned the fetishist apparel of sex shops. Punks followed bands with such alarming names as the Damned and the Clash, groups who represented a return to traditional rock 'n' roll (not that they would thank you for saying so) in the sense that they dispensed with the trappings of progressive rock, even disdaining keyboards, relying instead on guitar and drums to create short, fast, loud and often ferociously angry songs that addressed what it was to be young (and probably unemployed) in the crumbling Britain of 1976. The originators and stars of this movement, the Sex Pistols, could be seen most Tuesday nights at the 100 Club, a small basement venue on Oxford Street in London's West End. Outlandish, offensive and funny, the Pistols performed self-written power-chord numbers such as 'Anarchy in the UK', the extraordinary lyrics of which were enacted by a devilish youth named Johnny Rotten, the stage name of John Lydon: a skinny, carrot-haired urchin who screamed at his audience that he was the anti-Christ and he wanted to *destroy* everything. Only the roll of his yellowy eyes, and the faintest upturn of his lips, suggested this was not to be taken entirely seriously. The audience nodded their heads in fervent rhythmic agreement, some bouncing up and down energetically in the new punk dance, the pogo, others hawking up as much phlegm as they could muster and then spitting at Rotten in a ritual sign of appreciation, as he expectorated in turn on them. As a side show, John's half-witted friend Sid cut and smeared himself in his own blood. Meanwhile another fan(atic), Susan from Bromley, who had remade herself as the punk goddess

Siouxsie Sioux, paraded about with her breasts hanging free, a swastika band on one arm.

The scene at the 100 Club was outrageous. It was the crucible of the most significant movement in British pop music since the 1960s. Like that earlier musical renaissance, British punk was as much about clothes as music, and at its heart, working in the *shmata* business a generation on from Ossie Clark and Celia Birtwell, was a young couple whose sophisticated design ideas they utterly rejected, of course, but who were comparable to them nonetheless. Like Ossie and Celia, Malcolm McLaren and Vivienne Westwood were an odd couple united by a common interest in clothes. She was a former trainee school teacher from the North, a handsome, serious woman with a talent for design. Malcolm was a former art school student with a flair for self-promotion. Weedy and ginger-haired in appearance, fey in manner, Malcolm was a 20-year-old virgin when he met Vivienne in the 1960s. She was much more mature in many ways – five years his senior, already a single mother – but they saw enough in each other to set up home together.

By the early '70s Malcolm and Vivienne were running a boutique at 430 King's Road selling 1950s-style clothing to Teddy Boy revivalists, with Vivienne adding value to the garments by customising them with lettering and studs. Ever eager to stay ahead of the trends, Malcolm and Vivienne changed the shop name regularly. In 1974 they revamped it completely, putting naked mannequins in the window, and erecting over the door a sign made of inflated pink vinyl letters, reminiscent of Claes Oldenburg's soft sculptures, spelling out the word *SEX*. To venture inside was akin to entering one of the seedy shops in and around Soho that purveyed a familiar menu of *books, mags, movies and aids*. The walls were painted black, and genuine sex shop paraphernalia was for sale: tight rubber apparel, items that could be unzipped to reveal nipples or genitalia, bondage clothing fitted with buckles and straps. Saturday boy Glen Matlock, a student at Gilbert and George's alma mater, St Martin's School of Art, remembers that although Malcolm and Vivienne were aiming this rigmarole principally at the young and super-trendy, punters included traditional sex shop clientele. 'It was horrible,' recalls Matlock. 'You'd go into the changing rooms after someone had tried on some rubber tights and there'd be cum all over them. Vivienne would pick them up and say, *It's alright. I'll just wash them down and put them back on the rack.*' Also on sale was a range of T-shirts, including one devised by Malcolm that listed all the things he loved and hated, a kind of manifesto for what became punk culture. Cool dudes of the early '70s, David Hockney and Ossie Clark, were among the hates.

On a trip to New York to promote the clothes, Malcolm became friendly with members of the New York Dolls, a hybrid rock band that had the look of glam rock, but was irreverent and antagonistic in a wholly new way. The Dolls wore the swastika, for instance, and made cursing and vomiting into an artistic statement.* Musically, they were crude, almost inept, creating a fearful cacophony. Malcolm thought they were magnificent and became their manager briefly, in 1975, just before the group self-destructed. As a consequence he was in New York during a very significant period in the development of popular music in the city. A new generation of artists was pushing through (as Sam Shepard would glimpse during Dylan's 1976 tour), the best of whom could be heard at a former country music venue in the Bowery called CBGB. So-named because the owner originally intended it as a showcase for country, bluegrass and blues music, CBGB became the cradle of the new wave, with regular appearances by acts such as the Ramones and Television, that were the antithesis of singer-songwriter sensitivity and mainstream classical rock. These artists looked like hooligans, and their songs were for the most part short, fast and aggressive in tone. In common with the Dolls and the Tubes, they were *punks*, an evocative American term widely used to denote any kind of low life, and a term linked with this new music specifically when, in December 1975, a couple of guys from the underground comix movement launched a small music magazine called *Punk*. The cover of the first issue featured a wonderfully funny

---

*It should be noted that the prevalent flirtation with Nazi-style in rock at this time (Bowie as well as the Dolls and various punk bands) had a lot to do with the popularity of the 1972 movie *Cabaret*.

caricature of Lou Reed as a kind of insect in leather, an acknowledgement of the fact that Lou's work was a forerunner of this new music.

Returning to London richer for his experiences, Malcolm found his next managerial opportunity in the ragamuffin kids who used Sex as an unofficial hang-out. These included lads from the rougher parts of North and West London, two of whom, Steve Jones and Paul Cook, had a band called Strand (after the Roxy Music song 'Do The Strand'). Paul, an 18-year-old apprentice electrician from Shepherd's Bush, was a shy, nondescript youth who played drums. His best mate, Steve, who sang a bit and mucked about on guitar, was a thief by trade, with convictions for breaking and entering, who had stolen most of Strand's equipment from the homes of rock stars, picking on artists he admired such as Keith Richard. Most audaciously he even nicked part of David Bowie's sound system from the Hammersmith Odeon. Now he was in the process of helping himself to the stock from Sex. Taking an indulgent view of this pilfering, Malcolm suggested that Steve and Paul get serious about their music. Why not join forces with his Saturday boy, Glen? They needed a bass guitarist and Glen played bass. The boys were also about the same age, from the same part of West London. While all this was true, Glen was very different from Paul and, especially, Steve. Glen's background was working class, but he came from a strong and supportive family and had middle-class aspirations. He was after all at art college. Also, Glen was a more accomplished musician than either Paul or Steve. Despite these differences, the boys did team up. They also adopted a new name at Malcolm's suggestion. They would be the Sex Pistols: Sex, after the shop, and Pistols because, well, 'a pistol, a gun, assassins, young and vicious and sex,' Malcolm free-associated, getting excited. Next, he decided to find them a singer.

Calling on his New York contacts, Malcolm asked Richard Hell of Television if he wanted to come to London, but Richard wasn't interested. Then Vivienne pointed out that an interesting-looking youth named John came into the shop regularly. Maybe he could sing? 'And in walked a guy who I kept looking at, and I thought, well he's got something about [him],' recalls McLaren. John was a slightly built, pallid teenager with budgerigar-green hair (the accidental result of trying to turn his yellow hair blue with Crazy Color hair dye). He spoke in the manner of Malcolm McDowell's Alex in *A Clockwork Orange*, employing such odd phrases as 'hilarious good fun.' His clothes were similarly eccentric, including charity shop cast-offs, torn and pinned together. He modelled himself partly on the gentlemen of the road who drifted through London, destitute but retaining a ruined dignity. This particular day the lad wore a Pink Floyd T-shirt, which he had poked holes in and scrawled over in Biro, adding the prefix *I hate* before the band's name, expressing his dislike of the leading act of progressive rock. Intrigued, Malcolm asked John if he could sing. 'Like an outta tune violin,' came the surly reply. That was enough to get him an audition.

As we have touched on, John Lydon grew up working-class Irish, mainly in North London. He was born in 1956, and his family eventually moved to a council flat in an austere development off the Seven Sisters Road in Finsbury Park, a stone's throw from the Rainbow. The formative experience of John's young life came at age seven when he contracted meningitis. He was ill for almost a year and was left with a scrambled memory and impaired vision, which gave him a tendency to stare, as well as a problem with his sinuses which caused him (he says) to hawk up phlegm and spit regularly. Added to which, he was small and skinny with a slight hunchback. All told: a pathetic, sickly-looking runt. Marked for life by illness, and growing up poor, John became acutely aware of the gulf between his London life and the glamorous metropolitan world he saw on television and read about in the papers. As he says, 'That might as well have been a foreign country to me.' Like Charlie and Johnny Boy in *Mean Streets*, living in the shadow of the World Trade Center in New York, Lydon lived close enough to the wealthy heart of his city to walk into it, but he wasn't part of that lucky world. 'Flashy night life, easy money, etc. etc. It's like, *Well, there's no way I'm ever going to have access to that.*' Feeling excluded, and also kicking against aspects of his background such as the Catholic Church, Lydon became a natural iconoclast. But a literate one. Bright and inquisitive, he developed an appreciation of English literature at school, enjoying William Blake, Ted Hughes and, especially, Shakespeare, identifying strongly with Shakespeare's characterisation of Richard III as a twisted villain, and adoring the Laurence Olivier film of the play. ('I can see bits of me there. Fucking excellent. What a right bastard he was!') John also had wide-ranging taste in pop music, enjoying artists as diverse as Nico, the Doors and Miles Davis, most of whom he had seen perform live. Living opposite the Rainbow, and near the Roundhouse in Chalk Farm, he attended concerts almost every week, often worming his way in for free, and saw many landmark shows ranging from David Bowie's debut as Ziggy Stardust to Bob Marley at the Lyceum. 'That's why my tastes are very, very varied.' While he had never aspired to be a singer – knew he *couldn't* sing in the normal sense – John was also egocentric enough to say yes when asked if he wanted to audition for Malcolm's band.

So Malcolm and the three Pistols put John in front of a jukebox, and ordered him to sing to Alice Cooper's 'Eighteen', using a shower head as a pretend microphone. The primary idea was to see what he looked like. Totally ridiculous, and very embarrassing. 'It felt like the worst moment of my life,' shudders John, 'but I wouldn't back out of it.' Despite his nervousness, Lydon gave an astonishing audition: improvising lyrics, glaring dramatically at his small audience, and casting his limbs into weird poses. 'He was John Rotten from that very first moment,' Glen Matlock later observed admiringly, though it was Steve Jones who conferred the stage name on their new lead singer, in honour of his horrible-looking teeth. 'You're fucking rotten,' observed Jones disdainfully, and so Johnny Rotten it was.

It was only when Vivienne saw who Malcolm had picked to front the Sex Pistols that she informed him he'd made a mistake. 'That's not the John I meant,' she told her partner. 'There's another John.' In fact, there were a posse of Johns who hung out with Lydon, including lads named John Gray, John Simon Ritchie (aka John Beverley) and John Stevens. The youth Vivienne meant was Ritchie, a tall, skinny boy whom John called Sid, to distinguish him from all the other Johns. The nickname was derived from Lydon's belief that Ritchie – a friend from schooldays – was the most pathetic person he had ever known: a stupid and impressionable youth (during the recent glam-rock craze he had affected to be gay). Such low regard did he have for his friend, though friend he was, that John named him after his pet hamster, who was called Sid. When Sid the hamster went against type and bit John Lydon's dad, Sid the hamster and Sid the teenager both became known as Sid Vicious. Comical as this story is, Sid's background was a sad one. His mother, Anne, was a junkie, and she had dragged her only child up in a series of squalid homes, latterly in the poorer parts of inner London. By age fifteen, Sid was obliged to make a home for himself, living in squats. Sometimes he was so broke that he didn't have shoes to wear. Like his mother, he became a drug user, and made a fatal connection between drugs and rock-star chic. His musical heroes included Lou Reed, and the decadent New York scene that Reed wrote about was, as John Lydon recalls, 'a magic world for Sid.' Another idol was David Bowie, and though Sid could neither sing nor play an instrument he was sufficiently full of himself to think that he might one day be as big a star as Bowie, which made Lydon laugh. Malcolm saw another quality in Sid: 'He was a sex symbol, really; a weird one, but a good one. Very good. Really rock 'n' roll.' Sid's looks, such as they were, would eventually be his entrée into the world that he aspired to. That was still sometime off, however.

For now, Sid was just a weird-looking urchin whose mate Johnny was the leader of a band called the Sex Pistols, which no one had heard of. It was an opportunity, however, that John seized with both hands. 'It was immediately into writing songs. It was immediate access to me. Because I liked reading, and I liked writing, but I had nowhere to put it [until then],' explains Lydon. 'So I channelled all that immediately into the Sex Pistols and loved it, *loved* it. Never [saw] it as really ending in any *success* at all. I didn't think it would have any effect on the world in any way, shape or form. I didn't think it would frighten people, or seem violent, or nihilistic, or any of that. I thought it was a very, very positive, fun little thing that would just be ours, and no one would care, but lo and behold it turned into a monster.' Malcolm set the boys up in a seedy rehearsal room off Denmark Street, London's Tin Pan Alley. This got Jones off the street, and away from Sex, as Malcolm saw it, which meant he wasn't losing so much stock. In their garret, the boys began to build and rehearse a set-list comprised of covers of songs by favourite bands, such as the Who, and tunes of their own, the most significant of which was 'Pretty Vacant'.

The Pistols were not a band comprised of a group of mates. On the contrary. John thought the other three boys a bit thick, and they were unanimous in their opinion that John was a right nasty bastard. John, Paul and Steve were united, however, in their dislike of Glen. Steve in particular found the college boy incredibly irritating. It was the little things Glen did that got to Steve. 'He was always washing his feet,' Steve complained years later, with only a hint of a smile. Another bone of contention was that Glen was forever trying to improve Steve's guitar technique by showing him what Steve terms 'Beatles' chords,' which pissed him off. Nevertheless, it was the college boy who gave the Pistols their first significant song, 'Pretty Vacant', creating the guitar riff and working up the words, partly inspired by the title of a Richard Hell song about a blank generation, trying to express how young people in Britain felt at the time, with high unemployment and few opportunities, 'a blank, vacant kind of feeling going around [London],' as Matlock explains. Also, it was ironic to see a plug-ugly bastard like Lydon singing about how pretty he was. The band could also thank Glen (not that they did) for getting them their first gig. This took place in November 1975 at St Martin's School of Art, which Glen had dropped out of after his foundation year. They were supporting Bazooka Joe, featuring a young man named Stuart Goddard (later Adam Ant). Lydon wore his *I Hate Pink Floyd* T-Shirt for the show, which ended abruptly when Bazooka Joe pulled the plug on the boys. The Pistols left the stage without even a smattering of applause. But Lydon didn't care. 'We didn't do it to be loved,' as he says.

This fuck-you mentality was key to the success of the Pistols. It was an attitude totally different from most new bands, who want to ingratiate themselves with their audience in any way possible. The Pistols, and particularly John, gave the contrary impression that they hoped their audience dropped fucking dead, and this lent them a compelling negative charisma. Importantly, they also had a unique look. John had always been an eccentric dresser: part Dadaist, part Harold Pinter-tramp. With the patronage of Malcolm and Vivienne, all four Pistols now wore clothing that was the cutting-edge of 1975–76 King's Road fashion, including Vivienne's silkscreen T-shirts, printed with such outrageous images as the mask used by the recently-convicted Cambridge Rapist, and semi-pornographic pictures including two half-naked cowboys drawn in the style of the gay artist Tom of Finland. Finally, although they were inept musicians to begin with, the Pistols quickly became relatively proficient on their instruments. All in all, they had the makings of a good little act, and duly began to play increasingly prestigious London clubs, including the Nashville – one of the venues on London's so-called pub rock circuit.

The driving force behind 'pub rock' was Dave Robinson, a former road manager for Jimi Hendrix, who returned to London from several years in the United States in the early '70s. He found to his surprise that it was not easy to go out casually during the week in London and find a bar or club that had good live music, as one could in most American cities. So he cultivated a circuit of pubs – such as the Nashville in West Kensington and the Hope and Anchor in Islington – which had rooms large enough to accommodate a live show. Punters paid a small admission fee and hopefully spent more at the bar between the sets, which were deliberately short to encourage drinking, several little sets making up an evening's entertainment. The nature of the venues, with their beery male clientele, suited bands who played straightforward rhythm and blues music, or country blues, acts such as Dr Feelgood and Graham Parker and the Rumour. The latter featured an introspective young man from Camberley in Surrey who wrote literate, melodic songs such as 'Howlin' Wind' and 'Hey, Lord, Don't Ask Me Questions', and performed them with gusto and conviction. Graham Parker's musical influences included Van Morrison and the Stones, but were predominately American: Dylan, and the sound of Motown and Stax. With the Rumour, a multi-instrumental band that featured guitars, keyboards and horns, Parker blended these influences together – adding a dash of reggae – creating music that, for a short time in London in the mid-1970s, seemed to be the New Big Thing. 'In the hangover of the progressive [rock] era, I was bound to get attention,' notes

Graham, and indeed for a while he was the darling of the music press in Britain and also the USA, where *Rolling Stone* named Graham Parker and the Rumour the best new band of 1976. Signed to major labels on both sides of the Atlantic, Parker and his cohorts released two punchy albums in 1976, and toured energetically to promote them. The future looked bright from behind Parker's shades. 'I knew that I was using traditional stylings, but thought that my spin on them was so innovative that nothing could come along to equal it,' as he says. 'Boy, did I get it wrong!'

John Lydon saw acts like Graham Parker as fake, and in a fundamental sense he was right. Although these musicians were 100 percent British, from such homely places as Camberley (Parker) and Canvey Island in Essex (Dr Feelgood), they were all singing ersatz American songs, often in fake American accents, with a generous sprinkling of classic US covers, often about specific places in the United States such as 'Kansas City'. (As Lydon says astutely, 'I've yet to run into a band from Kansas writing about Canvey Island!') British bands have been putting on American airs for years, of course, the most shameless example being the Rolling Stones (with Mick and Keith coming from Dartford in Kent). One of the factors that makes the Pistols both unusual and very significant is that, unlike so many British bands, John and the boys did not pretend to be anything other than what they were, which was English, and in fact they expressed contempt for American culture.*

Another band on the pub rock circuit at this time was the 101ers, named for the address of the West London squat where the lead singer, John Mellor (aka Joe Strummer), and fellow members were living, which was 101 Walterton Road, W9. Like the Rumour, the 101ers were a multi-instrumental band who ingratiated themselves with audiences by playing familiar R&B tunes, in their case modelling their sound specifically on Van Morrison's great 1974 live album *It's Too Late to Stop Now*. In April 1976, the 101ers played the Nashville with the Pistols as their support act, and as Strummer watched the

---

*Though it should be said that both John Lydon and Steve Jones later made their homes in California, and show no signs of wanting to return to the UK.

Pistols perform he experienced an epiphany. 'The difference was, we played "Route 66" to the drunks at the bar, going "Please like us." But here was this quartet who were standing there going, "We don't give a toss what you think, you pricks, this is what we like to play and this is the way we're gonna play it" . . . They honestly didn't give a shit.' Strummer promptly quit the 101ers and became the front man of the Clash, who played their first show, on 4 July 1976, supporting the Pistols at a club in Sheffield, and became the *de facto* warm-up act for the Pistols thereafter, with Strummer emerging as one of the leading figures of this new musical scene. It didn't have a name yet but was, as Strummer told Graham Parker one night at the Marquee, a 'whole new thing.'

By the summer of 1976, the whole new thing had a name: *punk*. It was a term bestowed specifically in Britain by *Melody Maker* journalist Caroline Coon, but inspired by the American underground magazine *Punk* – to the irritation of Lydon for whom the music 'was totally nothing to do with America.' The punk label helped glue together a cohesive music and fashion movement, however. Apart from bands such as the Pistols and the Clash, punk already had a look, courtesy of the T-shirts and other items sold at Sex; punk also had a dance in the pogo, invented by crazy Sid Vicious when he started jumping up and down at the 100 Club to see his mates on stage; there was even a graphics style, designed by an art-school friend of Malcolm's named Jamie Reid who used collage and lithographic printing to create stickers, posters and record sleeves, often with lettering cut from newspapers and arranged in the style of a kidnap demand (at a time when there were several unpleasant kidnap cases, not least that of heiress Lesley Whittle). And the showcase for punk was the 100 Club, where the Pistols were playing regularly, building up a following of devotees, many of whom later fronted bands of their own: among them Siouxsie Sioux, of Siouxsie and the Banshees, and her pals from Bromley in Kent, the so-called Bromley Contingent, one of whom was the young Billy Idol. Another early Pistols fan was an art student from Torquay named Tim Smith, later TV Smith of the Adverts. 'The 100 Club gigs were fantastic,' reminisces Smith, 'a bunch of snotty-nosed kids full of energy, nothing to do with the music business, people [like me who] wanted to express themselves and didn't have anything to do with the whole pop star [syndrome].' Anybody who came to see the Pistols at the 100 Club inevitably saw the Clash, too. Taking their lead from the Pistols, Joe and the boys were now writing songs about the environment they were in, and shared the Pistols' antipathy to America, a prejudice best expressed in the Clash song 'I'm So Bored with the USA'. But to many 100 Club regulars the Clash in the early days seemed like poseurs, with Strummer's espousal of left-wing politics appearing particularly contrived, not least because he was from a very privileged background. John Lydon was dismissive of Joe's politics, and indeed all politics. As he says, 'left wing, the right wing, they were nothing to us.'

As the heatwave of '76 began to cool, the hype around the Pistols paid a dividend when Malcolm signed the band to EMI, a major company with interests in the music industry, television and film. EMI rock acts included the Beatles and Pink Floyd, and the company headquarters was a substantial building in Manchester Square, just north of Oxford Street, a short walk away from the 100 Club but also a world away. In fact, the Pistols and EMI were ill-matched from the start, but the company wanted a toehold in the new music, and the £40,000 they advanced the band was a modest investment. The next step was to hear what they sounded like in the studio. The producer chosen as midwife to the Pistols' debut album was Chris Thomas, he who had produced *The Dark Side of the Moon* and attended that long-ago David Bowie show at the Rainbow (in the same audience as Lydon, as it turned out).

That evening in 1972 was the first time that Chris Thomas had seen Roxy Music live. Soon afterwards he became their producer, working on all the Roxy albums from *For Your Pleasure* in 1973 until *Siren* in 1975. These LPs are among the most sophisticated records of the first half of the 1970s, and Thomas' reputation continued to flourish as a result, with his services being sought out by the biggest names in rock. When he was approached with the idea of producing the Pistols, Thomas was working with Paul McCartney on the Wings album *Back to the Egg* (1978). With a former Beatle as client, it might be assumed that Thomas might regard the Pistols as beneath him;

indeed, many of his contemporaries in the business took precisely that view. But Chris kept an open mind and was won over by the punk band. 'When I heard the demos,' he says of the Pistols, 'I thought, they've got the potential of being like one of these great English bands, like the Who, in the sense [of] one guitar, bass and drums . . . a stripped-down, fantastic English band.'

John Lydon wasn't at the initial meeting with Thomas, and wasn't in evidence when the band first came into Wessex Studios in Highbury in October 1976 to start recording with the producer. It seemed there was a plan afoot even at this early stage to kick Lydon out, or at least keep him away from the action, possibly because Malcolm found John, with his forceful character, so difficult to control. When John did finally appear in the studio, he was grumpy and suspicious. The song the band were working on was 'Anarchy in the UK'. It had taken quite a while to get the backing track down because the Pistols were so inexperienced in the studio, and now Lydon attempted to record a vocal. He couldn't hear himself properly through the headphones, which got him off on the wrong footing, and in frustration he screamed the lyric with a ferocity that rocked Thomas back in his chair in the control room behind the glass. 'He just sort of yelled incoherently over the track, and I thought, *What the heck?! What am I going to do with this?*' When Chris tried to speak to John about it, the singer snarled that *he* was the big-time producer so *he* could sort it out. Gradually, however, things settled down.

As recorded, 'Anarchy in the UK' is much slower than one expects a classic punk record to be, with Lydon sending the hair up on the back of the neck with his weird, rasping introductory phrase; '*Rigghhht* now . . .' following by a cackling laugh, and then the dramatic opening couplet in which he announces he is the Anti-Christ, rhyming this in the next line with the assertion that he is also an anarchist. The way that John sings this line, and indeed puts over all his lyrics, is reminiscent of musical theatre. He imbues every phrase with an abundance of expression, putting one in mind of a performer like Ron Moody playing Fagin. The forced Anti-Christ/anarchist rhyme made Glen Matlock wince, because it wasn't proper poetry to his sensible ears. But this was in fact a seminal example of Lydon's facility with language, taking delight in forcing words together that shouldn't rhyme, thus achieving an original and dramatic impression. He is in good company; Bob Dylan uses the same technique. The song is not meant to be taken literally. Lydon was never so delusional as to see himself as the Anti-Christ. Neither did he consider himself an anarchist, realising that anarchy was totally impractical. Rather, the lyrics were an expression of his *feelings*, which could indeed be nihilistic. The single 'Anarchy in the UK' was released on 26 November 1976, the week by chance that Dylan joined the Band on stage in San Francisco for their farewell concert, filmed by Martin Scorsese. As *The Last Waltz* was an adieu to the poetic folk-rock of the first half of the 1970s – with guest artists including Neil Young, Van Morrison and Joni Mitchell – 'Anarchy in the UK' ushered in the abrasive musical style that, along with disco, defined the second part of the decade.

Not that the public paid much attention at first. With little or no radio play, 'Anarchy in the UK' was selling very modestly in the United Kingdom and had made no impression at all beyond its shores when, five days after the record's release, the Pistols were invited to appear on the London-region television programme *Today*, hosted by Bill Grundy. Queen, another EMI act, had cancelled at the last minute, and EMI put the Sex Pistols up as a substitute, taking them out of a rehearsal room where they were getting ready for a promotional tour with the Clash, and sending them over to Thames Television in Euston. The boys would be the centrepiece of a short item about the phenomenon of punk, 'to find out why people put safety pins though their noses' as the producer later explained the thinking behind the item. The Bromley Contingent was rallied to appear with the lads, giving the bogus impression that this was a major youth movement, whereas in fact British punk had not yet grown beyond a tiny cult. John felt nervous entering the Thames TV tower. Here he was, a lad of eighteen, about to appear on a show that hundreds of thousands of people in the London area would see, not least his neighbours in Finsbury Park. *Today* was a programme many families switched on just after six p.m. before their evening meal – not a prestigious programme, but a staple of the weekday television routine. The 52-year-old host, Bill Grundy, was in that sense truly a household name in the capital. Prior to the broadcast, the band joined Grundy in the green room for drinks. Steve Jones set about the white wine with alacrity, drinking by his own reckoning three bottles of Blue Nun. John was already wired on speed, which he had been taking in rehearsals. (Amphetamines were the drug of choice for London punks, much cheaper and more readily available than cocaine.) Considering the Blue Nun and the speed, it was hardly surprising that trouble resulted when they went on air.

In the studio, the Pistols were seated opposite Bill Grundy, with members of the Bromley Contingent lined up behind the band. Steve wore one of Vivienne's provocative T-shirts, printed with a photograph of breasts. John was in a two-tone mohair jumper, looking young and innocent and a little over-awed. The boys might well have behaved themselves had Grundy kept a grip on proceedings, and had Jones not been pissed. As it was it all went terribly wrong (or not, depending on your point of view).

Grundy began by asking the band whether taking a £40,000 advance from EMI was not at variance with the anarchic spirit of punk. 'No. The more the merrier,' replied Glen Matlock.

Steve interjected, 'We've fuckin' spent it, ain't we?'

Grundy replied coolly: 'I don't know, have you?' The fact that in the first few moments Steve had already used the f-word – almost unheard of on British television at this time – seemed to have passed Grundy and everybody else by, as though it happened in a dream. The show went on regardless. At the conclusion of a nonsensical exchange between Grundy and Lydon about classical music, John muttered that it was 'tough shit' if people preferred that kind of music.

'It's what?' asked the presenter, this time turning like a school teacher on his naughty pupil.

'Nothing, a rude word,' sighed the boy. 'Next question.'

'No, no, what was the rude word?'

'Shit,' John repeated softy, not sure how far he should or could go.

'Was it really? Good heavens! You frighten me to death.'

Grundy then turned to the Bromley Contingent. Siouxsie told the presenter that she had always wanted to meet him. 'We'll meet afterwards, shall we?' leered Grundy in reply, which the boys picked up on immediately, having also noticed Grundy taking a keen interest in Siouxsie in the green room. 'You dirty sod,' said Jones indignantly. 'You dirty old man.'

'Well, keep going, Chief,' retorted Grundy, foolishly. 'Go on, you've got another five seconds, say something outrageous.'

'You dirty bastard.'

'Go on.'

'You dirty fucker . . .'

'What a clever boy!'

Now the floodgates were open. 'What a fuckin' rotter.' Odd choice of word that: rotter, like something Lydon would say, and it made the Bromley Contingent snigger.

As the programme credits rolled, Malcolm McLaren, amazed at what he had seen and heard, and fearful of the consequences, which he thought might involve the police, bundled his boys out of the Thames building and into the EMI getaway car, stopping only to drop Lydon at the nearest tube station. There, John stood on the pavement without even the money to buy a ticket to get home, penniless and unknown, while mayhem was erupting. For the obscene language had not been edited out of the broadcast, nor bleeped over, but beamed to the whole metropolis and its suburbs. Irate viewers immediately began to telephone Thames to complain, with one man in Essex becoming so incensed that he kicked his television set to pieces. Others rang the national newspapers. Sensing a big story breaking, editors changed their front pages. The *Daily Mirror* came up with the best headline. In the morning, on page one, it screamed the news of *THE FILTH AND THE FURY!* Punk rock had arrived.

21

GARY GILMORE'S EYES

FUCK, SHIT, PISS

GARY GILMORE

The morning after the *Today* show, packs of journalists descended on Denmark Street to photograph and interview the Sex Pistols, reporters noting down the band members' every cough and spit, especially the latter, of which there was plenty. All four ragamuffins suddenly found themselves infamous, but not equally so. It was Steve Jones who said *fuck* on television, but most of the attention fell on the singer with the magnetically negative charisma and memorable moniker. 'I [thought] it was hilarious. Hilarious! Loved the attention,' reflects John Lydon, on his apotheosis as anti-hero.

Meanwhile, over at EMI, press officers viewed the media furore initially as priceless publicity for 'Anarchy in the UK', and for the Sex Pistols' forthcoming promotional tour with the Clash. But to their surprise many promoters cancelled bookings in the days following the TV appearance, with the result that the Pistols were only able to play a handful of their scheduled dates. And though 'Anarchy in the UK' enjoyed a modest lift in sales, many stores wouldn't stock it because of the *Today* kerfuffle. There was even a problem manufacturing the disc when ladies working at an EMI pressing plant refused to handle such a vile item. In short, there was genuine and widespread shock in Britain in 1976 that these youths had gone on television and behaved so *uncouthly* (for in truth that's all it was). The chairman of EMI, Sir

John Read, not a rock 'n' roll person but a captain of industry, was deeply embarrassed, and when the Pistols again behaved loutishly at Heathrow airport in January 1977, *en route* to a gig in Amsterdam, he ordered that their contract be dropped. The band could keep the £40,000 advance, but there would be no more Sex Pistols records on EMI. Two months later the Pistols signed to A&M, but that label soon dropped them, too, for much the same reasons, leaving Malcolm McLaren to put a brave face on the situation. Which he did, telling the press, 'I keep walking in and out of offices being given cheques.' While this was true, the Pistols now had an album-worth of songs that they wanted to release, but no record company to manufacture and distribute it. And lesser punk bands were stealing a march on them.

Although there had only been a tiny punk scene when the Pistols went on the *Today* show in December 1976, the cult had expanded considerably in the weeks since, with the centre of the punk universe now being a club called the Roxy, a dingy former gay disco on Neal Street in Covent Garden, that quickly became to the London punk scene what CBGB was to New York new wave. 'There was this feeling that something was building and [when] the Roxy opened, in January 1977, suddenly there was a club where you could go to every night. That's when you really felt something had started. This was a real movement that was going on [with] the feeling of excitement and thrill of something new,' comments TV Smith of the Adverts, one of a plethora of punk bands performing regularly at the Roxy and, as a result, getting record deals. The Adverts signed to Stiff, a small label founded by pub rock king Dave Robinson. So did the Damned, who had the distinction of being the first punk band to get an album out: *Damned Damned Damned* being released on Stiff in February 1977. A&R men from mainstream record labels started to follow Robinson down the dingy stairs of the Roxy to see what was going on and lost little time in acquiring acts of their own, with the Clash making the most impressive deal when they signed to CBS for a £100,000 advance, releasing their debut album in April.

Crude in design and production, the two sides of *The Clash* LP contains the essential elements of the band's now familiar sound: the almost Phil Spector-ish effect of three guitars playing in unison while all three guitarists – Joe Strummer, Mick Jones and Paul Simonon on bass – also take turns on vocals, the words often delivered in a near shout by Joe Strummer. In his lyrics, Joe commented directly on the state of Britain from a left-wing point of view – sarcastically, as in 'Career Opportunities', and often topically, as in 'White Riot', which recalled the Notting Hill Carnival of 1976. Another important element in the Clash's music was the incorporation of reggae, with the band including a cover of the Junior Murvin song 'Police and Thieves' on their first LP. Simonon, a musician of limited ability, found reggae easy to play and, more significantly, reggae was increasingly part of the culture of urban Britain in the late 1970s. This was partly because of the recent success of Bob Marley, and partly a reflection of the fact that London and other major British cities included significant Afro-Caribbean communities, after decades of immigration to the UK from its former Caribbean colonies. It was friction between elements of the Caribbean community and London's Metropolitan Police that was at the root of the 1976 Notting Hill Carnival riot. An even more serious riot broke out in the summer of 1977 when the National Front (NF) attempted to exploit racial tensions in London by marching through multi-ethnic Lewisham. Race was suddenly a very hot topic, and opposition to the NF became a worthy cause for the Clash and similar left-leaning punk bands to rally behind, often in conjunction with the newly founded Anti-Nazi League.

In contrast, the Sex Pistols remained steadfastly apolitical, with John Lydon showing disregard for all sections of society equally as he completed the vocals for the Pistols' first LP at Wessex Studios, though who would release this notional disc was anybody's guess now that the band didn't have a record company. Furthermore, the Pistols were no longer the same group that had made 'Anarchy in the UK'. The antipathy John, Paul and Steve felt towards Glen Matlock had reached a crisis when he complained that *his mum* wasn't happy about the Bill Grundy débâcle. At the Gas Board, where Mrs Matlock worked, the other women were mocking her as *Mrs Sex Pistol*. It almost went without saying that Glen didn't like John's new lyrics (now that Lydon was writing virtually all the words). In return, John had no time at all for Glen. They disliked each other so intensely that they almost came to blows on stage. So Glen was pushed out and, in his stead, Lydon drafted in his imbecile friend Sid Vicious to play bass. The lad had always wanted to be a rock star and, with his padlock-chain necklace and leather jacket, he had the *look*. And though he had almost zero musical ability, Sid didn't have to do much: just learn the basics of playing the bass (the easiest of rock instruments) and stand in line, sneering, for photo-shoots. So limited was Sid as a musical force that there was no point having him at Wessex Studios. He had nothing to contribute to the Pistols' album. In fact, as the other three concluded recording what would be *Never Mind the Bollocks, Here's the Sex Pistols*, Sid was in hospital with yellow jaundice.

The absence of a functional bass player is, paradoxically, key to the sound achieved on *Never Mind the Bollocks*. With Sid on his back (not that he could play standing up), producer Chris Thomas asked Steve Jones to overdub the bass parts. Limited musician that he was, Jones proceeded to play the required pieces as he would on his regular guitar, because that's all he was capable of (whereas a professional bass player would naturally go for counterpoint). When this rudimentary bass was overdubbed on the existing tracks, Chris realised that he had stumbled upon something new and distinctive. '*That* was the sound. That was the key to everything,' he says referring to the big, double sound that resulted from Steve playing the same thing twice. This is also why 'Anarchy in the UK', recorded earlier with Glen Matlock on bass, sounds more conventional and thereby different from all the other tracks on *Never Mind the Bollocks*. After Glen, everything featured Steve Jones on guitar times two, his bass and lead guitar fusing together in the overdub to form a monumental *thrum*. As Chris Thomas remarks 'that became absolutely the sound of the Sex Pistols . . . this massive wall of energy.'

The second reason *Never Mind the Bollocks* is a great rock album is Lydon's lyrics and the astonishing way in which he delivers them. 'Holidays in the Sun', 'Liar' and 'EMI' (retribution for getting fired) are all impressive, with imaginative words performed in a vocal style that ranges from football terrace jeer to Music Hall, via the Teutonic chill of Nico. But the shocker was and remains 'Bodies', a song about abortion based on John's encounter with a Pistols fan named Pauline, who showed up at his door one night with the aborted foetus of her baby in a see-through plastic handbag. ('She thought, *Here, you might like this!*') Personally, John was of the view that it is up to a woman to do with her body as she will. But his song 'Bodies' went far beyond arguing the pros and cons of the abortion debate, with John choosing rather to crawl inside the heads of all involved. In recording different takes of the song with Chris Thomas at Wessex, John adopted all points of view so that in some versions the grammatical sense was that he was singing as Pauline; at times it sounded as if he was singing from the perspective of the father of the child (not that he *was* the father); and, most unsettlingly, he became the foetus – screaming that he was not merely a discharge, not an abortion, not a body, an animal, or a 'fucking bloody mess,' these lines being repeated maniacally, madly, and descending into a primal scream of rage and pain. By mixing the takes together, an extraordinary, disturbing song of multiple perspectives was created.

The other standout track on *Never Mind the Bollocks* is 'God Save the Queen'. Glen provided the riff before his departure, inspired by a track on *Ziggy Stardust*, but Lydon wrote the amazing words which constitute a seditious attack on Queen Elizabeth II in the twenty-fifth year of her reign, inventing a slogan in 'no future,' and delivering such unexpectedly poetic phrases as 'England's dreaming,' and 'God save your mad parade.' Where he got these vivid images from, John can not remember. 'England's dreaming' sounds like something William Blake might have written, in the sense of evoking a dream of a vanished, partly mythical England. 'William Blake was always there,' says John, 'because I studied him at school.' But the phrase wasn't lifted from Blake. It sprung from John's surprising brain, as far as he can recall his meaning being that England in 1977 was in a state of self-delusion: celebrating itself at a time when so much was wrong with the country. 'England's dreaming, you know, look at it!' Even if it was accidental, the double meaning adds to the interest of the song, while the splendid phrase 'mad parade' perfectly evokes the arcane rituals of British pageantry. In fact, there is an extraordinary richness of language in almost every line of 'God Save the Queen', even in the apparently throwaway remarks, such as when Lydon sneers that he and the boys mean it, *maaaan*. He invests the word 'man' with the visceral disdain he felt for the generation of liberal, middle-class, university-educated hippies (as he would term them) who had until recently made up the ranks of most rock bands. If the Pistols were against anything, it was those people and their corny language. 'It's a phrase I despise . . . a hippie cop-out. *Oh yeah, right on man* . . . a right dig at that.' At the same time, he really did mean it, man. Or did he? With his love of Shakespeare's history plays, it should not be a surprise that, deep down, John had respect for the royal family, in as much as he recognised that they are the living embodiment of a thousand years of English history. What John resented, and sought to express in 'God Save the Queen', was the expectation that he should automatically show deference to the monarch. 'It's understood that I hate them, and want them to go away. I don't at all,' he elucidates. '[But] they assume I owe them something. I owe them obedience, honour . . .You've no right to presume that you have that naturally from me.' And he didn't dislike the Queen personally. Looking at Elizabeth II, he couldn't help but notice that the Queen wore the same glasses as his mum, Eileen Lydon, though he tried not to let that soften his heart too much. As he says, 'I had a real mum, and I don't need a substitute, state-driven one.'

By now the Pistols had a new record company, Richard Branson's Virgin, the fortunes of which were founded on the stupendous success of Mike Oldfield's progressive rock album *Tubular Bells* (1973). With *Never Mind the Bollocks* almost finished, it was time for Virgin to start promoting the band, in which pursuit they benefited enormously from efficacious timing. The first Sex Pistols single on Virgin, 'God Save the Queen', was released in May 1977, shortly before the celebrations of Queen Elizabeth's Silver Jubilee, officially commemorated on 7 June with a service of thanksgiving at St Paul's Cathedral, with the populace encouraged to take the celebrations into their communities. Nobody could be sure in advance how the United Kingdom would react to the Jubilee, especially in light of the dire economic situation. In fact, it was a great success. Across the country, houses and streets were decorated with Union Jacks and bunting. Souvenir mugs, buttons, badges, hats and T-shirts sold briskly. Newspapers published fold-out portraits of the Queen, which many readers taped to their front windows, and one former art student found another use for altogether: Malcolm's pal Jamie Reid took a Cecil Beaton portrait of Her Majesty from the *Sunday People* and used it in a series of collages that formed a brilliant publicity campaign for 'God Save the Queen'. Tearing out Her Majesty's eyes and mouth, he replaced them with the name of the band and the song in kidnap lettering, superimposing the altered image on a Union Jack. The result was printed on postcards, flyers, posters and coffee mugs, in mockery of Jubilee souvenirs. Variations on the theme included an image whereby Her Majesty's lips were buttoned with a safety pin. There was a good deal of humour in this. Many kids thought it *hilarious good fun*, as John might say, and Reid's designs were indeed a work of art. (Like the Beatles, the Pistols were a complete artistic statement: a coming together of music, graphics and fashion, all of high quality.) However, so offensive were these images to many people that shops declined to stock 'God Save the Queen', and the BBC refused to broadcast the song. Still, the single sold sufficiently strongly for it to reach number two in the charts by mid-June, only prevented from hitting number one by the surprising popularity of Rod Stewart's rendition of 'I Don't Want to Talk About It'. Pistols supporters are still convinced that the chart was rigged.

The following month, the Pistols performed 'Pretty Vacant' on *Top of the Pops*: this being perhaps the moment when punk moved from a cult into the mainstream. Taking a break from recording his new single, 'Stick to Me', Graham Parker found himself at his parents' home in Surrey that Thursday evening watching TV. Like many members of the generation just ahead of the Pistols, Graham hadn't yet fully understood the significance of this new music. 'I actually paid very little attention to most punk music. It wasn't until I saw the Sex Pistols do "Pretty Vacant" on *Top of the Pops* that I realised I'd just been made redundant,' he says. 'Of course! This is what young people needed! Not old blokes like me re-treading '60s riffs.'

Punk came into full bloom in Britain in the summer of 1977, the summer that Elvis Presley died. In its brief flowering, one of the punk singles to enjoy chart success was a darkly comic song by the

Adverts entitled 'Gary Gilmore's Eyes', inspired by the story of the American murderer of the same name who was executed in Utah in January that year. The case of Gary Gilmore attracted more international media attention than any murderer since Charles Manson, specifically because Gilmore insisted on being executed for his crimes rather than have his death sentence commuted to life in prison. This created a moral and legal debate of widespread interest. Riding the tube on the Piccadilly line in London just after Gilmore's execution, TV Smith picked up a discarded copy of the *Sun* and read a report of how Gilmore had donated his organs, including his eyes, to a hospital. Revolted by how the *Sun* was using the story as light entertainment, as he saw it, Smith wrote a 'gothic punk horror song' from the point of view of the person who awoke after an ocular transplant to discover whose eyes they were now looking through. A weird thought indeed, and one that helped the song, 'Gary Gilmore's Eyes', become a notable punk hit. The Adverts were not alone in making use of Gilmore's name and image. In the King's Road, a trendy new boutique called BOY was selling Gary Gilmore T-shirts. And in America, Norman Mailer was embarking on a book about the killer, *The Executioner's Song*, which would be one of the most significant novels of the decade, and the book that revived Mailer's reputation as a writer.

Mailer's subject, Gary Gilmore, was born in 1940 and raised in a highly dysfunctional family in Provo, Utah, a family led and blighted by a violent, drunken, itinerant conman father. Gary was the second of four boys, all of whose lives were marked by their unstable and often alarming upbringing. Like their father, the three eldest Gilmore sons all drank heavily, drifted around the country for parts of their lives, and served time in prison. Only the youngest, Mikal, born in 1951, managed to make a relatively normal career for himself, perhaps because his father died when Mikal was still young, before he could poison his life as he had poisoned those of other family members; also, because Mikal was fortunate to meet a school teacher who encouraged his interest in literature, which in turn led to a career as a journalist for *Rolling Stone* magazine, and later as an author. (One of the most notable books about the life of Gary Gilmore is Mikal's

1994 memoir, *Shot in the Heart*.) Of all the Gilmore boys, Gary was the most difficult and volatile. Although he had a high IQ and a remarkable artistic talent, Gary was an aggressive, dishonest boy who was mixed up in crime from an early age and spent much of his young life in custody, culminating in a long sentence for armed robbery. While inside, he was subjected to Electro-convulsive Therapy to try and curb his wayward personality, but in fact he only seemed to become more twisted. Nevertheless, in April 1976, at the age of thirty-five, Gilmore was granted parole and returned to Provo to work in his uncle Vern Damico's shoe-mending business. He soon met and became obsessively involved with a young woman named Nicole Baker, but when he behaved violently towards Nicole she left him. It seems that Gilmore went on his final, deadly crime spree in a nihilistic rage as a result of this rejection.

An immediate problem for Gilmore was that he needed $400 (£220) to make a payment on a second-hand truck he had bought. Ever since getting out of jail, he had operated as a petty thief, stealing packs of beer and so forth from service stations. In order to raise the money for the truck payment, on 19 July 1976 Gilmore robbed a petrol station in a small town near Provo. The young man in charge of the station, Max Jensen, gave Gary all the money he had without putting up a struggle. Nevertheless, Gary ordered Jensen to lie down on the floor where he shot him twice in the head, saying the first bullet was for him and the second for Nicole (though Jensen didn't know either of them). Then Gilmore went to a drive-in to watch his favourite movie, *One Flew Over the Cuckoo's Nest* (in which Jack Nicholson's inmate character receives ECT). The next night Gilmore robbed the motel next to his Uncle's Vern's house. The manager, Benny Bushnell, was watching the Montreal Olympics on TV when Gary walked in. Bushnell's wife and baby daughter were in the back room. Again, Gary demanded and received what money there was in the till without any resistance from the manager. He then ordered Bushnell to lie down on the floor where he executed him. When Gilmore was arrested soon afterwards, all he had to show for these two callous and wholly unnecessary murders was $200 (£110) in change. 'I hope they execute me,' he told the cops. 'I ought to die for what I did.'

Gilmore was convicted swiftly of murder and sentenced to death in October 1976 (coincidentally around the same time that his straight kid brother Mikal had his first freelance article accepted by *Rolling Stone*, demonstrating the yawning difference in the lives of the siblings). A death sentence did not mean Gary would be killed, however. No convict had been executed in the United States since the 1960s, because many appeal judges considered state execution to be constitutionally unlawful. As a result, hundreds of men were languishing on Death Row, seemingly destined to die there of old age. Gilmore wouldn't accept this as his fate, and began a determined legal campaign – aided and abetted by pro-death-sentence lobbyists – to be shot. Initially, it seemed unlikely that he would succeed, and so he made an attempt to kill himself. He did so by entering into a suicide pact with Nicole Baker, who had re-established contact with Gary after his arrest. Nicole smuggled pills into jail for Gary, and they agreed to each take an overdose on 15 November 1976. She went ahead with her part of the bargain, taking the full overdose on schedule; he took less than the fatal dose, and waited until early morning to swallow his pills, when he knew a guard would soon discover him. As a result, Gary recovered easily, but Nicole almost died, and when she was resuscitated the authorities separated her from her children and committed her to a mental hospital.

This squalid and manipulative suicide pact made headline news across America and attracted the interest of a 39-year-old journalist-hustler named Larry Schiller, who had made his name with a series of sensational news events in recent years, signing up the protagonists and selling their stories in the most profitable way he could. He was a clumsy operator at times. During the Charles Manson case, for instance (the murders that had claimed the life of Roman Polanski's wife among others), Schiller made a deal with Susan Atkins, one of Manson's so-called family members and a witness in his Los Angeles trial, whereby Atkins' story was published *before* the trial started, thus jeopardising the prosecution (though she and Manson were later convicted of murder) and bringing Schiller into opprobrium with the LA court. By his own admission, Schiller *fucked up* that story. This time around, he determined to proceed with more care. Setting up his HQ in Utah, Schiller sought out, and made himself agreeable to, all the participants in the Gilmore case, including Nicole and Gary, signing them to formal agreements whereby he controlled the rights to their story. He paid Gary $50,000 (£27,500) in advance for his co-opera-tion, a morally dubious action of course. Schiller then sold Gilmore's love letters to the *National Enquirer* to recoup some of his outlay. Although they were not allowed to meet any more, Gary and Nicole were frequent correspondents and Gary used his letters to Nicole as a forum to discuss everything he was thinking about, though mostly to indulge in masturbatory fantasies. Sometimes his furious anger revealed itself. For instance, he became so enraged during the com-position of one missive to Nicole that he scrawled across the page in two-inch-high block capitals the obscene slogan FUCK, SHIT, PISS. What made Gary really mad was that the authorities' refused to allow him to see Nicole. As a result, he went on hunger strike late in 1976, which further increased media interest in the case. By the end of the year, Gary Gilmore was famous, featured in *Time* magazine as one of the faces of 1976, and parodied on the now hugely popular US comedy show *Saturday Night Live*. The press baron Rupert Murdoch was negotiating with Larry Schiller for his first-person account of the execution. This finally took place on 18 January 1977.

During the last months of his life, Gary Gilmore had been meat and drink to the tabloid media. Trash TV shows, supermarket magazines and red-top newspapers wallowed in the story, and showed no com-punction in paying for interviews, letters and photographs. In many ways, the exploitation of Gilmore's story was the prototype for the way the press has covered major crime cases ever since. After his death, Gilmore became the stuff of art: the low art of a punk rock song (which Mikal, now a reporter for *Rolling Stone*, loved) and the high art of literature. Although he controlled the rights to Gilmore's story, Schiller didn't feel able to write the book himself. In the past he had hired journalists and authors to do the writing for him. This time he went to Norman Mailer. The idea of a hustler like Schiller dealing with a distinguished author such as Mailer may seem strange, but Schiller had hired Mailer to write the text for two previous books, most notably a picture-based book about Marilyn Monroe. It was relatively easy, well paid work and Mailer had an expensive lifestyle to fund. The two men, though, didn't always get along. While Schiller was no writer he was not shy about giving authors the benefit of his opinions, and at times his relationship with Mailer was so tense that the author could hardly bear to speak to him. But there *was* a relationship. Also, Larry felt that Norman was peculiarly suited to the task of being Gary Gilmore's biographer. 'So why did I think of Mailer?' Schiller asks rhetorically, being the sort who likes to pose and answer his own questions. 'Because I understood and knew that Mailer had a very, very difficult relationship with his father, and that Mailer [had] exhibited through the years a certain violent side of his own behaviour.' (In this, Schiller was referring partly to the long-ago incident when Norman stabbed his second wife, Adele.) 'I felt that he understood now [at] this point in his life a lot about one's own inner violence, and the slight differences that tip people one way or the other, and that he might be able to understand Gilmore because of his own experiences, and that's why I thought of Mailer.'

An interview Schiller had conducted with Gary Gilmore was running in *Playboy* magazine, and the journalist sent an advance copy of the magazine to Norman's house at Cape Cod. After reading the material, Norman spoke to Larry on the telephone. 'I said, "This is a wonderful interview, I want to make a play out of it." And he said, "No, no, no, if you want to make a play out of it you've got to write the book first."' So Norman began to think of the story in another way, as the basis of a book exploring a notion he had that psychopaths like Gilmore were similar to saints. 'I had a psychological theory that saints and psychopaths had one profound element in common, which is they each had an enormous sense of the present, and were not that sharp about the future and the past. In other words they lived for the present . . . So I thought, *Alright, I'll write a 200-page book about* The Saint and The Psychopath, *that'll be perfect, taking Gilmore as my point of departure.*' Schiller envisaged the book very differently, of course, as a major and much more straightforward study of a murderer and his crimes. 'I always saw it as an immense project, an immense book,' says the journalist. To try and bring Mailer round to his way of thinking he brought Nicole Baker to New York to meet the author, introducing them over lunch at Trader Vic's restaurant. Norman was sufficiently intrigued by Nicole to make a deal whereby Larry would retain the underlying rights to the story and they would split the proceeds from the book.

It was only after he had secured Norman's co-operation that Schiller discovered American hardback publishers were wary of spending big money on a new Mailer book, giving Larry the impression that Norman's stock had fallen a long way since *The Naked and the Dead*. These days, the author was associated more with slim journalistic works, such as *The Prisoner of Sex*, which made a splash when they were published, but were ultimately ephemeral. 'So they didn't have the confidence to give me the money that I felt the project warranted.' Also, some people in the New York literary world were taken aback that Mailer was even considering the Gilmore story as subject matter, true crime being seen traditionally as low-rent, *National Enquirer* territory. ('This is the underbelly of America . . . with all its sweat,' as Schiller says.) It was with this background that a deal was finally done with the paperback publisher Warner Books for a $500,000 (£275,000) advance; the hardback rights sold later for a relatively small sum to Little, Brown.

Mailer then travelled with Larry to Provo to meet some of the key people in the story and conduct joint interviews with the families of the victims of Gilmore. Norman also began sifting through the hundreds of pages of transcripts of interviews Larry had done with Gary and Nicole, and virtually everybody else in the case including relatives, police officers and prison guards. The whole story was here in their words, and so Norman made a key decision. Rather than write in his characteristic authorial style, using his extensive vocabulary and introducing his personal views on the subject, he would tell the story of Gary Gilmore simply, without comment, in the plain vernacular speech of Provo. There was such an abundance of source material he could take quotes directly from the transcripts, as well as paraphrasing in the same style, creating a book that was highly evocative of life in this Mormon community in the west of America, exactly two hundred years on from the founding of the modern United States. This was an epic story of the West; that much was now clear to Norman.

'I realised I could never do the two-hundred page book,' he says, 'that this was going to be a big book, because the material was so wonderful.' In fact, the book would ultimately be over a thousand pages long.

While the writing in *The Executioner's Song* is deliberately simple, in keeping with the way that people speak in Provo, Mailer allowed himself to introduce flecks of lyrical description, such as the passage about night falling on Utah State Prison where Gilmore is held after being sentenced: 'Outside the prison, night had come, and the ridge of the mountain came down to the Interstate like a big dark animal laying out its paw.' The blend of flat but highly detailed and faithful reportage with fine writing created a truly grand book which, with multiple characters, a wealth of description and extensive dialogue, reads like an epic novel. Looking back on the project, Mailer says that the *writing* was the easy part. 'The hard work was the *editing*. I learned how to edit with that book. Because you'd have an interview that had good elements in it, but it went on for, let's say, twenty or thirty pages, and you just knew after a while that this was two or three pages at most in the book. So how do you boil it down, how do you reduce it? And it consisted of working through many drafts. In other words, it was a craftsman's task. And I think I've been a better craftsman as a writer ever since that book. I really learned how to put in the hours.'

Mailer did not spare his anti-hero, showing from the first how Gilmore was a devious, prison-hardened misfit. Like Travis Bickle in the then new movie *Taxi Driver* (1976), Gilmore looks down on people who he thinks are inferior to him, and who he believes he can push about – women and blacks among others – and ultimately kills stupidly, pointlessly, out of a sense of inadequacy. In describing the events leading up to the murders of Jensen and Bushnell in meticulous detail, in putting murder under the microscope as it were, Mailer helps the reader understand Gilmore. Nicole Baker is a major character in the first part of the book, her relationship with Gary being key to why he murdered. Mailer had a dramatic problem with the book in that, after their failed suicide pact, Gary and Nicole were separated. So, aside from their correspondence, their relationship stopped. The only people Gilmore met from then on were his jailers, lawyers, a few family members and Larry Schiller. It was for this reason that Norman turned the second part of the book into the story of how Larry and others in the mass media handled the case of Gary Gilmore, leading up to his execution. It was not a very edifying story and Norman did not spare his journalist friend and collaborator. By detailing the blood deal between Schiller and Gilmore, their often testy relationship and Schiller's selling of the intellectual property he had acquired, Mailer put not only murder under the microscope but the way murder stories are exploited, or at least how this started to work with the Gilmore case.

Finally, and perhaps most significantly, *The Executioner's Song* is the ultimate work of New Journalism, the form Tom Wolfe had so named in the 1960s, and which had dominated the literary world throughout the 1970s. With a wealth of interview material, Mailer was in an unprecedented position to create the perfect blend of fact and fiction in the sense that he told a factual story in a fictional style. It is not to all tastes. 'The real problem in the book, the argument in the book, the fundamental argument that people still do argue over, is whether this is fiction or non-fiction,' says Mailer, looking back on *The Executioner's Song*, which was such a mammoth task it was not published until 1979. 'Because, after all, the names are all the same as the original names. The facts were there. I wanted the book to be as factual as I could possibly make it. And yet I insisted it was a novel, and the reason I insisted it was a novel is it was written in the style of a novel. And once you write something so it's telling a story in novel-form it becomes a novel . . . I called it a true-life novel. I'm not happy with the phrase. But what I meant by that [was that] it was a novel that was trying to be as accurate to the events that had occurred as it could possibly be, but it still was a novel, because you can not capture reality in prose. Non-fiction is just another form of fiction as far as I'm concerned.'

22

INSIDE OUT/OUTSIDE IN

We haven't heard the end of this!

PRESIDENT GEORGES POMPIDOU

As Norman Mailer and other authors subverted the conventions of novel-writing in the seventies, turning real-life into books that read like fiction, architects turned the built environment inside out: putting what is usually inside a building on the outside, and bringing the outside in. The foremost example of this is the Pompidou Centre,* which was opened in Paris the month that Gary Gilmore was executed: a vast steel and glass shed, the size of a large department store, festooned with steel rods and coloured pipes, with an extraordinary see-through escalator hanging on its front façade. When France's President, Georges Pompidou, approved the design in 1971, he predicted: 'Ça va crier!' ('We haven't heard the end of this!') Upon its opening in January 1977, the centre named in his honour fulfilled his prophecy. Here was a structure, the like of which the world had never seen, that caused controversy at the time and still divides opinion between those who love the building and those who consider it monstrous. Still, on balance, it has become more beloved than reviled.

Like the Sydney Opera House, the Pompidou started with an open international competition to find a design for an arts centre that would

---

*Officially named Le Centre National d'art et de Culture Georges Pompidou, but referred to here by its common name.

enhance the image of a city and nation. In this case, there was also a specific political dimension in the violent student protests of May 1968. President Charles De Gaulle had quashed that uprising, which carried with it the threat of a Communist-led revolution, but he put it down at considerable political cost to himself and was obliged to retire from office the following year. His successor, Georges Pompidou, a long-term advisor to De Gaulle and a former Prime Minister of France (in which office he was instrumental in France's withdrawal from Algeria: the political decision that underpins *The Day of the Jackal*), had the task of healing the wounds of '68. One of his ideas was to give Paris a wonderful new library, one that would have free access to all, which was in itself a sop to students. This idea then expanded into a grander dream of a cultural palace that would, in part, serve to entertain and, hopefully, distract the youth of Paris from causing further civil unrest. This centre would also be the first of what became a succession of *grands projets* commissioned by French presidents for the glorification of Paris. Over the following decades these included I.M. Pei's glass pyramid entrance to the Louvre, a new opera house and the Arche de la Défense. Spectacular though all these structures are, none were quite so bold as the Pompidou Centre.

More than the other buildings featured in this book, the Pompidou is a quintessentially 1970s building. It was conceived ambitiously in the optimistic political climate of the early seventies before the international oil crisis began to depress Western economies; it was built with the very latest '70s technology, and completed, with appropriate cut-backs, in the more stringent latter years of the decade. The brief was drawn up in the summer of 1970, the competition announced soon thereafter. The site was the Plateau Beaubourg in the heart of the historic but dilapidated Marais district, adjacent to Les Halles food market, which was to be closed and redeveloped. The land was being used at the time as a parking area for trucks servicing the market. The brief called for a multi-purpose structure to include not only a public library, but a centre for experimental music, designed specifically to lure the French composer Pierre Boulez home from the United States. There would also be museum space to display artwork, including France's unrivalled collection of modern paintings; together with cinemas, book shops and restaurants. Finally, the building should be flexible enough to be able to accommodate as yet unforeseen developments in the arts. As with the Sydney Opera House, there was a cash reward for winning the architectural competition, plus the supreme prize of having one's building constructed in the heart of the world's most beautiful capital city.

Among those who took immediate interest in the competition was Ove Arup's engineering company. With their work on the Sydney Opera House finally nearing completion, senior partners at Arup decided that the Paris competition was a suitably ambitious, high-profile new challenge for the company. In order to compete, however, they would need to join forces with an architect, for architects traditionally lead such projects. It was Arup engineer Ted Happold who had the idea that the firm might collaborate with young Richard Rogers. As touched upon in Chapter 9, back in the 1960s Rogers was working in partnership with Norman Foster and others in a small, radical architectural firm in Britain named Team 4. As we have seen, one of their projects was the house that Stanley Kubrick used for the rape scene in *A Clockwork Orange*. To sketch in some more of Rogers' background, he was born in Florence in 1933, coming to England as a boy when his parents emigrated to escape the fascists. After studying at the Architectural Association in London, he completed his education in America at Yale, where he became friendly with a fellow scholarship student from England named Norman Foster. Rogers and Foster travelled extensively together in order to see the most notable modern buildings of the United States, experiences which had a significant influence on them both, though perhaps Rogers especially so. In his politics, Rogers was strongly left-wing, yet he admired greatly the energy of the USA, and the bold use of technology in every field of American life. Among his architectural heroes were such American innovators as Frank Lloyd Wright and, particularly, the husband-and-wife team of Charles and Ray Eames. From 1945–49, the Eames built a simple, flat-roofed, steel and glass home for themselves in Santa Monica, California, using commercially available components, rather as a child might bolt together a structure from pieces of Meccano. In doing so, they created a simple and delightful home which could be easily replicated or adapted. In this sense, the Eames House was eminently *flexible* (a key word in 1970s architecture, and with Rogers' architecture in particular). Around the same time that the Eames House was being built, the editor of the American journal *Arts and Architecture* commissioned a number of similar houses as 'case studies' in modern design, and these Case Study houses, by Craig Ellwood and others, also influenced Rogers significantly. In a sense, all these American architects were taking their lead from the seminal European modernists such as Mies van der Rohe, but their buildings were lighter, cheaper and more adaptable than those designed by the European masters of modernism, opening up a world of possibilities to Rogers who 'fell in love with the idea of a mass-produced house, made with standard industrial components.' Returning to England, Rogers and Foster formed Team 4 and began to design small houses and factory buildings that owed much to these American influences. In 1967, Foster left the partnership to pursue his own career (achieving great fame in the 1980s), and Rogers carried on in partnership with his wife, Su, designing simple but innovative steel and glass flat-roofed buildings, including a house for his parents in Wimbledon, south-west London, part of which was painted bright yellow, the use of colour being another Rogers trademark.

Clever though Rogers' design work was, commissions were modest in size and few in number. By 1970 he had so little work that he had to teach to make a living. Also, his marriage was in disarray, the architect having fallen for an American named Ruth Elias. However, it was in 1970 that Richard also met Renzo Piano, a 33-year-old Italian architect with whom he felt the same creative rapport he had once enjoyed with Norman Foster, and so the firm of Piano + Rogers was formed. 'We were both semi-unemployed, and we thought two unemployed [people] would get a better quality of life that one,' Rogers says of their early association. Still, there was practically no work. It was at this time that Ted Happold approached them with the suggestion that they collaborate on an entry for the exciting new Paris competition. Despite having little else to do, Rogers was not initially in favour. He had been appalled by the brutal way the French government suppressed the student demonstrations in 1968, and now here was Pompidou – one of the enemies of the Left during that crisis – presiding over a grandiose project that would glorify France and, inevitably, himself. As Rogers says: 'I didn't like the idea of doing what could be seen as a palace for a president.' However, Piano + Rogers was run in a spirit of democracy and it came down to a vote, taken in Rogers' flat in Belsize Grove. Despite the fact that Richard and Su were breaking up, she still played a part in his professional life at this time and she voted with him against the competition. Piano and Happold voted for, and when Su went to attend to the children Rogers found himself outnumbered by two to one on a second count. 'So, OK, the other two want to do it. I wasn't *that* much against it. We were all friends. So we started looking at it.'

They worked on the bid right up to the deadline, which was midnight on 15 June 1971. A colleague, Marco Goldschmied, ran the drawings round to the late-night post office in William IV Street, next to Trafalgar Square, only to be informed by the clerk on duty that the drawings were too big for the Royal Mail to handle. At the eleventh hour Goldschmied had to borrow a pair of scissors and cut the drawings down to size. (Philip Johnson, one of the judges, later said to Rogers that it looked like a dog had chewed his drawings.) This was in fact the first of a series of bad omens. Three days after the package went off to Paris it was returned to sender due to insufficient postage. When the team managed to post it off *again*, the French informed all the British entrants that they had mislaid their drawings. By this stage, Rogers was so exasperated that he told Piano it would hardly be worth the trouble re-submitting, if that's what it came to, his gloom deepened by the fact that he now knew there had been a total of 681 entries for the competition. 'We thought there'd be a handful.' In the end, the French *did* find the British entries and the telephone rang in July with the unexpected news that Piano + Rogers had won! Despite the fact that Su and Richard Rogers were about to divorce, they danced about their office in joy.

As with the Sydney Opera House, an open international competition judged blind had thrown up a young and mostly unknown winner, doubly so in the case of Piano and Rogers (aged thirty-three and thirty-seven respectively). Again in common with Sydney, theirs was an audacious design that was poetic and inspiring, but sketchily drawn. Boldly, Piano + Rogers had adapted the competition brief, imposing their own ideas on what Paris required, which they believed was a public meeting place at Beaubourg, almost a rallying point. Thus they turned over half the site to a piazza, to be shaped like an amphitheatre and drawing attention towards the structural centrepiece itself, which was to rise six storeys above ground. And what a structure it was! The big idea was to have huge, football pitch-like floors in the sky – measuring a massive 425 feet by 148 feet – that would be totally open. To achieve this, Peter Rice of Ove Arup & Partners, and a recent veteran of the Sydney Opera House saga, helped Piano + Rogers come up with a dramatic and poetic engineering solution. 'On one level there's very little difference between architecture and engineering,' comments Rogers. 'And certainly [Peter] was a poet of engineering.' Front and back of the structure would be two huge walls of steel. Between these walls would be slung the floors. In theory, the floors could be moved up and down to accommodate different uses. They would be supported underneath only (no internal pillars) by steel trusses attached to massive steel columns *outside* the skin of the structure: fourteen columns front and back, each spaced 42 feet apart. To join the trusses to the vertical columns, Rice had the idea of using gerberettes, a rocking joint named after its nineteenth-century German inventor, Heinrich Gerber. These units, which are normally small, would be enormous, weighing ten tons each, threaded on to the columns like bobbins, with a short inner arm that engaged with a floor truss while a longer, more delicate outer arm threaded into a tension rod anchored in the piazza. Finally, the whole system would be cross-braced against the wind. To keep the interior space clear, the pipes that usually clutter up the inside of a building would be outside the steel walls, forming a serpentine decoration concentrated on the back (or eastern) façade, facing Rue de Renard. Hanging off the front of the structure facing the piazza would be lifts and escalators, in transparent shells so that the people inside could see out, while those below in the piazza had the interest of watching people circulate around the building. For Rogers the escalators were akin to Rome's Spanish Steps: a means of getting from one place to another, but also a place to promenade. The views would be amazing, of course. As one rose up above the lead-grey roofs of the nineteenth-century buildings surrounding the Plateau Beaubourg, the magical panorama of Paris would be gradually revealed: from the nearby gothic eminence of Notre-Dame to the white dome of Sacré Coeur atop Montmartre. Also attached to this front (western) façade would be electronic display screens, like the animated advertising hoardings of Times Square, which impressed Rogers greatly when he first visited New York. These were intended to transmit art images, even films. Being of a radical disposition, Rogers used Leftist slogans and pictures from the Vietnam War to illustrate this feature in the competition plans. Pierre Boulez's music centre, IRCAM (Institut de Recherche & Co-ordination Acoustique Musique), would be built under the piazza, to eliminate exterior noise. There would also be subterranean levels of parking and storage. Summarising the salient points of the main structure, Rogers showed his considerable gift for rhetoric by invoking 'an ever changing framework, a Meccano kit, a climbing frame for the old and young ... a flexible, functional, transparent, inside out building.' He argued that it could be built relatively cheaply, for under 500 million French francs (roughly £50 million),★ and that like a big Case Study house it could be disassembled if need be, added to or adapted as requirements changed. In a hundred years time, an arts centre might become a hospital, say, or a university.

Excavation began in March 1972. Rogers moved to Paris and set up home near the job with Ruth, whom he married in 1973. Becoming immersed in the Parisian lifestyle was one of the joys of the project to the British architect. Richard and Renzo worked out of an amazing inflatable office – something like a giant bouncy castle, filled with the latest equipment and furnishing – next to the River Seine. In the evenings, Richard and Ruth frequented the cinema, and for vacations they slipped out of the city on the night train to the South of France. It was a delightfully romantic life in this sense, but the daily

★To construct and equip the main building actually cost a total of 750 million francs, plus the cost of the land, IRCAM and other bits and pieces. All told, the project cost 993 million francs, closer to £100 million.

grind of getting the Pompidou built proved almost as wearing on Rogers' nerves as the Sydney Opera House had with the unfortunate Jørn Utzon. Not only was the project vast and technically complex, the radical design caused consternation in sections of the French media, as Pompidou had predicted ('Ça va crier!'); journalists decried the design as being like an oil rig, and were antagonistic to the very fact that *their* arts centre was being designed by an Anglo-Italian team, with British engineers, and Germans manufacturing the gerberettes. Then, on 2 April 1974, Pompidou died, leaving Piano + Rogers politically exposed. The new President, Valéry Giscard d'Estaing, insisted on reductions to the budget and forbade Rogers' electronic screens, which he feared could be put to subversive use. The project had already been cut back in other respects: the building had lost a floor, and the planned glass-fronted elevators would not be built. Still, most of the key features remained: including the escalator with its transparent shell roof, which now ran all the way to the top of the building where it connected with a covered promenade. Although President Giscard d'Estaing made life difficult, the project continued, not least because of the unwavering commitment of a senior civil servant named Robert Bordaz who saw it as his duty to make sure that the wishes of his friend, the late President Pompidou, were carried out. It was Bordaz who guided Piano and Rogers through a political and legal maze, which the architects were too inexperienced to fully understand. In short, they didn't know how much trouble they were in until it was all over. As Rogers says, 'Naïveté has some advantages: you don't realise how naïve you are!'

Despite all the problems, the steel started to go up in the autumn of 1974 and by the following summer the Pompidou was assuming its distinctive appearance. The steel itself was a very strong visual element, the columns front and back being as thick as the trunks of mature trees. With their massive gerberette joints, interconnecting braces and tension rods, the steel articulates the façade, making it visually interesting, as does the see-through escalator. An equally important feature is the arrangement of the service pipes, particularly on the back where they are more numerous and larger than on the front: larger than necessary in order to make an aesthetic statement. For the same reason, the pipes are colour-co-ordinated: the uprights and cross-sections of structural steel are all painted white, as are the huge ship-like funnels designed to evacuate smoke in the event of fire; the massive air-conditioning pipes are painted blue, emerging on the roof again as funnels; the parts of the structure to do with the movement of people are red (the undersides of the escalators, and the boxes on the roof containing the winding mechanism for the service lifts); water pipes are green (for fire-extinguishing systems and so forth); finally the electricity conduit and fuse boxes are yellow. (See picture 31.) Piano was the prime mover behind this colour scheme, though Rogers had always been a bold user of colour, too. There is more inside: blue vinyl floors in the service areas and, originally, brightly coloured carpet for public spaces. The use of primary colour is one of the most striking features of the Pompidou Centre, and part of why the building is so dramatic to look at. It has been highly influential in architecture and design since 1977. However, such a bold use of colour was at variance with another important school of architecture at this time: that practised by those American architects known as *the whites*.

As Richard Rogers is a European architect influenced heavily by American design, Richard Meier is an American architect of distinction and influence who looks to Europe for his primary inspiration. Born into a Jewish family in New Jersey in 1934 (the year after Rogers), Meier fell under the spell of European modernism when he was studying at Cornell University, the dominant figure in architecture for him being Le Corbusier and what Meier calls his 'white, purist masterpieces.' As a young man, Meier travelled to Paris, where he sought out Le Corbusier, a pilgrimage Jørn Utzon had also once made. Meier offered the architect his services and was brusquely rejected, '. . . but at least I had the immense satisfaction of coming face-to-face with the great man.' In common with Utzon and Rogers, Meier also admired Frank Lloyd Wright, being profoundly influenced by an opportunity he had to be a weekend guest at Wright's masterpiece house, Fallingwater, in wooded hill country outside Pittsburgh. Fallingwater is built over a stream, with a natural waterfall. Numerous windows, some wrapped ingeniously around corners of the house, and cunningly-designed balconies, make one feel as if the house is part of nature, and nature is in the house. 'I was overwhelmed by this experience,' Meier wrote of his stay at Fallingwater, 'and fascinated by Wright's extension of the interior into the exterior.' Meier began his professional career in the New York office of the Bauhaus architect Marcel Breuer, thus establishing his connection to European modernism. Then, in the 1960s, he branched out on his own to build houses for wealthy clients, such as his Smith House (1965) overlooking Long Island Sound. These are generously-proportioned, box-like, wood-frame buildings with flat roofs, large windows and white-painted walls – *always* white because, as far as Meier is concerned, nothing reflects light so well. Meier also thought of the façades of his buildings as being a *taut skin*, the glass and white-painted walls forming a seamless smooth surface, so different from the Pompidou, which is a building *skinned* – the coloured arteries and veins of its circulatory system exposed.

In 1972, Meier and four like-minded New York architects published an influential book entitled *Five Architects*, in which they showcased their designs for starkly pure modernist buildings. The book earned Meier and his friends the collective term of *the whites*, in contrast to the postmodernist *grays* led by the Philadelphia-based architect Robert Venturi, who turned the European modernist maxim 'less is more' on its head, saying 'less is a bore.' Venturi championed busy, characterful buildings that were more like everyday America than the whites' designs, which to his mind were stuck in the Europe of half a century before, when Socialist architects had a vision of building a Utopia for working people with new mass-production techniques. Unfortunately, when their revolutionary ideas were applied to multi-storey apartment projects for the working classes of Europe and America, the structures were often compromised by budget. Built on the cheap, cities in the sky became high-rise slums. Crime, social alienation and despair resulted. In the early 1950s, two decades before the completion of his shimmering World Trade Center towers, Minoru Yamasaki was the architect responsible for one such disaster: the notorious Pruitt Igoe project in St Louis, Missouri, a high-rise city for 10,000 people that proved such a horrible place to live that its residents deliberately set fire to it. In 1972, the local housing department had the charred remains of the unloved complex dynamited. However, by tailoring similar modernist principles to the needs and budget of rich private clients, architects such as Richard Meier created handsome American mansions in the 1970s. Like the reviled projects, the homes were essentially box-like concrete buildings with flat roofs. But unlike the projects these structures were single-family dwellings built on a generous scale in beautiful locations (as opposed to the crowded urban landscape) where it was a pleasure to bring the outside in, via large windows, walkways and terraces.

Meier's Douglas House of 1971–73 was one such building. (See picture 30.) His client, a wealthy man named James Douglas, had admired magazine pictures of Meier's Smith House, and asked the architect to build an abode for himself and his wife on a dramatic plot of land overlooking Lake Michigan. 'The setting is quite unusual in that it is an extremely steep, sloping site down to the water,' explains Meier. 'It was so steep that one didn't want to remove any trees, because that would cause erosion of the earth. So the house was built with trees less than a foot away [from the walls]. It was almost like it was dropped by a helicopter into the site.' As with Frank Lloyd Wright's Fallingwater, the Douglas House feels as if it is part of the natural world. The visitor approaches from the back, via a ramp which joins the house at the top storey. Stairs lead down into the building which faces out on to the lake, the surface of which changes naturally with the weather and is reflected inside on the white walls. The feeling is of being on the water, an illusion emphasised by the deck-like wooden floors extending outside on every level beyond the glass windows, with nautical-style safety railings. 'Everyone who goes there feels that they're on a ship, but they don't get seasick,' the architect remarks. 'It doesn't move!'

The Douglas House is one of the most beautiful private houses to have been built in the 1970s, but it is large public buildings that make an architect's reputation. Although Meier was increasingly busy during the decade designing homes for wealthy, private clients, he received relatively few commissions for public buildings – that is, until 1979, when he was asked to design a new art gallery in Frankfurt, Germany.

In the rebuilding of postwar Germany, its modernist heritage had been discarded in favour of buildings designed in a less challenging, post-modern idiom. Now an American Jew (significantly, for German Jewish architects had suffered under Nazi rule) brought the stark clean lines of modernism back home, providing Frankfurt with a gleaming new white building that the German fathers of European modernism such as Mies van der Rohe would have been proud of. 'During the short speech that I gave during the inauguration of the museum at Frankfurt,' recalls Meier, 'I said how important it was for me to think about the great German architects [whose careers], unfortunately, and in some cases their lives, were extinguished during the Second World War, and this was a continuum of the work which [they did], and which was important to me.' The success of the Museum of the Decorative Arts led to commissions for Meier to build many more major public buildings, mostly in France and Germany where his style has become very much part of the modern urban landscape. Although he also went on to design a great new building for Los Angeles, in the Getty Centre, it is in Europe that Meier remains best-known and most appreciated. 'I think there is a different respect for architecture in Europe than there is in America,' he reasons. 'I think in America architecture is sort of seen as building, not as art. And I think that in Europe, you know, when people travel, what do they do? They go and look at architecture – whether it's from the Renaissance or the Middle Ages – that's art and cultural history. And somehow that attitude doesn't exist in the same way in the United States.'

The Pompidou Centre received a mostly negative reception from the European press when it opened in 1977, derided by many commentators as being ugly and overpowering. At a time when oil prices were rising and energy conservation was becoming more important, it was an inefficient building. Heat dissipated easily through the thin steel walls, while the sun turned the transparent escalators into greenhouses, making passengers feel sick. Free access and long opening hours had the unexpected result of providing shelter for the down-and-outs of Paris, who found the Pompidou a convenient place to doss. And although there was little indication of this when the building was new, it would deteriorate rapidly: the escalator coverings became discoloured by the sun, the metal panels rusted. All that was a problem for the future, however, and to some extent a reflection of the fact that the Pompidou had been built on the cheap. More importantly, the building proved immensely popular with the public.

As with the Sydney Opera House, the Pompidou Centre is a fantastic-looking edifice that excites the imagination. Tourists feel compelled to visit it, and be photographed in front of it. While the World Trade Center was awesome, and the shells of the Opera House have an immaculate and timeless beauty, the Pompidou Centre is also *fun*. Six million people visited the arts centre in its first year, making it the most popular tourist attraction in Paris; the see-through escalator was seized on from the first as the best free ride in the city, affording visitors splendid views of the capital. That many tourists treated the building almost as if it were an amusement ride delighted Richard Rogers, who wanted his building to be as accessible as possible. Meanwhile, the large numbers of students and academics using the library and other facilities on a daily basis for serious study proved that the building was functional as well as fun. The gallery spaces are popular and so are the cinemas and music centre. Piano and Rogers had also given the city an important new public space in the piazza, which continues to be one of the most pleasant open areas in central Paris. They did all this on budget and on schedule, remarkably for such a gigantic project, though the job took its toll.

'It was a helluva five years,' sighs Rogers, looking back on Beaubourg (as he calls the centre, never liking the fact that it was named for the glory of a politician). Despite the joy and excitement of living in Paris, every day on the job seemed to bring new crises, and after the opening ceremony in January 1977, Rogers sunk into a period of exhaustion, touching on depression, that puts one in mind of Jørn Utzon's Sydney experience. 'It took me one or two years after it was completed to recover. I was wiped out at the end of Beaubourg, totally wiped out.' It didn't help that there wasn't a rush of job offers at the end of the project, despite the international attention the Pompidou had attracted. Rogers began to think once again that his career was more or less over, that he would be known as a one-building architect, again like Utzon, and he spent an increasing amount of time teaching in the United States. His relationship with Renzo Piano cooled, and staff in the London office worried for their future. One of Rogers' senior colleagues, John Young, even contemplated becoming a cab driver.

As it turned out Young didn't have to start driving a taxi: in 1977 Richard Rogers was one of a select number of architects approached by Lloyd's of London to submit designs for a grand new headquarters for the organisation. Lloyd's, which is essentially a collective of self-employed insurance brokers and their employees, forming an insurance market of many thousands of people, had outgrown its existing building in the City of London and was in urgent need of a large, flexible new office that would provide masses of open space – particularly a central area for the brokers to mix and mingle and write business ('The Room') – and yet also take account of the fact that developments in computer technology might mean that in the near future the market would employ fewer people. A shortlist of six distinguished architects submitted plans, including I.M. Pei and Rogers' former partner, now rival, Norman Foster, with Rogers himself ultimately being given the go-ahead to design one of the most amazing new structures London had seen since the Victorian age. (See picture 32.)

The Lloyd's Building is associated primarily with the economic boom the City enjoyed in the 1980s. With its sleek metal façades and sexy lines – floodlit at night with blue, amber and white lamps – the building is often perceived as being a monument to, and symbol of, the resurgence of market force economics in Britain under the premiership of Margaret Thatcher. In fact, only in construction (1980–86) is Lloyd's a building of the eighties. In conception and design, it is a great 1970s building, for which Rogers' plans were published in June 1979. Though there were subsequent revisions and slight changes, this 1979 plan essentially became the building we see today. Like the Pompidou, Lloyd's is another inside-out Rogers structure, designed to give its occupants as much uncluttered space as possible. But unlike Pompidou, it is an inside-out building constructed to the highest specifications, partly because the client could afford the best. Also, the site demanded excellence: here in the ancient heart of the City of London, between Leadenhall and Lime Streets, neighbours to such time-honoured structures as St Helen Bishopsgate (parish church of William Shakespeare) and with Wren's Monument, St Paul's Cathedral and the Tower of London all within walking distance.

In recognition of the history and dense, gothic nature of the City, Rogers designed a building with the presence of a medieval fortress. At its heart is a central keep (about half a million square feet in area) surrounded by six towers. Being a modern office building, these are not defences but service towers and, this being a Rogers building, the towers are layered with fire escapes, see-through lifts, air-conditioning pipes and toilet pods all hanging on the outside, meaning the interior of the keep, so to say, is open and capacious. These were the same rev-olutionary design ideas behind Pompidou, but this time Rogers had a client relaxed about how much time he took to get the building absolutely right and, importantly, one that allowed him to use the best materials available. Another million pounds to clad the fire escape in stainless steel, rather than cheaper mild steel, because stainless steel weathers better and looks nicer? Rogers had his money. The toilet pods alone cost a million *each*, and the whole structure came in at the thumping price of £186 million. 'The Pompidou was an extremely low-cost building: the cost of a big shed in construction terms,' explains Rogers. 'The Lloyd's Building had a budget which was worthy of one of the world's great institutions – the biggest insurance house in the world – and it was in that sense [that] we could use dif-ferent types of materials, and the detailing is more perfect. It doesn't mean it's better; it's more *perfect*. The concrete is wonderful colours, the stainless steel, and so on. Whereas in Beaubourg we were using rough steel, plastic-coating paintwork and so on. It was just different.'

The Lloyd's Building is very exciting to be in, and to move around in. Standing on the marble floor of the Room, it is an exhilarating sensation to gaze up 220 feet to the barrel vault of the glass atrium ceiling. As with Pompidou, the means of getting about the building is its most thrilling feature: the escalators that transport one up through the first four floors of the atrium – which is a surprisingly large, clear space inside this complex structure. Best of all are the glass lifts that run up and down the exterior, accessing all twelve storeys. In Paris,

Rogers wanted glass elevators for the Pompidou (shades of Roald Dahl's 1972 book, *Charlie and the Great Glass Elevator*, though he can't recall whether or not that story influenced him), but didn't have the budget. Lloyd's could afford them. So insurance underwriters slide up and down the façades of their London tower in jewel-like glass elevator cases, gazing through transparent walls at a wonderful panorama of the vast and ancient metropolis: the view extending from Hampstead Hill in the north to Shooter's Hill in the south, the dome of St Paul's, the tower of Big Ben, and the brown swathe of the Thames in between. It is a shame that ordinary Londoners can't share in this glorious view of their city, which is beautiful to behold. When Lloyd's was designed, Rogers tried to give the public as much access to the building as possible (though it was never envisaged that they might use the lifts). He created a kind of dry moat around the outside, a step down from the pavement level, under the façades, where there are bars, cafés and shops. Originally there was also access to a viewing gallery on the fourth floor, but security threats caused this to be closed in 1992. More recently, Lloyd's has opened its doors to members of the public once a year. It is an indication of how much interest there is in this remarkable inside-out building, and architecture generally in Britain, that as many as 4,000 people come on these annual open days to look inside. Few office buildings inspire such interest and excitement, which is why – together with his work on the Pompidou Centre – Richard Rogers stands as a giant figure in 1970s architecture.

23

ALL IS VANITY

We went over to Studio 54 and just everyone was there.

THE ANDY WARHOL DIARIES

One of the first big-name artists to visit the Pompidou Centre after it opened in 1977 was Andy Warhol, who had become fond of taking the new Concorde service across the Atlantic from New York and spending a few days shopping, schmoozing and gallery-going in the French capital. In May 1977, the 48-year-old artist came to Paris primarily to attend the opening of a show of his new *Hammer and Sickle* pictures at the Daniel Templon Gallery in the Rue Beaubourg, adjacent to the arts centre. The pictures had been inspired by the artist seeing the Communist symbol of the hammer and sickle sprayed on walls and buildings in Europe, becoming such commonplace graffiti that Warhol decided the image was now abstract. The opening of the show, on 31 May, was akin to a Warholian happening of the past. The party was gate-crashed by a gang of rambunctious French punks who became deplorably drunk and used the raspberry sorbet being served to daub anarchist slogans on the walls. They also screamed for Warhol to come and talk to them. The punks' attitude to the artist was ambivalent. On one hand he was a hero iconoclast of the visual arts and mentor to the great Velvet Underground Band. Yet in middle age the American artist was also a member of the establishment, fawning over fellow celebrities, industrialists and European aristocracy, many of whom commissioned him to create flattering portraits of themselves.

At any rate, Warhol was too timid to meet the punks and hid away in a back office of the gallery, with the result that the punks grew so frustrated that they had a fight. Still, it was all publicity for the show. Indeed, the pictures sold briskly and received good reviews.

During this spring trip Warhol paid an extended visit to the Pompidou Centre. Firstly, there was a signing session of his relatively recent (1975) book, *The Philosophy of Andy Warhol (From A to B and Back Again)*, in the Pompidou gift shop. In many ways the book was a paradigm of the man. It was cleverly designed, but not by him; and though presented as Warhol's personal views on everything from Beauty to Death (two of the chapter titles) he had hardly written a word of it. His assistant Pat Hackett, using tapes of Andy's conversation, had done most of the writing. Yet Andy had the pleasure of signing *his book* and clearly relished any opportunity to do so. It was the essence of his art to reproduce an image endlessly. It was also pleasing to his cash-register mind to ponder the fact that every buyer waiting patiently in line was paying the equivalent of $7.95 (US cover price), so he was earning money, which is the way Andy liked it. Often, he rewarded fans with little drawings, sometimes leafing through the book and adding pictures to several pages. So much fun did he have with these signings that he astonished his publisher, Harcourt Brace Jovanovich, by signing *every one* of the first US print run of six thousand copies. And when those sold out, he signed another complete run.

With the Pompidou signing over, Andy was given a tour of the new building, which is when the other side of his mind was engaged: that of the serious artist. It was pleasing to see some of his own iconic works in the permanent national collection of modern art, alongside the great masters of the nineteenth and twentieth centuries. Warhol was also inspired by the newer work: the Jean Tinguely machine-sculpture on the ground floor and the Edward Kienholz exhibition. Warhol didn't race through the six levels of gallery space, but took his time, allowing the custodians to show him almost everything (which was a great deal). He became more and more excited and inspired, and yet at the same time was privately ruing the fact that he wasted so much of his time on nonsense: on parties, signings, society portraits and the other ephemeral activities of his life as artist-celebrity. Looking at all this great work gathered together in the Pompidou, Warhol knew in his heart that he should be in the studio more, working constantly, like Picasso. The next day he confessed as much to Pat Hackett (who had recently begun compiling an Andy Warhol diary from her daily telephone conversations with her boss), saying, '[I] wanted to just rush home and paint and stop doing society portraits.'

Warhol in the seventies is a conundrum. His reputation as an artist was in decline, overshadowed by his life as a celebrity, and he seemed increasingly to waste his talent on frivolous projects, motivated apparently only by a craving for money and the company of other famous people. The portraits he did to commission were the prime example of this. Yet there was serious work, too. And taken as a whole, his fine art, the commercial work and the peculiar life he led (documenting and archiving every day of that life as he did), form an impressive and cohesive *oeuvre* – interest in which has grown considerably in recent years.

From the early 1960s, when he first became famous as the leading figure in pop art, Warhol's daily life had been an ongoing work of conceptual art. The essential idea was artist-as-machine, producing art on an industrial scale *without emotion*. 'Andy's big pop point was taking the feeling out of painting,' explains Pat Hackett, who got to know this elusive man as well as anybody, 'that you don't have a big, deep feeling, and then try to express it on canvas the way the abstract expressionists did. That was his whole point.' By screen-printing such familiar images as Coca-Cola bottles or publicity portraits of Marilyn Monroe, Warhol achieved his breakthrough; the artist working in a mechanical way in a studio that he came to call his factory. As the '60s progressed, he took an interest in many other activities, becoming an *avant-garde* filmmaker and mentoring the Velvet Underground (for this alone he deserves his place in history). Then, in 1968, a crazed feminist named Valerie Solanis burst into the Factory and shot Warhol in the chest, an attack he was lucky to survive and which forced a change in direction. After the assassination attempt, he became more subdued and distant as a person and also more businesslike. The year after the shooting, Warhol launched his magazine, *Interview*, and shortly after that he began to undertake portrait commissions. The magazine and the portraits would be his most high-profile work throughout the 1970s.

Andy Warhol's *Interview* was inspired by the example of *Rolling Stone*, which the artist had seen his friend Jann Wenner build up from nothing to an extremely profitable brand name in just a few years, becoming a wealthy and influential man in the process. It was not lost on Andy that Jann had launched *Rolling Stone* on a shoestring budget with a small staff, printing the magazine initially on cheap paper. Andy decided to take the same low-rent approach with the launch of *Interview*, the primary subject of which was movie stars, who were *the* most exciting people in the world as far as Andy was concerned. 'He was star-struck his entire life. It didn't go away with him becoming famous,' notes Dennis Hopper, a longstanding friend of the artist and a shrewd art collector, who has the distinction of having bought the first soup-can painting, for all of $75 (£41), back in 1962. 'The glamour of Hollywood, and movie stars, and all these things, were so important to him,' Hopper adds. 'I mean, he was really a *fan*. He was a fan beyond [normality]. He would be trembling when he would see somebody [famous], like a little child. But he had that great childlike sensitivity, too.' In *Interview*, movie stars – later also rock singers, models, sports figures, almost anybody famous – would be interviewed at length, often by Andy or another celebrity, the conversation revolving around clothes, perfume, favourite night clubs, money and sex, though the questions were never intended to embarrass the subject. Rather, *Interview* celebrated fame. While circulation was never high and the magazine didn't start to turn a profit until the 1980s, it soon became fashionable for stars to appear in *Interview*, and advertisers followed the celebrities. *Interview* was a considerable success and it was the business of running the magazine, more than anything else he did, that kept Warhol current in the seventies, whereas he might otherwise have been relegated to a sixties' legend. *Interview* was a reason to put on his silver wig and go out on the town every night, to clubs and discos, in order to schmooze the stars he wanted in the magazine, and maybe get them to have their portrait done, too. And the more Warhol socialised, the more he became associated with what was hip and happening. As we shall see, he also came to create work that stands as a profound comment on the decade.

Away from the studio, and the nightclubs, the artist lived a remarkably private and quiet life, also one of luxury for by the mid-1970s Andy Warhol was a very rich man. The most visible evidence of his wealth was the house he had bought for cash during the recent Manhattan real-estate slump: an impressive brownstone at 57 East 66th Street. Apart from the prime location, between Madison and Park Avenues on the Upper East Side, the house was very large, six storeys, and soon became filled with valuable antique furniture and art. Warhol was a collector of early nineteenth-century American furniture in particular, also Art Deco. He shared this palace of good taste with a handsome young man named Jed Johnson, who had been his companion since the late 1960s, but they maintained separate bedrooms. One of the most curious aspects of Warhol's private life is that, although he was homosexual and worked in a flamboyantly gay milieu, it seems that he did not have sex for large parts of, or even all of, his life. 'There's not one person – and I knew him really well – there's not one person I know that can ever say they had sex with him, or they know anyone he had sex with,' remarks Dennis Hopper. 'So there's a great possibility that he went through his entire life celibate.' The artist's closest companion at East 66th Street was probably his dog, Archie, so-named after the TV character Archie Bunker, and later a second dachshund, Amos. The animals shared Andy's bedroom on the third floor. This most private of retreats had shuttered windows and an elaborate four-poster bed of dark polished wood, draped with silk. Next to the bed on a side table was a crucifix: a reminder of Warhol's enduring though little-known Catholicism.

After waking each morning around nine, the artist would telephone Pat Hackett, whom he referred to as 'Miss Diary.' The daily ritual of Warhol relating the events of the previous day to Pat started in 1976 as a means of keeping track of Andy's business expenditure for tax reasons – noting down the cabs he had taken, and other deductible business expenses – but it soon expanded into a quotidian summary, not only of what Andy had done the previous day, but who he had seen and what gossip he had heard. Though famously noncommittal in public, Warhol was opinionated and waspish in his diary, notably about famous friends such as Mick Jagger, Liza Minnelli, Truman Capote, and the dress designer Halston: he mocked their drinking, drug use and sex lives, and even admitted that their conversation could be boring (something he *never* would have said to their faces). Pat took notes, and later typed these up into diary entries, tidying and improving Andy's verbal accounts in the process, substituting appropriate adjectives for his bland stock phrases such as saying, typically, of an event he'd been to, 'Oh, it was so great!' Warhol was a creature of routine and once he started the diary he kept it up until the week, in February 1987, that he died. Edited with meticulous care by Pat, *The Andy Warhol Diaries* caused a sensation when they were published in 1989, initially because of tales told about celebrity friends. 'With time, that's not going to be important,' says Hackett. 'They will be – and they are already – a tremendous cultural document.' As such the book, begun in 1976, is one of Warhol's major achievements in the decade.

After speaking to Pat, Warhol showered, dressed and got into the elevator with Archie to ride down to the kitchen in the basement where he ate breakfast with his Filipino maids, Nena and Aurora. Warhol owned a Rolls-Royce, but usually left home on foot, meandering down Madison Avenue, calling at favourite antique and jewellery shops as he went, sometimes buying a bauble for his gem collection. Like many solitary people, Warhol was an obsessive collector – of a great many things ranging from cookie jars to old newspapers – and one of his collections was precious stones. He bought the largest and most expensive jewels he could afford and hoarded them in a safe in his bedroom as a hedge against going broke (his greatest fear). On this morning walk, he would also hand out back issues of *Interview* to managers of the stores he visited, to encourage them to advertise in the magazine. Towards lunchtime he stopped shopping, hailed a cab and completed his journey across midtown to 'the office' in Greenwich Village. Not 'the Factory,' a phrase Warhol had stopped using when he moved from 33 Union Square in 1974, having decided the term had become a cliché. Nowadays, 'the office' was in a building at 860 Broadway, at the corner of Union Square, which had ample space for himself and a large team of assistants, including Pat, office manager Vincent Fremont, and Bob Colacello, the executive editor of *Interview*.

Arriving around lunchtime, Warhol hung around the front office for a while, sitting on the windowsill in the sunshine, making telephone calls, and sorting through his mail, items from which he would place in what he called his 'time capsules,' plain cardboard boxes in which he archived the ephemera of his life, everything from party invitations to old airline tickets. By the time he died he had amassed hundreds of these capsules. Together with the *Diaries* and his tape-recorded conversations with friends, they constitute not so much a resource of Warholian information (for it would be difficult indeed to search for anything specific) as a conceptual artwork. The most surprising room at 860 Broadway (inasmuch as it was so conservatively furnished) was a formal, panelled dining room, dominated by a Victorian oil painting. Visitors were often given lunch here, and practically everybody who was anybody in the arts called by at one time or another in the 1970s, including many of the people we have looked at in this book. Jack Nicholson, Gilbert and George, David Bowie and Ossie Clark all passed through the door of Andy's office, and some of the personalities – David Hockney, Dennis Hopper and Mick Jagger, for example – became close friends with the artist. 'He was a centre in New York. So people came to him,' as Vincent Fremont explains. 'Publicists brought people. Society people brought society people. Artists brought other artists . . . Most people when they passed through New York had to see Andy Warhol.' Some just came to hang out, others to be interviewed for the magazine, or to pose for the Polaroid photographs which were the basis of the commissioned portraits Warhol was turning out at the rate of more than one a week.

There was a surprisingly involved production line process in making the portraits. Andy started by taking several dozen photographs of his subject, head and shoulders. He selected the best of these and had enlarged acetates made, which he cropped and doctored. Blemishes were removed, neck-lines stretched and smoothed.

This was one of the reasons he attracted so many portrait clients. The Shah of Iran's wife, Farah Diba Pahlavi, put her finger on Warhol's commercial success as a portraitist when she told the artist, 'Your portraits are so beautiful, much more beautiful than I am in reality.' Once Warhol had doctored an enlarged negative, the image was silk-screened on to a pre-painted canvas measuring 40 by 40 inches. Pistachio, pink, aquamarine and lilac were favourite backgrounds. Finally, Warhol shaded in details by hand. The combination of the photographic and the painted-in detail gave the portraits their dis-tinctively Warholian 3-D look. The standard fee for such a picture was $25,000 (£13,736). Warhol would sell a client two portraits for $30,000 (£16,483), and some buyers wanted many more than that. A single commission could therefore be very lucrative. Farah Diba was so pleased with her picture that twelve were ordered for the beautifi-cation of Iran.

Although many of his clients were famous, Warhol would paint vir-tually anybody who could afford his services, which set him apart from most of his contemporaries. Andy's friend, David Hockney, for example, accepted only one portrait commission in the 1970s: he was paid to paint a picture of Sir David Webster, the administrator of the Royal Opera House, Covent Garden. Hockney found painting a portrait of a man he neither knew nor had any particular interest in so unsatisfying that he vowed never to do it again, being wealthy enough to turn down work. Indeed, most well-known artists of the 1970s dis-dained portrait commissions. Warhol cast his eyes back through art history, however, and saw that the greatest artists – from Raphael to Velázquez – had done commissioned work, often with spectacular results. Some of the greatest portraits *ever* were painted to commission. On that basis, he didn't see why he should turn down such work. Also, Warhol was a commercial artist by background. Above and beyond famously drawing shoes in his youth, he had in fact been one of the busiest and most versatile commercial artists in all New York in the 1950s, creating book jackets, greetings cards, perfume ads, even flyers for a funeral director.

This commercial work continued into the 1970s, above and beyond the portraits. For example, Warhol designed two album covers for the

Rolling Stones in the 1970s, the jeans cover for *Sticky Fingers* in 1971 and, six years later, the artwork for the album *Love You Live*, for which he created a photo-montage of the band members apparently biting one another. As designed, there was no lettering on the front cover of the live LP, but Mick Jagger decided the band's name and album title had to be on the front for obvious reasons. *The Rolling Stones LOVE YOU LIVE* was duly scrawled across the Warhol montage in large yellow letters, whereupon Warhol complained to friends that this addition ruined the art, which it did. But there was nothing he could do about it because Mick was in charge. He had a similar experience when another rock-star friend, John Cale, formerly of the Velvet Underground Band, commissioned an LP cover, only to change the image from black and white to colour, again for marketing reasons, thus fundamentally altering the artist's work. Some years later, in a musical collaboration with Lou Reed called 'A Dream' (1990), Cale recalled Warhol's displeasure over this incident. In the song, Cale impersonates Warhol complaining about the LP cover, 'It would have been worth more if he'd left it my way, but you can never tell anybody anything; I've learned that.' While Cale depicts Warhol as grumbling about the way his friend and client has mucked about with his image, Andy maintained a phlegmatic attitude to commercial work, remembering that he was working for somebody else in these situations and it would not do to become too self-important about it all, though many of his artist contemporaries would.

What with coming to the office late and dealing with business, not much time was left in a day for what Andy considered his real art, the work, that is, which he kept distinct and separate from all the other commercial activities of Andy Warhol Enterprises. 'I would say that Andy thought that anything that had a *lot* of people involved was not art,' as Pat Hackett explains the subtle distinction Warhol made between his artistic activities. 'Sure, you could do a magazine artistically, but it's not art.' For the same reason, Warhol took the view that the films produced under his name were not art. This subject came up one day after Andy and Pat had been to a screening of Stanley Kubrick's luscious new movie *Barry Lyndon* (1975) and she asked her boss, 'Is a movie art?' Warhol replied, no, because there were too many people involved, and this held true for his movies, certainly in recent years when he had very little indeed to do with such productions as *Andy Warhol's Bad* (1977), which was in fact directed by his housemate Jed Johnson. 'I believe he thought his early, early movies were art,' says Pat, referring to Warhol films such as *Empire* (1965), which he had more of a hand in, 'but that the later feature-length movies were not art.' Warhol made the same distinction between the portraits he did to commission (with the help of assistants) and the artwork he did when he had time to himself, which were mostly images in series that could ultimately form the basis of a gallery show. With minimal help from assistants, he worked at these pictures in the office after five p.m. when most of the staff had gone home, and at weekends when he came into the office on his own. With this more private, personal art he returned to themes that had interested him for years, such as self-portraits and still-lifes, pictures of flowers, and his so-called *Death* and *Disaster* pictures: images to do with executions and accidental, violent demise. One of the important new series begun in 1972 were his portraits of the head and shoulders of Chairman Mao, ranging from simple line drawings to semi-abstract screen prints. By repeating Mao's face so many times, in many different ways, Warhol showed how Mao was like an omnipotent Chinese god. By colouring Mao's face purple and printing his visage on wallpaper he also made fun of the leader of the Chinese People's Republic. All in all, it was a clever and effective series, and together with the *Hammer and Sickle* pictures of 1976, the *Maos* were among the few picture series Warhol produced in the 1970s that art critics generally liked.

In contrast, some of his other series tended to the self-indulgent and whimsical. His 1976 pictures of cats and dogs were ridiculed in the art world, rightly so, for they are utterly banal; and the screen prints he did of his gem collection were also lamentable, serving to make his emeralds and sapphires look like so many boiled sweets. Then there were the more risqué pictures, including his so-called *Oxidization* paintings, 'piss paintings' as Andy referred to them when he was among friends. To make such pictures, he had an assistant pre-paint canvasses with metallic pigment. Then Andy urinated over the canvas, inviting his friends to likewise relieve themselves, the rivers of piss reacting with the paint to create abstract patterns. There was a strong link between this artwork and the gay club culture of New York at the time, which had become increasingly hedonistic. Apart from the aforementioned Continental Baths, the city that never sleeps now boasted such venues as the Toilet, where men lay down in baths for others to piss over them; and the Anvil, famed for its displays of fist-fucking. Warhol visited some of these places and seems to have been inspired, and indeed excited, by what he witnessed. Not long after visiting the Anvil, for instance, he embarked on the *Torso* pictures, which involved taking photographs in extreme close-up of homosexual sex. Warhol's friend the model Victor Hugo would help recruit men for private sex shows, some of which were conducted at the office after hours. Around 1977, it was almost commonplace for staff to come into 860 Broadway in the morning and find Polaroids of these sessions scattered about the desks. When Bob Colacello demurred, suggesting that some of the employees might find this offensive, Warhol replied, 'Just tell them it's art, Bob.'

Gay club culture was now mixed in with disco and drug culture. Cocaine and amphetamines helped give revellers the energy for manic dance sessions that, in the gay clubs of Manhattan and at the gay resort of Fire Island, were almost orgiastic in nature. Soon the disco craze spread to straight clubs, with songs such as Donna Summer's 1975 single 'Love to Love You Baby' becoming major crossover hits. Record producer Giorgio Moroder turned Bob Moog's box of tricks to a new use when he programmed the hypnotic synthesizer rhythm of Summer's 1977 follow-up, 'I Feel Love', which is perhaps the quintessential disco record. Then, at the end of 1977, John Travolta starred in *Saturday Night Fever* as Tony Manero, a working-class guy from Brooklyn who puts on his white suit at weekends and hits the dance floor at his local disco, 2001 Odyssey. The phenomenal international success of the movie, and its soundtrack, with songs by the Bee Gees, demonstrated that disco was *the* dominant new force in music, being both popular and hip.

The most fashionable new disco in America had opened earlier that year at a former television studio on West 54th Street in Manhattan.

The neighbourhood was a rough one, down by Eighth Avenue where you were liable to get mugged. Yet the rich and famous, and everybody who wanted to be like them, flocked to Studio 54 in 1977. Inside, the club was very large, with a domed ceiling and a balcony lounge area. There was a chrome bar and a monster sound and light system, the lights mounted on a gantry that hovered over the parquet dance floor like the space ship in Steven Spielberg's new film *Close Encounters of the Third Kind*. The club was the domain of Steve Rubell, a flamboyant former restaurateur whose clever idea it was to nurture an atmosphere in which patrons of all sexual persuasions would feel welcome. Another key to the club's popularity was the fact that drug use was celebrated at Studio 54, as was symbolised by the picture hanging over the dance floor. It showed the man in the moon grinning goofily with a coke spoon under his nose. When it first opened, Studio 54 didn't even have a liquor licence, but nobody cared because they could get high. (As Bob Colacello recalls in his excellent memoir *Holy Terror*, there were 'lines to do lines' in the toilets.) The final reason for the success of Studio 54 is that Rubell had an expert touch with celebrities, managing to befriend a coterie of stars who became regular guests at the club, separated from the many-headed at the door and taken down to the basement which became an unlikely celebrity inner sanctum. For some reason, stars enjoyed gathering in this dingy storage area to gossip and snort coke, and their presence night after night, though partially or wholly subterranean, lent Studio 54 a priceless aura of glamour.

Among these regulars were Andy Warhol and his friends Mick and Bianca Jagger, who held her thirty-third birthday party at Studio 54 shortly after it opened in 1977. Heralded by naked models in gold body paint, Bianca entered the main room through a screen of gold streamers, astride a white pony, as Mick danced with Mikhail Baryshnikov to a disco version of 'Happy Birthday'. There was a strong element of camp in all this, of course, but by association with disco culture, camp was finally becoming mainstream entertainment in America. A few years earlier David Bowie as Ziggy Stardust was seen as being too gay for popular tastes; now one of the biggest new acts in the USA was the Village People.

As the denizens of Studio 54 sniffed and stroked themselves to ecstasy in the semi-darkness of the balcony to the sounds of 'I Feel Love', 'Miss You' and 'Macho Man', with Steve Rubell signalling the DJ to ejaculate streams of fake snow on to the dance floor at the climax of the evening, Andy Warhol remained a voyeur. He avoided drugs for the most part (Colacello writes in *Holy Terror* that Warhol used cocaine surreptitiously), and he took no more active part in the sex than to feel the crutch of some of his younger acolytes as other clubbers walked past him buck-naked or fucked there and then. The artist also developed a trick of entering the club by the front door, in view of the press and public, doing a quick round of those people he felt he had to see, then slipping out the back to attend another club or party, or simply to return home where whoever was with him that evening was bid a firm farewell on the pavement. It was rare indeed for Warhol to invite anybody inside his home. With the door shut, he could relax in his fortress of quiet and good taste, taking himself up to bed with Archie and Amos, counting his diamonds if he had trouble sleeping after that bit of coke he'd rubbed guiltily on his gums. Life inside 57 East 66th Street was very different from the noisy, sticky messiness of Studio 54 yet, in his repressed way, Warhol took some of its abandoned behaviour into his private world, slept on his experiences, and when he got into the office the next day, expressed what he had seen in art. It is there, surely, in the *Oxidization* and *Torso* pictures, and most significantly it is in his *Skulls*. (See picture 34.)

Although Andy liked to play dumb when asked art questions, as if he was a complete naïve, he was in fact extremely knowledgeable about everything relating to art history, with a special interest in still life. This is the category in which he placed such work as his *Hammer and Sickle* pictures. He was certainly fully aware of the tradition of using skulls to represent the vanity of human life: pictures such as the Dutch 'vanitas' paintings of the seventeenth century, whereby artists juxtaposed a human skull with items associated with worldly pleasures. A typical example is Harmen Steenwyck's *Still Life: An Allegory of the Vanities of Human Life*, the title of which refers to Ecclesiastes (1:2): '. . . vanity of vanities; all is vanity.' Warhol the Catholic, who spent part of his life immersed in the sexual excess of modern New York and slept alone at night next to a crucifix, was acutely aware of the fact that in the midst of life we are in death; that behind every beautiful face is a grinning skull; that the most comely body is ultimately a sack of guts and bones.

It is with these sobering thoughts in mind that, in 1976, Warhol created a very important series of drawings and screen prints based on photographs of a human skull he acquired from a Parisian antique shop. Photographed, enlarged, silk-screened on to garish pre-painted canvasses, then shaded in by Warhol, his *Skulls* became a still life counterpoint to the commissioned portraits he did for his vain clients: the unfleshed skull seeming to laugh at the self-satisfied living heads (and who knows, to paraphrase Woody Allen, this skull might have belonged to *one of the beautiful people**). As with the seventeenth-century Dutch masters, Warhol was reminding himself, and anybody who cares to look at these pictures, that the gay parade of 1970s disco culture was merely a distraction from the fact that everybody, all the beautiful people, every one of us indeed, is on a short journey to the grave, and all the fuss we make, the wealth we accumulate and airs we put on, are ultimately of no account. That is the meaning of the old vanitas paintings. But these new pictures by Warhol have come to have an additional historical significance for us in the modern world, knowing as we now do that AIDS, as yet undiagnosed, was spreading through the gay community when Warhol made his *Skull* pictures in 1976. Soon, many of his friends from Studio 54 would be as dead as the first owner of that Parisian sconce.

*A joke from Woody Allen's *Manhattan* (1979). See the following chapter.

24

MANHATTAN

. . . the most fun I've ever had without laughing.
                                          ANNIE HALL

When the fiftieth annual Academy Awards were held in Los Angeles in April 1978, Polaroid threw a party at Studio 54 for the show business community of New York, and Andy Warhol found himself sitting through the telecast of the event, becoming increasingly aghast at the pictures that were given Oscars. Among the winners that year was *Star Wars*, not in the main categories, but for Art Direction, Costume Design, Editing and John Williams' music: some recognition of the stupendous commercial success of George Lucas' science-fiction movie. While *Star Wars* was not to Warhol's taste, his scorn was directed more particularly elsewhere. '. . . nobody good like John Travolta won,' the artist grumbled to Miss Diary the next day, referring to that fact that Travolta in *Saturday Night Fever* lost out as best leading actor to Richard Dreyfuss in *The Goodbye Girl*. 'I mean, Richard Dreyfuss? I mean, if he's a sex symbol, I don't know what the world is coming to,' spluttered the artist. 'And I can't stand Woody Allen movies,' he added, referring to the fact that *Annie Hall* was *the* big winner that year, garnering the prime Oscars for Best Picture, Best Director for Woody Allen, and Best Actress in a Leading Role for Allen's female star and former lover Diane Keaton. This was an astonishing sweep of the board for such a film, and a trick Woody Allen has never come near to repeating.

In many ways it is surprising that Warhol disliked Allen's pictures so, for the men had much in common. They were near one another in age, having been born into immigrant East European families shortly before the Second World War. Both were raised in working-class backwaters of the United States during the war, changing their names as soon as they were able – Andrew Warhola, born Pittsburgh 1928, becoming Andy Warhol; Allan Konigsberg, born Brooklyn 1935, renaming himself Woody Allen – and then reinventing themselves as super-sophisticated Manhattanites. Manhattan became part and parcel of both their lives and of their respective art. Both chose to live on the Upper East Side when they became rich; both made iconic New York movies; the parallels are numerous, significant and trivial. The men had met, of course, had been introduced earlier that year in fact at a swank party at the Dakota Building. Four separate people brought Woody over to talk to Andy, such a common assumption was it that the two men would get along, 'so I met him four times,' the artist noted without enthusiasm in his diary. As it happened, Allen liked Warhol's artwork. But Warhol couldn't relate to Allen's movies, didn't find them the least bit funny, having a dislike for what he called 'smart-alecky' humour, which was an apt description of the new direction Allen's career was taking with the release of *Annie Hall*.

By the mid-seventies, Allen had already enjoyed a very successful and surprisingly varied career, starting out in the 1950s as a gag writer for the likes of Sid Caesar. He then became a stand-up comedian, so popular that he played two-week residences in Las Vegas, and released three comedy albums. Allen was also well-known to television view-ers because of his appearances on *The Tonight Show*. An accomplished writer, he authored essays in *The New Yorker*, wrote movie scripts and Broadway plays. In 1969, Allen appeared in a successful movie adap-tation of his own Broadway comedy *Don't Drink the Water* and, that same year, wrote, directed and starred in *Take the Money and Run*, a slapstick movie about an inept bank robber. Made cheaply in New York, *Take the Money* owes much to Allen's love of the broad humour of the Marx Brothers, and his character is very much his nightclub persona of the time: a stuttering *nebbish* with a self-deprecating wit. He reprised the act in 1971 with the movie *Bananas*, but, in truth,

Allen was nothing like this character. Far from being a perennial loser, he was successful in almost everything he put his hand to and always had been: from athletics at school to filmmaking, from business to playing the jazz clarinet, which he did to near-professional standard. He also had little difficulty attracting women, though the fact that he was already twice divorced by the start of the 1970s was evidence of a problem in sustaining relationships. The key difference between the character Woody Allen portrayed in public life prior to *Annie Hall* and the man himself, however, was that Allen was not a clown but an intellectual, one who was largely self-educated (he had not gone to college) but nonetheless a serious man learned in philosophy and theology.

Since boyhood, Allen had wrestled with the mysteries of life and, more specifically, death. The big question that bothered him was that if there is no God – though raised a Jew, Woody was an agnostic in this respect – and we are all going to die, what is the purpose of life? He could not put aside this impossible problem and just get on with things, and rejected the notion that an artist in fact has an advantage over most people in that they get to leave behind a record of their existence – a book, a song, a film – that can be enjoyed posthumously. 'I've made this joke before, that I'm not interested in living on in the hearts of my countrymen,' he quipped. 'I'd rather live on in my apartment!' The serious kernel of this joke bothered Allen greatly, and was never far away in the films he made in the 1970s. At first he sneaked the philosophy in among the jokes, in pictures such as *Play it Again, Sam* (1972) and *Sleeper* (1973), keeping the comedy coming so thick and fast that audiences might be forgiven for overlooking the moments of introspection, or indeed laugh them off as just another aspect of their hero's endearingly angst-ridden persona. For instance, Allen's 1975 picture, *Love and Death*, was on the face of it a delightful spoof on Russian literary themes, a film with plenty of physical humour and many belly laughs. But what really interested Woody about the story was in the title. The film was about death. When Allen finished this picture he decided to make a clean break in his career. 'I said to myself, "I think I will try and make some deeper film and not be as funny in the same way. And maybe there will be other values that emerge, that will be interesting or nourishing for the audience."' Having spent so much time abroad in Europe filming *Love and Death*, he also determined to stay in New York for this new film, and for future projects, making New York stories.

From the day he was first brought into Manhattan as a child, back in 1941 by his best recollection, Woody had been bewitched by the wealth, architecture and vitality of the island-heart of New York City. 'I was in love with it from the second I came up from the subway into Times Square,' as he has said. As soon as he was able, Allen moved into Manhattan, and by 1970 he resided in a splendid eight-room penthouse on the Upper East Side, high above Fifth Avenue. Central Park was laid out below his terrace like a carpet, and on the other side of the park were the outlines of the grand apartment blocks of Central Park West, including the Dakota (where Roman Polanski filmed *Rosemary's Baby* and where John Lennon came to make his American home) and the twin towers of the San Remo where Diane Arbus grew up. It is intriguing to think that Diane and Woody must have passed each other many times strolling in Central Park, as Diane searched for unhappy subjects to photograph and Woody worked out his movie plots in his head before returning home to put pen to paper. It was in his exclusive East Side eyrie, sprawled across the counterpane of his bed, that Woody wrote the script of *Annie Hall*, one of the greatest romantic comedies ever to be set in the city, though it didn't start out quite like that.

Originally, Woody envisaged a darker picture, one about a middle-aged man such as himself reflecting on a series of failed relationships, and addressing his inability to embrace life and be happy – a picture that he wanted to call *Anhedonia* (the antitheses of hedonism). He didn't develop the script alone, but collaborated with an old friend named Marshall Brickman, a former folk musician Woody knew from his days working the clubs of Greenwich Village. Marshall had previously collaborated with Woody on *Sleeper*. Their working method was simply to talk about the film while strolling through Central Park and around the Upper East Side, resolving problems by a process of conversation. 'And then, when all the talking was done, I went and wrote the script,' explains Woody. 'Then I showed it to Marshall, and he made his comments: "*This seems quite good, but this scene is weak, why don't we try this instead.*" He provided new points of view and ideas, but I felt that I had to be the one to actually write it down. Because I had to say it, I wanted it written down the way I'm comfortable saying it.'

The original plot of *Anhedonia* was, strangely, a murder mystery with Allen in the lead as a comedian named Alvy Singer, the actor Tony Roberts as his debonair best friend, Rob, and Diane Keaton as the love interest. Woody, Tony and Diane had all become friends while appearing together on Broadway in Woody's play, *Play It Again, Sam*, which ran at the Broadhurst Theatre for almost a year in 1969–70, and was then made into a movie with the three principals reprising their roles. Diane had auditioned for the play as a 23-year-old unknown from Santa Ana, California. She and Woody began to date and Diane moved into his apartment, living with him there for a year before she moved into a place of her own and became increasingly absorbed in her burgeoning movie career, starting with her part in *The Godfather*. Woody and Diane remained friends, and to a great extent *Annie Hall* is about the actress.

Diane Keaton is a stage name. The actress' given name is Hall, and the character she plays in the film is close to who she was in life when she met Woody. Several of her characteristics are incorporated in the picture, including her quirky turns of phrase and her eccentric style of dressing, which at the time included wearing men's clothes – trousers, waistcoats, shirts with ties – with large, floppy hats. (See picture 37.) In the movie, as in their off-screen relationship, Allen becomes her lover and, in a sense, also her teacher. Also as in life, when Annie leaves Alvy she moves to California, a place that Alvy loathes as much as Woody really did. However the parallels with real life appear to have been largely unconscious, only fully coming home to Allen when filming was completed. It was when he came to cut the picture that he discovered, to his surprise, that the murder-mystery idea didn't hang together and what he had instead was the makings of a love story that mirrored his own romance with Keaton. As Tony Roberts says, 'He was more surprised than anybody, I think, to [discover] that he'd written a love affair.'

Fortunately for Woody, his production deal with United Artists gave him plenty of artistic freedom. So long as the studio approved the basic outline and he stayed within a modest budget (about £1.6 million at this time), Allen had total control over the script, who he cast and how he cut his pictures. Such an arrangement would not have suited a filmmaker like Francis Ford Coppola, who spent money expansively and tended to get lost in projects (as with *Apocalypse Now*, in which he was still embroiled in 1977–78). But Woody Allen was a very different filmmaker: a highly disciplined man who, United Artists knew, was unlikely to go over budget. If he did, the agreement was that he and his partners would cover the excess. This happened rarely, for there was little to spend money on. Allen did not seek exotic locations or demand elaborate sets, shooting instead mostly on the streets of New York. In the early years he eschewed big-name movie stars in favour of hiring character actors, many of whom were friends such as Tony Roberts. Woody himself was the star of his pictures, and in a sense he was working for free. With this inexpensive and efficient set-up, he could produce a movie a year, and he hoped that by continuing in this way he could work through the many story ideas he had stacked up in his mind (as Bob Rafelson and Martin Scorsese had projects stockpiled in their heads when producers finally gave them *permission*, as Rafelson puts it, in the 1970s, to do their work). Woody shot a new picture each autumn, editing during the winter for a spring release, by which time he was usually on to the next project.

Having finally decided what this particular movie with Diane Keaton was really about, Woody assembled a film that is filled with surprises. In the first place *Annie Hall* is announced, unconventionally for its day, with simple white-on-black titles: a style that Woody used here for the first time and retained for all his subsequent pictures (even using the same font for the most part). It seemed a lunatic waste of money to spend hundreds of thousands of dollars on elaborate title sequences (though this was fashionable in the 1970s). Rather, with the minimum of folderol, and at almost no cost, the audience is given the basic information and then we are straight into the picture, which begins in an equally unexpected way. Alvy Singer is addressing the audience directly, telling us a joke straight out of Woody's stand-up days, replete with characteristic nervous twitches:

There's an old joke. Uh, two elderly women are at a Catskills mountain resort, and one of 'em says: 'Boy, the food at this place is really terrible.' The other one says, 'Yeah, I know, and such small portions.' Well, that's essentially how I feel about life. Full of loneliness and misery and suffering and unhappiness, and it's all over much too quickly.

Having made us laugh (with a somewhat dark observation), Allen segues into the subject to hand. 'Annie and I broke up,' says Alvy with a sigh, and Woody the film director proceeds to tell the story of this failed romance, interspersed with scenes from Alvy's life before and after the affair, beginning with his childhood. Thus at the start of the film we are magically transported back to 1930s Brooklyn where we meet the precocious kid that Alvy (and Woody) was. In one of the film's most brilliant scenes, the three adult leads – Alvy, Annie and Alvy's best friend Rob – stand in Alvy's elementary school class, as phantoms, looking at the shades of young Alvy and his fellow pupils. As Alvy wonders what happened to his chums in adult life, his former classmates get up from their chairs and announce solemnly, and spookily, as if in a dream, what their fate has been. One boy is the president of a plumbing company. Another is a junkie. A little girl intones that she is 'into leather.'

The film is no less inventive when we come to the story of the romance, starting with Annie and Alvy having a drink together after meeting at a game of tennis. In order to show the characters' true feelings about one another Allen devised the conceit of having the couple make polite conversation while their private thoughts are revealed to the audience as subtitles. 'Photography's interesting,' Alvy says to Annie, 'it's a new art form . . .' (thinking: *I wonder what she looks like naked*). There are many such unexpected and clever devices in *Annie Hall*. For instance, when Alvy and Annie see their psychiatrists (as Allen and Keaton did), Woody uses a split screen to show both characters talking simultaneously to their respective shrinks, their conversations demonstrating how differently they see the relationship. Asked how often they have sex, *he* laments: 'Hardly ever. Maybe three times a week.' *She* complains: 'Constantly! I'd say three times a week . . .' Allen even inserts an animated sequence into the picture, depicting Annie as the Wicked Queen in *Snow White and the Seven Dwarfs*. These many and varied creative ideas help make *Annie Hall* a very surprising and indeed magical picture to watch.

Also, *Annie Hall* is a beautiful-looking film. Much of the credit for this belongs to cinematographer Gordon Willis, a veteran of the recent *Godfather* wars where he fought creatively with Francis Coppola. Unlike Coppola, Woody almost never raised his voice on set, which came as a relief to Willis. (As he remarks: 'Francis' life is an opera, Woody's is a walk through the park. Opera tires me out.') The collaboration between Woody and Gordon would be a long one, and the cinematographer's part in teaching Allen the finer points of filmmaking and guiding his hand on his most famous films, is often overlooked. 'I'm not afraid to do anything, and I fully embraced anything Woody wanted to do,' says Willis. 'I brought a great deal of structure as well as the visual concept to most of Woody's scripts, from *Annie Hall* through *The Purple Rose of Cairo*.★ He'd go over what he wanted to achieve, and I'd carve out the movie visually.' Gordon helped Woody perfect the long master shots that are a trademark of his mature work, and he gave Woody the confidence to be audacious in other respects. For example, in showing Alvy and Annie in their apartment it was a truthful and effective device to keep the camera on the living room even though the actors might walk out of shot (*both* do at times), leaving an empty room. They could still be heard talking, however, and a couple sharing an apartment will of course move between rooms and continue talking out of eyesight of one another. So a highly unusual technique produces a very natural impression, and indeed it is remarkable how real the characters in *Annie Hall* seem to be. Similarly, there is a sequence when Alvy and Rob are walking down the street together, Alvy complaining to Rob about people making comments about him being a Jew. What is so unusual here is that the camera focuses on one spot on the sidewalk, but the scene begins before the actors are in sight. We

---

★Released in 1985. When Allen was ready to shoot his next picture, *Hannah and Her Sisters* (1986), Willis had a conflicting schedule. As a result, the director began working with cinematographer Carlo di Palma.

hear them, and we see other pedestrians pass by, but several seconds elapse before Woody and Tony walk into view. Then they walk *through* the shot and out of view again, chatting as they do so. Again, this makes the scene seem very natural. Tony Roberts has another interesting observation: 'It makes you listen to the dialogue a little more when you don't know who's talking.'

The dialogue itself ranks among the best that Allen (with Brickman) ever wrote, with the actor-director insisting his actors overlap the lines, which makes the sharp verbal exchanges so natural. It does indeed seem that the characters are *chatting* all the time, though what they say is usually very clever indeed. There are many excellent jokes in the picture, including gags recycled from Woody's years as a stand-up comedian (not least the old chestnut about the boy in the metaphysics exam who cheats by looking within the soul of the student next to him). In fact, *Annie Hall* features some of Allen's most epigrammatic quips, especially on the subject of sex: 'The most fun I've ever had without laughing'; while masturbation is defended stoutly as 'sex with someone I love.'

While this is all highly entertaining, there is a darker side to *Annie Hall*. The classroom scene at the start of the picture is funny, but pessimistic and ultimately sad. And as we come to see, all Alvy's relationships have ended in failure. His romance with Annie Hall starts to go wrong as soon as she moves in with him, and she ultimately leaves him for a rock star (played by Paul Simon). When the affair begins to unravel, Alvy and Annie have an altercation in the street which concludes with her leaving in a taxi cab. 'I don't know what I did wrong,' laments Alvy when she has gone. An old crone passer-by stops to tell him sternly that it is never what *you* do; it's how people are. 'Love fades,' says the woman sagaciously.

'Love fades. God, that's a depressing thought,' Alvy mutters to himself as he wanders off. This is a funny moment, certainly, but moreover it is a profoundly pessimistic observation that gets to the heart of what bothers Woody Allen the man. Everything fades and ends. Even love. The greatest creative minds have been fixated with this idea since time immemorial, from the author of Ecclesiastes in the Holy Land in the third century BC to the painters of the vanitas pictures in seventeenth-century Europe to Andy Warhol and Woody Allen in New York in the 1970s. The carefree happiness of the scenes in *Annie Hall* when Alvy and Annie have just met – laughing together on holiday, enjoying a movie and so on – is quickly superseded by disillusionment, bickering, and finally the chill of loneliness. This loneliness, or *aloneness*, is a quality that becomes increasingly characteristic of Allen's movies from *Annie Hall* onward, influenced partly by his infatuation with Scandinavian cinema, specifically the work of the great Ingmar Bergman. It is also Allen's mien: a gloomy man half in love with depression, a man preoccupied with endings and thereby, ultimately, death.

That Woody Allen could pack all these many ideas and more into one 93-minute movie is remarkable. 'It's impressive, and it never would have happened if it had been a committee picture,' notes Tony Roberts, referring to the unique production deal Woody had with United Artists. 'Woody had the luxury of not having to tell anybody what [the film] was about before it was made, and could make it be exactly what he wanted, so he got away with all kinds of marvellous, imaginative, inventive things, which I'm sure the committees at the studios would have denied him the right to do.' His only compromise in fact was to change the movie's title from *Anhedonia* to *Annie Hall*, much to the relief of the studio executives. Though in truth the picture would more aptly be titled *Alvy Singer*, because it is really about Woody's character, and *his* perception of the world.

Although inventive, funny and moving, *Annie Hall* is at bottom a love story, and not a deeply profound one like Tolstoy's *Anna Karenina* (as Allen himself has pointed out by way of comparison). It is a romantic comedy, and one that appeals to a certain type of middle-class audience. For many people who went to see *Annie Hall* in 1977–78, Alvy, Annie and Rob were reflections of themselves, or people they aspired to be. While few men might want to *look* exactly like Woody Allen, most would admire his wit and many would covet his character's moneyed, metropolitan lifestyle. Meanwhile, Diane Keaton set a fashion for women with the clothes she wore in the picture, as well as presenting an attractive feminist archetype: an independent woman who moves between relationships in a modern,

civilised way, exploring herself and her feelings. 'It massages the prejudices of the middle-class,' Allen has said of the outstanding success
(by his standards) of the picture. 'It's nothing to be ashamed of, but
nothing special.' The fact that *Annie Hall* won in three of the most significant Academy Award categories is certainly impressive, to a point.
That point comes when Allen reminds us that Oscars are largely
bought by studio lobbying. Also, how can you compare pictures as
disparate as *Annie Hall* and *Star Wars* in a category as broad as Best
Picture? It is an absurdity. The evening of the Oscars ceremony in
April 1978, Woody made sure he did what he did most Monday
nights and played his clarinet at Michael's Pub on East 55th Street,
apparently taking less interest in the outcome of the awards than those
gathered at Studio 54.

Made on a small budget, *Annie Hall* turned a handsome profit, so
much so that Woody, like Andy Warhol, took to being chauffeured
around New York in a Rolls-Royce, one fitted with a car telephone
which was a rare item indeed in 1978. United Artists were delighted
with the film, and when Allen told them he wanted to do something
slightly different next time they did not hesitate to advance the money
that he required. Once more, Diane Keaton was cast in a leading
role, which inspired confidence. Allen himself would not appear in
this film, however, because he had come to believe that audiences had
a Pavlovian response to seeing his bespectacled face on screen: they felt
compelled to laugh. And this new picture, *Interiors*, was *not* to be a
romantic comedy in which weightier ideas are smuggled in among the
main cargo of humour. It would be deadly serious. 'I know I could
make a successful comic movie every year, and I could write a comic
play that would do very well on Broadway every year,' Allen commented in 1976. 'What I want to do is go to areas I'm insecure
about . . . I'd like to take chances.'

Interiors is a tragedy, the plot of which concerns a wealthy middle-
aged businessman named Arthur (E.G. Marshall) who decides he has
had enough of marriage to his cold, controlling wife, Eve (Geraldine
Page), and takes up with the vivacious Pearl (Maureen Stapleton). As
a result of her husband's rejection, Eve descends into depression,

eventually drowning herself. The meat of the movie is how the couple's three adult daughters react to the sea change in their parents' lives, and their mother's mental disintegration (one of the siblings being played by Diane Keaton). The sisters also grapple with sibling rivalry, relationships with the men in their lives and the contemplation of death without the solace of religion. 'In *Interiors* that theme occurs a few times,' Allen has observed. 'That really what we're all talking about is the tragedy of perishing. Aging and perishing. It's such a horrible, horrible thing for humans to contemplate, that they don't contemplate it. They start religions, they do all kinds of things not to contemplate it. They try to block it out in every way. But sometimes you can't block it out.'

Woody started work on this ambitious picture as soon as he had finished *Annie Hall*, shooting – again with Gordon Willis – scenes that are often sharply reminiscent of Ingmar Bergman movies. Then, just as *Annie Hall* was enjoying a second wind at theatres, thanks to its Oscar success, the public was presented with a new Woody Allen picture. But *Interiors* was a Woody Allen film without Woody Allen in it, and the *coup de grâce* came when audiences discovered that *Interiors* was a Woody Allen film *without any laughs*. Not only were there no jokes, there wasn't even a wry smile to be had.

Still, *Interiors* might have been a success on its own terms. The premise is certainly interesting: what are the repercussions when a man decides in mid-life that he has had enough of his wife and she can not accept his decision to start anew? But in its execution *Interiors* reveals Allen at his weakest and most pretentious. With the exception of Maureen Stapleton's Pearl, the characters are not believable, much less empathetic. They do not react to one another naturally, and their dialogue has little resemblance to the way people talk in life. Rather, they are ciphers voicing ideas that preoccupy Woody Allen. The film was a flop in all senses, confirming the suspicion many cinemagoers already had that Woody Allen was a smart-aleck (as Andy Warhol would have it) whose movies were best avoided. 'I failed, I failed,' bewailed the director, 'but the ambition was good, the ambition was high.' In a medium where compromise is the norm, it is surely commendable that a filmmaker like Allen has the freedom and desire to at least *try* and do something different. And though the film is not good, Allen was not put out of business by its failure. The fact that *Interiors*, like all his pictures, was made cheaply and quickly meant that the financial loss was comparatively modest and before anybody had time to brood on the disappointment he was on to his next project, which turned out to be the dazzling *Manhattan*, 'a serious picture [with] laughs in it,' as Allen says.

Writing again with Marshall Brickman, Woody's starting point this time was to celebrate the city he had loved since boyhood. To make New York look as beautiful as possible, Woody agreed with Gordon Willis to shoot in wide screen and black and white – 'I think we both perceive New York as a black and white city,' notes the cinematographer – the combination of wide screen and monochrome being particularly suited to the bravura opening and closing sequences in which a lengthy montage of classic b/w views of Manhattan is cut together with *Rhapsody in Blue*, culminating in a crescendo of Gershwin and a simultaneous explosion of fireworks over Central Park. (For these two ravishing sequences alone Allen and Willis deserve their place in cinema history.) Apart from being a love letter to New York, *Manhattan* is a love story, though one with a serious side, the balance between intellectual pretension and the creation of warm and entertaining characters better-realised than in almost any of Allen's previous films. This time, Allen was in front of the camera as well as behind it, his screen character a 42-year-old television writer named Isaac who is trying to get over the fact that his wife (Meryl Streep, in one of her first screen appearances) has left him for a lesbian – 'incredible sexual humiliation . . . enough to turn you off of women' – by having an affair with a 17-year-old beauty named Tracy, played by Mariel Hemingway. Meanwhile, his best friend, Yale (Michael Murphy) is having an adulterous affair with Mary, a woman more their age, played by Diane Keaton. When that affair cools, Isaac dates Mary, thereby cheating on Tracy, though he claims to believe that couples should mate for life 'like pigeons.'

Allen manages to combine serious ideas with good jokes in *Manhattan*, as in the scene when he discovers that Mary and Yale are seeing each other again, behind his back, and so decides to confront

Yale at the school where he teaches. Giving his friend a lecture on the need to maintain a degree of moral integrity in the way we behave, for the sake of posterity if nothing else (after all how do we want to be remembered?), Isaac points to a classroom skeleton Yale is standing next to and reminds his duplicitous friend of our universal fate: 'Some day we're gonna be like him,' he says of the bone man, '[and] he was probably one of the beautiful people. He was probably dancing and playing tennis and everything . . . I'll be hanging in a classroom one day. And I wanna make sure when I thin out that I'm well thought of!'

The picture does reveal some of Allen's flaws, it is true, especially those peculiar to his life. As film critic Pauline Kael asked, 'What man in his forties but Woody Allen could pass off a predilection for teenagers as a quest for true love values?' There is also a particularly unsatisfactory scene near the end when Isaac dictates an idea for a short story into a tape recorder, wondering as ever what makes life worth living, a question he attempts to answer by making a list of people and things he finds most delightful: Groucho Marx, a recording by Louis Armstrong, Swedish movies, 'Tracy's face . . .', at which point he breaks off, realising how much he loves the girl he has betrayed. In writing this scene Allen (and Marshall Brickman) evidently forgot that Isaac has a young son, a loveable little fellow whom the audience has indeed seen him with. Even the most solipsistic parent would put their child at or near the top of a list of things that make life worth living. But Woody hadn't yet become a father in real life. If he had, he might have seen that procreation and parenthood is in itself a reason for living, in a Godless universe or otherwise. That this does not cross Isaac's mind marks *Manhattan* down slightly, perhaps being indicative of something lacking in Woody Allen personally. Nevertheless, Allen succeeded with *Annie Hall* and *Manhattan* in creating two classics of 1970s cinema, films that have moreover transcended the decade. They are beautiful, funny, romantic, philosophical and magical entertainments which will be enjoyed as long as people watch movies.

25

RICH AND STRANGE

. . . oh all those wonderful glittering absolutely vanished pantomimes!

THE SEA, THE SEA

Magic is ever-present in the musical theatre, never more so than in Mozart's opera *The Magic Flute*, the story of which has a prince and his helper, Papageno, armed with a magic flute and music box, on a quest to rescue a princess from a magician. Comical, magical and religious, this eighteenth-century opera was presented in a spectacular new production in England in 1978 with sets by David Hockney.

Because of the ephemeral nature of theatrical performances, theatre plays small part in this journey through the 1970s. A play, ballet or opera lives on the stage, and when a run closes the magic evaporates, as is well-expressed by Charles Arrowby, the hero of Iris Murdoch's 1978 novel *The Sea, The Sea*, as he retires from a life in theatreland with a lament for 'all those wonderful glittering absolutely vanished pantomimes!' This particular production of *The Magic Flute* is worth recalling, however, principally because of Hockney's sets, which made such an impression when the opera opened at Glyndebourne in May 1978 that audiences broke into spontaneous applause, causing the conductor Andrew Davis to pause the music. The set designs endure as important artworks in their own right and, moreover, this move into designing opera was a significant shift in the career of the most notable British painter of the decade.

In fact, David Hockney designed two operas for the English stage in the 1970s, both of which went on to tour the world. The first commission came in the spring of 1974, at a time when Hockney was living in Paris and feeling in need of a change. The naturalistic double portraits he had become famous for, primarily *Mr and Mrs Clark and Percy*, had led to an ever more obsessive search for perfection in his work, and the artist was starting to feel trapped in his own pursuit of excellence. One day he received a letter from John Cox, a producer with the Glyndebourne Festival Opera, the opera company situated in a country house near Lewes in Sussex, offering a timely distraction from his problems. Cox inquired as to whether Hockney might like to design a forthcoming production of Igor Stravinksy's *The Rake's Progress*. Written between 1948 and 1951 while Stravinsky was living in Los Angeles, with a libretto by W.H. Auden and Chester Kallman, the opera is based loosely on William Hogarth's *A Rake's Progress* of 1735, the moralistic picture series illustrating the tragedy of a young aristocrat named Tom Rakewell who inherits and then squanders a fortune, ending his life in penury and madness. As John Cox knew, Hockney had created a series of etchings in the '60s based on Hogarth's picture-story, relocating Rakewell to modern-day New York. Cox was also aware that Hockney had previous theatrical experience, though limited, in that he designed the sets for a 1966 production of Alfred Jarry's play *Ubu Roi*. Furthermore, uncommonly for an artist of his generation, Hockney was a devotee of classical music.

Hockney didn't know Stravinsky's opera, however, and found the music austere at first. But he loved the libretto and accepted the commission, soon becoming completely engrossed in the project. Glyndebourne expected the artist simply to produce drawings of what he thought the sets and costumes might look like, sketches which they could then work from. But Hockney wanted to have much more control than that: he took the advice of a friend to build a model for himself of Glyndebourne's shoe-box theatre, and filled it with everything he wanted to show on stage in order to get an idea of the scale, and to make sure that the final production adhered to his mind's eye vision of what the sets should look like.

Listening to the opera repeatedly, the artist noticed that although Stravinsky's *Rake* is a modern piece the score has elements of eighteenth-century pastiche, which is appropriate considering Hogarth painted his *Rake* in 1735, the work becoming famous thereafter in engravings. Thus Hockney had his big idea: 'I talked a lot with John Cox and then I made this suggestion: since *The Rake's Progress* was from Hogarth, could we not stylise the designs with crosshatching, like Hogarth's engravings?' Unlike Hogarth, however, Hockney decided to introduce colour to the etchings, but sparingly – only red, blue and green – and using inks available in Hogarth's time. This was a highly imaginative approach, yet also slightly old-fashioned in that Hockney was essentially creating painted backdrops of naturalistic scenes rather than using lighting and simple props to represent locations, which had been the predominant style in theatre since the 1950s. Hockney's designs for the *Rake* went against this abstract trend, as his drawings and paintings did for contemporary gallery shows. 'It was time to change because, in a way, the abstract had become literal. So I thought, here was an opportunity to introduce the pictorial element again.'

The 1974 Glyndebourne production of *The Rake's Progress* was a triumph, remaining in repertory for years to come, and is now regarded as a classic. 'What I didn't know at the time was Glyndebourne didn't think it would be,' admits Hockney. In fact, the company had been very concerned that the artist had over-reached himself, but all misgivings were set aside with the success of opening night. Hockney celebrated the occasion with an expansive and expensive gourmet picnic for a host of friends on the lawns of Glyndebourne, a feast begun in the long interval and concluded after the show on a beautiful midsummer's evening. 'The performance ended at about nine-thirty, and because it was Midsummer Day we came back out, back to the food, and there was this wonderful, glorious sunset over the Sussex Downs, absolutely beautiful. And as the sun set, the moon came up and it was so bright that it cast shadows on the lawn . . . I'll never forget it.'

During this magical evening, John Cox asked the artist whether he would like to design a production of *The Magic Flute* for the 1978 season, and Hockney gladly seized the chance, delighted to work on an opera he knew and loved. Also, he was starting to feel that the collaborative experience of working in the theatre was good for him creatively, freeing him from his obsessive pursuit of naturalism and opening up a whole new career. So it was that he set about creating a cavalcade of painted drops that rank with his best work of the 1970s. 'I begin with the music. That's what you've got to match,' Hockney says of his starting point in designing opera, which became a second career that occupied much of his time into the early 1980s. In the case of the *Flute*, the artist also went back to the stage directions by Emanuel Schikaneder, the Viennese impresario who commissioned the score from Mozart in 1789, when the composer was entering the final, wretched years of his life, penurious and ill. (Considering Mozart's straitened circumstances, it is amazing how joyful the music is.) Schikaneder was a man of multiple talents. Not only did he commission the music from Mozart, he wrote the libretto (which tells a preposterous story, even by operatic standards), he acted the part of the bird-catcher Papageno in the original production, and he wrote the stage directions. Since the eighteenth century, Schikaneder's directions had been largely disregarded as far too busy. But Hockney saw the logic behind Schikaneder's many scene changes. 'I'd seen quite a few *Magic Flutes*. I loved it, but if the second act is not done with a lot of variety . . . it can get a bit boring,' he says. 'The music isn't boring. I mean, the music is fabulous [but the story can get lost]. I thought, I *think you should put all these scenes in. I see why you need them.* Mozart and Schikaneder were right. To make it entertaining, you've got to have all these changes.'

In this spirit, Hockney designed and oversaw the painting of approximately thirty-five old-fashioned *painted flats*, so that his production of the *Flute* became like a slide-show of images, in literal interpretation of the events of the story. When the libretto indicates the characters are in a garden, a garden drops down, and so forth. By the 1970s, very few theatres were still using painted flats and they created many problems, including the fact that there was insufficient drop space at Glyndebourne. The flats were also difficult to light (or rather the skill of lighting flats had been lost). In many ways the sets are best viewed as a series of huge paintings, some of them truly spectacular, especially towards the end of the second act with the fire and water scenes, the night-time garden and the great climax. The opera culminates in a joyful marriage between the Prince and Princess, who join the magician Sarastro and his followers in a state of enlightenment, which Hockney dramatised with a brilliant sunburst – golden rays of light radiating out from the centre of the set to the edges of the proscenium arch. (See picture 35.) This brought applauding audiences to their feet night after night. As Stephen Spender commented, having attended the opening in May 1978, Hockney sets for Mozart's *Magic Flute* proved to be 'a true marriage of the arts.'

Whimsy, commonplace in opera, plays a strong part in the novels of Iris Murdoch which 'as well as being brilliant,' as the critic and Murdoch's friend A.N. Wilson has observed, 'are also surely pretty good tosh.' That same summer, Murdoch's latest book, *The Sea, The Sea*, appeared in the shops, and it has come to be perhaps the best-known of her many novels, receiving particular attention because it won the 1978 Booker Prize.

Murdoch's is a very different style of writing to the other novelists and novels we have looked at so far: the racy bestsellers of Peter Benchley, Frederick Forsyth and Mario Puzo; Updike's elegant *Rabbit* stories; the New Journalism practised in its various forms by Wolfe, Thompson and Mailer (the latter then still working on *The Executioner's Song*). In truth, Murdoch was a writer out of time. She turned fifty-nine in 1978, but might have been twenty years older for all the connection she had with the modern world. Iris took no interest in popular culture; she disregarded modern art, music, film and television, and didn't even trouble herself to read the great contemporary novelists. She *never* read Americans such as Updike and Mailer, and only occasionally dipped into books by contemporary British authors – Kingsley Amis for example, and then chiefly because Kingsley was a friend. Aside from reading for work (that is as background to her work as an academic), recreational reading consisted of refreshing dips into the familiar waters of Austen, Dostoyevsky and James. Above all, however, Iris wallowed in Shakespeare, basing three of her novels on Shakespeare plays, with *The Sea, The Sea* using *The Tempest* as its wellspring.★ 'Everything comes out of Shakespeare: pure romance, melodrama, marvellous characters, poetry, and wisdom about life,' Murdoch stated in 1978. 'I read the plays again and again hoping something will rub off.'

As well as immuring herself mentally from modern culture, Iris and her husband, John Bayley, lived physically in a world of their own, in a dilapidated old house named Cedar Lodge, a short distance from Oxford, the city that was the epicentre of their lives. Both had been students at Oxford colleges and were distinguished lecturers in adult life. Iris was a philosopher, an expert on existentialism, and Honorary Fellow of St Anne's. John was a Fellow of New College and later Warton Professor of English Literature at St Catherine's. The couple, who married in 1956, had no children, their relationship being child-like in itself. They lived in a glorious muddle at Cedar Lodge, chattering back and forth entertainingly like clever children (as house-guests recall), Iris occasionally breaking into spontaneous song (and a dance, if she'd had a drink). John's conversation was illustrated liberally with quotes, jokes and laughter; his speech also was marked by a pronounced stammer that made a gentle, open-faced man seem vulnerable as a boy, belying his impressive biography. Born into a notable family, John Bayley was educated at Eton and Oxford, served as an officer in the Grenadier Guards during the Second World War and, as mentioned, was a distinguished Oxford don. On top of which he was a renowned critic and novelist in his own right. Still, he would be the first to admit that his readership paled in comparison to that of his wife, to whom he deferred as being *the most intelligent woman in England*. This was only a slight exaggeration.

Born in Dublin in 1919, Iris Murdoch had been an outstanding undergraduate at Oxford, gaining a double first in literature and classics in 1942. She then worked at a senior level in the Treasury during the war, becoming a Fellow of St Anne's in 1948. Shortly thereafter she launched a second, extremely successful career as a

---

★*A Fairly Honourable Defeat* (1970) reworks *Much Ado About Nothing*. *The Black Prince* (1973) is inspired by *Hamlet*.

playwright and novelist. Her most popular books, such as *The Bell* (1958), are on one level superior melodramas, with clever young people falling in and out of love. Above and beyond their basic entertainment value, however, the books are also rich in symbolism, philosophy and all things fabulous. Murdoch believed magic and mystery are part of the human experience: we live our daily lives in a linear, logical way, but at the same time we are drifting through a mysterious universe. Who knows what is possible? Perhaps there are sea monsters (as in *The Sea, The Sea*); our pets may have thoughts and abilities we do not fully appreciate; even inanimate objects, such as stones, may have a *personality*. The point is we don't have a perfect understanding of existence.

Murdoch, who was after all a working philosopher, thought very deeply about such (some might say dotty) ideas, and she worked her considerable mental preoccupations into her novels. The quirky and original fiction that resulted sold very well in the 1950s, but fell out of favour during the 1960s when her literary career entered 'a period of eclipse,' as her friend and biographer Peter J. Conradi terms it. There was also a feeling among some critics that Murdoch, a prolific author who produced a new book almost every year, would do better to slow down and take more time perfecting her work, rather than keep knocking out eccentric and unruly books at such a rate (and some of her novels of the 1960s were substandard). This is a belief shared to a degree by her husband, who was best placed to observe her method of working. 'I sometimes feel that she spent too long pondering and getting the thing right in her head, and maybe not enough time [rewriting]. She never changed anything,' comments John Bayley, though he is hesitant to be too critical of Iris even after her death (in 1999 at the age of seventy-nine, after succumbing to Alzheimer's disease). He recalls that his wife would approach each new novel as she would a philosophical problem, first constructing a theorem during a lengthy period of rumination, without discussing the matter with anyone, even John. One time he had the temerity to break in on his wife's thoughts to ask: 'H-h-how's the novel going?'

'Oh, it's finished.'

'F-f-f-finished? But you've hardly begun to write it!'

'Oh, no. But it's all done,' she replied, meaning the novel was complete *in her head*. 'I've only got to write it down now.'

Having thought through her theorem, and its solution, Iris would sit down to write in a room on the first floor of Cedar Lodge overlooking the untidy garden. Her work area was almost as wild as the garden: piled about with books, old newspapers and sundry inanimate objects collected on her travels: especially stones she had brought home because they seemed to her somehow to be possessed. Wind whistled through holes in the widows (panes patched with Sellotape). Rats could be heard in the attic. Military aircraft thundered overhead, bound for the USAF base at Upper Heyford. Despite such conditions and distractions, Iris would write rapidly, dashing off a first draft in longhand in a notebook. After corrections, she would take another run through the story, writing on loose pages which would in turn be given to a typist, the result being presented to her publisher, Chatto & Windus. John believes that the writing of *The Sea, The Sea* took no more than three months in total, which was very fast work for such a long (502 pages) and complicated book, but quite normal for his hasty wife. Such speed resulted in irregular spellings and errors of fact, which the editorial staff at Chatto had to correct discreetly, knowing that Iris disliked anybody tampering with her words. Still, the 1970s saw a renewed imaginative energy and intellectual rigour entering her novels. *The Black Prince* (1973) was a triumph, and *The Sea, The Sea* is even better.

Like the sorcerer Prospero in her source story *The Tempest*, Charles Arrowby, the hero of Murdoch's nineteenth novel, *The Sea, The Sea*, abjures his magic – theatrical magic in his case – to live as a hermit in retirement by the sea, only to find that he has, by chance, bought a house near to the home of his first love, a girl he used to know simply as Hartley. Now in late middle age, Hartley is married to a fellow called Ben Fitch, and they have a son named Titus. Arrowby uses Titus to help him in a misguided quest to woo Hartley away from her husband, whom Arrowby has decided is an ogre, with ridiculous and ultimately tragic results. As the melodrama unfolds, many people from Arrowby's past life in London come to stay in his cottage, which is situated on a stretch of coast in an unspecified part of northern England.

Theatrical acolytes, ex-lovers, would-be lovers; also, importantly, his cousin James, a retired military man and a Buddhist (a recurring type in Murdoch's novel), all pitch up for a house party. Arrowby uses his guests as Prospero manipulates the characters who inhabit and visit his island kingdom. The demonic character of Arrowby also recalls a more temporal manipulator in Murdoch's own life.

Directly before her marriage to John, Iris had had an affair with the writer Elias Canetti, an East European émigré to England who won the Nobel Prize for Literature in 1981. A brilliant, but severe and rather monstrous-looking little man, Canetti tended to attract followers, whom he treated badly, *using* them as opposed to cherishing their friendship. This was an egocentricity that repelled some acquaintances but bewitched others, including Iris, who became besotted with the man despite the fact that he was married. As both John Bayley and Peter J. Conradi point out, it would be a mistake to draw very close comparisons between Murdoch's biography and the stories she weaves in her extraordinary novels, and indeed she disliked readers and critics doing exactly that. Nevertheless there *is* a link here, as Conradi cautiously agrees: 'Yes, she does use bits of her life. But she makes it, to quote from *The Tempest*, into something "rich and strange." Nothing of it but the stuff of "sea change" – the song "Full Fathom Five", which she loved.' In fact, Elias Canetti appears in more than one of Iris' books. He is clearly the model for the egocentric Mischa Fox in *The Flight from the Enchanter* (1956), and a good deal of his personality is in Charles Arrowby. 'I think the quality of demonism, of being determined to get what you want, and to make it part of your possessions, that's very true of Canetti,' concedes John Bayley, who was not fond of Iris's former l-l-lover (he can't help but stumble over *that* word). 'He regarded his friends not really as friends, but as possessions.'

As the book's title indicates – and it is a splendid title, suitably wave-like in its repetition* – *The Sea, The Sea* is much to do with the sea, the best part of the book being, for John Bayley, the evocation of the English seaside. He and Iris loved to swim or, more specifically, to

---

*The title is inspired by a line in the poem 'The Graveyard by the Sea' by Paul Valéry.

wallow in water. They took almost every opportunity to slip into rivers, lakes or swimming pools, at home and abroad, with Iris deriving particular pleasure from dipping into the seas off the English coast. She was fascinated by the darkness of the water, the cold, and its tidal pull. Iris had almost drowned once, swimming off Dorset, and had a peculiar fantasy of rescuing somebody from drowning. 'If I could rescue somebody, John, before I died,' she would tell her husband enigmatically (though it was *he* who had to rescue *her* in Dorset), 'I should die happy.' Near-drowning, and death by drowning, occurs in several of her books, including *The Sea, The Sea* in which Titus is drowned, and the hero Arrowby almost meets a watery grave but is saved miraculously by cousin James, who seems to possess supernatural powers. When Arrowby looks back on the incident, he is certain that a sea monster was in the water with him. This is one of the more fantastical aspects of the novel, having something of the quality of magic realism, a literary genre which was starting to become very fashionable in the mid-1970s, following the translation into English in 1970 of Gabriel Garciá Márquez's novel *One Hundred Years of Solitude*. In fact, the fantastical had always been part of Murdoch's story telling since the 1950s, when nobody talked about magic realism – and it runs through Shakespeare, too, of course. Anyway, 'magic realism' wasn't a literary device for Murdoch so much as how she saw the world. And sea monsters had long held a fascination for her. Once, on holiday in Scotland, she sat by Loch Ness a whole morning, apparently half-expecting its famed monster to rise up and greet her. 'You know, she did it with such seriousness we began to feel perhaps there is something in this after all,' says John. It is also worth noting that one of Murdoch's inspirations for *The Sea, The Sea* was Titian's sixteenth-century painting *Perseus and Andromeda*, illustrating the myth of Perseus rescuing Andromeda from a sea serpent. During the mid-1970s, particularly around the time of writing *The Sea, The Sea*, the author often went to look at this painting in the Wallace Collection at Hertford House, Manchester Square, which is adjacent to the London headquarters of EMI, thus conjuring up the unexpected image of Iris and the Sex Pistols crossing paths.

Although eccentric in many ways, the Bayleys shared a remarkable love affair, and *The Sea, The Sea* is a close study of love, though not in a conventional sense. Charles Arrowby is *obsessed* with Hartley, infatuated beyond all reason, an obsession that brings no joy to either of them. At the same time he is an ambiguous and androgynous figure who admits towards the end of the book, 'I have not had all that many love affairs, and the women I pursued successfully did not always please me in bed.' Murdoch had had lesbian relationships, and homosexual/bisexual characters abound in her fiction, androgynous men being a Murdoch speciality. This is partly inadvertent, perhaps, as a woman who often wrote from a male perspective, a trick she achieved by following Henry James' advice not to try to *be* the opposite sex, but to forget that this is a problem. The result is of course sexually uncertain characters. That was fine as far as Murdoch was concerned, believing as she did that too much is made of the differences between the sexes, especially in fiction. 'She would have said, "But, look, in terms of imagination, and the imagination of the novel in particular, they are just people . . ."' comments John Bayley. 'She always hated the idea of feminism. Or masculinity,' he adds, because for Iris that was an over-simplification. The complexity of human beings, and her over-riding belief that the universe itself is infinitely complex, precluded narrow human types such as 'gay' or 'straight.' 'You know, all the characters are, in a sense, androgynous,' says Bayley. 'Particularly [the hero of] *The Sea, The Sea*. Very much so.' In this sense her books were in tune with the 1970s when, as Lou Reed observed, it was a very fashionable view that everybody was, to some extent, bisexual.

Like most of Murdoch's novels, *The Sea, The Sea* is also a forum to work through *specific* philosophical ideas. At least that was the theory, and one of the philosophical problems she addresses in the novel is obsessional love and its effects. However, in practice, like most of her novels, *The Sea, The Sea* becomes a hold-all in which the author places the many ideas currently occupying her mind and sets her characters to rummage around in them, bringing forth finds with cries of excitement and then discussing them with relish. There are lengthy passages in which Arrowby and his houseguests debate such pet Murdochian subjects as the history of Ireland; the importance of art; the meaning of love; the power of inanimate objects; the relationship between humans and animals (especially their dogs, which Iris suspected know much more than we give them credit for); existentialism; and religion, always *religion*. Raised as a Protestant, Iris jettisoned her Christian faith at an early age and became an atheist, in common with her husband and many Oxford people of their generation. Lack of faith did not preclude her from being fascinated by religion, though, and indeed the author took an almost prurient interest in the beliefs of others, finding Buddhists (such as her friend Peter Conradi) particularly fascinating. One gets the impression that, if she could, she would have brought Buddhists she met on her travels home with her, along with the stones and books and other objects she collected, and piled them up in the general clutter of her study. Her novels are absolutely stuffed with religion, thereby proving, as A.N. Wilson observes wittily in *Iris Murdoch As I Knew Her*, that 'it is possible to be a religious maniac who doesn't believe in God.'

The profusion of ideas in the books is not entirely accidental. In a way it was modelled on a quality Murdoch admired greatly in Shakespeare: the way the dramatist packs all human life into his plays, the tragedy of *Hamlet* for example incorporating a ghost story, a love story, a murder mystery, philosophy and comedy. She tried to emulate this multiformity in her books, and achieves her aim better in *The Sea, The Sea* than in any other of her twenty-six novels. Here indeed is a tragedy, a love story, philosophy, religion and comedy, as well as an abundance of English pastoral charm (the messing about in and on the water and a loving attention to detail in the description of Arrowby's diet, has a delightful *Wind in the Willows*-ish quality). For some readers, Charles Arrowby's pursuit of Hartley is not Murdoch's strongest plot. ('I don't quite believe in the story,' says John Bayley). But *The Sea, The Sea* is certainly a very full book, one that can be enjoyed on many levels, and it is written with tremendous panache. Published during the summer of 1978, the novel was well-reviewed, it sold strongly and was short-listed for the Booker Prize.

Back in 1978, the Booker Prize was far from being the considerable media event it is today. It was a relatively new institution, having first been awarded in 1969, and the announcement was not televised. It wouldn't be until 1980, when two titans of literature, William Golding and Anthony Burgess, came head-to-head (with Golding winning for *Rites of Passage*), that the Booker came to widespread attention. Still, it was an award of growing consequence, and the appellation of Booker Prize Winner has never done an author any harm. The theory behind the Booker, as its organiser Martyn Goff reminds the members of the judging panel each year, is to award a prize for *the book of the year*, not to honour grand figures of English literature for past achievements. However, the judges, who change each year, have shown themselves to be wonderfully wilful and eccentric, and they frequently discount Goff's advice. When it came to the 1978 awards, Goff believes that there was a strong sentiment among the judges not so much that *The Sea, The Sea* was the best book of the year – though it was and is very good indeed – but that it was dear old Iris's *turn*.

Having fallen out of favour with critics in the 1960s, Murdoch was moving into that period of life when honours are bestowed, if they are ever coming. She had recently received two other significant awards, and was given the CBE in 1976. Soon she would be promoted to Dame. She had also been short-listed no fewer than three times for the Booker (in 1969, 1970 and 1973) without winning. Of the five judges in 1978, novelist Angela Huth was the only one who *didn't* vote for *The Sea, The Sea*, for this reason: 'I thought it was one of Iris' best books, but not *the* best.' The other four judges* decided that Iris' time had indeed finally come, and so she was given the award and a cheque for £10,000 (which she spent on paintings). Iris' acceptance speech at the dinner at Claridge's on 22 November 1978 was brief and modest, but privately she felt that the award was her due, telling friends that she would have very much minded *not* to have won. 'She had a quiet pride, you know,' says John Bayley, who didn't attend the dinner, choosing to stay home at Oxford while his wife went up to London. As he says, Iris liked to do things like that – 't'ings like that' she would have said, her Irishness creeping in – on her own.

---

*The other four being Sir Alfred Ayer (Chairman of panel), Derwent May, P.H. Newby, and Clare Boylan.

Although Iris Murdoch may have won the Booker in 1978 partly out of a sense of it being her turn – and anyway all prizes are something of a nonsense – the stamp of approval that goes with the Booker has helped make *The Sea, The Sea* one of the most renowned English novels of the decade. This is quite appropriate as far as her biographer Peter J. Conradi is concerned, ranking it as he does as being one of her very best books and one that stands a good chance of being read a century from now. *The Sea, The Sea* is also much admired by the most eminent contemporary writers who Murdoch herself chose to ignore. John Updike, for example, is fulsome in his praise, recalling that he read *The Sea, The Sea* with great pleasure and admiration for the feat of imagination that is, after all, what novel-writing is all about. 'I was a fan,' he says, in simple endorsement. 'Her ability to imagine was awesome.'

26

BRIAN OF NAZARETH

He's not the Messiah, he's a very naughty boy!
MONTY PYTHON'S LIFE OF BRIAN

Asked about her religious beliefs at the Booker Prize dinner, Iris Murdoch told a reporter: 'I am not a believer in the sense of believing in God the Father, or Jesus Christ as divine. But I believe that religion is terribly important in people's lives, because it tries to look at the world not veiled by the obsessions, fears, and egoism of everyday life. Various priests now tell me that this is what they believe. If only they work fast enough, Christianity can become like Buddhism, before people forget it entirely.' This was a sagacious observation on the state of religion – mainstream Christianity in particular – in the West in the 1970s, a decade that saw a decline in established churches and a simultaneous blooming of esoteric and extreme faiths.

Since the Second World War, the old Christian churches had been losing authority throughout Northern Europe. England was a Christian country only in name by the late 1970s. The Church of England had been established on dubious foundations, of course, under the reign of Henry VIII, and by the late twentieth century the institution was a crumbling if picturesque ruin. Two world wars had eroded faith in God generally. And in the postwar world, more sophisticated, better educated generations of indigenous Britons had less time for church, while immigrants from Britain's former colonies brought their own religious superstitions with them. The architecture of Christianity in England often became simply that: beautiful old buildings opened (sometimes for a fee) as museums. The ineffectual C of E clergy were regarded by many as no longer moral leaders so much as characters of light entertainment: mostly harmless, intrinsically absurd.

Although, taken as a whole, the United States is a more religious country than the United Kingdom, the established churches were also failing there. Like the marriage rate, church attendance rose in the USA during the 1950s and early 1960s, before beginning its long decline in the 1970s. Catholic, Methodist, Lutheran, Presbyterian and Episcopalian, all these churches experienced falls in attendance figures: for example, in the late 1950s, seventy-five percent of American Catholics claimed to have attended mass in the past week; by 1975, that number was down to fifty-four percent. A 1967 survey of American Catholics and Protestants found that forty percent said that they had a 'great deal' of confidence in organised religion. By 1979, only twenty percent felt so strongly. At the same time, however, there was an upsurge of evangelical churches across America, especially in the South where pastors broadcast their sermons on radio and television, lending them a specious authority and disproportionate political influence, usually of a conservative kind. One such noisy right-wing tele-evangelist was the Baptist minister Jerry Falwell of Lynchburg, Virginia, who in the late 1970s bridged the gap between religion and politics by founding the Moral Majority, an anti-libertarian pressure group that made it abundantly clear they were anti a lot of things including abortion, pornography and homosexuality. This then was the flipside of gay bath-houses, pan-sexuality, piss paintings, and all the other excesses characteristic of the decade.

Outside of the southern states, many Americans who might hitherto have attended established churches turned to esoteric sects and beliefs, ranging from the ancient, such as Buddhism, to new cults like Hare Krishna, Rastafarianism, the so-called Moonies, and the Church of Scientology. The latter had been founded in the 1950s by a hack science-fiction writer named L. Ron Hubbard who, despite being exposed as a con man, attracted a great number of followers in the

1970s, including such personalities as John Travolta, who was one of the biggest new movie stars of the decade.* At the most extreme end of the spectrum of cult religion in America were the unfortunate followers of the Reverend Jim Jones of San Francisco. In the mid-1970s, Reverend Jim led adherents of his People's Temple to Guyana where he persuaded nine hundred of these deluded souls to commit mass suicide with him.

Fringe groups aside, what might be termed *extreme belief* was generally in the ascendant in the seventies, especially in the United States. Born-again Christianity was one aspect of this phenomenon, 'born-again' being a catch-all for those charismatic churches which, by converting people to their faith, like to think that they remake them so fundamentally it is as if they are born anew. Born-again Christianity was not a marginal type of faith, however. Far from it. In November 1977, America chose a born-again Christian as its President, in 53-year-old Georgia peanut farmer Jimmy Carter. During his election campaign, Carter had used his faith to win over Christian voters, while at the same time quoting the lyrics of Bob Dylan as a sign to a younger, more secular audience that he was in touch with them, too. This was not as contradictory as might be imagined. Surprisingly, Carter and Dylan were *both* born-again Christians. Though born and raised a Jew, in the wake of a stressful divorce from Sara Dylan in the late 1970s Dylan had been herded into Jesus' flock by a pastor at the Vineyard Fellowship, one of the new evangelical churches that had recently sprung up like weeds in Southern California. The Fellowship was informal in character, meeting not in church but in rented halls, even down at the beach in LA where the pastor was likely to wear shorts and play the guitar. To the mortification of his Jewish family and friends, Dylan accepted an invitation from the group to have a 'lifestyle relationship' with Jesus in January 1979, shortly thereafter releasing an extraordinary Christian rock album titled *Slow Train Coming* (1979), which remains one of the most extreme career changes of any mainstream rock star of the decade (making David

---

*Following *Saturday Night Fever* (1977), Travolta hit the jackpot in 1978 with the lead role in *Grease*.

Bowie's changes of image seem utterly superficial by comparison). An unpleasant aspect of Dylan's new-found and evidently heartfelt faith, and typical of born-again Christianity generally, was that Bob now judged everybody on the basis of whether they believed as he did. Those that didn't accept Jesus Christ as their saviour were headed straight for Hell, as he made clear in lyrics to songs such as 'Gotta Serve Somebody', a surprise hit single for Dylan in the US in June 1979.★ And time was apparently pressing for those who had not yet made up their minds whose side they were on. In his conviction that Judgement Day was nigh, Dylan and his fellow born-again Christians were influenced not only by the New Testament but by the religious bestseller of the decade, Hal Lindsay's *The Late Great Planet Earth* (1970). Using the Book of Revelation as his source material, Lindsay wrote that the long-prophesied Biblical battle between the forces of good and evil would happen in the Middle East *imminently*: the Apocalypse if not *now*, coming very soon. This prediction literally put the fear of God into millions of Americans during the decade (Lindsay's book reputedly sold ten million copies in the States by 1977). Countless Americans, Dylan included, now lived in daily expectation of the end of the world, believing that they, the faithful, would be swept up to heaven in 'the rapture' while everybody else was destroyed in the battle of Armageddon.

Such was the prevailing hysterical religious climate in America in 1979 when the *Monty Python* team unveiled their most contentious movie, *Monty Python's Life of Brian*. Little wonder then that the Pythons' satire on religion caused such controversy.

By the late 1970s, *Monty Python* was an international success story. The four television series the team made for the BBC between 1969 and 1974 had been sold to more than twenty countries, and the spin-off stage shows, comedy albums and *Python* books had also proved enormously popular. The team's second feature film, the Arthurian spoof *Monty Python and the Holy Grail*, lifted *Python* to a new level of success, though the picture was a nightmare to make. The team had

★To date, this is also his last hit single.

only a minuscule budget to work with (partly constituted of modest twenty-thousand-pound investments from sympathetic rock groups such as Led Zeppelin). And they filmed on location in Scotland during particularly miserable, rainy weather. In the process, the patience of all concerned was tested to the limit. King Arthur was played by Graham Chapman, who was often so drunk that he could not remember his lines. The chain mail that the knights wore was fabricated from wool, which absorbed the wet and meant the actors were permanently sodden. Behind the camera were neophyte directors Terry Jones and Terry Gilliam, Gilliam making a somewhat uneasy transition from studio-bound animation to live-action filmmaking. 'I remember getting very cross with Terry Gilliam one day,' John Cleese recalls in *The Pythons Autobiography*. 'He was lining up a shot, and we were kneeling on the ground, which didn't help in all that [woollen] armour, and it was very uncomfortable. And I remember he kept moving us about three-eighths of an inch this way, and then a quarter of an inch that way, and then he said, "No, can you come back a little bit there?" By the end I remember saying to him when I was so uncomfortable, on the verge of pain, "For God's sake, get on and shoot the fucking thing; you know, we're not bits of paper." I think he was so used to doing animation that he was trying to do the same with us . . .' Despite such problems, *Holy Grail* was a big hit when it was released in 1975, doing particularly well in America where the showing of the BBC television series on PBS (the American Public Broadcasting Service) in recent years, and the cult popularity of *Monty Python* comedy albums, had established a sizeable fan base for the team. Made for less than a quarter of a million pounds, *Holy Grail* grossed over six million, largely as a result of its American success, which increased the pressure on the Pythons to work together again.

John Cleese refused to countenance further television series, and in fact he hadn't appeared in the fourth and last BBC series in 1974, believing that the format had already become stale. Without Cleese, the final six episodes of *Monty Python's Flying Circus* are unbalanced. Not only do the shows lack the distinctive manic sketches Cleese and Chapman formerly contributed, but the physical absence of Cleese is akin to watching the Rolling Stones perform sans Mick Jagger. It isn't the same thing *at all*. Meanwhile, Cleese channelled his energy into solo projects, notably his brilliant sitcom *Fawlty Towers*, inspired as we have seen by his experience of staying at the Hotel Gleneagles in Torquay. Hotelier Donald Sinclair became Basil Fawlty, a study in suppressed rage, which was a subject that fascinated both Cleese and his American wife, Connie Booth, who co-wrote the show and played Polly the chambermaid. Basil was furious with the world, but he was forced to sublimate his rage in order to run his hotel, exploding when he came under intolerable pressure. Although *Fawlty Towers* received mixed reviews when it premiered in September 1975, it was repeated time and again and became a beloved national institution. Eventually, it was also an international success, its lines quoted like comedic holy writ. Classic episodes such as 'The Germans' – in which Basil suffers a head injury and in his concussed state wrestles with his subconscious impulse to associate German guests with the Second World War (reminding himself 'Don't mention the war!' but eventually assuming moral and military superiority 'Who won the bloody war anyway?') – make *Fawlty Towers* among the greatest of all television situation comedies, British or American. Cleese and Booth separated in 1976, but they continued to work together and were developing the equally successful and equally funny second series when the next major Python project emerged.

At the premiere of *Monty Python and the Holy Grail*, a reporter had asked Eric Idle what the team's next movie would be. '*Jesus Christ: Lust for Glory*,' Idle shot back, a throwaway gag which was the genesis of the idea that Python should indeed tackle religion which, as we have seen, was a hot topic in the 1970s – not just the decline of established churches and the proliferation of wacky faith: in Ireland and the Middle East, religion was being used as a pernicious argument for terrorism and murder.

Reading into the life of Christ, the Pythons came to agree that Jesus himself wasn't an ideal target for comedy: the words and actions ascribed to Christ were, they thought, mostly commendable. What *was* worthy of satire, however, was the way in which Christ's supposed utterances were twisted to fit the purposes of the myriad churches founded in His name. By June the basic idea was in place. The central character of this religious spoof would be a fellow living in Judaea at the same time as Christ, who is *mistaken* for the Messiah. He is not Jesus of Nazareth, but *Brian of Nazareth* (as the Pythons originally intended to call the picture). Brian Cohen is, in summary, a 40-year-old unemployed nonentity, living at home with his mum. To play this dull but likeable innocent, the team nominated Graham Chapman, their best straight actor, even though Chapman's drinking had made him erratic and unreliable on set, especially so on the *Holy Grail*. Seeing the trust that his friends had placed in him yet again, and realising that this would be their biggest film to date, Chapman stopped drinking once and for all, which transformed him into a much nicer and more focused person. To complete the script the whole team flew to Barbados in January 1978, to spend a fortnight together in a rented beach house. As we have seen, in the past their working method had been to write in their individual teams, coming together for group meetings to finalise what material they would use and how they would play it. But as their individual success grew, and outside interests took up more of their time, it had become increasingly difficult to get all the members together in London. By going away as a group for two weeks, without the distraction of wives and lovers with them, the Pythons were forced into an intensive collaboration such as they hadn't experienced for many years; as a result they quickly produced their most mature and consistently funny script.

More than a collection of sketches, *Brian* would be a cohesive and compelling story. As planned, the film would start with the three wise men, bearing gifts, being drawn to Bethlehem by a guiding star (echoes of Gilliam's animated Christmas cards for *Do Not Adjust Your Set*), only to call in mistakenly on the home of a certain Mrs Cohen (Terry Jones wonderful as always in drag), whose new-born babe, Brian, is in his crib. The wise men soon realise their error, snatch back their presents from Mrs C, and go next door to worship baby Jesus. The film would then flash forward to a Saturday afternoon in Judaea, AD 33, 'around tea time,' Judaea being a land under the yoke of the Roman Empire, with a plethora of local prophets most of whom are obvious frauds. In this atmosphere, Jesus is glimpsed giving his Sermon on the Mount. Standing at the back of His audience, and finding it difficult to make out what is being said, Mrs Cohen yells for Jesus to *speak up!* Meanwhile, a mangled version of the sermon is relayed through the crowd. One of Jesus' pronouncements comes through to the people at the back as: 'Blessed are the Greek'

'The *Greek*?' asks one spectator of another.

'Well, apparently he's going to inherit the Earth.'

Brian falls for Judith, a member of an inept revolutionary group, the People's Front of Judaea (PFJ). The group leader, Reg, is played by John Cleese as one of those stroppy, ideological union leaders all too familiar in the strike-bound Britain of the 1970s. Reg is also an amoral zealot, willing to incite kidnap and murder to achieve his self-righteous ends. In this respect, the PFJ is a lampoon of sectarian groups who were committing outrages across Europe and the Middle East during the 1970s (e.g. kamikaze terrorists who blew twenty-six people up on a plane in Tel Aviv in the name of the Popular Front for the Liberation of Palestine [PFLP] in 1972; the IRA murdering seventeen people in the Birmingham pub blasts of 1974). Reg persuades Brian to take part in a kidnap attempt on Pontius Pilate's wife. As he explains, the PFJ plan to kill her and send her dismembered parts back to Pilate on the hour every hour until he accedes to their demands (merely the dismantling of the Roman Empire). During this operation Brian is caught by the Romans, escapes, and on the spur of the moment assumes the identity of a prophet so as to blend in with the holy fools holding forth in the forum. While mimicking these maniacs, he is mistaken for a true Messiah, becomes the focus of an exasperating cult, and ultimately – wouldn't you know it? – is crucified. Jesus Christ himself would only appear in the film twice, fleetingly as a baby in the manger, and then giving the Sermon on the Mount. The main target of the Pythons' satire was, in fact, religious and political zealotry; also – a facet of the film often overlooked – the Roman Empire. Roman antiquity provided the team with an abundance of excellent comic material. They derived endless fun from jokes about centurions, circuses, first-century food and barbaric punishments – notably crucifixion – which would be shown being carried out almost casually, and treated as such by perpetrators and victims. ('At least it gets you out in the open air,' philosophises one such, stoically.)

As the Pythons polished the script in Barbados, they received several celebrity visitors, including Mick Jagger and his new love, the Texan model Jerry Hall, as well as Keith Moon of the Who. The drummer was an old drinking buddy of Graham Chapman, who had promised Moon a small part as a prophet in *Brian* even though Keith was in terrible physical and mental shape, his body and mind broken by years of alcohol and drug abuse. Despite his problems, Moonie was still a lively and loveable companion, and during the Barbados fortnight he would hang out on the beach at Heron Bay waiting for the boys to break from writing and come out to play at lunchtime. In this convivial, social and relaxed atmosphere the script of *Life of Brian* was soon completed to everybody's satisfaction. Upon their return to London, the team had little trouble raising the funds to make the picture, though they required far more money than had been spent on *Holy Grail*. To film on location in Tunisia, to hire sufficient extras and to build proper sets would cost approximately four million pounds. EMI guaranteed the money in full, without quibble, and the team were about to commence filming when Lord Delfont, the Chairman of EMI, reviewed the script and announced at the eleventh hour that *Life of Brian* was too iconoclastic a project for his company. Just as with the Sex Pistols eighteen months before, EMI simply lost its nerve and reneged on its deal, which was the first indication that *Life of Brian* would be more than just a funny film.

Indeed, it would be a sensation . . . if the team could find the money to get it made. Graham's friend Keith Moon thought that he might be able to rescue *Life of Brian*. Living wildly beyond his means, Moon didn't have anything like the financial wherewithal to finance *Life of Brian* personally, but the Who was awash with cash. Also, the group had a significant interest in the British film industry at this time. With the direction of Ken Russell, the Who had recently turned their rock opera *Tommy* into a successful movie (with Roger Daltrey making a creditable job of the title role), and plans were afoot for the group to appear in and produce further British-made pictures. The drummer was working on a deal when he died at home in London on 7 September 1978. Moon had been using prescription medication to try and stop drinking and made the fatal mistake of mixing the pills with booze. Aged only thirty-two, he was the latest in a long line of rock stars who died prematurely in the decade, victims of the culture of excess that marred the music business at this time.

Ultimately, it was another rock star, George Harrison, who saved the day. The former Beatle had been a great fan of *Holy Grail* and had become close friends with Eric Idle. He announced to Idle that he was willing to pay to see *Life of Brian*, even if that meant footing the bill for the entire production – which he literally did, forming an independent production company called HandMade Films. As Idle has said, it might be the most money anybody's ever paid for a cinema ticket. With Harrison's millions behind them, filming commenced in Tunisia in September 1978, with Terry Jones directing and Gilliam in charge of art direction, a division of labour intended to avoid some of the problems that arose during the making of *Holy Grail*. It turned out to be the most enjoyable filming experience the team ever had. For once, they had sufficient money to ensure high production values, unlike most British comedy films and in contrast to previous Python pictures. They had their best ever script: coherent, cohesive, funny and saying something significant. And now that he was sober, their leading man knew his lines. Indeed, in his sobriety Graham Chapman had the energy to function again as a doctor, running a surgery for cast and crew on location.

One of the features of *Life of Brian*, as with previous Python films, is that the team members play multiple roles. John Cleese in particular shines in many parts, not least as Reg, leader of the PFJ, who makes Brian prove his commitment to the cause by daubing 'Romans Go Home' in Latin on the walls of the forum at night. While Brian is engaged in this nocturnal graffiti, he is seized by centurion Cleese, whose reaction is one of shock: not at the vandalism, but at Brian's atrocious Latin grammar. As a result he instructs Brian how to express 'Romans Go Home' correctly, ordering him to write it out one hundred times on the walls as a lesson. This is a fine joke on the Roman oppressors, who are characterised in *Life of Brian* as being close to the British comedy view of Germans: efficient but overbearing, and humourless to the point of stupidity.

Perhaps the best comic sequence – one of *the* classic comic scenes in modern cinema – again involves Cleese, as Reg, addressing the PFJ on the subject of the enemy. When he asks his followers rhetorically what the Romans have ever done for the people of Judaea, his comrades pour forth a stream of examples: the aqueduct, sanitation, wine, roads, education, public order, improvements *ad infinitum*. It is a classic Chapman–Cleese list gag, the flow stemmed only when Reg summarises grumpily: 'Alright! Apart from the sanitation, the medicine, education, wine, public order, irrigation, roads, the fresh water system and public health, what have the Romans ever done for us?'

'Brought peace,' suggests a follower, timidly.

Up to this point, *Life of Brian* is mostly concerned with lampooning the Roman Empire and its subjects. It is only in the last forty minutes of the film that the religious story is developed fully, starting with Brian being taken up by the impressionable inhabitants of Judaea as their Messiah, his band of devotees pursuing him into the desert, then gathering outside his home while he sleeps. One of the highlights of the film comes when Mrs Cohen complains to Brian about the multitude milling about outside and discovers, to her disgust, that her son has spent the night with his girlfriend, Judith. Mrs C flings open the shutters on the mob – who are chanting *Messiah! Messiah!* – and admonishes them: 'Now, you listen here. He's not the Messiah, he's a very naughty boy! Now go away!'

When Brian appears at the window to tell his followers that they've got it all wrong, that they don't need to follow anybody, because *they're all individuals*, the mob chant in unison by reply: 'Yes, we are all individuals.'

'You've all got to work it out for yourselves.'

'Yes, we've got to work it out for ourselves . . . Tell us more!'

This was Cleese's favourite line in the whole picture, because he thought it so aptly summed up the zealot mentality: the urge religious people have to abrogate independent thought in favour of following somebody, something, *anything*, and their willingness to blinker themselves to flaws in their chosen idol. It is because the team tackle such important ideas in *Monty Python's Life of Brian* that it is a special film above and beyond being very funny. At the same time, this was also innovative and stylish filmmaking in the technical sense, though the Pythons were given little or no credit for such, to their disappointment. Terry Gilliam recalls how angry he was when he read a history of British filmmaking written by an eminent critic, and saw the *Python* pictures of the '70s relegated to a footnote, '[as if] it wasn't serious film-making. It was, like, very serious film-making!'

The sequence leading up to the climactic crucifixion is suitably irreverent, with Michael Palin as the concerned Roman in charge of a crucifixion party simpering over his victims, Idle and Gilliam as grotesque jailers, and Idle appearing as a nonchalant condemned man, bantering with the Romans on his way to the execution site. It is Idle who brings the film to its remarkable conclusion by leading his fellow victims in a sing-song. 'Always Look on the Bright Side of Life' is one of Idle's best ditties, created by the Python with the feeling that he had to write something 'very cheery' to end the picture. Granted life is a piece of shit, as Idle sings, you might as well make the best of it, even banged-up on the cross. The image of a group of crucified men singing and whistling philosophically as the camera pulls away is one of the strangest endings to any movie, especially as the effect was to send cinema audiences home with a curious feeling of having been uplifted. Well, some of them felt that way. Others loathed the picture.

From the start, the team were very clear about what and whom they were satirising. *Life of Brian* was not about Jesus Christ, it was about Brian Cohen. It was not a work of blasphemy, but heresy: a word little used in 1979, but a clear distinction in their minds, for it meant that they were mocking church-based religion rather than a deity. Nevertheless, many religious leaders decided that this was mere sophistry and *Monty Python's Life of Brian* was blatantly and outrageously blasphemous. When the picture opened in America in August 1979 – an America where Bible-based religious groups had become so much more extreme in recent years – it was met with vociferous protests. Some were bizarre and comical, such as the nuns who paraded with banners outside a New York theatre. Offence was, however, deeply and widely felt. The Catholic Archdiocese of New York complained bitterly that the movie held Christ up for 'comic ridicule.' Jews were also offended, according to Rabbi Abraham Hecht of the

Rabbinical Alliance of America, who commented hotly: 'We have never come across such a foul, disgusting blasphemous film before. *Life of Brian* is a vicious attack upon Judaism and the Bible and a cruel mockery of the religious feelings of Christians as well.' So deep did feeling run down in Baptist South Carolina, that the Republican senator Strom Thurmond managed to have the picture pulled from all the theatres in the state.

As the film opened in countries around the world, controversy followed it, with many local politicians succeeding in having the film blacklisted in their regions. The picture was banned *nationwide* in Norway, with the inadvertently comic result that in neighbouring, liberal Sweden *Brian* was promoted as the film too funny for the unsophisticated Norwegians. In most cases, those most vehemently opposed to *Life of Brian* had never seen it, or only seen bits of it. This was demonstrated during a British television debate that pitted John Cleese and Michael Palin against Mervyn Stockwood, then the Bishop of Southwark, and the writer, broadcaster and Catholic convert Malcolm Muggeridge.

In preparation for the show, *Friday Night, Saturday Morning* – which was broadcast on BBC-2 on 9 November 1979 – Muggeridge and the bishop were sent to a screening of *Life of Brian*. Unfortunately, they arrived late at the theatre and so missed the vital first few minutes of the picture in which the distinction between Brian Cohen and his neighbour and contemporary Jesus Christ is established. As a result, the two men entered into the TV show with a less than perfect understanding of what they were talking about, and encountered a stout debater in John Cleese, whose background as a Cambridge-educated lawyer came to the fore. When Muggeridge asserted piously during the programme that Christianity had been a font of goodness for centuries, Cleese countered with 'What about the Spanish Inquisition?' In another lawyerly exchange, Cleese told Muggeridge: 'Four hundred years ago we would have been burned for this film. Now, I'm suggesting that we've made an advance.' Michael Palin was quieter than Cleese during the debate, having been taken aback by the vehemence and nastiness of the criticism, with Malcolm Muggeridge sniping at their 'making a tenth-rate film' (which *Life of Brian* evidently is not), and the Bishop of Southwark making the jibe that he supposed that Cleese and Palin had earned their thirty pieces of silver. After such a fierce encounter Palin was surprised, and indeed appalled, that Muggeridge and Southwark behaved in a perfectly friendly way towards him and Cleese off-screen, saying how well they thought the programme had gone 'as though we'd all been "showbiz" together,' as Palin says. 'I hadn't realised they weren't actually being vindictive, they were just performing for the crowd.'

The outraged reaction, in public at least, of figures such as the Bishop of Southwark to *Monty Python's Life of Brian* only served to give the film welcome publicity, of course, making it a picture that many people felt compelled to see in 1979. And the consensus among those who did see the film, the *whole* film, is that it was a triumph. *Life of Brian* was certainly a major commercial hit, especially in the UK, and it is considered by most British *Python* fans to be the best work that the team ever did, a view with which John Cleese concurs. 'I'm always surprised the Americans prefer *Holy Grail*,' Cleese has commented. 'The English much prefer *Life of Brian* and so do I. I think it's mature and I also think it's because we were making some very good jokes about very important things.'

Like *Jaws* (though for different reasons), *Life of Brian* has lost its power to shock over the ensuing years. It has become a familiar old friend. The routines and gags are now part of the common stock of British comedy, part of our cultural life, quoted from casually as we quote from such well-loved if diverse sources as Shakespeare's plays and, indeed, episodes of *Fawlty Towers*. All the more reason then to recall that *Life of Brian* was once viewed in some sections of society as being utterly outrageous. Others considered it to be brilliant and risky cinema. It is evidence of how far ahead of its time *Life of Brian* was in 1979 that it was not until 1991, fully twelve years later, that regulators finally permitted it to be broadcast on British television.

27

NOW THE END IS NEAR

He took it all too far and, boy, he couldn't play guitar

JOHN LYDON

Religion had always played a part in John Lydon's life, right back as far as his childhood in North London where his Irish-Catholic parents wanted him to be an altar boy. John, who kicked against the old beliefs, remembers wishing the priest would die, so that he wouldn't have to serve in church. 'And, luckily, the priest died that very night, before I had to go in, so that cancelled my altar boy duty.' In adult life, Lydon came to believe that the Roman Catholic Church is abusive, and goes against nature in its doctrines on sex. And when John walked away from the Sex Pistols in 1978 and formed a new band, Public Image Ltd, one of the first songs he recorded was a denunciation of Christianity, a song called 'Religion'. Working with friends, including guitarists Keith Levene and Jah Wobble, Public Image reached its artistic peak a year later with the multi-disc release known as *Metal Box*, so-called because the discs were originally sold in a metal canister. This is strange and ambitious music, flavoured by reggae and Euro-disco, with Lydon's vocals sounding weirder than ever before. In the song 'Chant', he wails that one word repeatedly over a sludge of drum and guitar, like a soul in purgatory. In contrast the last track in *Metal Box*, 'Radio 4', is an ambient instrumental that might have been scored by Michael Nyman, the synthesizer creating delicate washes of sound that ebb and flow like the tide of time at the end of the decade. Suitably, the album was released in December 1979, despite the misgivings of the executives at Virgin Records who didn't think that it would sell.* 'It's nothing like the Sex Pistols,' they told Lydon, who replied that that was the point; he wanted to get as far away from the Pistols as possible, now that his role in that band had ended in acrimony, and tragedy.

To step back in time for a moment, the Sex Pistols' debut album, *Never Mind the Bollocks*, had finally been released in Britain in November 1977, by which point several of the best songs on the LP were familiar to the public as singles. Nevertheless, it was an astonishing album, almost as remarkable for its graphic design as its musical content. Jamie Reid had created an eye-catching pop art cover, using cut-out newspaper letters, and Day-Glo yellow and pink as his background colours, taking his inspiration from supermarket packaging. 'It was very much the sort of colour of "SALE",' he says. 'It's very much the colour of "BUY NOW."' The album went to number one in the British charts, and early in 1978 the Pistols' American record company, Warner Brothers, brought the group to the US for a promotional tour.

The trip was trouble from the start. Due to the fact that the band members had several petty criminal convictions, the US embassy in London was loath to grant them entry visas, and eventually allowed the band into the country for only two weeks. Police were called at Heathrow when the boys did their usual trick of upsetting their fellow travellers *en route* to their destination, and when they arrived in the States on 3 January 1978, the Pistols soon had reason to wish themselves home again. They were certainly not welcomed as pop heroes in the USA. Huge though punk was in Britain, it had at best only a cult following in America. The mainstream music press was bemused by the genre, and by the Sex Pistols in particular. Typically, Jann Wenner listened once to 'God Save the Queen' and pronounced it 'fucking noise.' Nevertheless, he had been persuaded to give the Pistols one *Rolling Stone* cover, back in October 1977. When that issue died on the news-stands, the publisher felt that his intuition had been

---

*In fact, it did reasonably well reaching number 18 in the UK album charts.

vindicated. The Pistols were of marginal interest to his readers. 'Look, they were a small group,' he says, on reflection. 'They didn't sell records.' This was true to an extent – *Never Mind the Bollocks* rose no higher than number 106 in the US album charts – but Jann's attitude was a symptom of the fact that *Rolling Stone* was no longer the hip counter-culture publication it had been. In 1977, the magazine had relocated from San Francisco to New York, shedding many of the old hands and old ideals, and Jann was now part of another world: a rich man in his thirties who partied at Studio 54 with Andy Warhol and Mick Jagger and put his rock star buddies on the cover of his magazine. (When punk was in its heyday, *Rolling Stone* had cover stories on figures such as Boz Scaggs.) In short, Jann was now far removed from the young people who create and consume new pop music. Some younger members of the editorial staff at *Rolling Stone* championed punk, notably Charles M. Young and Mikal Gilmore, who rated *Never Mind the Bollocks* the best album ever made. But their boss was not convinced, and few Americans were converted by the Pistols' 1978 visit to the USA.

Perversely, the tour didn't start in the rock 'n' roll heartland of America – the urban north-east, or even California – but down south, where many rock bands never venture because musical tastes are so narrowly defined for the most part in the southern states. Malcolm McLaren decided that the Pistols should play Georgia, Tennessee and Texas, and, for once, he and John Lydon were in agreement. John liked the cheekiness of such a wayward itinerary, which was also sure to garner publicity. Typical of the gigs was their third concert on the evening of 8 January 1978. It was at Randy's Rodeo, a country and western venue in San Antonio, Texas. John wore a Vivienne Westwood T-shirt, the one showing two cowboys with their cocks almost touching. In case anybody in the club missed the inference, Sid Vicious told the audience, 'You cowboys are all faggots.' The Texans yelled 'Cocksuckers!' in return and pelted the band with beer cans. When a member of the audience tried to grab Sid, the guitarist smacked him over the head with his bass. Such ructions made headlines and reinforced the band's anarchic image for anybody at all interested, but relatively few Americans *were* interested, and more to the point the chaos on stage was an expression of an increasingly ugly situation behind the scenes.

John felt alienated from Steve Jones and Paul Cook during the tour, and he had no trust left in Malcolm, who wanted Sid to take over as front man of the band. Visions of himself as a proper rock star curdled Sid's feeble brain and wrecked his friendship with John. 'He felt the need to compete with me rather than go in and have his own place in [the band],' Lydon says of his childhood friend. Apart from becoming obsessed with his own prominence in the group – against all reason, as he could neither sing nor play – Sid was now a junkie. Roadies were employed to keep him away from heroin on tour, but he still managed to score with predictably disastrous consequences. When the Pistols played the Winterland Ballroom in San Francisco on Saturday 14 January, Sid was obviously stoned. This was the last show on the tour, the band's only show on the West Coast, and they were playing to their biggest-ever audience, a crowd of 5,000, comprised of a cross-section of Bay Area music fans with a hard core of Californian punks. Now was the time for the Pistols to unite and give the show of their lives. Instead, they performed one of their worst ever sets. The band had rarely sounded more discordant, partly because of Sid who, in his stupefied state, was slashing at his guitar almost at random; and also because of a lousy sound system. John struggled to hold the show together, but eventually gave up on the evening – and on the Sex Pistols. Squatting on the skirt of the cage, almost on the verge of tears as it seemed, his famous parting words to the crowd reflected his own thoughts about Malcolm and the way that the Pistols had been managed. Before walking out on the gig, he asked the audience rhetorically, 'Ever get the feeling you've been cheated?'

After the show, Steve Jones and Paul Cook flew to Brazil with Malcolm McLaren to film scenes for a Sex Pistols movie, *The Great Rock 'n' Roll Swindle*, the premise of which was that the Pistols had been a con, masterminded by Malcolm, to gull record companies and the public out of their money. *The Swindle*, released in 1979, was a very poor film, shoddily made and tedious to watch, the main purpose of which was to give Malcolm a platform on which to display his risible attempts to act and – even worse – sing. Meanwhile, Steve and Paul came across as a couple of dullards who didn't mind what tawdry nonsense they went along with so long as there was the reward of beer and birds. Sid didn't travel with the team to Brazil, not because of any artistic discrimination on his part, but because he overdosed after the Winterland show and had to be hospitalised. After a period of recuperation, he travelled to France in March to record his main contribution to the movie, a sequence which turned out to be – along with some documentary footage of the Pistols on stage – the only matter of interest in *The Great Rock 'n' Roll Swindle*, as well as being Sid's only significant artistic contribution to the whole Sex Pistols project. This was his twisted cover of 'My Way', the lounge bar ballad beloved by people who delude themselves that they have carved a unique path through life.

Sid was filmed miming to 'My Way' at a theatre in Paris, dressed in a white tuxedo jacket and bondage trousers. At the start of the sequence, director Julian Temple has Sid walk down a flight of illuminated stairs to a concert stage as orchestra strings swell and then subside: the sound of something winding down, dying. In what John Simon Ritchie's long-suffering teachers back in London might have called *a deliberately stupid voice*, Sid then begins to warble the familiar hubristic lyrics about having no regrets now that the end is near. As he sings, his voice breaking, the lyrics about having lived a full life were grimly ironic. Sid had hardly lived at all. Dragged into the world by an itinerant junkie mother, he was a street urchin of no discernible talent who got caught up in the luck of some mates. Like a fool he fell for the first groupie he slept with, a junkie-hooker named Nancy Spungeon. Aged twenty-one, he was the self-medicating, self-mutilating front man of a band that didn't really exist any more, deluded by his own ego-dreams into thinking that he could become a rock star in the tradition of David Bowie (prompting John Lydon to pun, 'He took it all too far and, boy, he couldn't play guitar'). Sid's pathetic braggadocio found its perfect expression in this song, with the band kicking in hard on the second verse and Sid abandoning his mock-serious voice to sneer out the rest of the lyrics in punk parody: cursing and making puking noises, scatting stupid lines about killing cats and John Lydon's silly hats. Anarchic, ridiculous, and apparently tossed off without much thought, Sid nevertheless managed to reinterpret a standard, one that the mighty Frank Sinatra no less had all but made his own, making 'My Way' Sid's song too. 'My Way' was Sid's best moment, and also his requiem, for now the recording was done so was he.

Sid and Nancy flew to New York in the autumn of 1978 and checked into the Hotel Chelsea. We can picture them stumbling into the ornate lobby of this venerable New York institution, filled as it is with artwork, and presenting themselves bleary-eyed at the desk to sign the requisite paperwork and collect their key. Then they make their way unsteadily up the marble stairs, following in the footsteps of so many legendary Chelsea guests of the past: of Dylan Thomas, and Bob Dylan, who rested here between tours during the height of his mid-'60s fame; *Look Homeward Angel* author Thomas Wolfe also stayed here; Arthur C. Clarke wrote *2001* at the Chelsea; William Burroughs and Andy Warhol still flitted in and out; and as recently as 1971 tragic Diane Arbus climbed these same marble stairs to photograph Germaine Greer (*Feminist in her hotel room, NYC, 1971*). Throughout the twentieth century the Chelsea had been home from home to some of the world's most luminous artists. At the same time it was a seedy hide-out for the dissolute. Once they had checked into Room 100, Sid and Nancy went on a drug spree, culminating in a squalid night of scoring and shooting-up in their room, which smudged into the early hours of 12 October 1978 when Nancy was found dead under the bathroom sink, having been stabbed in the stomach. A hunting knife was in her side, and a trail of blood led to the bedroom she shared with Sid. When the police arrived, Sid admitted to them that he had stabbed Nancy, though he was so befuddled it would never be entirely clear what had happened. Charged with second-degree murder, he was held initially in the prison on Riker's Island, where he detoxed in the hospital and was later released on bail. After a suicide attempt, he was sent to a psychiatric unit at Bellevue Hospital. Discharged from there in November, he got into a fight and was sent back to Riker's, where he detoxed again. On 1 February 1979, he was released on bail, this time into the company of his mother, Anne Beverley, who had brought her son a present of heroin. Retiring to a friend's apartment in Greenwich Village, Sid made use of the gift and shot up. 'Jesus, son, that must have been a good hit,' Mum exclaimed when she saw her son aglow with the smack. Later that night, he injected himself again and died of an overdose while Anne was in the adjacent room. 'I'm glad he died,' his mother said. 'Nothing can hurt him anymore.'

The death of Sid Vicious is surely the most pitiful of the many rock star fatalities of this dangerous decade in pop music – even more wretched than those of Jimi Hendrix, Jim Morrison, Janis Joplin and Keith Moon – and it has a suitably squalid coda. Although accounts differ in the details, Anne had Sid cremated in New York and brought his ashes home to England via Heathrow where she was obliged to open the urn for customs inspectors, who were no doubt searching for narcotics. The ashes were spilt, with the result that Sid's remains were disposed of finally in an airport bin, with stray particles of his dust drifting into the air vents of the terminal building. As John Lydon observes, bits of Sid may still be circulating in Heathrow's air-conditioning, '. . . which Sidney, I think, would take as a great laugh,' cackles John, whose attitude to the tragedy of Sid is characterised by irreverence mixed with moments of regret. 'The shame of it is, of course, that I brought Sid into that pressure, and that really twisted him. It twisted his head. He couldn't cope with it. I always feel a regret about that,' he says, more quietly. 'He became terribly lost. He got lost.'*

The Clash were on a promotional visit to the United States when they heard that Sid, a friend back to 100 Club days, had died. Joe Strummer tossed his coffee across the room and exclaimed, 'Fucking idiot!' Yet in many ways the self-destruction of the Pistols liberated the Clash and allowed them to emerge as a great band in their own right, reaching their peak in 1979 with one of the most impressive rock 'n' roll records of the decade: *London Calling*.

For many, the Clash had always been inferior to the Sex Pistols so

*Other versions of the story have Sid's ashes dumped in an airport bin in New York.

long as the Pistols were active, with John Lydon rarely failing to seize an opportunity to put Joe's band in its place. 'A let-down for me, the Clash,' he sneers. 'They appealed mostly to kids from suburbia.' There is some truth in this. Despite the posturing and image-making, the Pistols *were* of the streets. In Dickensian London, the likes of John Lydon and Steve Jones might have been picking pockets for Fagin. They were urchins, from a rough urban background, and that lent authenticity to their image and to the songs. By contrast, Joe Strummer came from a solidly middle-class family, having been raised in suburban Surrey and educated privately, all of which undermined his working-class-hero act. Meanwhile there was a good deal of art school poseur about his fellow band members Paul Simonon and Mick Jones. Though it has its fans, the Clash's debut album sounds thin and contrived next to *Never Mind the Bollocks*, and the band's follow-up, *Give 'em Enough Rope* (1978) was a step backward. The situation is the Beatles versus the Rolling Stones reprised: at the time when the Beatles got everything right – music, image, graphics – the Stones played catch-up. Then the Beatles disbanded, and the Stones kept going, ultimately assuming a grandeur they never had while the Beatles were recording. And just as the Stones came into their own with a loose double album, *Exile on Main Street*, recorded shortly after their arch-rivals left the stage, so did the Clash with *London Calling*.

Also, like the Stones in 1972, the Clash were in financial difficulty in 1979 when they made their masterpiece. They had recently split acrimoniously with their manager, Bernie Rhodes, and were out of favour with their record company, CBS, who had signed them for a large advance when punk was the New Big Thing. Now CBS was looking at mediocre sales figures. The Clash didn't give up, however. Indeed, they worked harder than ever, writing more new material than CBS had an appetite to release, and touring relentlessly. Often they played small venues, and the reviews were not always positive, with sections of the British music press who had worshipped them back in 1977 marking them down as second-rate in 1978. Unlike the Pistols, however, the guys in the Clash liked each other; they were stronger in that sense, strong enough to weather this change in their fortunes. By touring almost constantly they became an increasingly tight musical unit. The songs improved considerably, too, with the principal writers, Strummer and Jones, placing less emphasis on sententious Leftist dogma in favour of writing songs of more general interest. And despite their earlier avowed aversion to all things American ('I'm So Bored with the USA') the band began to incorporate a positive American influence in their music, releasing, for example, a swaggering cover of the US rocker 'I Fought the Law' in the summer of 1979. With little support from CBS, the band toured the USA twice that year, initially in the frigid months of January and February, a tour that culminated on Saturday, 17 February 1979, in snow-bound New York with a show at the Palladium. Local celebrities who attended the gig included the ubiquitous Andy Warhol, who noted in his diary, 'The Clash are cute but they all have bad teeth, sticks and stumps. And they scream about getting rid of the rich.' This didn't stop Joe Strummer asking Warhol to take him out on the town after the concert, as the artist recalls: 'One of them said he didn't want to go anywhere downtown – that he wanted to be shown uptown. So I said okay, we'd go to Xenon and Studio 54.' Thus Joe the quasi-revolutionary, who had appeared on stage the year before wearing a Red Brigade T-shirt (at the Anti-Nazi League show in Victoria Park, London), spent the evening hobnobbing with the cocaine cowboys of Studio 54. (Like a man who has woken after sleeping with a whore, Strummer confessed to his roadie the next day, 'I've done something terrible . . . I went out with Andy Warhol last night to Studio 54.')

When they got back to London, the Clash were in many ways at their lowest ebb, bereft of hit records, written off by sections of the fickle music press, and in bad odour with CBS. Because of management changes, they couldn't even use their customary rehearsal hall to work on new material. So it was that they came to hire two rooms behind a garage at 36 Causton Street, just north of the River Thames near Vauxhall Bridge, a humble, semi-industrial space that went by the name of Vanilla Studios. It was here that the boys began working on a batch of new songs that would constitute the best double studio album any British band had made since *Exile on Main Street*; certainly the best-*value* double album of the decade, in that the band insisted that the nineteen-track, two-disc set that was *London Calling* should sell for the price of one LP, retailing in Britain in 1979 at a fiver (discounted to three pounds at Virgin stores). Due to its release in the last month of the last year of the decade, with copies going into shops in the US some time later, *London Calling* was also a record, like *Metal Box*, of the new decade. In fact, it was voted best album of the 1980s by *Rolling Stone* when that publication came to appreciate retrospectively the significance of British punk. But *London Calling* wasn't really a punk album, of course. It was an album made by a band that happened to start in the punk era, a band matured by years on the road, who now believed that they could make 'any kind of music,' as Mick Jones says.

Importantly, the Clash were now back in their home town. *London Calling* is a London record. Joe could walk to Vanilla Studios from his flat in Chelsea. During breaks in the sessions, former art school student Paul would amuse himself by going around the corner to look at pictures in the Tate Gallery, where *Mr and Mrs Clark and Percy* was now on display. And each day's work was prefaced with a relaxing kick-about football session in a Pimlico playground. After soccer, the boys warmed up in the studio by playing covers such as 'Louie Louie', 'Revolution Rock' and 'Brand New Cadillac', the latter created by Vince Taylor, a wild man of the British music scene in the 1950s and '60s who was a model for *Ziggy Stardust*. During the warm-ups Simonon usually practised his reggae riffs, one of which became his song, 'The Guns of Brixton'. Meanwhile Joe and Mick were prolific as ever in providing material for the band, Mick writing most of the music for their new songs and Joe the words, though not invariably that way around. By mid-summer the Clash had so much new material that they persuaded CBS to advance them the money for recording sessions, going into Wessex in Highbury with the eccentric record producer Guy Stevens, who made his name working with such acts as Traffic and Mott the Hoople. A heavy drinker, Stevens famously trashed a studio during a Hoople session when told that he had gone into overtime. The Wessex sessions with the Clash were no less eventful. Stevens had a habit of prowling around the studio with the band when they were recording, picking up items of furniture and swinging them round his head, and one time poured a bottle of booze over the studio piano while Joe was trying to play it.

By acting the fool, Stevens kept the boys laughing throughout the sessions, with the result that *London Calling* has a happy, relaxed feel. Stevens' manic behaviour was also no doubt an expression of the fact that he cared about the music. Certainly, the producer made excellent choices when it came to the songs. It was he, for example, who persuaded the Clash to include on the album a take of 'Brand New Cadillac'. The boys protested that the version of the song he proposed to use on the album (and did) was too rough, with many mistakes, but Stevens pointed out correctly that it was better than perfect; the recording had the joyful abandonment that rock records *must* have in order to be great, but which too often gets lost in the pursuit of excellence. Meanwhile, there was an abundance of first-class new Clash songs to play with, too. The tunes that the band brought into Wessex were particularly strong because the boys had already worked them up to a high standard at Vanilla. Now, Stevens encouraged them to polish the songs until they were *perfect*, without losing the freshness of the material. In particular, he encouraged Joe to do more work on his words, with the result that the lyrics on *London Calling* are superior to any other Clash LP – the metaphor of 'Lost in the Supermarket' being typically elegant. Then there was the amazing *range* of songs, and the contrast between the moods. Full-force punk rock is represented by tracks such as 'Death or Glory' and 'Clampdown', with the three guitars and Topper Headon's martial drums coming in like a tank division. Contrast this with the softly whistled introduction to 'Jimmy Jazz', a saloon bar ballad that ends with a breezy horn section. No Clash album had horns on it before, but they blow through all four sides of *London Calling*. Another new texture was provided by Mickey Gallagher on keyboards, his piano being particularly effective on 'The Card Cheat', which the band recorded twice and overdubbed on itself to get a bigger sound. Again in contrast, the tribute to the actor Montgomery Clift, 'The Right Profile', is as light as a feather, with Joe's slurry scat singing evocative of the narcotic miasma in which Clift ended his days. Drugs were part of the story of the Clash, too, and drug references carry through the album, on tracks including

'Koka Kola' and 'Hateful', which might be the best song about an addict's relationship with his dealer since 'I'm Waiting for My Man'. Several tracks have a reggae feel, with the band taking a traditional folk song in 'Stagger Lee' and breathing new life into it as a ska number called 'Wrong 'em Boyo'. Somehow all these different types of songs, and the sound of the horns, the keyboards, Topper's percussion, and the thunder of the guitars, blend happily together in *London Calling*. The Clash's vocals are also superb. None of the band members were great singers in the conventional sense. Paul was hardly a singer at all, as was demonstrated by his weak vocal on 'Guns of Brixton'. Mick had a modest voice and Joe tended to scream when he became excited. The Clash sounded strongest when they combined their voices in harmony, as they do on many tracks on *London Calling*, or when they took turns on a vocal as in 'Rudie Can't Fail'. The many spoken asides add to the loose feel that makes the album so infectious and ultimately uplifting, despite the apocalyptic undercurrent.

At one point, the band considered naming the album *The Last Testament*, seeing this collection of songs as representing the capstone on the tomb of a musical genre that had been taken as far as it could go. (This conceit was part of the ethos of punk – 'I thought we ended rock 'n' roll,' as John Lydon says.) In fact, the Clash settled on a different and much better title in *London Calling*, but the cover art retains something of the original concept of the LP commemorating the demise of a type of music. The cover features a photograph of Paul Simonon smashing his bass guitar on stage at the Palladium in New York. The word *LONDON* is in pink letters running up the left hand side of the sleeve, and *CALLING* is in green along the bottom. This typography and colour scheme echoes a classic Elvis Presley record sleeve from the 1950s. The point is that, at the birth of rock 'n' roll, Elvis is seen holding his guitar aloft, heroically, setting out on the great adventure; a quarter of a century later Simonon deals rock 'n' roll its death blow by bringing his bass down in an act of spontaneous violence. (In fact, Clash roadie Johnny Green recalls that Paul was showing off for Debbie Harry, of new wave band Blondie, who was watching the concert that night.)

It wasn't the end of rock 'n' roll, of course. But the Clash had a weakness for Big Ideas, and this one fitted Joe's pessimistic view of the end of the seventies, with world events in 1979 giving him cause for foreboding. This was the year of the meltdown at the Three Mile Island nuclear power station at Harrisburg, Pennsylvania (which Joe mentions in 'Clampdown'); the killing fields of Pol Pot's Khmer Rouge were being uncovered; closer to home was the squalor of Britain's 'winter of discontent,' during which industrial action caused hospitals to turn away patients and refuse to be left uncollected in the streets, with London alive with rats as a result (even more than usual that is). Finally, partly in response to the fact that this chaotic domestic situation had been allowed to develop under a Labour government, Margaret Thatcher was elected Prime Minister in May 1979, ushering in what turned out to be eighteen years of Conservative rule. The failure of old-style socialist Labour, and the strong resurgence of the Conservative Party, was perhaps the most deeply depressing turn of events for Joe Strummer. Partly as a result, 'Clampdown', 'Four Horsemen' and the album's eponymous title track are all doom-laden songs.

This dark mood is balanced and lightened however by songs such as 'Brand New Cadillac', 'Jimmy Jazz' and the uplifting final three tracks on the LP: 'I'm Not Down', 'Revolution Rock' and 'Train in Vain (Stand by Me)', which became the band's first hit single in the United States, where *London Calling* sold strongly. The album broke through in the US no doubt partly because it had more of a transatlantic sound than previous Clash LPs. At its heart, however, *London Calling* is a London record, written, rehearsed and recorded (in demo form) by the Thames. Suitably, its title track makes direct reference to the Thames and further incorporates a burst of Morse code invoking the old call sign of the BBC World Service, broadcasting from Bush House down river ('This is London Calling . . .') The Clash told Guy Stevens that they wanted the album mixed to sound like a foggy morning on the Thames, acknowledging the inspiration that the river had injected into their music, as it had in so much work created by generations of musicians, painters and writers. Not least among these distinguished forebears was Joseph Conrad, who took as the starting point of his novel *Heart of Darkness* a gloomy evening on the sea reach of the Thames, around Gravesend, where the river joins the watery network that carries Conrad's narrator to Kurtz.

By the summer of 1979, Francis Ford Coppola had been on his journey into the heart of darkness for four years. In the process, he had transformed John Milius' original concept for a Vietnam War film into a picture based much more closely on Joseph Conrad's novella, creating a story in which the characters – notably Marlon Brando's Walter E. Kurtz – try to fathom man's primal nature. The picture had been extremely difficult to make in all respects, and was such a stressful experience for Coppola that he almost had a nervous breakdown on the set. One rainy day in the Philippines when Brando was being particularly exasperating, Coppola climbed up on to a lighting tower and lay down on it, in the rain, unable to carry on. 'Let me out of here, let me just quit and go home,' he muttered to himself in misery as his crew stood around waiting for direction. 'I can't do it.'

The cast had been through an ordeal, too, even more so than Coppola in the case of Martin Sheen who almost died on location. Seven months after tearing himself apart emotionally for the extraordinary Saigon hotel scene, Sheen suffered a heart attack and had to be flown home to the United States for treatment. Considering the seriousness of his condition, he returned surprisingly quickly and was back in the Philippines in April 1978 to finish filming. Soon afterwards Coppola finally wrapped the production and limped back to California, more than eight million pounds over budget. He knew that his homes were at risk if he didn't cut the mass of footage he had shot into something that was profound (the material demanded nothing less) and at the same time sensational enough to be a major box-office hit. However, while Coppola had been lost in the jungle, Hollywood had moved on from its love affair with the artistic, intellectual and personal films of the early 1970s, which was the climate in which *Apocalypse* had been planned and financed. Now a new ethos was in place.

The recent blockbusters directed by Steven Spielberg and George Lucas had created a demand for more broadly entertaining, some might say simplistic, movies that could be enjoyed by vast audiences comprised largely of teenagers and very young adults – films that lent themselves to merchandising and sequels, and could be sold all around the world. In November 1977, Francis Coppola, George Lucas and Steven Spielberg were all on a flight from California to Washington DC to attend a White House function when they fell to talking about their great commercial successes of the decade now coming to an end: *The Godfather*, *Jaws* and *Star Wars*, which together had grossed more than a billion dollars. As their aeroplane carried them eastward, Spielberg gave his friends an example of the global success of *Jaws*. He told the others that he had gone on a world tour after the film had been released and that in every single country he visited – aside from India and Russia – it was impossible to get away from *Jaws*. Not only was the movie itself ubiquitous, the world was papered with *Jaws* posters, and a myriad promotional items advertised the film's existence. Now *Jaws 2* was in production (to be released in 1978), and in due course there would be *Jaws 3-D* (1983) and *Jaws – The Revenge* (1987). The film studios had always been in business to make money, of course, but they had seldom conducted themselves in such a rapacious way. Now intensive exploitation of a single popular idea became the norm in the industry, and it has remained so, with *Star Wars* introducing the added and very significant commercial dimension of spin-off plastic toys. For his part, George Lucas argued that the modern blockbuster – which he and Spielberg had essentially created in the last couple of years – had saved Hollywood. Lucas' point was that a proportion of the millions generated by a movie like *Star Wars* went as profit to the theatre owners, who invested some of their revenue in the new multiplex cinemas, thereby creating numerous small screens on which art films could find a home. This is an interesting and persuasive theory, until one reflects upon personal experience that most multiplexes are clogged with mass-market fodder, too.

At any rate, this was the change taking place in Hollywood as Coppola neared the end of the odyssey of *Apocalypse Now*: a New Hollywood-type film with intellectual pretensions, artistic camerawork and high-flown dialogue, that now seemed old-fashioned in what was truly the *new* Hollywood. When Francis embarked upon his journey to find Kurtz in the mid-'70s, he was also looking forward to coming back from his voyage with the *first* big Vietnam picture. But *Apocalypse* had taken so long to make that he had lost that important advantage. In the spring of 1979, Coppola appeared on stage at the Academy Awards in Los Angeles to open the envelope for best director of a picture released in the previous year, and found himself giving the statuette to Michael Cimino for *his* Vietnam War film *The Deer Hunter*, featuring Robert De Niro as one of a trio of friends from a Pennsylvania steel town who volunteer for service in the war, and Meryl Streep (in her first starring role) as one of the girlfriends the boys leave behind. In fact, *The Deer Hunter* won Best Director *and* Best Picture, with the awards for actors in leading roles going to Jon Voight and Jane Fonda for still another Vietnam movie, *Coming Home*. Would cinema audiences have any interest in seeing a third major Vietnam picture in 1979?

Apocalypse Now premiered at the Cannes Film Festival in the spring of 1979, winning the Palme d'Or, and opened in the US in August that year. The critical consensus in America was that the first two-thirds of the movie were terrific, with several brilliant bravura scenes such as the helicopter attack on the Vietcong village to the music of *Die Walküre*. (Robert Duvall was universally considered outstanding as Kilgore.) But critics felt that Coppola lost his grip on the movie from the point when Marlon Brando appeared on screen as Colonel Kurtz. 'Like the Vietnam War, it gets out of control at the end,' commented Arthur Schlesinger Jr in *The Saturday Review*. Brando was criticised for acting in shadow, and accused of mumbling dialogue which seemed, at times, merely pretentious. The picture fared respectably at the US box office, nonetheless, and was nominated for eight Academy Awards, ultimately winning in two categories. But the picture wasn't a smash hit and did not bring home the premium Oscars that Coppola coveted and which Cimino had won for *The Deer Hunter* the previous year. 'Of course, now it's a great classic,' says *Apocalypse* cast member Frederic Forrest. 'But at the time it wasn't considered near as good as *The Deer Hunter.*'

Coppola could not help but feel disappointed with the reception of his movie, observing that audiences were split between those who saw *Apocalypse Now* as a masterpiece and others who regarded it as a 'piece of shit.' For the former group, especially those who saw *Apocalypse Now* during their impressionable youth, the movie is filled with wonder. The main characters played by Brando, Duvall, Hopper and Sheen are all unforgettable; the use of music, not least 'The End', is a triumph; set pieces such as Willard's briefing, the *Playboy* show and the scenes at Kurtz's compound are all superbly realised; while the narrative written late in the day by *Dispatches* author Michael Herr, and spoken by Sheen as a voice-over, is a very powerful addition to the picture, winding through the movie like the river that carries Willard into the heart of darkness. Ultimately, the literary and philosophical references are the chief interest of the film. But in truth they are also the reason why it is a flawed masterpiece, because of course there *is* a degree of pretension to the movie, and Coppola does not conquer the challenge he sets himself. The whole picture leads up to the point when we meet Kurtz, and we expect Kurtz to say something profound about the abyss at the heart of man. While Brando and Coppola did their best to identify and convey a profound truth, they ultimately fail in this endeavour, as they were bound to. Conrad himself could only hint at what he wanted to say in *Heart of Darkness*, which is why Kurtz is such an elusive figure in his book. The subject matter is virtually impossible.

The very fact that Coppola should have tried to integrate Conrad's metaphysics with the story of the Vietnam War, and then attacked the ideas with such verve and imagination, is nonetheless impressive. In its finest moments, certainly for the first two acts leading up to the arrival at Kurtz's compound, *Apocalypse Now* is a transcendent war movie: one that is exciting and entertaining and makes one think about war in a different way. In its final act, the film is an audacious attempt to go even further. The picture is also the ultimate work of the school of maverick American filmmaking which began in the late 1960s/ early 1970s, where directors (such as Bob Rafelson with *Five Easy Pieces*) felt able to tackle the most difficult ideas and complex feelings without feeling obliged to arrive at neat or happy endings. For all its flaws, *Apocalypse Now* still outclasses nearly every other movie made during this extraordinary decade in film. No other picture was quite so exhilarating an experience to watch when it was released, and no other film of the decade – the luscious *Godfather* movies, Nic Roeg's beautiful time-twisting pictures, Martin Scorsese's gritty and poetic films, and Woody Allen's sophisticated New York stories notwithstanding – remains such a visual and intellectual feast all these years later.

28

THE '70s ARE DEAD!

Woody Allen requests the pleasure of your company for
New Year's Eve.

In the newspaper round-ups of the year, the consensus among New York film critics was that *Manhattan* and *Kramer vs Kramer* – two New York pictures, of course – were the best films of 1979. Few American critics even included *Apocalypse Now* in their top ten list, though Alexander Walker of the London *Evening Standard* made it his number one, with *Manhattan* as best comedy. The reputation of *Apocalypse Now* would grow with time. But what was already evident was that Woody Allen had enjoyed a triumphant comeback with *Manhattan* after the calamity of *Interiors*, and that he had very good reason to celebrate the end of a decade in which his career had been transformed from comic to film *auteur*. So it was that Allen threw the swellest, swankiest, starriest party New York had seen in years. The weighty, cream-coloured invitation cards, printed by Cartier, read simply: 'Woody Allen requests the pleasure of your company for New Year's Eve.'

Rather than host the party at home, Woody hired a spectacular mansion for the evening. At 4 East 75th Street, the next block up from Allen's apartment building, stood a fabulous five-storey town-house built in the late 1890s for a railroad tycoon and later acquired by the oil-rich Harkness family. The house had an imposing canopied entrance and was decorated in the opulent style of a renaissance palace. All through the afternoon of Monday, 31 December 1979, caterers, cleaners and florists scurried about the mansion, busily preparing for the party. The chandeliers were dusted and lit and, finally, Woody changed into his tuxedo, with the comic touch that he also wore tennis shoes for the evening. Thus attired, he took his place as host in the magnificent marble lobby to welcome his guests, confident that his status as the maker and star of *Annie Hall* and *Manhattan* would draw a gathering of talent this evening to compare favourably – it was said afterwards – with Truman Capote's legendary Black & White Ball at the Plaza Hotel back in 1966.

New Year's eve was mild and dry in New York, with temperatures in the low forties. So pleasant was the weather that some guests walked over to the party from their nearby apartments. Others came by limousine and taxi. Leonard Bernstein, Lauren Bacall, Robert De Niro, Lillian Hellman and Stephen Sondheim were among the early arrivals. Woody shook hands with each, thanking them for coming, but keeping a special look-out for his personal heroes: mostly jazz musicians and sports stars. He was also keen to renew his acquaintance with a famous actress who lived on the opposite side of Central Park, a woman who had come over to his table at Elaine's restaurant recently to say hello. Newly divorced from André Previn, and the wife of Frank Sinatra before that (an association which thrilled Sinatra-fan Woody), Mia Farrow told Woody at Elaine's that she had absolutely loved *Manhattan*. Of course, she had a family connection to the movie. Her sister Tisa played the bit part of Polly in the film, Polly being the girl who says sadly, 'I finally had an orgasm and my doctor told me it was the wrong kind,' setting-up a classic Allen rejoinder: 'Did you have the wrong kind? Oh, really? I've never had the wrong kind . . . my worst one was right on the money.' Not long after meeting Woody, Mia received an invitation to his New Year's party (later remarking, 'I think practically everybody in New York got one'.) Now here she was, with another Farrow sister, Stephanie, and the actor Tony Perkins (*Psycho*) and his wife. Woody didn't get a chance to say much to Mia during the party, but this was nonetheless the beginning of a life-changing relationship for them both, one that would see Woody become a father for the first time, and ultimately the man whom Mia reviled most in the world, after it emerged that he was having an affair with one of her adopted daughters. All that was as yet undreamt of, however. Mia only had fond thoughts about Woody as she ascended the elegant stairs of his rented mansion, noticing how beautifully her host had arranged everything.

Hyacinths scented the rooms, which were themed inasmuch as there was a suite of rooms turned over to dining, with a buffet serving lobster and *filet mignon*; there were conversation rooms; a large television was switched on in another area so that guests could gather at midnight to watch the ritual of the white ball descend the pole atop the Allied Chemical Building in Times Square; music was provided, naturally, with a jazz band playing Dixieland-style in one room, and a disco set up in another. Looking out through the tall windows of these gilded salons, the guests could already see occasional fireworks ejaculating prematurely over Manhattan. And down on the sidewalk roller-skaters were whizzing along 75th Street to join a throng – dressed in the new brightly coloured leggings that were so fashionable – celebrating New Year's Eve by spinning around Central Park. Many of the skaters had tiny headphones clamped to their ears and a small tape recorder strapped to their waist. Roller-skating with the brand-new Sony Walkman was *the* new youth craze as the seventies segued into the eighties.

As the hands of the antique Harkness clocks hurried to meet at the midnight hour, more guests came surging in to celebrate with Woody, the five floors of the mansion buzzing with excited conversation, everybody looking around to see who was there, eager to hear and relay the latest gossip. Many guests were lamenting the sad news that Richard Rodgers had died on Sunday night, right here in New York; the loss of the composer of *Oklahoma!* and *Pal Joey* concluded an era of American hegemony in musical theatre. The new dominant force on both Broadway and in London's West End was the Englishman Andrew Lloyd Webber. Sombre words in memory of Rodgers were soon subsumed by excited party chatter and jokes, however. It was hard to be sad for long with Bette Midler in the house, throwing back her head and emitting peels of bawdy laughter as she told stories.

(Bette had come a long way from entertaining swingers at the Continental Baths!) Another veritable one-man show was provided by party guest Robin Williams, young star of the TV series *Mork and Mindy* and just beginning his movie career. Williams, who would appear in 1980 as Popeye in Robert Altman's new movie of that name, was regaling his circle with Hollywood anecdotes told in an amazing range of funny voices. It was truly impressive how many brilliant and diverse people Woody's Cartier invitations had drawn together for this one night. 'It was probably the best party I ever went to,' recalls the actor Tony Roberts who, having appeared as Rob in *Annie Hall*, was pleased to be playing a part in Woody's forthcoming picture, *Stardust Memories* (1980). 'The stairways were the best place to be because they offered the best chance to smile back at a steady flow of familiar faces [all] night.'

Guests came from all areas of the arts. From the literary world, they included Kurt Vonnegut, Arthur Miller and Norman Mailer, the latter buoyant with the success of his newly-published opus *The Executioner's Song*. (See picture 38.) The big book about Gary Gilmore had been worth all the effort that Norman and Larry Schiller had invested in it over the past few years, for it was receiving more acclaim than anything Norman had written since his youth, and would win him his second Pulitzer Prize in 1980. Everybody seemed to be reading *The Executioner's Song* that winter. Mia Farrow had a copy over at her apartment. Having just returned from London, where he had been filming *The Shining* with Stanley Kubrick, Jack Nicholson was also reading the new book, as research for his next movie. Jack was going to be working with Bob Rafelson again, remaking *The Postman Always Rings Twice* (1981) and he figured that Gilmore was akin to the amoral antihero of that story. Norman was congratulated repeatedly as he worked the rooms of the Harkness House with his wife. A rare critic of the book – not at the party – was Norman's contemporary John Updike, who did not enjoy Mailer's melding of real-life events with the novel-form to create what Mailer was calling in interviews *true-life novels*. 'It seemed too long to me,' Updike says of the book, 'and Nicole was more interesting than the hero.'

Updike was working on *Rabbit is Rich*, the third book in his tetralogy of the life of Harry Angstrom. In the novel Harry bids farewell to the 1970s, as Woody's guests were doing, and it is an ambivalent farewell. Like many people at Woody's party, Harry feels sad saying goodbye to the heavenly wonder of the moon shots and Skylab; the car dealer also feels melancholy saying adieu to the earthly pleasure of watching Farrah Fawcett-Majors on TV in *Charlie's Angels*; and it looks like Harry and Janice will have to refrain in future from their habit of sunbathing on vacation until their skin is toasted. Almost everybody who could afford the time, and air travel, worked hard on their tan in the '70s – several of Woody's guests are unseasonably brown this winter evening – but now doctors were warning that sunburn caused skin cancer. This was too bad! Harry felt good baking his middle-aged bones down in Florida, and girls looked sexier to Harry with a deep tan. Meanwhile, for the Angstroms, as for so many Americans, the end of the decade also closed the book on much that they were only too happy to put aside for ever: not least Vietnam, Richard Nixon and Watergate. Also, hopefully, they could say so long to the energy crisis and double-digit inflation. Reflecting the fears of his fellow citizens, Updike had Harry buy gold in *Rabbit is Rich* as a hedge against his savings at a time of an increasingly-devalued dollar. Many of Woody's party guests were doing the same.

In fact, the phenomenal rise in the gold price was a staple of party conversation this evening. Back in 1977 Woody's well-heeled guests could buy an ounce for $200 (£110). Those wise enough to invest saw their ingots and coins worth an astronomical $524 an ounce in December 1979, and smart money was now going into silver. This scramble into precious metals was a sign of international insecurity, not only because of the fall of the US dollar, but also in response to unrest in the oil-producing Middle East where Islamic fundamentalism was on the rise with alarming consequences. Amidst the celebrations in New York this New Year's Eve there were thoughts – and indeed a candle-lit vigil across town – for American diplomatic staff being held hostage by followers of the Ayatollah Khomeini at the US Embassy in Tehran. The hostages had been seized after the January revolution that dramatically swept the Shah of Iran from power. His wife, Farah Diba Pahlavi, went with him into exile in

Egypt (leaving Andy Warhol – who was on Woody's guest list, naturally, but hadn't shown up yet – with unwanted and unpaid-for
portraits of the royal couple). The way in which the US Marines
guarding the Tehran embassy had been so lightly brushed aside by
the Iranian revolutionaries, and the subsequent cruel treatment of
the American hostages, with apparently nothing that the ineffectual
President Carter could do about it, was the final indignity for many
Americans in a decade that had seen US pride much dented.

All told, despite the many cultural achievements of the decade – all
the glorious works of art, literature, architecture, film and music we
have looked at – many of Woody's guests would be glad to see the
back of the 1970s for political and economic reasons. The same was
true for ordinary Americans, and indeed many people around the
world. Celebrating in Times Square on 31 January, Ray Bollig, a
young man from Ohio, expressed a commonplace view when he told
a reporter from the *New York Times* that he had come into town to say
goodbye to what he called, 'the depressing 1970s,' adding this jubilant
cry: 'No more oil crisis, no more Irans – the '70s are dead!'

At midnight, Woody Allen's guests hailed the arrival of 1980 with
cheers and the popping of champagne corks, as motorists sounded
their horns down on Fifth Avenue and fireworks exploded over the
city in virtual facsimile of the credits to *Manhattan*. And people were
still arriving at Woody's party, the very fashionable coming very late
indeed. At three a.m., beautiful Bianca Jagger persuaded her walker
for the evening, Andy Warhol, to leave a party hosted by their good
friend Halston and accompany her to Woody's do. Warhol told Miss
Diary the next day that he wished they'd arrived earlier. 'Woody's was
the best party, wall-to-wall famous people,' he gushed, impressed as
always by fame, and delighting in such a concentration of it at 4 East
75th Street. 'Mia Farrow is so charming and such a beauty. Bobby De
Niro was there and he's so fat. Really fat.'

There was much comment at the party on De Niro's appearance.
Normally such a slim man, the actor was positively gross. To those
who had the temerity to ask what had happened to him, De Niro
explained in his quiet way that he had made himself fat purposefully

for a boxing picture he had been working on. After the success of *Rocky* in 1976, fight films had become as ubiquitous as Vietnam pictures in the closing years of the decade. *Rocky II* was the highest-grossing movie of the year in America, having earned over a hundred million dollars, and *The Champ* was another big 1979 hit. De Niro explained to people at Woody's party that his forthcoming picture, *Raging Bull*, was something quite different, however: not so much a film about boxing as an in-depth study of a tortured man who happened to be a fighter. The character under scrutiny was Jake La Motta, a middleweight champion of the 1940s in New York, when he was known as the Bronx Bull. Having become fascinated with La Motta, whom he had also befriended, De Niro had worked assiduously over the past few years to persuade his friend Martin Scorsese to direct him as the boxer in an adaptation of La Motta's autobiography, charting both his fight career and long subsequent decline. Scorsese had been chary of the project at first, considering fight films to be cliché-ridden, and having enough problems to deal with, including the failure of his first big-budget Hollywood picture, *New York, New York* (1977). While making this flop, Marty had moonlighted as director of the rock documentary *The Last Waltz*, a much more successful enterprise (indeed it may be the best rock concert movie ever made), but one steeped in cocaine use, which had become a bad habit for Scorsese as he entered his mid-thirties. On a recent coke-fuelled vacation into the Rocky Mountains, with his screenwriter friend Mardik Martin and their respective partners, high altitude plus excessive tooting caused the film director to start haemorrhaging. As Mardik recalls, 'Marty almost died.'

The gossip at the party was that when Scorsese was at his nadir he began to see parallels between himself and the disintegration of Jake La Motta – two guilty Catholics being punished for their sins – and with this characteristic thought in mind Martin resolved to make Bobby's movie. The director suspected pessimistically that it might be his last Hollywood project, doubting that LA studios would advance him the budgets to make feature films again after the disaster of *New York, New York*. They were only financing this film because of De Niro, who was now a very big star in Hollywood. In this sense, *Raging Bull* became

Scorsese's *London Calling*: a project made when there seemed to be no future in the mainstream of his industry, which gave him the carefree confidence to do whatever he felt was right – to shoot in black and white, for example, lending the fight scenes the quality he remembered from watching sports on TV in the '40s, even though this would almost certainly harm the picture commercially. Never mind. He would make his last American feature the best picture he could. As De Niro explained to everybody who asked him at Woody's do, the first scenes to be shot were La Motta's early bouts when he was the raging bull, performing a brutal ballet in the ring. At thirty-six, De Niro said he had been just young enough to get into condition for the mock fights, training himself down to a lean ten stones. Then he went on a four-month gastronomic tour of France and Italy, eating himself into the latter scenes when La Motta is a fat, drunken has-been. Sure, he could have put on a body suit, as most actors would, but Bobby wanted to make the extra effort to become the character. As it happened, De Niro had just finished work on the fat scenes and so was tipping the scales at fifteen stone on New Year's Eve. Looking askance at the movie star at the party, a mischievous thought crossed Andy Warhol's mind, as he told his diary the next day: 'I *know* he gained weight for the boxing movie, but wouldn't it be funny if he could never lose it?'

De Niro would indeed lose the weight, and he was rewarded in 1980 for his remarkable portrayal of La Motta with his second Oscar. Though *Raging Bull* itself met an ambiguous critical reception it has come to be judged by many commentators as *the* best picture of the eighties. In fact, *Raging Bull* was the last really significant movie of the decade now coming to its close, having been conceived, written and filmed in the 1970s, by one of the great actor-director teams of that halcyon decade in the arts, in the '70s tradition of naturalist, character-driven movies. Such authentic pictures would be rare indeed in the 1980s, a decade when American cinema became dominated by formulaic films aimed predominantly at teenagers. Some of the biggest movies of the '80s starred child actors, or actors who looked like children, such as Michael J. Fox in the Steven Spielberg-produced *Back to the Future* series. There was little room for naturalism or introspection in this future. It was thrills, effects and box-office receipts that counted. And if a movie was a hit, the studios kept remaking the story until it was worn out. Another prominent member of the film community at Woody's party was the suave movie producer David Brown, who had the dubious distinction of recently giving *Jaws 2* (1978) to the world – a film which shamelessly exploited, and thereby debased the currency of, the original, which he had also produced. Who cared that the sequel was rubbish? It was all money.

Brown was telling people how he and his partner Richard D. Zanuck were working with the author Peter Benchley again now, on an adaptation of his new novel *The Island*, which they hoped would be as big a smash as *Jaws* (which it certainly wasn't). The star of the picture was Michael Caine, who had been having dinner with Mia Farrow and Mick Jagger the fateful night that Woody and Mia met at Elaine's. And now here was Mick, sweeping into Woody's party in the very small hours with girlfriend Jerry Hall. (See picture 40.) It wasn't long since Jerry had been Bryan Ferry's partner. Bryan had put her picture on the sleeve of Roxy Music's terrific 1975 album, *Siren*, after which Roxy broke up and Jerry went off with Mick. Now Ferry had his group together again and a new disco-slick Roxy Music record was out called *Manifesto*. Wanting to keep up with the trends, Mick was also making disco part of the sound of the Rolling Stones. The band's first single of the eighties would be the bouncing disco ball 'Emotional Rescue', from the album of the same name. It surely wasn't the greatest record that the Stones had ever made, but it wasn't their worst either and at least the band was still in business.

In fact the Stones were in good shape for the decade ahead, largely due to Mick's astute business choices and an *esprit de corps* within the band that many of their fellow British rock 'n' rollers lacked. Their great rivals the Beatles were now scattered to the four winds. Despite having recently released a very successful new album in *The Wall*, there was also a fatal clash of personalities within Pink Floyd, as Mick knew. When Roger Waters left Floyd to launch his solo career, the group that had set the high watermark in progressive rock in the '70s was effectively finished. Excess had also taken its toll on the British rock community during the 1970s. When Led Zeppelin drummer

John Bonham drank himself to death in September 1980, the three surviving members of that great band would call it a day. The Who also crumbled after Keith Moon destroyed himself in 1978. Meanwhile, Mick's old friend and rival David Bowie was not the force he was, having chosen to make increasingly esoteric music. David's buddy, the innovative Lou Reed, released only one further significant studio album in the '70s, *Street Hassle* (1978), and one remarkable live album, *Take No Prisoners* (1979), which showed him both at his best and worst as a performer. But these records were a long way from the glory of *Transformer*, and indeed a reunion between Bowie and Reed around this time resulted not in *Transformer Redux* but in Lou slapping David in the face.

In fact, many luminaries of American popular music were in decline at the turn of the decade. Joni Mitchell's jazz-rock experiments, especially her most recent LP *Mingus* (1979), left most people cold, though the music continued to be exceptional. Bob Dylan enjoyed a surprise hit in 1979 with his amazing Christian rock album *Slow Train Coming*, but subsequent religious records sold poorly. As for Stevie Wonder – who had supported the Stones on tour in 1972 at a time when Stevie was turning out one brilliant LP after another – he released a concept album in 1979 called *Journey Through the Secret Life of Plants* that baffled and alienated many fans. Meanwhile, there was a new song leaping up the charts in December 1979 that would show the way forward for black music, and indeed pop in the '80s: the Sugarhill Gang with 'Rapper's Delight', the first rap record to reach a mainstream audience. Chameleon though he was, even Mick Jagger hadn't latched on to rap yet.

When Mick breezed into Woody's party in the small hours of 1 January, elegantly attired in a dinner suit, his former spouse Bianca Jagger found herself in a potentially embarrassing social situation. It was only eight years since she and Mick had married in the South of France, with Bianca wearing a white wedding suit designed by Ossie Clark (now divorced from Celia, and in dire financial straits, literally homeless since his London house had been repossessed). Mick and Bianca's divorce had come through as recently as November. Now here was Mick with Jerry at Woody's party. It was a test for even the most confident of women, but the former Mrs Jagger was equal to the challenge and went straight up to Mick and his new partner to say *Hi*. 'Bianca ran over and was charming. I don't know how she did it, but she got it over with, she broke the ice,' Andy told Miss Diary admiringly. 'She wanted to get Jerry nervous, which she did.'

At four in the morning, as waiters began to serve Woody's guests a scrambled-egg breakfast to soak up all that champagne, Andy and Bianca slipped away from the house at East 75th Street to visit the underworld of Studio 54. The club's theme for New Year was ice – ice sculptures, ice on the walls – dripping now in the small hours as the guests boogied on to the pulsating sound of Blondie. Studio 54 *looked* like the club of old, but the establishment was in serious trouble. A recent FBI raid had uncovered bundles of undeclared cash earnings on the premises, and during the ensuing criminal investigation stories had leaked to the press about drugs being supplied to celebrities at the club and important Studio 54 clients, such as Andy Warhol, receiving cash back-handers. Within the past month, Steve Rubell and his business partner had pleaded guilty in court to tax evasion charges and both were awaiting sentencing, which was due in January. 'They were hoping for some sort of community service in lieu of prison,' recalls their friend Bob Colacello. 'Building discos on naval bases was one suggestion . . .' Despite the gay banter, Warhol noticed how much had changed when he came by the club in the early hours of New Year's day. The basement had always been a peculiar place for stars to gather. In the past, Steve had attempted to make this subterranean storeroom a tad more comfortable with a scattering of cushions. This evening the basement was just plain and dirty. It was also slightly rank with the smell of garbage. And when Steve asked his friends if anybody had any cocaine, he was answered by nervous laughter, as if the FBI were listening. 'He wanted it to be like the good old days,' noted Warhol. But it wasn't. A couple of weeks later Rubell was sentenced to three years in prison for tax evasion. He was paroled early, and tried to resurrect his career, but the party of the decade was over. Studio 54 closed for good. Diagnosed HIV-positive, Rubell died in 1989.

Andy left Studio 54 at six a.m., just as Woody's party was winding up across town. The artist made one final stop at a friend's house for breakfast, before getting home as the sun was rising. He wanted a couple of hours sleep before going into the office, which he did at eleven that morning, feeling thankful that he had abstained from alcohol the night before. Warhol's head was clear, as were the streets on New Year's day, with most of the shops shut. So there were no opportunities to browse for jewels and no one to hand out copies of *Interview* to as he headed downtown. Most people were taking a day of rest, not least most of the guests who had been up all night at Woody's do. But Andy had learned long ago that creative work is a blessing – filling up a life, displacing depression and loneliness – and for that reason he worked as much as he could whenever he could. Travelling into the office on 1 January 1980, Warhol knew that the artwork he had done during the 1970s would be remembered long after all the night clubs of the decade had closed, long after even the most glamorous parties had been forgotten. Meanwhile, pictures – like books, films, music, sculpture and architecture – endure. They are how we mark and remember our lives. And Warhol was fortunate enough to be one of those individuals who had added significantly to the culture of his time, creating work that helps us all to see and understand the multi-faceted and often brilliant decade that had just passed into history. Now he was eager to explore a new age.

SOURCE NOTES

CHAPTER 1. AUSPICIOUS BEGINNINGS

Epigraph: author's interview with Bob Rafelson.

Jack Nicholson's dialogue: 'I don't know . . .' etc. *Five Easy Pieces* (1970).

Nicholson draws on his own family history to play crying scene: Nicholson's interview with *Time* magazine, 12 August 1974.

Jack Nicholson's conversation with Bob Rafelson: recalled by Rafelson in interviews with the author.

Nicholson background: author's interviews; Nicholson press interviews (including *Time*, 12 August 1974); *Jack's Life* (McGilligan); *The Films of Jack Nicholson* (Brode); *Jack Nicholson: Face to Face* (Crane and Fryer); *Jack Nicholson* (Dickens).

Nicholson's mother thought him a 'bum': in an interview quoted by Patrick McGilligan in *Jack's Life*, Nicholson says his mother 'saw me as a bum.'

All Bob Rafelson quotes: author's interviews with Rafelson. Additional background on Rafelson from *Easy Riders, Raging Bulls* (Biskind).

Dennis Hopper quotation: 'Rafelson and Bert Schneider . . .': author's interview with Hopper.

All Karen Black quotes: author's interview with Black.

Changes in attitudes to marriage and divorce in the 1970s/US divorce law: *How We Got Here: The '70s* (Frum); *Oxford Companion to United States History* (Boyer, ed.).

Nicholson's dialogue: 'What do you mean . . .' etc. *Five Easy Pieces* (1970).

CHAPTER 2. MR HOCKNEY, MR AND MRS CLARK AND PERCY

All David Hockney quotes, including the epigraph, and the remark about painting versus photography: author's interview with David Hockney.

Ossie Clark/Celia Birtwell background and Celia's quotes: author's interview with Celia Birtwell. Additional background from *The Ossie Clark Diaries* (Rous, ed.).

Hockney background: author interviews with Celia Birtwell, David Hockney, Kasmin and Peter Schlesinger; also from *Portrait of David Hockney* (Webb); *David Hockney by David Hockney.*

Kasmin quotes: author's interviews, except 'I adored . . .' which is from *Portrait of David Hockney* (Webb).

Ossie Clark quotation: 'I can't bear . . .' recalled by Celia Birtwell in interview with the author.

Ossie Clark quotation: 'like glass' from *The Ossie Clark Diaries* (Rous, ed.).

Ten most popular: BBC Radio 4 *Today* programme poll, 2005.

E.H. Gombrich quotation: 'A simple corner . . .' from *The Story of Art* (Gombrich).

History of the *Arnolfini Portrait*: *The Arnolfini Betrothal* (Hall) and *Paintings in the National Gallery* (Gentili, Barcham and Whiteley).

CHAPTER 3. AND NOW FOR SOMETHING COMPLETELY DIFFERENT

Epigraph: the 'Dead Parrot' sketch from Episode Eight of the first BBC series of *Monty Python's Flying Circus*, first broadcast in December, 1969.

Incident at the Hotel Gleneagles and dialogue with Donald Sinclair: based on the author's interview with Terry Gilliam (who established when, in the *Python* chronology, the team stayed at the hotel, differing from dates given in other published accounts). Thanks also to Ray Marks, of the Hotel Gleneagles. Background: *Cleese Encounters* (Margolis); *A Liar's Autobiography* (Chapman); and John Cleese's interview accompanying the double DVD set of *Fawlty Towers* (BBC Worldwide Ltd, 2003); also an interview with the Sinclairs published in *Daily Mail*, 20 February 1979.

Terry Gilliam quotes: author's interview with Gilliam (unless otherwise indicated).

Donald Sinclair's exchanges with Idle and Cleese: recalled by Cleese in the *Fawlty Towers* DVD documentary (BBC Worldwide Ltd, 2003).

Betty Sinclair quotation: 'They didn't fit . . .' as reported by Margolis in *Cleese Encounters*.

Graham Chapman quotations: 'The owner . . .', 'But no mincing . . .' and 'We were . . .' from *A Liar's Autobiography* (Chapman).

Python background: author's interviews; also, *The Pythons Autobiography* (McCabe, ed.); *Monty Python Encyclopaedia* (Ross); *A Liar's Autobiography* (Chapman); *Cleese Encounters* (Margolis). Also documentary films, *The Pythons* (BBC, 1979) and *It's the Monty Python Story* (BBC/A&E Network, 1999); plus various newspaper interviews.

Founding of *Gay News*: *Monty Python Encyclopaedia* (Ross).

Eric Idle quotation: 'Graham was . . .' and 'There was . . .' from *The Pythons Autobiography* (McCabe, ed.).

Graham Chapman quotation: 'I do remember . . .' from *The Pythons Autobiography* (McCabe, ed.). Also *paucity of language*.

Robert Crumb quotation: 'It was not . . .' from author's correspondence with Crumb.

Huw Weldon quote: recalled by Terry Jones in *The Pythons Autobiography* (McCabe, ed.).

'Dead Parrot' sketch: '. . . I wish to complain . . .' etc from *Monty Python's Flying Circus: Just the Words* (Wilmut, ed.).

Cleese on Jones: 'bit of a control freak' and Cleese's arrogance: from *The Pythons Autobiography* (McCabe, ed.).

Terry Gilliam quotation: 'very patronizingly . . .' *The Pythons Autobiography* (McCabe, ed.).

Ministry of Silly Walks dialogue: '*Times*, please . . .' etc from *Monty Python's Flying Circus: Just the Words* (Wilmut, ed.).

Public reaction to 'Silly Walk' sketch: *Cleese Encounters* (Margolis).

CHAPTER 4. EAST AND WEST

Epigraph: Alexander Solzhenitsyn's 1970 Nobel lecture: Nobel *e*-museum (www.nobel.se).

Isle of Wight Festival background: author's interview with organiser Ray Foulk. Also film footage of the festival, and the DVD *Blue Wild Angel: Jimi Hendrix Live at the Isle of Wight* (Experience Hendrix, 2003).

Joni Mitchell quotation: 'It looks like . . .' etc and background from *Shadows and Light: Joni Mitchell* (O'Brien).

Ossie Clark at Isle of Wight: author's interviews with Celia Birtwell.

Jimi Hendrix's comments from stage: *Blue Wild Angel: Jimi Hendrix Live at the Isle of Wight* (Experience Hendrix, 2003).

Hendrix's death: *The Encyclopaedia of Rock Obituaries* (Talevski).

Alexander Solzhenitsyn quotations: 'I put no . . .' and 'No one . . .', and conversation with the Norwegian journalist from *The Oak and the Calf* (Solzhenitsyn).

Alexander Solzhenitsyn quotation: 'Will you . . .' from *Alexander Solzhenitsyn* (Thomas).

Stalin quotation: 'blood for blood' from *Alexander Solzhenitsyn* (Thomas).

Alexander Solzhenitsyn quotations: 'Arrest! Need it . . .', 'the black maw . . .' and 'Eight years!' from *The Gulag Archipelago* (Solzhenitsyn).

250,000 died on the Belomor Canal: *The Gulag Archipelago* (Solzhenitsyn).

'Are you from freedom?': *The Gulag Archipelago* (Solzhenitsyn).

Alexander Solzhenitsyn quotation: 'I hate to think . . .' from *The Oak and the Calf* (Solzhenitsyn).

Alexander Solzhenitsyn quotations: 'And that is why . . .' and 'The grass has grown . . .' from *The Gulag Archipelago* (Solzhenitsyn).

Alexander Solzhenitsyn quotation: 'I've always been . . .' from *Solzhenitsyn: A Soul in Exile* (Pearce).

'The skilly was . . .': *One Day in the Life of Ivan Denisovich* (Solzhenitsyn).

Alexander Solzhenitsyn quotation: 'Dust off . . .' from *The Oak and the Calf* (Solzhenitsyn).

Mstislav Rostropovich quotation: 'At first . . .' from an interview in *Daily Telegraph*, 28 October 2004.

Nobel citation: 'ethical force . . .' as quoted by Pearce in *Solzhenitsyn: A Soul in Exile*.

Mstislav Rostropovich quotation: 'I know . . .' from *Solzhenitsyn: A Soul in Exile* (Pearce).

Solzhenitsyn's Nobel lecture: Nobel e-museum (www.nobel.se).

CHAPTER 5. MONUMENTAL

Epigraph: Richard Serra's *Verb List* (1967–68).

Richard Serra quotation: 'It's not going . . .' from *Richard Serra: The Coagula Interview* www.coagula.com

Serra background: *Richard Serra* (Foster); *Sculpture Magazine*, Jan./Feb. 1999; and *American Art in the Twentieth Century* (Joachimides and Rosenthal, eds).

Richard Serra quotation: 'bounced into the sea . . .' from *Richard Serra* (Foster).

'to roll, to crease . . .': Richard Serra's *Verb List* (1967–68).

Richard Serra: 'I started . . .' from *Richard Serra: The Coagula Interview* www.coagula.com

Accidents: *New York Times*, 2 May 2001; *Sculpture Magazine*, Jan./Feb. 1999.

Spiral Jetty: *A History of Modern Art* (Arnason).

Richard Serra quotation: 'sinister [place] used . . .' and dislike of modern architecture from *Richard Serra* (Foster).

Background on Minoru Yamasaki and the World Trade Center, including figures and statistics (sometimes differing from those published elsewhere), based primarily on the author's interviews with Henry Guthard of Yamasaki Associates, Inc. Background reading includes *The Seventy Architectural Wonders of Our World* (Parkyn).

TV reception affected by twin towers: *New York Times*, 24 December 1970.

St Louis Airport influenced Utzon: *Jørn Utzon: The Sydney Opera House* (Fromonot).

Yamasaki: 'Was the rose . . .' etc, as recalled by Henry Guthard.

All Henry Guthard quotations: author's interviews and correspondence with Guthard. Also Yamasaki's recalled conversation with colleagues ('One day . . . etc).

Background to World Trade Center commission/concerns of owners of Empire State Building: *Casting Giant Shadows: The Politics of Building the World Trade Center*, by Roger Cohen, first published in the winter 1990/91 issue of *Portfolio* magazine, and on the Web at www.greatbuildings.com

Tenants move into twin towers: *New York Times*, 17 December 1970.

Topping-out ceremony: *New York Times*, 24 December 1970.

US weather, 24 December 1970: Northeast Regional Climate Center at Cornell University. Also *New York Times*. UK weather, 24 December 1970: BBCi (www.bbc.co.uk).

Minoru Yamasaki quotation: 'I feel . . .' at www.greatbuildings.com

Solzhenitsyn's son born: *The Oak and the Calf* (Solzhenitsyn).

CHAPTER 6. ADAPTED FROM THE NOVEL

Epigraph: author's interview with the late Peter Benchley.

Mario Puzo quotation: '*The Godfather* is . . .' from *The Godfather Papers* (Puzo).

All Peter Benchley quotes: author's interview with Benchley.

All Frederick Forsyth quotes, and recalled conversation: author's interview with Forsyth.

Mario Puzo quotations: 'I never . . .', 'Honey . . .', 'I wished . . .' and 'That was like . . .' from *The Godfather Papers* (Puzo).

'Her hand closed around . . . ': *The Godfather* (Puzo).

Mardik Martin quotation: '[It] was really terrible . . .' from author's interview with Martin.

Robert Evans quotation: 'smell the spaghetti . . .' from *The Kid Stays in the Picture* (Evans).

Francis Ford Coppola quotation: 'hunk of trash' from *Coppola* (Cowie).

Detail on the *Notebook*: *The Making of The Godfather* documentary accompanying the 2001 DVD box-set edition of the three *Godfather* films.

All Gordon Willis quotes: author's correspondence with Willis.

'Michael spoke very quickly . . .': *The Godfather* (Puzo).

'"You know my father? . . ."': *The Godfather* (1971).

Puzo first sends the book to Brando: *Songs My Mother Taught Me* (Brando).

Francis Ford Coppola quotation: 'People had . . .' in *Imagine: Brando* television documentary (BBC-TV, 2004).

Stanley Jaffe quote: recalled by Francis Coppola in *Imagine: Brando* documentary (BBC-TV, 2004).

Jack Nicholson quotation: 'my only real . . .' from *Time* magazine, 12 August 1974.

Brando, 'of a bulldog': as recalled by Coppola in *The Making of The Godfather* documentary. Also 'This was Sonny . . .'

Altercation with Willis as reported in *Francis Ford Coppola* (Schumacher) and elsewhere. (Willis confirms that there was an incident, and that Coppola tore his office door from its hinges, but says he does not recall saying, 'You don't know how to do anything right!')

Francis Ford Coppola quotation: 'That film made me . . .' in *Imagine: Brando* documentary (BBC-TV, 2004).

Frederick Forsyth's conversations with Harold Harris: recalled by Forsyth in an interview with the author.

Peter Benchley quotations, and recalled conversation with his editor: author's interview with Benchley. Additional Benchley background: *People*, 15 April 1974.

CHAPTER 7. WOMEN OF THE YEAR

Epigraph: Germaine Greer as quoted in *Diane Arbus: A Biography* (Bosworth).

Diane Arbus background: author's interview and correspondence with Allan Arbus; *Diane Arbus: Revelations* (Estate of Diane Arbus, eds); *Diane Arbus: A Biography* (Bosworth); and *Diane Arbus: Family Albums* (Lee and Pultz).

All Allan Arbus quotes: author's interview and correspondence with Mr Arbus.

Diane Arbus quotation: 'Most people go through . . .' in *Newsweek*, 20 March 1967, reproduced in *Diane Arbus* (Bosworth).

Dennis Hopper quotation: 'she'd just . . .' from author's interview with Hopper.

Conversation in Central Park: *Diane Arbus* (Bosworth).

'shaved and deodorized . . .' etc: *The Female Eunuch* (Greer).

Diane Arbus quotations: 'I'm a photographer . . .' and 'You know . . .' from *Diane Arbus* (Bosworth).

Norman Mailer quotes, and his recalled conversation: author's interview with Mailer (except where indicated).

Norman Mailer quotation: 'low, sloppy beasts' from *Mailer: A Biography* (Mills).

Norman Mailer quotation: 'He grinned broadly . . .' from *The Prisoner of Sex* (Mailer).

1971 Town Hall debate: film of event; *Mailer: A Biography* (Mills); *Mailer* (Manso).

Germaine Greer quotation: 'It developed . . .' from *Diane Arbus: A Biography* (Bosworth).

Diane Arbus quotations: 'fun and terrific . . .' and 'They cry . . .' from *Diane Arbus: Revelations* (Estate of Diane Arbus, eds).

Diane Arbus quotation: 'My work . . .' from *Diane Arbus: A Biography* (Bosworth).

Death of Diane Arbus: author's interview with Allan Arbus; *Diane Arbus: Revelations* (Estate of Diane Arbus, eds); and *Diane Arbus: A Biography* (Bosworth). Also 1972 show attendance.

CHAPTER 8. SEX AND FEAR AND LOATHING

Epigraph: *Fear and Loathing in Las Vegas* (Thompson).

'All the vulgar . . .': *The Female Eunuch* (Greer).

Frederick Forsyth quotation: 'They're awful . . .' from author's interview with Forsyth.

All John Updike quotes: correspondence with author.

'Harry, I'm sorry . . .': *Rabbit Redux* (Updike).

Richard Locke quotation: 'Updike was always there . . .' in *New York Times Book Review*, 14 November 1971.

All Jann Wenner quotes: author's interview with Wenner. Additional background on Wenner and *Rolling Stone*: *The Rolling Stone Story* (Draper).

Norman Mailer quotation: 'Tom Wolfe and I . . .' from author's interview with Mailer.

Tom Wolfe quotation: 'Over the past . . .' from *The New Journalism* (Wolfe).

Background on Hunter S. Thompson: author's interviews; *Hunter S. Thompson* (McKeen).

Doctor of Divinity: Thompson obituary in *Daily Telegraph*, 22 February, 2005.

Jann Wenner: 'Look, I . . .' from *Hunter S. Thompson* (McKeen).

Hunter S. Thompson quotation: 'writing could be . . .' from *The Rolling Stone Story* (Draper).

All Ralph Steadman quotes: author's interviews with Steadman. Also dialogue with *Scanlon's* editor, and Thompson.

'fear and loathing . . .' and 'We Can . . .': *The Kentucky Derby is Decadent and Depraved* (Thompson).

'If the Pigs . . .': *Fear and Loathing in Las Vegas* (Thompson).

Writing of *Fear and Loathing in Las Vegas*: author's interviews, and *The Great Shark Hunt* (Thompson).

Sandra Thompson quotation: 'It was a very . . .' from *Hunter* (Carroll).

Terry Gilliam quotation: 'That's what . . .' from author's interview with Gilliam.

CHAPTER 9. QUEER AS . . .

Epigraph: dialogue from *A Clockwork Orange* (1971).

Sonnabend opening: author's correspondence with Ileana Sonnabend and Antonio Homem; *Gilbert & George: The Singing Sculpture* (Ratcliff and

Rosenblum); *Gilbert & George: A Portrait* (Farson); *New York Times*, 27 September 1971; *The Village Voice*, 12–18 July 2000; *The New Yorker*, 9 October 1971.

Mrs Castelli and Douglas Davis quotes, and G&G explanation: *The New Yorker*, 9 October 1971.

'Underneath the Arches': Flanagan & Allen, 1932.

Gilbert quotation: 'love at first . . .' from *Gilbert & George: A Portrait* (Farson). Also George's marriage.

St Martin's background: documentary film *Art and The '60s* (BBC-TV, 2004); *Gilbert & George: A Portrait* (Farson).

Caro and tutor: *Gilbert & George: A Portrait* (Farson).

Drunkenness and footnote quote (Gilbert's): *Gilbert & George: A Portrait* (Farson).

'So do contact . . .': reported in *Guardian*, 20 November 1970.

Kasmin quote: author's interview with Kasmin.

Peter Schlesinger quotes: author's interviews with Schlesinger.

David Hockney quote: author's interview with Hockney.

Guardian review: 20 November 1970.

George Melly story: *Gilbert & George: A Portrait* (Farson).

Antonio Homem quotation: 'The public in New York . . .' from author's correspondence with Homem.

'atrocious': *Studio International*, November 1971.

Biggest figure they could think of: *Gilbert & George: A Portrait* (Farson).

Gilbert and George's answer-machine message: as of 27/7/04.

Bob Moog/synthesizer background: author's correspondence with Moog (also Moog quotes); profile of the late Dr Moog 25 April 2000, by Frank Houston published on the Internet at salon.com; and *Rolling Stone*, 13 February 1975.

Robbie Robertson: 'It seemed . . .' from *Down the Highway: The Life of Bob Dylan* (Sounes).

Led Zeppelin's use of theremin: *Hammer of the Gods* (Davis).

Walter Carlos background: author's correspondence with Dr Moog; *Analog Days* (Pinch and Trocco); also www.biographybase.com, and www.wendy-carlos.com

TONTO: author's interviews with Robert Margouleff and Malcolm Cecil.

Who's Next background: *Dear Boy* (Fletcher); *The Who: Maximum R&B* (Barnes); and the DVD documentary *Classic Albums: Who's Next* (Classic Albums, 1999).

Background to Anthony Burgess' *A Clockwork Orange*: various articles including *Independent*, 2 December 1999; *Times Saturday Review*, 30 January 1993.

Anthony Burgess quotation: 'good to Alex . . .' in *Rolling Stone*, 8 June 1972.

Anthony Burgess quotation: 'The question was . . .' in *Observer*, 21 March 1993.

Si Litvinoff involvement: author's interview with Litvinoff.

Nic Roeg's involvement in *A Clockwork Orange* and quote: author's interview with Roeg.

Location filming: *Stanley Kubrick* (Baxter).

Architecture of Thamesmead: *The Buildings of England: London 2: South* (Cherry & Pevsner, eds).

Architecture of the Jaffe House: *Richard Rogers: Complete Works: Volume 1.* (Powell).

'Viddy well . . .': *A Clockwork Orange* (1971)

John Lydon quotation: 'Arsenal went Clockwork' from author's interview with Lydon.

Palmer case: *Daily Express*, 4 July 1973.

Pensioner beaten: *Daily Telegraph*, 20 November 1973.

Lancashire rape: *Times Saturday Review*, 30 January 1993.

Kubrick's decision to withdraw the movie: *Daily Telegraph*, 4 March 2000.

CHAPTER 10. STEVIE AND THE STONES

Epigraph: Stevie Wonder interview in *Rolling Stone*, 26 April 1973.

All Malcom Cecil and Robert Margouleff quotes, and recalled dialogue with Stevie Wonder and others: author's interviews with Cecil and Margouleff.

Stevie Wonder background: author's interviews; *Stevie Wonder* (Davis); *Rolling Stone*, 26 April 1973; and an article by Joel Selvin published in *Mojo*, April 2003.

Stevie Wonder quotation: 'I wanted . . .' in *Rolling Stone*, 26 April 1973.

Wonder tried marijuana, but it made his head feel 'tight': author's interview with Margouleff.

Stevie Wonder quotation: 'It's the same . . .' in *Rolling Stone*, 26 April 1973.

Bobbye Hall: I have drawn on my interview with Hall for my book *Down the Highway: The Life of Bob Dylan*.

In his remarks, Malcolm Cecil quotes from the lyric to Stevie Wonder's song 'Big Brother' (Jobete Music/Black Bull Music 1972).

Jann Wenner quotation: 'The Stones were brilliant . . .' from author's interview with Wenner.

Rolling Stones' move to France: *Symphony for the Devil* (Norman).

Mick Jagger quotations: 'The thing about . . .' and 'I'd love to . . .' from *According to the Rolling Stones* (Loewenstein and Dodd, eds). Also Keith Richard's quotation, 'The point is that . . .'

Mick Jagger quotation: 'scared shitless' from *Symphony for the Devil* (Norman).

Wolfman Jack quote and staging of the 1972 tour: *Rolling Stone*, 6 July 1972.

Cocksucker Blues: *Guardian*, 9 October 2004, and *The Rolling Stone Illustrated History of Rock 'n' Roll* (Miller, ed.).

CHAPTER 11. THE TRANSFORMERS

Epigraph: Lou Reed interview published in *New Musical Express Greatest Hits, 1975* (Scott, ed.).

Rainbow show: author's interviews; various reviews; www.5years.com

All John Lydon quotes: author's interviews with Lydon.

Chris Thomas background and quotes: author's interview with Thomas.

Angie Bowie background and quotes: author's interviews with Angie Bowie (unless otherwise stated).

David Bowie background: author's interviews; *Strange Fascination* (Buckley); *Backstage Passes* (Bowie).

Angie Bowie quotation: 'the best-known . . .' from *Backstage Passes* (Bowie)

Background on recording Bowie and Reed at Trident and Ken Scott quotes: author's interview with Scott.

Lou Reed background: *Lou Reed* (Bockris).

David Bowie discussion with William Burroughs: 'The time is . . .' in *Rolling Stone*, 28 February 1974.

Trip to New York: *Backstage Passes* (Bowie).

Meeting with Warhol: author's interviews with former Warhol employees; Bowie's dialogue with Warhol as recalled by Bowie in an interview in *Rolling Stone*, 28 February 1974; also *Backstage Passes* (Bowie).

Andy Warhol quotation: 'Can he use . . .' from *Holy Terror* (Colacello).

Transformer background: author's interview with Ken Scott; also the DVD documentary *Lou Reed: Transformer* (Classic Albums, 2001).

Lou Reed recalls Warhol saying 'It would be so . . .': *New Musical Express Greatest Hits, 1975.* (Scott, ed.)

David Bowie quotation: 'Lou's really got . . .' in *Rolling Stone*, 8 June 1972.

David Bowie quotation: 'I'm gay and always . . .' in *Melody Maker*, 22 January 1972.

Dana Gillespie quotation: 'He was always . . .' from author's interview with Gillespie.

Charles Shaar Murray review: *New Musical Express*, 26 August 1972.

Alexander Stuart review, *Plays and Players*, November 1972.

Elton John remark: recalled by Ken Scott in interview with the author.

CHAPTER 12. DOWN THE MEAN STREETS

Epigraph: Robert Towne's screenplay of *Chinatown*, as published by Faber & Faber.

Jonathan Taplin meeting with Scorsese and all Taplin quotes: author's interview and correspondence with Taplin.

Background on Martin Scorsese: author's interviews, including interviews with Mardik Martin and Jonathan Taplin. Background material: *Scorsese on Scorsese* (Christie and Thompson, eds); *Martin Scorsese Interviews* (Brunette, ed.).

Mardik Martin background and quotes: author's interview with Martin.

Raymond Chandler quotation: *The Simple Art of Murder* (Chandler).

Conversation between Scorsese and Spielberg about the ocean: *Easy Riders, Raging Bulls* (Biskind).

LA acting group: author's interviews with Richard Romanus and Jonathan Taplin.

Robert De Niro background, and Scorsese's quote about De Niro: 'We were both . . .' from *De Niro: A Biography* (Baxter).

All Richard Romanus quotes: author's interview with Romanus.

Martin Scorsese quotation: 'I played on it . . .' from *Scorsese on Scorsese* (Christie and Thompson, eds).

Voice-over 'You don't make up . . .': *Mean Streets* (1973).

Brando dialogue: 'A name? . . .' from *Last Tango in Paris* (1972)

Marlon Brando's background and quotations: 'I felt I had . . .' and 'In subsequent pictures . . .' from *Songs My Mother Taught Me* (Brando).

Rock Around the Block: recalled by Candy Clark in interview with the author.

Francis Coppola quotation: 'You'll see . . .' from *Easy Riders, Raging Bulls* (Biskind).

Candy Clark quotation: 'It kind of . . .' from author's interview with Clark.

Selling *Mean Streets* and quotes: author's interview and correspondence with Taplin.

Background on *Chinatown*: author's interviews; *Roman* (Polanski); *Jack Nicholson* (Dickens); *Jack's Life* (McGilligan); *The Films of Jack Nicholson* (Brode); *The Kid Stays in the Picture* (Evans); *Looking For Gatsby: My Life* (Dunaway); and the documentary accompanying the 2004 DVD of *Chinatown*.

Robert Towne quotation: 'temperament, his manner . . .' on *Chinatown* DVD.

Evans discussion with Towne, etc: *The Kid Stays in the Picture* (Evans).

'as little as possible': recalled by Towne on *Chinatown* DVD.

Roman Polanski quotation: 'Unlike Bob Evans . . .' from *Roman* (Polanski).

Faye Dunaway's wardrobe: author's interview with *Chinatown* costume designer Anthea Sylbert.

Robert Evans quotation: 'World War III . . .' from *The Kid Stays in the Picture* (Evans).

Dreaded Dunaway: *Looking for Gatsby: My Life* (Dunaway).

Restaurant row: *Roman* (Polanski); *Looking For Gatsby: My Life* (Dunaway); and *Jack's Life* (McGilligan).

Faye Dunaway quotation: 'I don't believe . . .' from *Roman* (Polanski).

Polanski's chess analogy: *Jack's Life* (McGilligan).

Polanski on Nicholson: 'and he's . . .' from *Roman* (Polanski). Also Roman Polanski quotation, 'Know what you . . .'

Jack Nicholson quotation: 'One of the . . .' from *The Films of Jack Nicholson* (Brode).

Noah Cross dialogue: 'I don't blame myself . . .' *Chinatown* (1974). Also: 'Forget it, Jake . . .'

Robert Towne barred: *The Kid Stays in the Picture* (Evans).

Polanski on the ending: *Chinatown* DVD documentary.

CHAPTER 13. THE SYDNEY OPERA HOUSE

Epigraph: Jørn Utzon as quoted in *Jørn Utzon: The Sydney Opera House* (Fromonot).

Sydney Opera House opening ceremony: author's interviews; various press reports, including the *Sun-Herald*'s Special Opera House Souvenir Issue, 21 October 1973.

Queen's speech as published in *Sydney Morning Herald*, 22 October 1973.

Background on the Opera House competition, design and construction: author's interviews with Michael Lewis and Sir Jack Zunz, both formerly of Ove Arup & Partners; and Peter Myers, formerly of Jørn Utzon's office. Background reading: *The Saga of the Sydney Opera House* (Murray); *Jørn Utzon: The Sydney Opera House* (Fromonot); *Sydney Opera House* (Drew); *The Arup Journal*, October 1973 issue.

Robert Hughes remark: *The Saga of the Sydney Opera House* (Murray).

Utzon win announced: *Sydney Morning Herald*, 30 January 1957.

Frank Lloyd Wright's appraisal: 'This circus tent . . .' in the (Sydney) *Sun*, 26 February 1957.

Mies van der Rohe's reaction: *The Saga of the Sydney Opera House* (Murray).

All Jack Zunz quotes: author's interviews with Sir Jack.

All Peter Myers quotes: author's interview with Myers.

Jørn Utzon quotation 'I've solved it!': as recalled by Sir Jack Zunz in an interview with the author.

Mick Lewis quotes: author's interview with Lewis (unless otherwise indicated).

Richard Meier quotation: 'White has always been . . .' from *Building the Getty* (Meier).

Françoise Fromonot quotation: 'the pale violet . . .' from *Jørn Utzon: The Sydney Opera House* (Fromonot).

Bricked-up: *The Saga of the Sydney Opera House* (Murray). Also Zunz.

Lewis' exasperating conversation with Utzon: recalled by Lewis in author's interview.

Utzon's 'resignation' announced: *Sydney Morning Herald*, 1 March 1966.

Mick Lewis quotation: 'a grain of . . .' from *The Saga of the Sydney Opera House* (Murray). Also Lis Utzon's quotation, '. . . please do not . . .'

Utzon's recent work on the renovations to the Opera House: *Guardian*, 10 October 2005, and www.sydneyoperahouse.com

Jørn Utzon quotation 'the Sydney Opera . . .': card to Ove Arup quoted in *The Saga of the Sydney Opera House* (Murray).

Frank Gehry has said 'without [Utzon's] vision, there would hardly be the Guggenheim in Bilbao today': *The Saga of the Sydney Opera House* (Murray).

CHAPTER 14. EXILE

Epigraph: a retort to reporters in Switzerland in 1974, as quoted by D.M. Thomas in his superb biography, *Alexander Solzhenitsyn: A Century in His Life*.

Primary sources for Alexander Solzhenitsyn: *The Oak and the Calf* (Solzhenitsyn); *Alexander Solzhenitsyn: A Century in His Life* (Thomas); *Solzhenitsyn: A Soul in Exile* (Pearce); and contemporaneous press reports.

The 'Solzhenitsyn problem': a Kremlin memorandum quoted by Thomas in his book *Alexander Solzhenitsyn: A Century in His Life*. Also the alleged assassination attempt.

All Solzhenitsyn quotes and dialogue with others are from *The Oak and the Calf* (unless otherwise indicated).

Natalya Reshetovskaya quotation: 'I was never . . .' – *Alexander Solzhenitsyn: A Century in His Life* (Thomas).

'the jerkiness of the book . . .' etc: *The Gulag Archipelago* (Solzhenitsyn).

Leonid Brezhnev quotation: 'Solzhenitsyn is becoming . . .' from *Alexander Solzhenitsyn: A Century in His Life* (Thomas). Also Solzhenitsyn to reporters.

Baryshnikov's defection: *Chronicle of the 20th Century* (Mercer, ed.).

Professor Ronald Grigor Suny (Department of Political Science, University of Chicago) quotes: correspondence with author.

Professor Stephen G. Wheatcroft (Department of History, University of Melbourne) quotes: correspondence with author. Also 650,000 shot.

Bob Marley background: author's interview with Chris Blackwell; *Catch a Fire* (White); the DVD documentary *Catch a Fire* (Classic Albums, 1999); *No Woman, No Cry: My Life with Bob Marley* (Rita Marley); and various press reports.

Bob Marley quotation: 'There is something . . .' from *Catch a Fire* (White).

All Rita Marley quotes: *No Woman, No Cry: My Life with Bob Marley* (Marley).

Bob Marley quotations: 'When you smoke . . .' and 'War and peace . . .' in *Rolling Stone*, 11 September 1975.

Haile Selassie visits Jamaica: *Catch a Fire* (White).

All Chris Blackwell quotes: author's interview with Blackwell.

Bunny Wailer quotation: 'a hard driving rhythm . . .' in the documentary *Classic Albums: Catch a Fire* (Classic Albums, 1999).

Recording of 'Boogie on Reggae Woman': *Analog Days* (Pinch and Trocco).

CHAPTER 15. GOOD GRIEF!

Epigraph: A White House spokesman parodied in a May 1973 *Doonesbury* strip, reproduced in *Flashback: Twenty-Five Years of Doonesbury* (Trudeau).

Charles Schulz: author's interview and correspondence with the cartoonist's widow, Mrs Jean Schulz; *Peanuts Jubilee: My Life and Art with Charlie Brown and Others* (Schulz); and *Good Grief: The Story of Charles M. Schulz* (Grimsley Johnson).

All Jean Schulz quotes: author's interview with Mrs Schulz.

Charles M. Schulz quotations: 'I can think . . .', 'The idea of . . .' and 'I deal in . . .' from *Good Grief: The Story of Charles M. Schulz* (Grimsley Johnson).

Charles M. Schulz quotations: 'The initial . . .', 'combination of . . .' and 'I do not . . .' – *Peanuts Jubilee: My Life and Art with Charlie Brown and Others* (Schulz).

Charles M. Schulz quotation: 'I've never done . . .' – 1988 interview with Michael Barrier, www.michaelbarrier.com

G.B. Trudeau background: *Flashback: Twenty-Five Years of Doonesbury* (Trudeau); *The Doonesbury Chronicles* (Trudeau); *Contemporary Authors*; *Time* cover story (9 February 1976); *Newsweek* cover story (15 October 1990); also www.amuniversal.com and www.doonesbury.com

Al Capp quotation: 'Anybody who can . . .' from *Flashback: Twenty-Five Years of Doonesbury* (Trudeau).

Phred quotation: 'I hope you can live . . .' in a 1972 *Doonesbury* strip published in *Flashback: Twenty-Five Years of Doonesbury* (Trudeau).

Joan Caucus quotation: 'At the end of the meal . . .' in a 1972 *Doonesbury* strip published in *The Doonesbury Chronicles* (Trudeau).

Washington Post pulls May 1973 strip, and explanation: *Guilty, Guilty, Guilty* (Trudeau).

Uncle Duke is introduced: 'What's he like?' etc: *The Doonesbury Chronicles* (Trudeau).

Hunter S. Thompson quotation: 'There was not a . . .' and his political reporting from *The Great Shark Hunt* (Thompson).

Hunter S. Thompson quotation: '. . . I heard them . . .' from *Flashback: Twenty-Five Years of Doonesbury* (Trudeau).

President Ford quotation: 'There are only . . .' from *The Doonesbury Chronicles* (Trudeau). Also Garry Wills' comment, 'The strip says . . .'

Pulitzer prize: www.pulitzer.org

CHAPTER 16. WATERSHED

Epigraph: one of the original theatrical trailers for *Jaws*.

Background material for *Jaws*: author's interviews with the late Peter Benchley and Carl Gottlieb. Additional material: *The Jaws Log* (Gottlieb); *The Making of Jaws* (Universal, 2000) documentary, produced for the 25th anniversary of the film.

All Peter Benchley quotes, and recalled dialogue: author's interview with Benchley (unless otherwise stated).

Richard D. Zanuck quotation: 'We both read it . . .' from *The Making of Jaws* (Universal, 2000).

Richard D. Zanuck quotation: 'The first thing . . .', recalled by Peter Benchley in interview with the author.

Steven Spielberg quotation: 'I didn't know what that meant . . .' from *The Making of Jaws* (Universal, 2000).

'things with teeth' and Steven Spielberg's quotation: 'I didn't know who I was . . .' from *Easy Riders, Raging Bulls* (Biskind).

David Brown quotation: 'Everything that could go wrong . . .' from *The Making of Jaws* (Universal, 2000).

Quint's speech 'Eleven hundred men . . .': *Jaws* (1975).

All Carl Gottlieb quotes: author's interview with Gottlieb.

Steven Spielberg quotation: 'in alphabetical order' and Peter Benchley's response in the *LA Times*: as reported by Gottlieb in his *Jaws Log*.

Brody dialogue 'You're gonna need . . .': *Jaws* (1975).

Richard Dreyfuss quotation: 'turkey' from *Easy Riders, Raging Bulls* (Biskind).

'None of man's fantasies . . .': original theatrical trailer.

Andy Warhol story and quote: related by Warhol associate Vincent Fremont in an interview with the author.

Spielberg visits cinema in Hollywood: author's interview with Gottlieb.

CHAPTER 17. CENTREPIECE

Epigraph: Dylan's question to his bass player Rob Stoner, when informed that Bruce Springsteen was coming to see him in concert in November 1975. As recalled by Stoner in an interview with the author. NB: For the sections of this chapter concerning Bob Dylan, I have drawn on interviews conducted for my 2001 biography of Dylan, *Down the Highway: The Life of Bob Dylan.*

Bob Dylan to Ramblin' Jack Elliott: 'I'm gonna . . .' recalled by Elliott in an interview with the author (as above).

David Mansfield quotation: 'voracious, although . . .' from author's interview with Mansfield (as above).

Allen Ginsberg's admiration for Dylan's lyrics: Larry Sloman's liner notes for the CD *The Bootleg Series Vol. 5: Bob Dylan Live 1975: The Rolling Thunder Revue*; also *Rolling Stone*, 15 January 1976.

Lyric 'We're idiots, babe': 'Idiot Wind' by Bob Dylan (Ram's Horn Music, 1975).

Jon Landau's *Rolling Stone* review of *Blood on the Tracks*: as reported in *Bob Dylan: Behind the Shades – Take Two* (Heylin).

All Jacques Levy quotations: author's interview with Levy (as per introductory note).

Larry Poons' quotation: author's interview with Poons (as above).

Sam Shepard quotation: 'TV sets flashing . . .' from *Rolling Thunder Logbook* (Shepard).

Sam Shepard quotation: 'One impression . . .' from author's interview with Shepard (as per introductory note).

Rob Stoner quotation: author's interview with Stoner (as above).

Joni Mitchell background: *Shadows and Light: Joni Mitchell* (O'Brien); the TV documentary, *Joni Mitchell: A Woman of Heart and Mind* (Eagle Rock Entertainment, 2003).

Stephen Holden's review of *Summer Lawns*: *Rolling Stone*, 15 January 1976.

Prince's liking for *Summer Lawns*: *Shadows and Light* (O'Brien).

Lyric 'I've had no one over me': 'Don't Interrupt the Sorrow' by Joni Mitchell (Warner Brothers Music Ltd, 1975).

Lyric 'working cheap': 'The Boho Dance' by Joni Mitchell (Warner Brothers Music Ltd, 1975).

Lyric 'the hissing of summer lawns': 'The Hissing of Summer Lawns' by John Guerin and Joni Mitchell (Warner Brothers Music Ltd, 1975).

Lyric 'like a dragonfly on a tomb': 'Harry's House' by Joni Mitchell (Warner Brothers Music Ltd, 1975).

Paul Simon's home: *Rolling Stone*, 23 September 1976.

Bob Dylan quotation: 'Who's this guy, *Springfield*?' recalled by Rob Stoner in interview with the author.

Jon Landau's review in the *Boston Real Paper*, as reported in *The Mansion on the Hill* (Goodman).

Jon Landau quotation: '*great* rock 'n' roll . . .' from author's conversation with Landau.

Advertisement for *Born to Run*: *Rolling Stone*, 20 November 1975.
Gold and platinum records: www.riaa.com

CHAPTER 18. SPACED-OUT

Epigraph: author's interview with Nic Roeg.

Bowie on stage in 1976: *Strange Fascination* (Buckley); *RAM* magazine (March 1976); *Hit Parader* (August, 1976); *Rolling Stone* (12 February and 11 March 1976).

David Bowie quotation: 'I think I might have . . .' in *Rolling Stone*, 12 February 1976.

All Nic Roeg quotes: author's interview with Roeg. Background on the making of *The Man Who Fell to Earth*: author's interviews with Candy Clark, Buck Henry, Nic Roeg and Si Litvinoff. Also the DVD documentary *Watching the Alien* (Blue Underground, Inc., 2002).

Walter Tevis background: *My Life with The Hustler* (Griggs Tevis). My thanks also to Tevis enthusiast Kacey Kowars.

'He was not a man . . .': *The Man Who Fell to Earth* (Tevis).

Jann Wenner quotes: author's interview with Wenner.

Stephen Ostrow and his club: *Rolling Stone*, 6 May 1976.

Angie Bowie quotes: author's interview with Angie Bowie. Except 'a dark, horrible house' from *Backstage Passes* (Bowie).

Bowie quotation: 'Let me know when you want me' recalled by Roeg in interview with the author.

Candy Clark quotes: author's interview with Clark.

Dialogue 'somewhere down there . . .' and 'I think Mr Newton . . .': *The Man Who Fell to Earth* (1976).

Si Litvinoff quote: author's interview with Litvinoff.

Buck Henry quote: author's interview with Henry.

Background on *Star Wars*: George Lucas interview for the 1995 video edition; *George Lucas* (Baxter). Also, Harrison Ford's quotation 'You can type . . .'

CHAPTER 19. APOCALYPSE NOW

Epigraph: *The Nigger of the 'Narcissus'* (Conrad).

Background on the making of *Apocalypse Now*: author's interviews with Frederic Forrest and Dennis Hopper; *Notes* (Eleanor Coppola); *Coppola* (Cowie); *Francis Ford Coppola* (Schumacher); *Songs My Mother Taught Me* (Brando); *George Lucas: A Biography* (Baxter); and the documentary movie *Hearts of Darkness* (1991).

Sofia Coppola quotation: 'It looks like . . .' from *Notes* (Eleanor Coppola).

Also Eleanor Coppola's quotation, 'Francis feels frustrated . . .'

All Frederic Forrest quotes: author's interviews with Forrest (who also recalled his conversation with Monty Cox, with Coppola, and Brando's comments on set, 'meat rack.')

Sam Bottoms' drug use: as interviewed for the documentary *Hearts of Darkness*.

Dean Tavoularis quotation: 'We sat around . . .' from *Coppola* (Cowie).

Martin Sheen's state of health and quotes: 'I was in a chaotic . . .' etc in *Hearts of Darkness*.

Dennis Hopper background, quotes and recalled conversation with Brando and Coppola: author's interview with Hopper.

Marlon Brando quotation 'I lied . . .': *Notes* (Coppola).

Marlon Brando quotation 'simply didn't make . . .': *Songs My Mother Taught Me* (Brando).

Francis Coppola quotation 'This film is a . . .': *Hearts of Darkness*.

'enthusiastic, fabulous' and subsequent quotes from the Penguin edition of *Heart of Darkness* (Conrad).

Hopper's dialogue: 'Sometimes he goes too far . . .' in *Apocalypse Now* (1979).

James Guetti quote: the introduction to the 1973 Penguin edition of Conrad's *Heart of Darkness*.

Dialogue 'The horror! The horror!': *Apocalypse Now* (1979). And Hopper dialogue, 'This is the way . . .'

Marlon Brando quotations: 'I made it all up . . .' and 'It was probably . . .' from *Songs My Mother Taught Me* (Brando).

CHAPTER 20. THE FILTH AND THE FURY

Epigraph: As quoted in *England's Dreaming* (Savage).

Social and economic events in 1976: *Chronicle of the 20th Century* (Mercer, ed.).

The Sex Pistols background: author's interviews with John Lydon and others; *England's Dreaming* (Savage); *I Was a Teenage Sex Pistol* (Matlock); *No Irish, No Blacks, No Dogs* (Lydon); *The Sex Pistols Diary* (Woods). Also the *Classic Albums* making-of DVD *Never Mind the Bollocks* (Eagle Rock Entertainment, 2002); and the TV documentary *Blood on the Turntables* (BBC, 2004).

Glen Matlock quotation: 'It was horrible . . .' from *I Was a Teenage Sex Pistol* (Matlock).

Malcolm McLaren quotation: 'a pistol, a gun . . .' in *England's Dreaming* (Savage).

Malcolm McLaren quotation: 'And in walked . . .' in *Blood on the Turntables* (BBC, 2004).

John Lydon quotation 'hilarious good fun': *No Irish, No Blacks, No Dogs* (Lydon).

John Lydon quotation 'Like an outta tune violin': recalled by McLaren in *Blood on the Turntables* (BBC, 2004).

John Lydon quotations: 'That might as well . . .' etc from author's interviews with Lydon (all further Lydon quotes from these interviews unless otherwise stated).

John Lydon quotation 'I can see bits . . .': *No Irish, No Blacks, No Dogs* (Lydon).

Glen Matlock quotation: 'He was John Rotten . . .' from *I Was a Teenage Sex Pistol* (Matlock).

Steve Jones quotation: 'You're fucking rotten' from *No Irish, No Blacks, No Dogs* (Lydon).

Vivienne Westwood quotation: 'That's not the John . . .' as recalled by Malcolm McLaren in *Blood on the Turntables* (BBC, 2004).

Malcolm McLaren quotation 'He was a sex symbol . . .': *Never Mind the Bollocks* DVD (Eagle Rock Entertainment, 2002).

John Lydon background and quotes: author's interviews with Lydon, unless otherwise stated.

Steve Jones quotations: 'He was always washing . . .' and 'Beatles' chords' from *Never Mind the Bollocks* DVD (Eagle Rock Entertainment, 2002).

Glen Matlock quotation 'a blank, vacant . . .': *I Was a Teenage Sex Pistol* (Matlock).

John Lydon quotation 'We didn't do it . . .': *No Irish, No Blacks, No Dogs* (Lydon).

Dave Robinson and pub rock: author's interview with Robinson.

Graham Parker background and quotes: author's correspondence with Parker. Also a 'whole new thing'.

Joe Strummer quotation 'The difference was . . .': *England's Dreaming* (Savage). Background source: *The Clash: The Last Gang in Town* (Gray).

TV Smith quotations: author's interview with Smith.

All Chris Thomas quotations: author's interview with Thomas.

Today producer quotation: 'to find out why . . .' from *The Q/Omnibus Press Rock 'n' Roll Reader* (Kelly, ed.).

Exchange with Bill Grundy: videotape of the *Today* show, 1 December 1976.

Dropped at a tube station: author's interview with Lydon.

CHAPTER 21. GARY GILMORE'S EYES

Epigraph: from Gary Gilmore's prison correspondence, as reported by Norman Mailer in *The Executioner's Song*.

All John Lydon quotes: author's interviews with Lydon.

Sex Pistols section of this chapter: author's interviews; *The Sex Pistols Diary* (Wood); *England's Dreaming* (Savage); *I Was a Teenage Sex Pistol* (Matlock); *No Irish, No Blacks, No Dogs* (Lydon). Also the *Classic Albums* making of *Never Mind the Bollocks* DVD (Eagle Rock Entertainment, 2002), and the TV documentary *Blood on the Turntables* (BBC, 2004).

Malcolm McLaren quotation 'I keep walking . . .': *The Sex Pistols Diary* (Wood).

All TV Smith quotes: author's interview with Smith.

Stiff Records: author's interview with Dave Robinson.

The Clash background: *The Clash: The Last Gang in Town* (Gray); *Uncut Presents The Clash* (A special edition of *Uncut* magazine published in 2003).

Glen Matlock's mum: *England's Dreaming* (Savage).

All Chris Thomas quotes: author's interview with Thomas.

Lyric 'fucking bloody mess . . .': 'Bodies' by the Sex Pistols (Sex Pistols Residuals, 1977).

Lyrics 'no future', 'England's Dreaming' and 'God save your mad parade': 'God Save the Queen' by the Sex Pistols (Sex Pistols Residuals, 1977).

Jamie Reid graphics: author's interview with Reid.

Graham Parker quotation: author's correspondence with Parker.

Gary Gilmore section of this chapter: author's interviews with Norman Mailer and Larry Schiller (all quotes); *The Executioner's Song* (Mailer); *Shot in the Heart* (Mikal Gilmore). Additional background from *Mailer* (Manso), and *Mailer* (Mills).

Gary Gilmore quotation 'I hope they execute . . .': *The Executioner's Song* (Mailer).

Schiller and the Manson trial: *Helter Skelter* (Bugliosi). (In an interview with the author, Schiller spoke about how he had 'fucked' this story.)

FUCK, SHIT, PISS: *The Executioner's Song* (Mailer).

Mikal Gilmore on 'Gary Gilmore's Eyes': *Shot in the Heart* (Gilmore).

'Outside the prison . . .': *The Executioner's Song* (Mailer).

CHAPTER 22. INSIDE OUT/OUTSIDE IN

Epigraph: President Pompidou as quoted by Bryan Appleyard in his book *Richard Rogers*.

The Pompidou Centre sources include, primarily, the author's interview with Lord Rogers. Philippe Lê, an architect on the staff of the Pompidou Centre, gave me an extensive guided tour of the building in 2005, and provided blueprints of the building and other information. Thanks also to Sir Jack Zunz, formerly of Ove Arup & Partners. Background reading: *Richard Rogers: Complete Works: Volume One* (Powell); *Richard Rogers* (Appleyard); *The Seventy Architectural Wonders of Our World* (Parkyn).

Georges Pompidou quotation 'Ça va crier!': *Richard Rogers* (Appleyard).

Richard Rogers quotation 'fell in love with . . .': *Richard Rogers* (Appleyard). All subsequent Rogers' quotes: author's interview with Lord Rogers (unless otherwise indicated).

Philip Johnson's remark: recalled by Lord Rogers in an interview with the author.

Richard Rogers quotation 'an ever changing . . .': *Richard Rogers: Complete Works: Volume One* (Powell).

Costings: thanks to Philippe Lê at the Pompidou Centre.

Richard Meier background and quotes: author's interview with Meier, unless otherwise attributed. Background reading: *Five Architects* (Eisenman *et al*); *Building the Getty* (Meier); *Richard Meir Architect* (Green, ed.).

Richard Meier quotations: 'white purist masterpieces', '. . . but at least . . .' and 'I was overwhelmed . . .' from *Building the Getty* (Meier).

Robert Venturi's quip 'less is a bore': *Modern Architecture Since 1900* (Curtis). Also Pruitt Igoe.

Lloyd's of London section: author's interview with Lord Rogers (all quotes); thanks also to Martin Leach of Lloyd's. Background reading: *Richard Rogers: Complete Works: Volume One* (Powell); *Richard Rogers* (Appleyard); *The Buildings of England: London 1: The City of London* (Bradley and Pevsner).

Costings of Lloyd's: thanks again to Martin Leach.

CHAPTER 23. ALL IS VANITY

Epigraph: *The Andy Warhol Diaries* (Hackett, ed.).

This chapter is based on the author's interviews with former members of Warhol's office/factory including Vincent Fremont and Pat Hackett, and friends of Warhol including David Hockney and Dennis Hopper. Background reading: *The Andy Warhol Diaries* (Hackett, ed.); *Holy Terror* (Colacello); *Andy Warhol: 365 Takes* (Staff of the Andy Warhol Museum, eds).

NB: there has long been uncertainty in biographical sources about Warhol's place and date of birth; I have taken it as Pittsburgh, 6 August 1928 (*Holy Terror*, Colacello), which makes Warhol forty-eight in the spring of 1977.

Andy Warhol quotation '[I] wanted to . . .': *The Andy Warhol Diaries* (Hackett, ed.).
All Pat Hackett quotes: author's interview and correspondence with Hackett.
Dennis Hopper quotes: author's interview with Hopper.
Description of Warhol's home: partly based on exhibits at the Andy Warhol Museum in Pittsburgh, particularly the 2002 exhibition *Possession Obsession*.
Vincent Fremont quote: author's interview with Fremont.
Farah Diba Pahlavi quotation 'Your portraits . . .': *Holy Terror* (Colacello).
David Hockney's portrait of Sir David Webster: *David Hockney by David Hockney*.
Love You Live commission: *The Andy Warhol Diaries* (Hackett, ed.).
John Cale story and quotation comes from a monologue by Cale on the track 'A Dream,' from the 1990 album *Songs for Drella* by Lou Reed and John Cale.
Andy Warhol quotation 'Just tell them it's art . . .': as reported by Bob Colacello in *Holy Terror*.
Background on Studio 54: *Rolling Stone*, 19 April 1979.
'lines to do lines': *Holy Terror* (Colacello).

CHAPTER 24. MANHATTAN

Epigraph: *Annie Hall* (1977).
All Andy Warhol quotes: *The Andy Warhol Diaries* (Hackett, ed.).
As with the previous chapter, regarding Warhol's place and date of birth I have taken it as Pittsburgh, 6 August 1928 (*Holy Terror*, Colacello).
In an interview with the author, Pat Hackett characterised Warhol's view of Woody Allen's humour as 'smart-alecky.'
Woody Allen material: author's interviews. Background reading: *Woody Allen* (Lax); *Woody Allen on Woody Allen* (Björkman); *Woody Allen: His Films and Career* (Brode); *The Unruly Life of Woody Allen* (Meade).
Woody Allen quotations: 'I've made this joke . . .', 'I said to myself . . .', 'And then, when all the talking . . .', 'In *Interiors* . . .' and 'I failed, I failed . . .' from *Woody Allen on Woody Allen* (Björkman).
Woody Allen quotations: 'I was in love . . .' and 'It massages . . .' from *Woody Allen* (Lax).
All Tony Roberts quotes: author's interview with Roberts.
'There's an old joke. Uh . . .': *Annie Hall* (1977). Also, 'Photography's interesting . . .' and 'Hardly ever . . .' etc.
All Gordon Willis quotes: author's correspondence with Willis.
Woody Allen quotations: 'I know I could . . .' and 'a serious picture . . .' from *Woody Allen: His Films and Career* (Brode). Also Pauline

Kael's quotation, 'What man . . .'

Movie dialogue: 'the most fun . . .', 'sex with . . .' and 'I don't know . . .' etc from *Annie Hall* (1977).

'incredible sexual humiliation . . .' and 'Some day we're gonna be . . .' etc: *Manhattan* (1979).

CHAPTER 25. RICH AND STRANGE

Epigraph: 'oh all those wonderful . . .' from *The Sea, The Sea* (Murdoch).

David Hockney's Glyndebourne productions: author's interviews with Hockney and friends. Background reading: *Hockney Paints the Stage* (Friedman); *That's the Way I See It* (Hockney); *Portrait of David Hockney* (Webb); and the Art Haus Musik DVD of *The Magic Flute* (Glyndebourne, 1978).

Reviews of/reaction to Hockney's Glyndebourne *Magic Flute*: *Guardian*, 29 May 1978; *Daily Telegraph*, 30 May 1978.

David Hockney quotes: author's interview with Hockney unless otherwise indicated.

David Hockney quotations: 'I talked a lot . . .', 'It was time . . .' and 'The performance ended . . .' from *That's the Way I See It* (Hockney).

Stephen Spender quotation 'a true marriage . . .': *Hockney Paints the Stage* (Friedman).

Iris Murdoch section: author's interviews and/or correspondence with the late Iris Murdoch's husband John Bayley and her biographer Peter J. Conradi; also Martyn Goff, Angela Huth, the late Bernice Rubens, and Murdoch's editor Jane Turner. Background reading: *The Sea, The Sea* (Murdoch); *Iris Murdoch: A Life* (Conradi); *The Saint & The Artist* (Conradi); *Iris Murdoch As I Knew Her* (Wilson); *Iris* (Bayley).

A.N. Wilson quotations: 'as well as being . . .' and 'it is possible to . . .' from *Iris Murdoch As I Knew Her* (Wilson).

Iris Murdoch quotation 'Everything comes out of Shakespeare . . .': *The Times*, 23 November 1978.

All Peter J. Conradi quotes: author's interview with Conradi.

All John Bayley quotes (and Bayley's recalled conversation with his late wife): author's interview with Bayley.

Murdoch's relationship with Chatto & Windus: author's interviews with John Bayley and Murdoch's editor Jane Turner.

Lou Reed comment: from an interview published in *New Musical Express Greatest Hits, 1975* (Scott, ed.). See Chapter 11.

1978 Booker Prize: author's interview with Martyn Goff, correspondence with Angela Huth (her quote); two booklets giving the history of the Booker Prize, privately published by the Booker Prize Foundation (*Booker*

30 and *The Man Booker Prize*); *The Times*, 23 November 1978.

John Updike quote: 'I was a fan . . .': author's correspondence with Updike.

Epigraph: *Monty Python's Life of Brian* (1979)

Iris Murdoch quotation 'I am not . . .': *The Times*, 23 November 1978.

Percentages regarding church attendance and faith in the United States: as quoted by David Frum in his book *How We Got Here: The '70s: The Decade That Brought You Modern Life – For Better or Worse.*

Jerry Falwell's Moral Majority: *America's Century* (Daniel, ed.).

Born again Jimmy Carter: *Mauve Gloves & Madmen, Clutter & Vine* (Wolfe).

Born-again Bob Dylan: from research for my biography of Dylan, *Down the Highway.* (In describing Dylan's conversion, Pastor Kenn Gulliksen of the Vineyard Fellowship told me that Dylan indicated he wanted a 'lifestyle relationship' with the Christian God.)

Monty Python's Life of Brian section: author's interview with Terry Gilliam. Background: *The Pythons Autobiography* (McCabe, ed.); *Cleese Encounters* (Margolis); *Monty Python Encyclopaedia* (Ross); various press reports and two documentary films: *It's the Monty Python Story* (BBC/A&E Network, 1999), and *The Pythons* (BBC, 1979).

John Cleese quotations: 'I remember getting very cross . . .' and 'I'm always surprised . . .' from *The Pythons Autobiography* (McCabe, ed.).

'Don't mention the war . . .' etc: 'The Germans' episode in the first series of *Fawlty Towers* (BBC-TV, 1975).

Eric Idle quotation: '*Jesus Christ: Lust for Glory*' – *It's the Monty Python Story* (BBC/A&E Network, 1999).

'around tea time' and 'Blessed are the Greek' etc: *Monty Python's Life of Brian* (1979).

Terrorist outrages: *Chronicle of the 20th Century* (Mercer, ed.).

'At least it gets . . .': *Monty Python's Life of Brian* (1979).

Keith Moon background: *Dear Boy* (Fletcher) and *A Liar's Autobiography* (Chapman).

'Alright! Apart from . . .' and 'Now, you listen here . . .' etc: *Monty Python's Life of Brian* (1979).

Terry Gilliam quote: author's interview.

Michael Palin quotation: 'as though we'd . . .' from *The Pythons Autobiography* (McCabe, ed.).

Eric Idle quotation: 'very cheery': *The Pythons Autobiography* (McCabe, ed.).

American protests and reaction: *Daily Mail*, 5 October 1979; *Daily Express*, 26 October 1979.

Catholic Archdiocese of New York: 'comic ridicule' in (London) *Evening*

News, 29 August 1979.

Rabbi Hecht quotation: 'We have never . . .' in *Evening News*, 31 August 1979.

Exchange with Malcolm Muggeridge and the Bishop of Southwark: various reports including *The Pythons Autobiography* (McCabe, ed.) and *Cleese Encounters* (Margolis).

First British television broadcast: *Observer*, 3 March 1991.

CHAPTER 27. NOW THE END IS NEAR

Epigraph: 'He took it . . .' from *No Irish, No Blacks, No Dogs* (Lydon).

All subsequent John Lydon quotes, and recalled conversation with record executives: author's interviews with Lydon (unless otherwise stated).

Jamie Reid quotation 'It was very much . . .': author's interview with Reid.

Sex Pistols' background: author's interviews; *No Irish, No Blacks, No Dogs* (Lydon); *England's Dreaming* (Savage); *The Sex Pistols Diary* (Wood). Also the television documentary *Blood on the Turntables* (BBC, 2004) and the *Classic Albums* making of *Never Mind the Bollocks* (Eagle Rock Entertainment, 2002).

Criminal convictions/visa problems: *England's Dreaming* (Savage).

Jann Wenner quotation 'fucking noise': *The Rolling Stone Story* (Draper).

Jann Wenner quotation 'Look, they were a . . .': author's interview with Wenner.

Mikal Gilmore voted *Never Mind the Bollocks* the best album ever made for the 1987 edition of *Top 100 Albums* (Gambaccini, ed.).

Sex Pistols at Randy's Rodeo, and Vicious' comment from the stage: sources include Charles M. Young's report in *Rolling Stone* (23 February 1978) and *The Sex Pistols Diary* (Wood).

John Lydon quotation 'Ever get the feeling . . .': on video-tape of the Pistols at Winterland, San Francisco, 14 January 1978.

John Lydon's pun 'He took it all too far . . .': *No Irish, No Blacks, No Dogs* (Lydon).

Death of Sid Vicious: author's interviews and background sources including *England's Dreaming* (Savage) and *The Encyclopaedia of Rock Obituaries* (Talevski).

Anne Beverley quotes: 'Jesus, son . . .' and 'I'm glad he died . . .' from *England's Dreaming* (Savage).

Sid's ashes: in his interview with the author, and in his autobiography, John Lydon tells the Heathrow Airport story. Slightly differing versions are reported in *The Encyclopaedia of Rock Obituaries* (Talevski) and elsewhere.

Joe Strummer's reaction to Sid Vicious' death: *A Riot of Our Own: Night and Day with the Clash* (Green).

Clash background: *The Clash: Return of the Last Gang in Town* (Gray); *A Riot of Our Own: Night and Day with the Clash* (Green); the 25th Anniversary

Edition of *London Calling* and its booklet and DVD documentary, *The Last Testament*; press reports, including *New Musical Express* articles collected and published as a magazine special by *Uncut* in 2003.

Andy Warhol quotation: 'The Clash are cute . . .' from *The Andy Warhol Diaries* (Hackett, ed.).

Joe Strummer quotation: 'I've done something terrible . . .' from *A Riot of Our Own: Night and Day with the Clash* (Green).

Mick Jones quotation: 'any kind of music' from *The Last Testament*.

Paul Simonon smashing his guitar: *A Riot of Our Own: Night and Day with the Clash* (Green).

Completion and release of *Apocalypse Now*: author's interviews; *Notes* (Eleanor Coppola); *Francis Ford Coppola* (Schumacher); *Coppola* (Cowie).

Francis Ford Coppola: 'Let me out of here . . .' from *Notes* (Eleanor Coppola). Also the flight to Washington.

George Lucas and the multiplexes: *Easy Riders, Raging Bulls* (Biskind).

Arthur Schlesinger Jr's review, and Coppola's 'piece of shit' comment as reported in *Francis Ford Coppola* (Schumacher).

Frederic Forrest quotation 'Of course, now . . .': author's interview with Forrest.

CHAPTER 28. THE '70S ARE DEAD!

Epigraph: invitation to Woody Allen's New Year's party, 31 December 1979, as reported that day in *New York Times*.

Films of 1979: *Variety*, 2 January 1980.

Background on Woody Allen's New Year's party: author's correspondence with Tony Roberts; *New York Times*, 31 December 1979; *The Unruly Life of Woody Allen* (Meade); *Woody Allen* (Lax); *The Andy Warhol Diaries* (Hackett, ed.).

Dialogue: 'I finally had an orgasm . . .' etc in *Manhattan* (1979).

Roller-skating craze: *New York Times*, 31 December 1979.

Introduction of the Sony Walkman: *The Oxford History of the Twentieth Century* (Howard & Louis).

Richard Rodgers dies: *Variety*, 2 January 1980.

Tony Roberts quotation 'It was probably . . .': author's correspondence with Roberts.

Jack Nicholson reading *The Executioner's Song*: *Jack's Life* (McGilligan).

John Updike on *The Executioner's Song*: 'It seemed too long . . .' from author's correspondence with Updike.

Gold prices: *How We Got Here: The '70s: The Decade That Brought You Modern Life – For Better or Worse* (Frum); *America's Century* (Daniel, ed.)

Shah of Iran deposed: *Chronicle of the 20th Century* (Mercer, ed.).

Warhol portraits unwanted: *Holy Terror* (Colacello).

Ray Bollig quotation: 'the depressing 1970s . . .' in *New York Times*, 1 January 1980.

Andy Warhol on the Woody Allen party and subsequent quotes: *The Andy Warhol Diaries* (Hackett, ed.).

Making of *Raging Bull*: author's interview with Mardik Martin; *Scorsese on Scorsese* (Christie and Thompson, eds); *Martin Scorsese Interviews* (Brunette, ed.); *De Niro: A Biography* (Baxter); the DVD documentary *The Bronx Bull* (Blue Source, undated).

Mardik Martin quotation 'Marty almost died': author's interview with Martin.

'Rapper's Delight': *Variety*, 2 January 1980.

Decline of Ossie Clark: *The Ossie Clark Diaries* (Rous, ed.).

FBI investigation and Bob Colacello quotation: 'They were hoping . . .' from *Holy Terror* (Colacello).

BIBLIOGRAPHY

Allen, Woody. *Four Films of Woody Allen*. London: Faber & Faber, 1983.

Andy Warhol Museum (Staff of, eds). *Andy Warhol: 365 Takes*. London: Thames & Hudson, 2004.

Appleyard, Bryan. *Richard Rogers*. London: Faber & Faber, 1986.

Arbus, Diane (Estate of, eds). *Diane Arbus: Revelations*. London: Jonathan Cape, 2003.

Arnason, H.H. *A History of Modern Art (Third Edition)*. London: Thames & Hudson, 1986.

Augarde, Tony, ed. *The Oxford Dictionary of Modern Quotations*. Oxford: Oxford University Press, 1991.

Barnes, Richard. *The Who: Maximum R&B*. London: Plexus, 2000.

Baxter, John. *De Niro: A Biography*. London: HarperCollins, 2003.

Baxter, John. *George Lucas: A Biography*. London: HarperCollins, 1999.

Baxter, John. *Stanley Kubrick: A Biography*. London: HarperCollins, 1998.

Bayley, John. *Iris: A Memoir of Iris Murdoch*. London: Abacus, 1999.

Benchley, Peter. *Jaws*. London: Pan, 1975.

Biskind, Peter. *Easy Riders, Raging Bulls*. London: Bloomsbury, 1999.

Björkman, Stig. *Woody Allen on Woody Allen*. London: Faber & Faber, 1995.

Bockris, Victor. *Lou Reed: The Biography*. London: Hutchinson, 1994.

Bosworth, Patricia. *Diane Arbus: A Biography*. New York: Knopf, 1984.

Bowie, Angela, with Patrick Carr. *Backstage Passes: Life on the Wild Side with David Bowie*. New York: Cooper Square Press, 2000.

Boyer, Paul S., ed. *The Oxford Companion to United States History*. New York: Oxford, 2001.

Bradley, Simon, and Nikolaus Pevsner. *The Buildings of England: London 1: The City of London*. Harmondsworth: Penguin, 1999.

Brando, Marlon. *Songs My Mother Taught Me*. London: Century, 1994.

Brode, Douglas. *The Films of Jack Nicholson*. London: Columbus, 1987.

Brode, Douglas. *Woody Allen: His Films and Career*. London: Columbus, 1985.

Brunette, Peter, ed. *Martin Scorsese Interviews*. Jackson (Mississippi): University Press of Mississippi, 1999.

Buckley, David. *Strange Fascination: David Bowie: The Definitive Story*. London: Virgin, 2001.

Bugliosi, Vincent, with Curt Gentry. *Helter Skelter*. London: Arrow, 1992.

Burgess, Anthony. *A Clockwork Orange*. Harmondsworth: Penguin, 1972.

Carroll, E. Jean. *Hunter: The Strange and Savage Life of Hunter S. Thompson*. New York: Dutton, 1993.

Chapman, Graham. *A Liar's Autobiography, Volume VI*. London: Methuen, 1999.

Cherry, Bridget, and Nikolaus Pevsner. *The Buildings of England: London 2: South*. Harmondsworth: Penguin, 1999.

Christie, Ian, and David Thompson, eds. *Scorsese on Scorsese*. London: Faber & Faber, 2003.

Colacello, Bob. *Holy Terror: Andy Warhol Close Up*. New York: HarperCollins, 1990.

Conrad, Joseph. *The Nigger of the 'Narcissus'*. Harmondsworth: Penguin, 1989.

Conrad, Joseph. *Heart of Darkness*. Harmondsworth: Penguin, 1973.

Conradi, Peter J. *The Saint & The Artist*. London: HarperCollins, 2001.

Conradi, Peter J. *Iris Murdoch: A Life*. London: HarperCollins, 2001.

Coppola, Eleanor. *Notes: On the Making of Apocalypse Now*. London: Faber & Faber, 1995.

Cowie, Peter. *Coppola*. London: André Deutsch, 1989.

Crane, Robert David, and Christopher Fryer. *Jack Nicholson: Face to Face*. New York: M. Evans & Co., 1975.

Curtis, William J.R. *Modern Architecture Since 1900 (Third Edition)*: London: Phaidon, 1996.

Daniel, Clifton, ed. *America's Century*. New York: Dorling Kindersley, 2000.

Davis, Sharon. *Stevie Wonder: Rhythms of Wonder*. London: Robson Books, 2003.

Davis, Stephen. *Hammer of the Gods*. London: Pan Books, 1995.

Dickens, Norman. *Jack Nicholson: The Search for a Superstar*. New York: Signet, 1975.

Draper, Robert. *The Rolling Stone Story: The Magazine That Moved a Generation*. Edinburgh: Mainstream, 1990.

Drew, Philip. *Sydney Opera House: Jørn Utzon*. London: Phaidon, 1995.

Dunaway, Faye, with Betsy Sharkey. *Looking for Gatsby: My Life*. London: HarperCollins, 1995.

Dylan, Bob. *Lyrics 1962–1985*. London: Paladin, 1988.

Eisenman, Peter, with Michael Graves, Charles Gwathmey, John Hejduk and Richard Meier. *Five Architects*. New York: Oxford University Press, 1975.

Evans, Robert. *The Kid Stays in the Picture (Revised Edition)*. London: Faber & Faber, 2003.

Ewan, David. *The Complete Book of Classical Music*. London: Robert Hale, 1989.

Farson, Daniel. *Gilbert & George*. London: HarperCollins, 1999.

Fleming, John, Hugh Honour and Nikolaus Pevsner. The *Penguin Dictionary of Architecture (Third Edition)*. Harmondsworth: Penguin, 1980.

Fletcher, Tony. *Dear Boy: The Life of Keith Moon*. London: Omnibus, 1999.

Foster, Hal, with Gordon Hughes, eds. *Richard Serra*. Cambridge (Massachusetts): The MIT Press, 2000.

Friedman, Martin. *Hockney Paints the Stage*. London: Thames & Hudson, 1983.

Fromonot, Françoise. *Jørn Utzon: The Sydney Opera House*. Milan: Electa, 2000.

Frum, David. *How We Got Here: The '70s: The Decade That Brought You Modern Life – For Better or Worse*. New York: Basic Books, 2000.

Gambaccini, Paul, ed. *Top 100 Albums*. London: GRR/Pavilion, 1987.

Gentili, Augusto, William Barcham and Linda Whiteley. *Paintings in the National Gallery*. London: Little, Brown, 2000.

Gilmore, Mikal. *Shot in the Heart*. London: Viking, 1994.

Gombrich, E.H. *The Story of Art (Fifteenth Edition)*. London: Phaidon, 1991.

Goodman, Fred. *The Mansion on the Hill*. London: Jonathan Cape, 1997.

Gottlieb, Carl. *The Jaws Log: 25th Anniversary Edition*. London: Faber & Faber, 2001.

Gray, Marcus. *The Clash: The Return of the Last Gang in Town*. London: Helter Skelter, 2003.

Green, Johnny, with Garry Barker. *A Riot of Our Own: Night and Day with the Clash – And After*. London: Orion, 2000.

Green, Lisa J., ed. *Richard Meier: Architect*. New York: The Monacelli Press, 1999.

Greer, Germaine. *The Female Eunuch*. London: Flamingo Seventies Classic, 2003.

Grimsley Johnson, Rheta. *Good Grief: The Story of Charles M. Schulz*. London: Ravette Books, 1990.

Grobel, Lawrence. *The Hustons*. London: Bloomsbury, 1990.

Guralnick, Peter. *Careless Love*. London: Little, Brown, 1999.

Hackett, Pat, ed. *The Andy Warhol Diaries*. London: Simon & Schuster, 1989.

Hall, Edwin. *The Arnolfini Betrothal*. Berkeley: University of California Press, 1997.

Heylin, Clinton. *Bob Dylan: Behind the Shades: The Biography – Take Two*. London: Viking, 2000.

Hockney, David. *David Hockney by David Hockney*. London: Thames & Hudson, 1977.

Hockney, David. *That's the Way I See It*. London: Thames & Hudson, 1993.

Howard, Michael, and Wm. Roger Louis, eds. *The Oxford History of the Twentieth Century*. Oxford: Oxford University Press, 1998.

Joachimides, Christos M., and Norman Rosenthal. *American Art in the 20th Century: Painting and Sculpture 1913–1993*. Munich: Prestel-Verlag, 1993.

Katz, Ephraim. *The Macmillan International Film Encylopedia*. London: Macmillan, 1998.

Kelly, Danny, ed. *The Q/Omnibus Press Rock 'n' Roll Reader*. London: Q Magazine, 1994.

Kingston, Victoria. *Simon & Garfunkel: The Biography*. New York: Fromm International, 1998.

Lax, Eric. *Woody Allen: A Biography*. London: Jonathan Cape, 1991.

Lee, Anthony W. and John Pultz. *Diane Arbus: Family Albums*. New Haven (Connecticut): Yale University Press, 2003.

Levey, Michael. *The National Gallery Collection*. London: National Gallery Publications, 1987.

Loewenstein, Dora, and Philip Dodd, eds. *According to the Rolling Stones*. London: Phoenix, 2004.

Lydon, John, with Keith and Kent Zimmerman. *No Irish, No Blacks, No Dogs*. London: Plexus, 1994.

McCabe, Bob, ed. *The Pythons Autobiography*. London: Orion, 2003.

McGilligan, Patrick. *Jack's Life: A Biography of Jack Nicholson*. New York: Norton, 1994.

McKeen, William. *Hunter S. Thompson*. Boston: Twayne, 1991.

Mailer, Norman. *The Executioner's Song*. London: Hutchinson, 1979.

Mailer, Norman. *The Prisoner of Sex*. New York: Signet, 1971.

Manso, Peter. *Brando: The Biography*. New York: Hyperion, 1994.

Manso, Peter. *Mailer: His Life and Times*. New York: Simon & Schuster, 1985.

Margolis, Jonathan. *Cleese Encounters*. London: Orion, 2003.

Marley, Rita, with Hettie Jones. *No Woman, No Cry: My Life with Bob Marley*. London: Pan, 2005.

Marsh, Dave, and John Swenson, eds. *The New Rolling Stone Record Guide*. New York: Random House, 1983.

Matlock, Glen, with Peter Silverton. *I Was a Teenage Sex Pistol*. London: Virgin, 1996.

Meade, Marion. *The Unruly Life of Woody Allen*. London: Phoenix, 2001.

Meier, Richard. *Building the Getty*. New York: Knopf, 1997.

Mercer, Derrik, ed. *Chronicle of the 20th Century*. Harlow: Longman, 1988.

Miles, Barry. *Paul McCartney: Many Years from Now*. London: Vintage, 1998.

Miller, Jim, ed. *The Rolling Stone Illustrated History of Rock 'n' Roll*. London: Picador, 1981.

Murdoch, Iris. *The Sea, The Sea*. Harmondsworth: Penguin, 1980.

Murray, Peter. *The Saga of the Sydney Opera House*, London: Spon Press, 2004.

Norman, Philip. *Symphony for the Devil: The Rolling Stones Story*. New York: Linden Press, 1984.

O'Brien, Karen. *Joni Mitchell: Shadows and Light: The Definitive Biography*. London: Virgin Books, 2001.

Orgel, Stephen, and A.R. Braunmuller, eds. *The Complete Pelican Shakespeare*. Harmondsworth: Penguin, 2002.

Parkyn, Neil, ed. *The Seventy Architectural Wonders of Our World*. London: Thames & Hudson, 2002.

Pearce, Joseph. *Solzhenitsyn: A Soul in Exile*. London: HarperCollins, 2000.

Pinch, Trevor, and Frank Trocco. *Analog Days: The Invention and Impact of the Moog Synthesizer*. Cambridge (Massachusetts): Harvard University Press, 2002.

Polanski, Roman. *Roman*. London: Pan, 1985.

Powell, Kenneth. *Richard Rogers: Complete Works, Vol 1*. London: Phaidon, 2000.

Puzo, Mario. *The Godfather*. London: Arrow, 1991.

Puzo, Mario: *The Godfather Papers and Other Confessions*. London: Pan, 1973.

Pym, John, ed. *Time Out Film Guide (Thirteenth Edition)*. London: Ebury, 2004.

Ratcliff, Carter, and Robert Rosenblum. *Gilbert & George: The Singing Sculpture*. London: Thames & Hudson, 1993.

Ross, Robert. *Monty Python Encyclopaedia*. London: Batsford, 2001.

Rous, Lady Henrietta, ed. *The Ossie Clark Diaries*. London: Bloomsbury, 1998.

Savage, Jon. *England's Dreaming: Anarchy, Sex Pistols, Punk Rock, and Beyond*. New York: St Martin's Press, 2001.

Schlesinger, Peter. *A Chequered Past*. London: Thames & Hudson, 2003.

Schulman, Bruce J. *The Seventies: The Great Shift in American Culture, Society, and Politics*. New York: Da Capo Press, 2001.

Schulz, Charles M. *Peanuts Jubilee: My Life and Art with Charlie Brown and Others*. Harmondsworth: Penguin, 1976.

Schumacher, Michael. *Francis Ford Coppola: A Filmmaker's Life*. New York: Crown, 1999.

Scott, Jack, ed. *New Musical Express Greatest Hits 1975 (Annual)*. London: IPC Magazines, 1974.

Shepard, Sam. *The Rolling Thunder Logbook*. Harmondsworth: Penguin, 1978.

Shone, Tom. *Blockbuster: How Hollywood Learned to Stop Worrying and Love the Summer*. London: Simon & Schuster, 2004.

Solzhenitsyn, Alexander. *The Gulag Archipelago* (Abridged). London: Harvill, 2003.

Solzhenitsyn, Alexander. *The Oak and the Calf.* London: Collins, 1980.

Solzhenitsyn, Alexander. *One Day in the Life of Ivan Denisovich.* Harmondsworth: Penguin, 1963.

Sounes, Howard. *Down the Highway: The Life of Bob Dylan:* New York: Grove, 2001.

Steadman, Ralph. *Between the Eyes.* London: Jonathan Cape, 1984.

Strong, Martin C. *The Great Rock Discography (Fourth Edition).* Edinburgh: Canongate, 1999.

Talevski, Nick. *The Encyclopaedia of Rock Obituaries.* London: Omnibus, 1999.

Tevis, Jamie Griggs. *My Life with The Hustler.* Athens (Ohio): GreatUnpublished.com, 2003.

Tevis, Walter. *The Man Who Fell to Earth.* London: Bloomsbury, 1999.

Thomas, D.M. *Alexander Solzhenitsyn: A Century in His Life.* New York: St Martin's Press, 1998.

Thompson, Hunter S. *The Great Shark Hunt.* London: Picador, 1980.

Thompson, Hunter S. *Fear and Loathing in Las Vegas,* London: Paladin, 1972.

Thompson, Hunter S. *Hell's Angels.* Harmondsworth: Penguin, 1967.

Towne, Robert. *Chinatown.* London: Faber & Faber, 1998.

Trudeau, G.B. *The Doonesbury Chronicles.* New York: Holt, Rinehart and Winston, 1975.

Trudeau, G.B. *Flashback: Twenty-Five Years of Doonesbury.* Kansas City (Missouri): Andrews & McNeel, 1995.

Updike, John. *Rabbit is Rich.* Harmondsworth: Penguin, 1982.

Updike, John. *Rabbit Redux.* Harmondsworth: Penguin, 1973.

Updike, John. *Rabbit, Run.* Harmondsworth: Penguin, 1964.

Warhol, Andy. *The Philosophy of Andy Warhol (From A to B & Back Again).* New York: Harcourt Brace Jovanovich, 1975.

Webb, Peter. *Portrait of David Hockney.* London: Paladin, 1990.

Whitburn, Joel. *The Billboard Book of Top 40 Hits.* New York: Billboard, 1996.

White, Timothy. *Catch a Fire: The Life of Bob Marley.* London: Omnibus, 2000.

Wilmut, Roger, ed. *Monty Python's Flying Circus: Just the Words (Volume 1).* London: Methuen, 1999.

Wilson, A.N. *Iris Murdoch As I Knew Her.* London: Arrow, 2004.

Wolfe, Tom. *Mauve Gloves & Madmen, Clutter & Vine.* New York: Bantam Books, 1977.

Wolfe, Tom, and E.W. Johnson, eds. *The New Journalism.* London: Picador, 1996.

Wood, Lee. *The Sex Pistols Diary: Sex Pistols Day by Day.* London: Omnibus Press, 1988.

PICTURE CREDITS

INDEX